THE OFFICIAL RED BOOK
OF UNITED STATES COINS ®

—————— *1991* ——————

A GUIDE BOOK
of
UNITED STATES COINS

By R. S. YEOMAN

44th Revised Edition

Edited by Kenneth Bressett

Fully Illustrated
Catalog and Valuation List — 1616 to Date

A BRIEF HISTORY OF AMERICAN COINAGE
EARLY AMERICAN COINS AND TOKENS
EARLY MINT ISSUES   REGULAR MINT ISSUES
PRIVATE, STATE AND TERRITORIAL GOLD
SILVER AND GOLD COMMEMORATIVE ISSUES
PROOFS

9051-91   ISBN: 0-307-19892-8   Printed in U.S.A.

WHITMAN COIN PRODUCTS

CONTRIBUTORS TO THE FORTY-FOURTH EDITION

KERRY EMMRICH, *Project Coordinator*

Gary Adkins
Michael Aron
Richard August
Richard A. Bagg
Robert F. Batchelder
Gerald L. Bauman
Aubrey E. Bebee
Lee J. Bellisario
Philip E. Benedetti, Sr.
Neil S. Berman
Jack H. Beymer
George H. Blonker
Q. David Bowers
Phil Bressett
Hy Brown
Mike G. Brownlee
Bill Causey
J. H. Cline
Alan R. Cohen
Jerry Cohen
John W. Dannreuther
Larry Demerer
Silvano DiGenova
Marc A. Dixon
Dennis J. Forgue
Chuck Furjanic
Henry G. Garrett
Jeff Garrett
William G. Gay
Dorothy Gershenson

Dennis M. Gillio
Ronald J. Gillio
Harry Gittelson
Ira Goldberg
Lawrence S. Goldberg
Kenneth M. Goldman
Paul Grosz
James L. Halperin
David J. Hendrickson
Leon E. Hendrickson
Gene L. Henry
Karl D. Hirtzinger
Ronald M. Howard
Jesse Iskowitz
Curtis Iversen
Steve Ivy
Robert Jacobs
Floyd O. Janney
James J. Jelinski
A. M. Kagin
Donald H. Kagin
Paul S. Kagin
Jack Klausen
Mike Kliman
Paul L. Koppenhaver
Abner Kreisberg
Julian Leidman
David Leventhal
Edwin Leventhal
Dana Linett

Bruce R. Longyear
Denis W. Loring
Virg Marshall III
Robert T. McIntire
Raymond N. Merena
Bill Mertes
Michael C. Moline
Sylvia Novack
Paul B. Nugget
Sidney L. Nusbaum
Robert M. Paul
William P. Paul
Joe Person
Joel D. Rettew
Maurice Rosen
Richard J. Schwary
Robert R. Shaw
Michael W. Sherman
James A. Simek
William J. Spencer
Maurice A. Storck, Sr.
Charles Surasky
Anthony Terranova
Frank Van Valen
Russell P. Vaughn
Robert E. Wilhite
Douglas A. Winter
Mark S. Yaffe
Gary L. Young

Special credit is due to the following for service and data in this book:
Harry X Boosel, Walter Breen, Dan Brown, Malcolm O. E. Chell-Frost, Ted F. Clark, Roger S. Cohen, Jr., Mike Danish, Tom DeLorey, Bill Fivaz, George Fuld, Natalie Halpern, V. M. Hanks, Jr., James A. Haxby, Herbert Hicks, Michael J. Hodder, Robert W. Julian, Jerry Kimmell, Lonesome John, Lester Merkin, Ed Metzger, Raymond D. Munde, Eric P. Newman, Andrew W. Pollock, Mary Sauvain, Earl Schill, Neil Shafer, Arlie Slabaugh, Leonard W. Stark, Anthony Swiatek, Thomas Underwood, Holland Wallace, Stewart P. Witham, John Wright, and Leo A. Young.

Those now deceased, but whose contributions have been a part of this book since early editions, include:
Kamal M. Ahwash, Herbert Bergen, David M. Bullowa, William L. Clark, Ben M. Douglas, Ben Dreiske, Charles E. Green, Abe Kosoff, Steve Kosoff, Kenneth W. Lee, Ken Nichols, Jerome Nusbaum, Al C. Overton, Richard Picker, Hubert L. Polzer, Lewis M. Reagan, Norman Shultz, Mulford B. Simons, and Sidney Smith.

Auction price data furnished by "Auction Prices Realized: U.S. Coins," various editions, Krause Publications, Inc., and often reflect prices realized without commission adjustments.

THE SPANISH MILLED DOLLAR
The Coin of Our Nation's Founders

The Spanish Milled Dollar valued at 8 *reales,* otherwise known as the "pillar dollar" or "piece of eight," has been given a place in romantic fiction unequaled by any other coin.

This time-honored piece and its fractional parts of ½ and 1 *real,* 2 and 4 *reales* were the principal coins of the American colonists, and were the forerunners of our own silver dollar and its fractional divisions.

The coin shown above bears the M̃ mint mark for Mexico City. Similar pieces with other mint marks were struck in Bolivia, Chile, Colombia, Guatemala and Peru. For details see listings in Whitman's *Coins of the World 1750-1850* by W. D. Craig and *Silver Dollars of North and South America* by Wayte Raymond. Average value for an 8 *reales* of common date and mint is about $125.00 in Fine to Very Fine condition. Dates range from 1732 to 1772.

Note: Many modern copies of the 8 *reales* exist. These are produced mostly as souvenirs and have little or no value.

THE PURPOSE OF THIS BOOK

Coin values listed in the Guide Book are averaged from data supplied by contributors several months before publication. The coin market is so active in some categories that values can easily change during this period. Prices are shown as a guide and are not intended to serve as a price-list for any dealer's stock. A dash appearing in a price column indicates the existence of coins in that grade, whose current values cannot be determined. It does not necessarily mean that such coins are excessively rare. Italicized prices indicate unsettled values. A number of listings of rare coins do not have prices or dashes in certain grades. This indicates that they are not available or known in those grades.

Prices rise when: 1. The economic trend is inflationary. 2. The number of collectors increases, while coin supplies remain stationary or decrease through attrition or melting. 3. Dealers replace their stocks of coins only from collectors or other dealers, who expect a profit over what they originally paid.

Prices decline when: 1. Changes in collecting habits may alter demand for certain coins. 2. Speculators buy and sell in large quantities. 3. Hoards or large holdings are suddenly released and cannot be quickly absorbed by the normal market. 4. Bullion gold and silver prices decline sharply.

Those who edit, contribute to, and publish this book advocate the collecting of coins for pleasure and educational benefits. A secondary consideration is that of investment, the profits from which are realized over the long term based on intelligent purchases.

The *Handbook of United States Coins* by R. S. Yeoman, Western Publishing Company, Inc. Racine, WI. containing average prices dealers will pay for these coins, is obtainable at most coin dealers, hobby shops and bookstores.

[4]

CONDITION OF COINS
Essential elements of the A.N.A. grading system

PROOF — A specially made coin distinguished by sharpness of detail and usually with a brilliant mirrorlike surface. Proof refers to the method of manufacture and is not a condition, but normally the term implies perfect mint state unless otherwise noted and graded as below. See pages 60 and 61 for details.

MINT STATE — The terms Mint State (MS) and Uncirculated (Unc.) are interchangeably used to describe coins showing no trace of wear. Such coins may vary to some degree because of blemishes, toning or slight imperfections as described in the following subdivisions.

PERFECT UNCIRCULATED (MS-70) — Perfect new condition, showing no trace of wear. The finest quality possible, with no evidence of scratches, handling or contact with other coins. Very few regular issue coins are ever found in this condition.

CHOICE UNCIRCULATED (MS-65) — An above average Uncirculated coin which may be brilliant or lightly toned and has very few contact marks on the surface or rim. MS-67 through MS-62 indicate a slightly higher or lower grade of preservation.

UNCIRCULATED (MS-60) — Has no trace of wear but may show a number of contact marks, and surface may be spotted or lack some luster.

CHOICE ABOUT UNCIRCULATED (AU-55) — Barest evidence of light wear on only the highest points of the design. Most of the mint luster remains.

ABOUT UNCIRCULATED (AU-50) — Has traces of light wear on many of the high points. At least half of the mint luster is still present.

CHOICE EXTREMELY FINE (EF-45) —- Light overall wear shows on highest points. All design details are very sharp. Some of the mint luster is evident.

EXTREMELY FINE (EF-40) — Design is lightly worn throughout, but all features are sharp and well defined. Traces of luster may show.

CHOICE VERY FINE (VF-30) — Light even wear on the surface and highest parts of the design. All lettering and major features are sharp.

VERY FINE (VF-20) — Shows moderate wear on high points of design. All major details are clear.

FINE (F-12) — Moderate to considerable even wear. Entire design is bold with overall pleasing appearance.

VERY GOOD (VG-8) — Well worn with main features clear and bold although rather flat.

GOOD (G-4) — Heavily worn with design visible but faint in areas. Many details are flat.

ABOUT GOOD (AG-3) — Very heavily worn with portions of lettering, date and legends worn smooth. The date may be barely readable.

IMPORTANT: Damaged coins, such as those which are bent, corroded, scratched, holed, nicked, stained, or mutilated, are worth less than those without defects. *Flawless uncirculated coins are generally worth more than values quoted in this book.* Slightly worn coins ("sliders") which have been cleaned and conditioned ("whizzed") to simulate uncirculated luster are worth considerably less than perfect pieces.

Unlike damage inflicted after striking, manufacturing defects do not always lessen values. Examples are: Colonial coins with planchet flaws and weakly struck designs; early silver and gold with weight adjustment "file marks" (parallel cuts made prior to striking); and coins with "lint marks" (dust or other foreign matter which may mar the surface during striking).

Brief guides to grading are placed before each major coin type in this book. For those readers who desire more detailed descriptions of all coin grades, we recommend OFFICIAL A.N.A. GRADING STANDARDS FOR UNITED STATES COINS, by the American Numismatic Association.

RARE COINS AS AN INVESTMENT

Investing in rare coins can be a rewarding experience for anyone who approaches the calling armed with the right attitude and background knowledge about this exciting field. It can just as easily become a costly mistake for anyone who attempts to profit from coins without giving serious thought to the idiosyncrasies of this unique market.

The best advice that can be given to anyone considering investing in rare coins is to use common sense precautions that would apply to any contemplated purchase. No thinking person would consider buying a diamond ring from a street peddler, or an art masterpiece from a pawn shop. The chances of finding a good buy in such an off beat place are just not worth the risk. It is just the same with rare coins, and the more careful you are in selecting a qualified dealer and making an educated evaluation of the coins that you purchased, the greater will be your chance of making a profitable investment.

The opportunities for successful collecting and investing in quality numismatic items are greater today than ever before. Inexperienced buyers can now rely upon the integrity and skill of a third-party grading services to assure them that the grade of any coin that they purchase will be up to industry standards, and saleable at that grade when it is time to liquidate. The pricing of rare coins is also more competitive than ever before, and the chance of being overcharged has been greatly diminished by the general availability of pricing guides and rarity information presented in numismatic publications. The investment market potential has also been further strengthened through active participation by Wall Street interests, thus providing an even broader audience for investment coins in the future. In addition to these safeguards, the industry has done a creditable job of upgrading the quality of service provided by dealers through organizations and associations that promote professional conduct and ethics.

For hundreds of years rare coins and precious metals have proven themselves to be an excellent hedge against inflation, and source of ready money in times of disaster. There is no reason to think that this will change in the future. Gone are the days when coin collecting was only a passive hobby for those who would study the history and artistry of these enjoyable objects. It has now grown into an investment arena where speculation on the future demand for rare coins has made them a standard part of nearly every well rounded investment portfolio.

With this change in attitude about collecting coins has come a measure of concern for those who purchase coins without the background or experience necessary to avoid costly mistakes in accepting over priced or over graded coins that simply are not worth what is paid for them. Extreme caution is advised for anyone considering an investment in rare coins. Investigate the person or firm with whom you are dealing, and seek professional non-biased help with grading determinations. Satisfy yourself that the coins you select are not priced considerably higher than is being charged by other dealers, and determine that you will be able to sell your coins when it is time to liquidate your holdings.

Collectors and investors alike can profit by investigating the background and history of the coins they buy. These are not just inanimate objects akin to stock certificates or gems. Coins are a mirror of history and art that tell the story of mankind over the past 2,600 years, reflecting economic struggles, wars, prosperity and creativity of every major nation on earth. We are but the custodians of these historical relics, and must appreciate and care for them while they are in our possession. Those who treat rare coins with the consideration and respect they deserve will profit in many ways, not the least of which can be in the form of a sound financial return on ones investment of time and money.

AN INTRODUCTION TO UNITED STATES COINS

Money of the Early Americans

The story of American money, which occupies a period of over three centuries, began when the early settlers in New England carried on their fur trade with the Indians through the use of wampum, which had been fashioned from mussel shells in the form of "beads." Beaver skins, wampum, and in Virginia, tobacco, soon became the commonly accepted media of exchange for all other available commodities. The immigrants, in fact, had little use for coined money at first, but when traders arrived from foreign lands, coins were usually demanded in payment for goods. Any foreign coins were usually accepted, such as French louis, English guineas, German thalers, Dutch ducats, and various Spanish coins, including doubloons and particularly the Spanish milled dollar, or piece of eight. The piece of eight continued to be a standard money unit throughout the entire colonial period. Even after the Revolutionary War, the Spanish dollar and its fractional parts circulated in this country with official sanction until 1857. One *real* equaled 12½ cents and was known as a "bit." A quarter of the dollar thus became known as "two bits," a term still in use.

England consistently ignored the plight of the colonists and made no effort to provide gold or silver coins, or a small-change currency for them. Although coins known as "Hogge Money" were provided for the Sommer Islands, now known as the Bermudas, about the year 1616, the first coins minted in America were minted by John Hull in the Massachusetts Bay Colony. The General Court of the colony granted him authority to begin coinage. Starting in 1652 the Boston mint provided the famous N.E., pine tree, and similar shillings, with their fractional parts, for the hardpressed colonists. Other colonies tried similar projects but failed.

As time went by, coins and tokens of many types were introduced and employed by the colonists in their daily course of business. Lord Baltimore in Maryland was responsible for a series of silver pieces, which were probably struck in England in 1658. Mark Newby introduced a piece known as St. Patrick's Halfpence into the province of New Jersey in 1682. Coins dated 1722 to 1724, known as Rosa Americana and Hibernia coppers, were produced by William Wood in England and were widely circulated in America. The Carolina and New England Elephant Tokens were current in the years following 1694. There were also a few issues of uncertain date and origin, such as the New Yorke Token, which circulated among the Dutch settlers and was probably sent over from Holland.

Enterprising American individuals were responsible for some of the copper pieces that circulated during the eighteenth century. The Gloucester Token, about which little is known, was one of these. John Higley of Granby, Connecticut, made an interesting series of threepence pieces during the period from 1737 to 1739. J. Chalmers, a goldsmith in Annapolis, Maryland, issued silver shillings, sixpence, and threepence pieces in 1783. In 1787 Ephraim Brasher, a New York goldsmith, struck a gold piece of the value of a doubloon (about $16.00). Standish Barry of Baltimore, Maryland, made a curious silver token threepence in 1790.

Still other tokens, struck in England, reached our shores in Revolutionary times and were for the most part speculative ventures. These much-needed, small-denomination coppers were readily circulated because of the great scarcity of fractional coins. Included in this category were the Nova Constellatio and the Bar copper pieces.

During the period of confederation following the War of Independence, still more English tokens were added to the great variety of coins and tokens employed in the new nation. In 1787 the Nova Eboracs, known as New York Coppers, the Georgius Triumpho, the Auctori Plebis, and later the Kentucky, Myddelton and Franklin Press tokens were introduced.

Another interesting series, historically important because of its close association with our first president, consists of those tokens bearing the portrait of Washington. Although most of these pieces are dated from 1783 to 1795, many of them were made in England around the turn of the century.

Coinage of the States

The Articles of Confederation, adopted March 1, 1781, provided that Congress should have the sole right to regulate the alloy and value of coin struck by its own authority or by that of the respective states.

Each state, therefore, had the right to coin money, but Congress served as a regulating authority. New Hampshire was the first state to consider coinage, but few if any coins were placed in circulation. The only specimens known bear the date 1776.

Vermont, Connecticut, and New Jersey granted coining privileges to companies or individuals. Massachusetts erected its own mint in which copper coins were produced. A number of interesting varieties of these state issues, most of which were struck in fairly large quantities, can still be acquired, and form the basis for many present day collections of early American coins.

The Beginnings of United States Coinage

Throughout the Colonial years, Americans had become accustomed to the use of the Spanish dollar and its fractional parts, the *real,* the medio (half-*real*), etc. It was only natural, therefore, that when a national coinage was under consideration the dollar was mentioned most frequently. In earlier years currency statutes in many of the colonies had given first consideration to the Spanish dollar. Connecticut, Massachusetts, and Virginia, particularly, passed laws making Spanish coins a legal tender. The first issue of Continental paper money May 10, 1775, offers further evidence that the dollar was to be our basic money unit, for it provided that the notes should be payable in "Spanish Milled Dollars or the value thereof in gold or silver."

The Assistant Financier of the Confederation, Gouverneur Morris, proposed a decimal coinage ratio, and his plan was incorporated in a report presented by Robert Morris, Superintendent of Finance, to the Congress, January 15, 1782. Plans for a mint were advanced, and a uniform national currency to relieve the confused money conditions was outlined. Morris's unit, 1/1440 of a dollar, was calculated to agree without a fraction with all the different valuations of the Spanish Milled Dollar in the various States. Although a government mint was approved February 21, 1782, no immediate action was taken. During 1784 Thomas Jefferson, then a member of the House of Representatives, brought in a report concerning the plan, and expressed disagreement with Morris' complicated money unit. He advocated the simple dollar unit because he believed the dollar was already as familiar and convenient a unit of value as the British pound. He favored the decimal system and remarked that, "The most easy ratio of multiplication and division is that of ten. George Washington referred to it as 'a measure, which in my opinion, has become indispensibly necessary.' "

The Grand Committee in May 1785 recommended a gold five-dollar piece; a dollar of silver with fractional coins, of the same metal, in denominations of half, quarter, tenth, and twentieth parts of a dollar; and copper pieces valued at one-hundredth and one two-hundredth of a dollar.

In 1783 Robert Morris submitted a series of pattern pieces in silver which were designed by Benjamin Dudley to carry out the decimal idea for United States money. These are known as the Nova Constellatio Patterns and consist of the "Mark" or 1,000 units, the "Quint" or 500 units, the "Bit" or 100 units, and a copper "five". The unit was to be a quarter grain of silver. This was not the first attempt at a dollar coin, for the Continental Currency piece of dollar size, dated 1776, had been struck in such metals as brass, pewter, and silver. The variety in silver probably saw limited service as a dollar.

Congress gave formal approval to the basic dollar unit and decimal coinage ratio in its resolution of July 6, 1785, but other more pressing matters delayed further action. Not until the Constitutional Convention had placed the country on firm ground and the new nation had elected George Washington President, did the Congress again turn attention to the subject of currency, a mint, and a coinage system.

The Massachusetts cents and half cents struck in 1787 and 1788 were the first official coins to bear a stated value in terms of decimal parts of the dollar unit in this country. The cent represented a hundredth part of a Spanish dollar.

The first federally authorized coin was the Fugio Cent, sometimes called the Franklin Cent, as he was supposed to have supplied the design and composed the legends. This piece, similar in design to the Continental Currency dollar of 1776, was privately struck in 1787 by contract with the government.

Alexander Hamilton, then Secretary of the Treasury, reported his views on monetary matters January 21, 1791. He concurred in all essentials with the decimal subdivisions and multiples of the dollar contained in the earlier resolutions and urged the use of both gold and silver in our standard money.

Congress passed a resolution March 3, 1791, that a mint be established, and authorized the President to engage artists and procure machinery for the making of coins. No immediate steps were taken, but when Washington delivered his third annual address, he recommended immediate establishment of a mint.

On April 2, 1792, a bill was finally passed providing "that the money of account of the United States should be expressed in dollars or units, dismes or tenths, cents or hundredths, and milles or thousandths; a disme being the tenth part of a dollar, a cent the hundredth part of a dollar, a mille the thousandth part of a dollar . . . "

Denominations specified in the act were as follows:

	Value of	Grains Pure	Grains Standard
Gold Eagle	$10.00	247 - 4/8	270
Gold Half Eagle	5.00	123 - 6/8	135
Gold Quarter Eagle	2.50	61 - 7/8	67 - 4/8
Silver Dollar	1.00	371 - 4/16	416
Silver Half Dollar	.50	185 - 10/16	208
Silver Quarter Dollar	.25	92 - 13/16	104
Silver Disme (dime)	.10	37 - 2/16	41 - 3/5
Silver Half Disme	.05	18 - 9/16	20 - 4/5
Copper Cent	.01	11 pennyweights	
Copper Half Cent	.005	5½ pennyweights	

The word "pure" meant unalloyed metal; "standard" meant, in the case of gold, 11/12 fine or 11 parts pure metal to one part alloy, which was mixed with the pure metal to improve the wearing qualities of the coins. The fineness for silver coins was 1485/1664 or approximately 892.43 thousandths, in contrast with the gold coins of 22 karats, or 916 2/3 thousandths fine.

The law also provided for free coinage of gold and silver coins at the fixed ratio of 15 to one, and a token coinage of copper cents and half cents. Under the free coinage provision no charge was to be made for converting gold or silver bullion into coins "weight for weight." At the depositor's option, however, he could demand an immediate exchange of coins for his bullion, for which privilege a deduction of one-half of one percent was to be imposed.

Washington appointed David Rittenhouse, a well-known philosopher and scientist, as the first Director of the Mint. Construction began on a mint building nearly four months after the passage of the Act of April 2, 1792. The building was located on Seventh Street near Arch in Philadelphia.

The first coin struck by the government was the half disme. Fifteen hundred of these pieces were produced during the month of July 1792 before the mint was completed. Washington supplied some of his own silver to the value of about one hundred dollars for those first coins. Dismes also were probably struck at this time or a short while later. The portrait on these pieces may have been modeled by Martha Washington.

Copper for cents and half cents was covered in the Act of May 8, 1792 when the purchase of not over 150 tons was authorized. On September 11, 1792, six pounds of old copper were purchased, this being the first purchase of copper for coinage, which was probably used for the striking of patterns.

Planchets with upset rims for cents and half cents were purchased from Boulton of Birmingham, England from 1798 to 1838.

Several pattern coins were prepared in 1792 before regular mint operations commenced. These included the silver center cent by Henry Voigt, a smaller piece than that of regular issue. The small plug of silver, worth about three-quarters of a cent, was evidently intended to bring the intrinsic value of the coin up to the value of one cent and permit production of a coin of more convenient size. Alexander Hamilton had mentioned a year before that the proposed "intrinsic value" cent would be too large, and suggested that the amount of copper could be reduced and a trace of silver added. The pattern cent with a silver center may have been designed to conform to this recommendation.

The cents by Robert Birch are equally interesting. These patterns are identified by their legends which read "LIBERTY PARENT OF SCIENCE AND INDUSTRY" and "TO BE ESTEEMED BE USEFUL." The quarter with an eagle on the reverse side belongs among the early patterns devised before regular issues were struck.

The Bank of Maryland deposited the first silver, sending $80,715.73½ in French coins to the mint July 18, 1794. Moses Brown, a Boston merchant, deposited the first gold in the form of ingots, February 12, 1795, amounting to $2,276.22, receiving silver coin in payment. The first coins transferred to the Treasurer consisted of 11,178 cents on March 1, 1793. The first return of coined silver was made on October 15, 1794, and the first gold coins, 744 half eagles, were delivered July 31, 1795.

File marks on early U. S. coins are a result of the mint process of weight adjustment.

Regular Mint Issues

Cents and half-cents exclusively were coined during the year 1793, and by 1799 approximately $50,000 in these coins had been placed in circulation. This amount proved insufficient for the requirements of commerce, and small denomination coins of the states and of foreign countries continued in use during the first few years of the nineteenth century.

One of the most serious problems confronting the commercial interests during the early years was the failure of the government to provide a sufficient volume of circulating coins. The fault, contrary to popular opinion at the time, did not lie with any lack of effort on the part of the mint. Other circumstances tended to interfere with the expected steady flow of new coinage into the channels of trade.

Free circulation of United States gold and silver coins was greatly hindered by speculators. For example, worn Spanish dollars of reduced weight and value were easily exchanged for U. S. silver dollars, which meant the export of most of the new dollars as fast as they were minted, and a complete loss to American trade channels.

Gold coins failed to circulate for similar reasons. The ratio of 15 to 1 between gold and silver was close to the world ratio when Hamilton recommended it, but by 1799 the ratio in European commercial centers had reached 15¾ to 1. At this rate the undervalued gold coins tended to flow out of the country, or were reduced for bullion. After 1800, therefore, United States gold coins were rarely seen in general circulation. As no remedy could be found, coinage of the

Eagle and the silver dollar was suspended by President Jefferson in 1804 and 1806 respectively. It is generally conceded that the silver dollar was discontinued in 1804, although the last coins minted for the period were dated 1803.

Lacking gold coins and silver dollars, the half dollar became the desirable coin for large transactions, bank reserves, and foreign payments. Until 1830, in fact, half dollars circulated very little as they were mainly transferred from bank to bank. This will account for the relatively good supply of half dollars of this period which are still available to collectors in better than average condition. A senate committee of 1830 reported that United States silver coins were considered so much bullion and were accordingly "lost to the community as coins."

There was only a negligible coinage of quarters, dimes, and half dimes from 1794 to 1834. It has been estimated that there was less than one piece for each person in the country in the year 1830. This period has been described as one of nondescript currency made up of banknotes, underweight foreign gold coins, foreign silver coins of many varieties, and domestic fractional silver coins. Notes of "wildcat banks" flooded the country before 1830 and were much more common than silver coins.

On June 28, 1834, a new law was passed reducing the weight of standard gold, which had the effect of placing our money on a gold standard. Trade and finance were greatly benefited by this act, which also proved a boon to the gold mines of Georgia and North Carolina. Branch mints in Dahlonega, Georgia, and Charlotte, North Carolina, were established two or three years later to handle the newly mined gold at the source. The Templeton Reid and Bechtler issues of private gold coins were struck in this area.

The law of January 18, 1837, completely revised and standardized the mint and coinage laws. Legal standards, mint charges, legal tender, mint procedure, tolerance in coin weights, accounting methods, a bullion fund, standardization of gold and silver coins to 900 thousandths fine, and other desirable regulations were covered by the new legislation. Results of importance to the collector were the changes in type for the various coin denominations and the resumption of coinage of the eagle shortly thereafter.

The political and financial elements underwent a crisis at about this time. The familiar "Jackson Tokens" and fractional notes of banks and commercial establishments completely eclipsed the circulation of metallic currency. This was the era of "shinplasters."

The California gold discovery in 1848 was responsible for an interesting series of private, state, and territorial gold issues in the Western states, culminating in the establishment of a branch mint at San Francisco in 1854.

Two new regular gold issues were adopted in 1849. In that year the double eagle and gold dollar joined our American family of coins. The California gold fields greatly influenced the world gold market, making the exportation of silver profitable. For example, the silver in two half dollars was worth $1.03½ in gold. The newly introduced gold dollars soon took over the burden and hastened the disappearance of silver coins from trade channels. This was the situation when the new three cent postage rate brought about the bill authorizing the coinage of the silver three cent piece in 1851. This was our country's first subsidiary coin, for its value was intrinsically 86% of its face value, an expedient designed to prevent its withdrawal from circulation.

The three dollar gold piece was authorized by the act of February 21, 1853. Never a popular or necessary coin, it nevertheless was issued regularly until 1889.

On February 21, 1853, fractional silver coins were made subsidiary resulting from the fact that the weight of all silver pieces, excepting the dollar, was reduced. As the coins were now worth less than their face value free coinage of silver was prohibited, and the mint was authorized to purchase its silver requirements on its own account using the bullion fund of the mint, and, according to law, "the profit of said coinage shall be, . . . transferred to the account of the treasury of the United States."

Arrows were placed at the date on all silver coins except three cent pieces and dollars, and on the quarters and half dollars rays were added on the reverse side to denote the change of weight. In 1854 the rays were removed, and in 1856 the arrows disappeared. Production of silver coins in large quantities during this period greatly relieved the demands on gold dollars and three cent pieces. Consequently for the first time in our nation's history there was a sufficient supply of fractional coins in general circulation.

The law of 1857 was designed primarily to reform the copper coinage. No matter how interesting and valuable the large cents and half cents may have become in the eyes of the modern collector, they were very unpopular with the people and cost the mint too much to produce.

The new law abolished the half cent piece, and reduced the size and changed the design of the cent. The new Flying Eagle cent contained 88% copper and 12% nickel. Several hundred experimental cents were stamped from dies bearing the date 1856 although no authority for the issue existed before 1857. Other important effects of the law were the retirement of the Spanish silver coins from circulation, and dispersal of the new cents in such excessive quantities as to create a nuisance to business houses, particularly in the eastern cities. The Indian head device replaced the Eagle in 1859, and in 1864 the weight of the cent was further reduced and its composition changed to a proportion of 95% copper and 5% tin and zinc. This bronze composition was the standard for our cent except for the years 1943, and 1944 to 1946. In 1962 the alloy was changed to 95% copper and 5% zinc. In 1982 the composition was changed to 97.5% zinc and 2.5% copper.

Both Jefferson and Hamilton had contended in their day that the currency of money of small value benefits society. The history of our cent and its daily use proves the soundness of this principle.

Abundance turned to scarcity following the outbreak of the Civil War. Anticipation of a scarcity and depreciation of the paper money was sufficient to induce hoarding. The large volume of greenbacks in circulation caused a premium on gold, and subsidiary silver as a result of the sudden depreciation quickly vanished in the North. Resort was soon made to postage stamps for small change. All types of fractional notes were put out at this time by municipalities and the government. "Postage currency" became widely used, and in 1863 a great variety of tokens appeared to help fill the vacuum. Like the tokens of 1837 they were of two general classes, tradesmen's coins and imitations of legal cents. Many of the latter were political or patriotic in character, carried slogans typical of the times, and were usually produced at a profit.

The Law of 1864, which effected changes in the cent, provided also for the new bronze two cent piece. The act, moreover, provided legal tender status for these two coins up to ten times their value. The two cent piece was the first coin to bear the motto IN GOD WE TRUST. The new coin was readily accepted by the people but proved an unnecessary denomination, going out of fashion and being discontinued only nine years later.

Secretary Chase had issued a great many currency notes of three cent denomination early in 1865. The nickel interests seized upon this circumstance to fight for a new three cent coin for redemption of the paper money. A law was quickly passed and signed by the president as of March 3, 1865, providing for a three cent coin of 75-25 copper-nickel composition. Our country now possessed two types of three cent pieces. The nickel three cent piece was struck continuously until 1889; the three cent silver until 1873.

The new copper-nickel alloy ratio was selected for the five cent coin, adopted May 16, 1866, to be thereafter known as a "nickel." Again the people had a coin value available in two forms. The silver half dime, like the three cent piece, was retired from service in 1873.

The Carson City Mint was established in 1870 as a convenient depository for the miners in that area and operated until 1893.

The Law of March 3, 1871, was a redemption measure and was passed to provide a means for the disposal to the United States Treasury of millions of minor coins which had accumulated in the hands of postmasters, newsdealers, and others. Small-denomination coins as a result of this new law were placed on an equal footing and could be redeemed when presented in lots of twenty dollars.

There was a general revision of the coinage laws in 1873. Several years of study and debate preceded the final enactment. The legislative history of the bill occupies hundreds of pages of the Congressional Globe, and the result was considered by many a clumsy attempt and a failure. The law has sometimes been referred to as the "Crime of '73." One consequence of the bill, which achieved final enactment February 12, 1873, was the elimination of the silver dollar. In its stead the Trade dollar of greater weight was provided for use in commerce with the Orient in competition with the Mexican dollar. The legal tender provision, which unintentionally gave the Trade dollar currency within our borders, was repealed the following year.

The charge for converting standard gold bullion into coin was reduced by the act to one-fifth of one percent. The same rate was imposed on silver bullion for coining Trade dollars only.

It may be a surprise to some collectors to learn that the silver dollar had not circulated to any great extent in the United States after 1803. The coin had been turned out steadily since 1840, but for various reasons such as exportation, melting, and holding in bank vaults, the dollar was virtually an unknown coin. The Law of 1873 in effect demonetized silver and committed our country to a gold standard. The silver mining interests came to realize what had occurred a little later, and the ensuing quarter century of political and monetary history was filled with their voluble protests. There was a constant bitter struggle for the return to bimetallism.

From an economic point of view the inadequate supply of gold was responsible for a gradual decline in prices throughout the world. This brought about a gradual business depression in our country, particularly in the South and Middle-West. Private silver interests influenced great sections of the West for bimetallism as a remedy for the failing price level. Authorities have concluded that a world-wide adoption of bimetallism would have improved economic conditions, but the United States alone proceeding to place its money on a double standard at the old 16 to 1 ratio would have led only to a worse situation.

Of particular importance to collectors, however, were those features of the Law of 1873 which affected the status and physical properties of the individual coins. The weight of the half-dollar, quarter, and dime, was slightly changed and arrows were placed at the date for the ensuing two years to indicate the difference in weight. Silver three-cent pieces, half-dimes, and two-cent pieces were abolished by the act, and the manufacture of minor coins was restricted to the Mint at Philadelphia.

The short-lived twenty-cent piece was authorized March 3, 1875. It was created for the Western states where the Spanish "bit" had become equivalent to a U. S. dime. The five-cent piece did not circulate there, so when a quarter was offered for a "bit" purchase, only a dime change was returned. However, it was confused with the quarter-dollar and was discontinued after 1878.

The Bland-Allison Act of February 28, 1878, gave the Secretary authority to purchase two to four million dollars worth of silver bullion each month to be coined into silver dollars. The coin, never popular, was produced in minimum quantitites. This was not a bimetallic law, nor was it a free coinage act. Strictly speaking it was a subsidiary coinage law, called by some "a wretched compromise."

The North and East so disliked the silver dollars that they did not actively circulate there and eventually found their way back to the Treasury, mostly through tax payments. Secretary Manning transferred ownership to the people and removed them from Treasury holdings by the simple expedient of issuing silver certificates in small bills to effect a wide circulation.

The Bland-Allison Act was repealed in 1890 and the Sherman Act took its place. Under this new law 4,500,000 ounces of silver per month could be paid for with Treasury Notes that were to be legal tender, and redeemable in gold or silver dollars coined from the bullion purchased. Important in this case was the fact that the notes were constantly being redeemed for gold which was mainly exported. The measure was actually a government subsidy for the silver miners and as such it was marked for failure, and was hastily repealed. The Bland-Allison Act and the Sherman Act gave a total of 570 million silver dollars to our monetary stocks.

The "Gold Standard Act" of 1900 gave our country a single standard, but reaffirmed the fiction that the silver dollar was a standard coin. It still enjoyed unlimited legal tender, but was as much a subsidiary coin, practically speaking, as the dime, for its value in terms of standard gold, even before the gold surrender executive order, was far below its face value.

The lapse in coinage after 1904 and until 1921 was due to lack of bullion. Legislation authorizing further metal supplies for silver dollars was not forthcoming until 1918 when the Pittman Act provided silver for the new dollars.

Before the first World War the value of gold was equal to the value of gold coined into money. In order to encourage a steady flow of gold to the mints the government (with the exception of the period 1853-1873) had adopted a policy of gratuitous coinage. The cost of converting gold into coin had generally been considered an expense chargeable to the government.

In practice the mint made fine bars for commercial use or mint bars for coinage at its discretion. The bars in later years were stored in vaults and gold or silver certificates issued in place of the coins.

On April 5, 1933 President Roosevelt issued an order prohibiting banks from paying out gold and gold certificates without permission, and gold currency was thus kept for reserve purposes. Gold imports and newly mined domestic gold could be sold only to the government. Gold bullion and coins may now be collected and saved by anyone as all restrictions were removed in 1975.

Under the Coinage Act of 1965, the composition of dimes, quarters and half dollars was changed to eliminate or reduce the silver content of these coins. The "clad" dimes and quarters were composed of an outer layer of copper-nickel (75% copper and 25% nickel) bonded to an inner core of pure copper. Starting 1971 the half dollar and dollar composition was changed to that of the dime and quarter. All silver clad coins have an outer layer of 80% silver bonded to an inner core of 21% silver, with a total content of 40% silver.

By the Law of September 26, 1890, changes in designs of United States coins cannot be made more often than once every twenty-five years. Since that date, there have been design changes in all denominations and there have been many gold and silver commemorative issues. These factors are largely responsible for the ever increasing interest in coin collecting.

QUANTITIES OF COINS STRUCK

Collectors are cautioned that mint reports are not always reliable for estimating the rarity of coins. In the early years of the mint, dies of previous years were often used until they became worn or broken.

It should also be emphasized that quantities reported, particularly for gold and silver, cover the number of coins struck and have no reference to the quantity reaching actual circulation. Many issues were deposited in the treasury as backing for paper currency and were later melted.

The rarity of gold pieces struck before 1834, particularly half eagles, can be traced to the fact that the gold content was reduced in 1834, making previous issues greater in value than face, causing melting and reminting.

The quantities reported by the mint of three dollar gold pieces from 1873 to 1877 and half cents from 1832 to 1836 are subject to doubt.

Coinage figures shown for 1964 through 1966 are for coins bearing those dates. Some of them were struck in more than one year and at various mints, both with and without mint marks.

Mint quantities are shown adjacent to each date throughout the book. Figures shown in *italic* are estimates based on the most accurate information available. PROOF TOTALS ARE SHOWN IN PARENTHESES.

I. THE BRITISH COLONIES IN AMERICA
SOMMER ISLANDS (Bermuda)

This coinage, the first struck for the English colonies in America, was issued about 1616. The coins were known as "Hogge Money" or "Hoggies."

The pieces were made of copper lightly silvered, in four denominations; shilling, sixpence, threepence and twopence, indicated by Roman numerals. The hog is the main device and appears on the obverse side of each. SOMMER ISLANDS is inscribed within beaded circles. The reverse shows a full-rigged galleon with the flag of St. George on each of four masts.

The islands were named for Sir George Sommers who was shipwrecked there in 1609 while enroute to the Virginia Plantations. Shakespeare's *The Tempest* was possibly based on this incident.

The Bermuda Islands, as they are known today, were named for Juan Bermudez who is believed to have stopped there in 1515. A few hogs which he carried for delivery to the West Indies were left behind. When Somers and his party arrived, the islands were overrun with the animals which served as a welcome source of food for the expedition.

Twopence   Threepence

Sixpence   Large Portholes   Small Portholes

Shilling ★   Small Sail   Large Sail

	Good	V. Good	Fine	V. Fine
Twopence	$1,750	$2,750	$5,000	$7,500
Threepence (V. Rare)	——	——	——	70,000
Sixpence, small portholes	1,750	2,500	4,200	7,000
Sixpence, large portholes	1,500	2,400	4,000	6,500
Shilling, small sail	2,000	3,000	4,750	8,000
Shilling, large sail	2,250	3,200	5,000	8,500

★Star throughout colonial section indicates that struck copies exist

Copies of certain American issues were made after 1850 to provide facsimiles of rarer issues which would otherwise be unobtainable. A star has been placed adjacent to those pieces of which deceptive copies exist. Many crude imitations have also been made in recent years, as well as forgeries intended to deceive collectors. The specimens illustrated are genuine.

MASSACHUSETTS
"NEW ENGLAND" COINAGE (1652)

The earliest medium of exchange in the New England settlements was wampum. The General Court of Massachusetts in 1637 ordered "that wampamege should passe at 6 a penny for any sume under 12 d." Wampum consisted of shells of various colors ground to the size of a grain of corn. A hole was drilled through each piece so they could be strung on leather thongs for convenience and adornment.

Corn, pelts, and bullets were frequently used in lieu of coins, which were rarely available. Silver and gold coins brought over from England, Holland and other countries tended to flow back across the Atlantic to purchase needed supplies. The colonists thus left to their own resources dealt with the friendly Indians in kind. In 1661 the law making wampum legal tender was repealed.

Agitation for a standard coinage reached its height in 1651. England, with a civil war pending between the Puritans and Royalists, ignored the colonists, who took matters into their own hands in 1652.

The General Court in 1652 ordered the first metallic currency to be struck in the English Americas (the Spaniards had established a mint in Mexico City in 1535), the New England silver threepence, sixpence, and shilling. Silver bullion was procured principally from the West Indies. Joseph Jenks made the punches for the first coins at his Iron Works in Saugus, Massachusetts, close to Boston where the mint was located. John Hull was appointed mintmaster; his assistant was Robert Sanderson (or Saunderson). Mintmaster Hull received one shilling threepence for every twenty shillings coined as his compensation. This fee was adjusted several times during his term as mintmaster.

NE Threepence (1652)   **NE Sixpence (1652) ★**

Note: Early American coins are rare in conditions better than listed and valued much higher.

NE Shilling (1652) ★

	V. Good	Fine	V. Fine
NE Threepence *(2 known)*	—	—	
NE Sixpence *(7 known)* — Garrett Sale 1980...	—	—	$75,000
NE Shilling	$7,500	$11,500	24,000

[16]

MASSACHUSETTS
WILLOW TREE COINAGE (1653-1660)

The simplicity of the design on the N.E. coins invited counterfeiting and clipping of the edges. Therefore, they were soon replaced by the Willow, Oak and Pine Tree series. The Willow Tree coins were struck from 1653 to 1660, the Oak Trees 1660 to 1667, and the Pine Trees 1667 to 1682. All of them (with the exception of the Oak Tree twopence) bore the date 1652, however. This evasion was to give them the appearance of having been struck during the English civil war, when Cromwell was in power.

The coinage was abandoned in 1682; a proposal to renew coinage in 1686 was rejected by the General Court.

Many varieties of all of these coins exist.

Threepence   **Sixpence**

Shilling

	Fair	Good	Fine	E. Fine
Willow Tree Threepence 1652 *(3 known)*	—	—		
Willow Tree Sixpence 1652	—	—	$20,000	$45,000
Willow Tree Shilling 1652	$2,500	$5,500	17,000	40,000

OAK TREE COINAGE (1660-1667)

Twopence ★   **Threepence**

	Good	V. Good	Fine	V. Fine
Oak Tree Twopence 1662	$350.00	$650.00	$1,250	$2,500
Oak Tree Threepence 1652	425.00	800.00	1,750	3,500

MASSACHUSETTS

Sixpence

Shilling ★

	Good	V. Good	Fine	V. Fine
Oak Tree Sixpence 1652..........	$300.00	$700.00	$1,450	$3,200
Oak Tree Shilling 1652...........	325.00	750.00	1,600	3,300

PINE TREE COINAGE (1667-1682)

The first pine tree coins were minted on the same size planchets as the Oak Tree pieces. Subsequent issues of the shilling were narrower and thicker to conform to the size of English coins.

Threepence ★

Sixpence ★

**Shilling,
Large Planchet
(1667-1674) ★**

**Shilling,
Small Planchet
(1675-1682)**

	Good	V. Good	Fine	V. Fine
Pine Tree Threepence 1652..............	275.00	550.00	850.00	2,000
Pine Tree Sixpence 1652	325.00	650.00	1,100	2,200
Pine Tree Shilling, large planchet 1652...	425.00	750.00	1,300	2,800
Pine Tree Shilling, small planchet 1652...	350.00	650.00	1,100	2,600

MARYLAND

In 1658 Cecil Calvert, the second Lord Baltimore and "Lord Proprietor of Maryland," had coinage struck in England for use in Maryland.

There were four denominations: shillings, sixpence, and fourpence (groat) in silver, and a copper penny (denarium). The silver coins have the bust of Lord Baltimore on the obverse, and the Baltimore family Arms with the denomination in Roman numerals and the legend CRESCITE ET MULTIPLICAMINI (Increase and be multiplied) on the reverse. The obverse of the penny is similar, but the reverse has a ducal coronet with two pennants and the inscription DENARIUM, TERRAE-MARIAE (Penny, Maryland). Numerous die varieties and patterns exist.

Fourpence (groat)

Lord Baltimore Shilling

Sixpence

Penny (denarium) ★

	Good	V. Good	Fine	V. Fine
Penny (Copper) (Ex. Rare)........	—	—	—	—
Fourpence.....................	$1,000	$1,750	$4,500	$7,000
Sixpence	900.00	1,500	3,500	5,000
Shilling	1,200	2,000	4,750	7,500

NEW JERSEY
ST. PATRICK OR MARK NEWBY COINAGE

Mark Newby, who came to America from Dublin, Ireland, in November 1681, brought copper pieces believed by numismatists to have been struck in Dublin c. 1670-1675. These are called St. Patrick coppers.

The coinage was made legal tender by the General Assembly of New Jersey in May, 1682. The legislature did not specify which size piece could circulate, only that the coin was to be worth a halfpenny in trade. Most numismatists believe the larger size coin was intended. However, as many more farthing size pieces are known than halfpennies, some believe that the smaller size piece was meant. Copper coins often circulated in the colonies at twice what they would have been worth in England.

The obverses show a crowned king kneeling playing a harp. The legend FLOREAT REX (May the King prosper) is separated by a crown. The reverse side of the halfpence shows St. Patrick with a crozier in his left hand and a trefoil in his right, surrounded by people. At his left is a shield. The legend is ECCE GREX (Behold the flock). The farthing reverse shows St. Patrick driving away reptiles and serpents, as he holds a Metropolitan cross in his left hand. The legend reads QUIESCAT PLEBS (May the people be at ease).

The large size piece, called a halfpenny, bears the arms of the City of Dublin on the shield on the reverse; the smaller size piece, called a farthing, does not.

NEW JERSEY

The decorative brass insert found on the coinage, usually over the crown on the obverse, was put there to make conterfeiting more difficult. On some pieces this decoration has been removed or does not show. Numerous die variations exist.

St. Patrick "Farthing"

St. Patrick "Halfpenny"

	V. Good	Fine	V. Fine
St. Patrick "Farthing"	$75.00	$175.00	$450.00
St. Patrick "Farthing" — Silver....................	750.00	1,500	2,500
St. Patrick "Farthing" — Gold....................			(Unique)
St. Patrick "Halfpenny"..........................	125.00	300.00	700.00

II. COINAGE AUTHORIZED BY ROYAL PATENT
AMERICAN PLANTATIONS TOKEN

These tokens struck in nearly pure tin were the first authorized coinage for the British colonies in America. They were made under a franchise granted in 1688 to Richard Holt. Bright, unblemished specimens are more valuable. Restrikes were made about 1828 from original dies.

	Fine	E. Fine	Unc.
(1688) James II Plantation Token farthing,			
1/24 PART REAL — Tin	$300.00	$800.00	$2,250
1/24 PART REAL — Tin. Sidewise 4 in 24	750.00	2,300	——
Restrike	200.00	450.00	1,000

COINAGE OF WILLIAM WOOD
ROSA AMERICANA COINS

William Wood, an Englishman, obtained a patent from George I to make tokens for Ireland and the American Colonies.

The first pieces struck were undated; others bear the dates 1722, 1723, 1724

ROSA AMERICANA

and 1733. The Rosa Americana pieces were issued in three denominations, halfpenny, penny and twopence, and were intended for America. This type had a full-blown rose on the reverse with the words ROSA AMERICANA UTILE DULCI (American Rose — useful and pleasant).

The obverse, common to both Rosa Americana and Hibernia pieces, shows the head of George I and the legend GEORGIUS D:G: MAG: BRI: FRA: ET. HIB: REX. (George, by the Grace of God, King of Great Britain, France and Ireland) or abbreviations thereof. Rosa Americana tokens, however, were rejected by the American colonists. The coins are made of a composition of 75% copper, 24.7% zinc, and .3% silver known as Bath metal.

	V. Good	Fine	V. Fine	E. Fine
Twopence (no date) (illustrated)	$110.00	$250.00	$500.00	$800.00
Twopence (no date) motto without label (*3 known*)	—	—	—	—

1722 Halfpenny VTILE DVLCI	1,000	2,500	—	—
1722 Halfpenny D. G. REX ROSA AMERI.				
UTILE DULCI	100.00	225.00	450.00	725.00
1722 Halfpenny DEI GRATIA REX UTILE DULCI	85.00	175.00	275.00	600.00

1722 Penny GEORGIVS				—
1722 Penny VTILE DVLCI	85.00	175.00	275.00	575.00
1722 Penny UTILE DULCI	70.00	135.00	225.00	525.00

ROSA AMERICANA

	V. Good	Fine	V. Fine	E. Fine
1722 Twopence, period after REX...........	$100.00	$225.00	$350.00	$650.00
1722 Twopence, no period after REX........	100.00	225.00	350.00	675.00

1723 Halfpenny, uncrowned rose	1,500	2,500	——	——
1723 Halfpenny	80.00	175.00	275.00	600.00

1723 Penny	75.00	150.00	250.00	500.00
1723 Twopence (illustrated)	110.00	225.00	425.00	750.00

1724, 4 over 3 Penny (Pattern) DEI GRATIA....................	5,000
1724, 4 over 3 Penny (Pattern) D GRATIA	6,000
1724 Penny (undated) ROSA: SINE: SPINA. (3 known)..........	7,000

ROSA AMERICANA

1724 Twopence (Pattern).. $6,500

★

1733 Twopence (Pattern) Proof 20,000

The 1733 twopence is a pattern piece and bears the bust of George II facing to the left. Issued by the successors to the coinage patent, since William Wood had died in 1730.

WOOD'S HIBERNIA COINAGE

The type intended for Ireland had a seated figure with a harp on the reverse side and the word HIBERNIA. Denominations struck were halfpenny and farthing with dates 1722, 1723 and 1724. Hibernia coins were unpopular in Ireland, so many of them were sent to the American colonies.

	First Type	Second Type	1723 over 22	
		V. Good	V. Fine	E. Fine
1722 Farthing, D: G: REX		$135.00	$325.00	$700.00
1722 Halfpenny, D: G: REX, rocks at right (Pattern)..		——	——	
1722 Halfpenny, first type, harp at left.............		40.00	125.00	275.00
1722 Halfpenny, second type, harp at right........		40.00	125.00	275.00
1723 Farthing — D.G.REX.........................		80.00	150.00	475.00
1723 Farthing — DEI. GRATIA. REX		30.00	75.00	200.00
1723 Farthing — Silver pattern...................		700.00	1,750	2,750

WOOD'S HIBERNIA COINAGE

1723 Hibernia Farthing	1724 Hibernia Halfpenny

	V. Good	Fine	V. Fine	E. Fine
1723 over 22 Halfpenny....................	$55.00	$100.00	$200.00	$400.00
1723 Halfpenny	25.00	40.00	70.00	200.00
1723 Halfpenny — Silver pattern..........	—	—	—	—
1724 Farthing...........................	60.00	100.00	175.00	350.00
1724 Halfpenny	50.00	80.00	125.00	325.00

VIRGINIA HALFPENNY

In 1773 coinage of a copper halfpenny was authorized for Virginia by the Crown. The pattern in proof struck on a large planchet with wide milled border is often referred to as a penny.

The silver piece dated 1774 is referred to as a shilling, but may have been a pattern or trial for a halfpenny or a guinea.

Red uncirculated pieces without spots are worth considerably more.

	V. Good	Fine	V. Fine	Unc.
1773 Halfpenny, period after GEORGIVS......	$45.00	$75.00	$150.00	$750.00
1773 Halfpenny, no period after GEORGIVS...	50.00	85.00	175.00	900.00

Proof
1773 "Penny" $5,250

Proof
1774 "Shilling" (*6 known*)...... $18,000

III. EARLY AMERICAN TOKENS
Struck in America or England for use by American Merchants

LONDON ELEPHANT TOKENS

The London Elephant tokens were struck circa 1672-1684. Although undated, two examples are known struck over 1672 British halfpennies. The legend on this piece, GOD PRESERVE LONDON, is probably just a general plea for divine aid and·not a reference to the outbreak of plague in 1665 or the Great Fire of 1666.

These pieces were not struck for the colonies, and probably did not circulate widely in America, although a few may have been carried here by colonists. They are associated with the 1694 Carolina and New England Elephant tokens, through a shared obverse die.

	V. Good	Fine	V. Fine	E. Fine
(1680) Halfpenny GOD PRESERVE LONDON (Thick planchet)	$ 100.00	$200.00	$350.00	$800.00
(1680) Halfpenny GOD PRESERVE LONDON (Thin planchet)	150.00	400.00	650.00	1,200
(1680) Halfpenny GOD PRESERVE LONDON (Diagonals in center of shield)	250.00	450.00	750.00	1,400
(1680) Halfpenny, similar. Variety with sword in second quarter of shield instead of first....	—	—	—	—
(1680) Halfpenny LON DON......................	475.00	1,200	1,900	3,400

CAROLINA AND NEW ENGLAND ELEPHANT TOKENS

Although no law is known authorizing coinage for Carolina, two very interesting pieces known as Elephant Tokens were made with the date 1694. These copper tokens were of halfpenny denomination. The reverse reads GOD PRESERVE CAROLINA AND THE LORDS PROPRIETERS. 1694.

The second and more common variety has the last word spelled PROPRIETORS. The correction was made on the original die, for the E shows plainly beneath the O. The elephant's tusks nearly touch the milling on the second variety.

The Carolina pieces were probably struck in England and perhaps intended only as tokens, or possibly as advertising to heighten interest in the Carolina Plantation.

Like the Carolina Tokens, the New England Elephant Tokens were believed to have been struck in England as a promotional piece to increase interest in the American Colonies.

CAROLINA ELEPHANT TOKENS

	V. Good	V. Fine
1694 PROPRIETERS.....................................		$7,500
1694 PROPRIETORS, O OVER E	$2,000	5,000

NEW ENGLAND ELEPHANT TOKEN

1694 NEW ENGLAND..................................	16,000	30,000

THE NEW YORKE TOKEN

Little is known about the origin of this token. The style of design and execution seem to be Dutch, and it is probable that the dies were prepared in Holland. There is no date on the piece which evidently belongs to the period between 1664, when the name New Yorke was first adopted, and the 1770's after which it was rarely spelled that way.

UNDATED

	V. Good	Fine
Brass	$3,250	$6,500
Pewter...........	3,500	7,250

GLOUCESTER TOKENS

S. S. Crosby, in his book "The Early Coins of America" stated that this coin appears to have been intended as a pattern for a shilling; a private coinage by Richard Dawson of Gloucester (county), Virginia. The only specimens known are struck in brass, although the denomination XII indicates that a silver coinage (one shilling) may have been planned. The building may represent some public building, possibly the court house.

Although neither of the two known examples shows the full legends, combining the pieces shows GLOVCESTER COVRTHOVSE VIRGINIA / RIGHAVLT DAWSON-.ANNO.DOM. 1714. This recent discovery has provided a new interpretation of the legends, as a Righault family once owned land near the Gloucester Courthouse.

GLOUCESTER TOKENS

1714 Shilling Brass $25,000

HIGLEY OR GRANBY COPPERS

Dr. Samuel Higley owned a private copper mine near Granby, Connecticut. He worked the mine as an individual, smelting his own ore and making his own dies for the coins that he issued. After his death in 1737 his brother John continued the coinage.

The Higley coppers were never officially authorized. All the tokens were made of pure copper. There were seven obverse and four reverse dies. The first issue, in 1737, bore the legend THE VALUE OF THREEPENCE. After a time the quantity exceeded the local demand, and a protest arose against the value of

the piece. Higley, a resourceful individual, promptly created a new design, still with the Roman III, but with the inscription VALUE ME AS YOU PLEASE. On the reverse appeared the words I AM GOOD COPPER.

(Electrotypes and Casts Exist)

★

	Good	*Fine*
1737 THE • VALVE • OF • THREE • PENCE. —		
3 Hammers — CONNECTICVT	$4,200	$9,000
1737 THE • VALVE • OF • THREE • PENCE. —		
3 Hammers — I • AM • GOOD • COPPER	5,500	11,000
1737 VALUE • ME • AS • YOU • PLEASE —		
3 Hammers — I • AM • GOOD • COPPER	4,200	9,000

1737 VALVE • ME • AS • YOU • PLEASE —		
3 Hammers — I • AM • GOOD • COPPER	(Ex. Rare)	
(1737) VALUE • ME • AS • YOU • PLEASE —		
Broad Axe — J • CUT • MY • WAY • THROUGH	4,750	9,500
(1737) THE • WHEELE • GOES • ROUND •, Rev.		
as above (Unique)................................		40,000
1739 VALUE • ME • AS • YOU • PLEASE —		
Broad Axe — J • CUT • MY • WAY • THROUGH	6,000	12,000

HIBERNIA-VOCE POPULI

These coins, struck in the year 1760, were prepared by Roche, of King Street, Dublin, who was at that period engaged in the manufacture of buttons for the army. Like other Irish tokens, some of these pieces found their way to Colonial America and possibly circulated in Colonies with numerous other counterfeit halfpence and "Bungtown Tokens." The piece apparently dated 1700 is from a defective die.

There are two distinct issues. The first, with a "short bust" on the obverse, range in weight from 87 to 120 grains. The second, with a "long bust" on the obverse, range in weight from 129 to 154 grains. Most of the "long bust" varieties have the letter P on the obverse. None of the "short bust" varieties bear the letter P and judging from their weight may have been contemporary counterfeits.

Farthing 1760

Halfpenny 1760

Halfpenny "1700"   **VOOE POPULI**

	Good	Fine	V. Fine	E. Fine
1760 Farthing, large letters (illustrated)	$150.00	$350.00	$600.00	$1,500
1760 Farthing, small letters	350.00	700.00	1,600	3,200
1700 Halfpenny	—	—	—	—
1760 Halfpenny	45.00	100.00	175.00	375.00
1760 Halfpenny VOOE POPULI	50.00	125.00	200.00	450.00
1760 Halfpenny, P below bust	85.00	175.00	250.00	500.00
1760 Halfpenny, P in front of face	85.00	175.00	250.00	500.00

PITT TOKENS

William Pitt, who endeared himself to America, is the subject of these pieces, probably intended as commemorative medalets. The halfpenny served as currency during a shortage of regular coinage. The reverse legend refers to Pitt's efforts to have the stamp act repealed. The Pitt farthing-size tokens, struck in brass or copper on cast planchets, are rare.

1766 Farthing...... E.F. $6,500

1766 Halfpenny .... (illustrated)

V. Good	Fine	E. Fine
$160.00	$350.00	$1,450

RHODE ISLAND SHIP MEDAL

The obverse type shows the flagship of British Admiral Howe at anchor, while the reverse depicts the retreat of American forces from Rhode Island in 1778. The inscriptions show that it was meant for a Dutch speaking audience. It is believed that the token was struck in England c. 1779-1780 for the Dutch market, as propaganda to pursuade the Dutch not to sign the Treaty of Armed Neutrality (December, 1780). Specimens are known in brass, copper, tin and pewter.

1778-1779
Rhode Island
Ship Medal

★

	V. Fine	E. Fine
VLUGTENDE (fleeing) below ship		$12,500
Wreath below ship..	$775.00	1,250
Without wreath below ship...............................	700.00	1,100

J. CHALMERS — Annapolis, Maryland

John Chalmers, a goldsmith, struck a series of silver tokens at Annapolis in 1783. The shortage of change and the refusal of the people to use underweight cut Spanish coins, or "bits," prompted the issuance of these pieces.

The shilling with rings on the reverse is very rare. The common type shilling has two clasped hands on the obverse. The reverse shows two doves competing for a worm.

The sixpence has a star within a wreath on the obverse, and a cross with hands clasped on the reverse. The threepence has the clasped hands on the obverse side, and the reverse shows a branch encircled by a wreath.

	V. Good	V. Fine
1783 Threepence	$850.00	$2,300
1783 Sixpence, small date	1,000	3,000
1783 Sixpence, large date	950.00	2,800

1783 Shilling — Birds, long worm.........................	725.00	2,500
1783 Shilling — Birds, short worm (illustrated)	650.00	2,400
1783 Shilling — Rings — Roper Sale, 1983	——	24,200

IV. THE FRENCH COLONIES

None of the coins of the French regime is strictly American. They were all general issues for the French colonies of the New World. The coinage of 1670 was authorized by an edict of Louis XIV dated February 19, 1670, for use in New France, Acadia, the French settlements in Newfoundland, and the French West Indies. The copper of 1717 to 1722 was authorized by edicts of 1716 and 1721 for use in New France, Louisiana, and the French West Indies.

ISSUE OF 1670

The coinage of 1670 consisted of silver 5 and 15 sols. A copper 2 deniers was also authorized but never struck. A total of 200,000 of the 5 sols was struck, and 40,000 of the 15 sols, at Paris. Nantes was to have coined the copper, but did not; the reasons for this may never be known, since the archives of the Nantes mint before 1700 were destroyed. The only known specimen is a pattern struck at Paris. The silver coins were raised in value by a third in 1672 to keep them circulating, but in vain. They rapidly disappeared, and by 1680 none was to be seen. Later they were restored to their original value.

	V. Good	Fine	V. Fine	E. Fine	Unc.
5 Sols 1670 (200,000) ..	$225.00	$500.00	$1,000	$1,600	——
15 Sols 1670 (40,000) ...	6,000	10,000	18,000	——	——

COINAGE OF 1717-1720

The copper 6 and 12 deniers of 1717 were authorized by an edict of Louis XV dated December 1716, to be struck at Perpignan. The order could not be carried out, for the supply of copper was too brassy. A second attempt in 1720 also failed, probably for the same reason. All these coins are extremely rare.

"COLONIES" and no crowned arms on reverse

Copper

	V. Fine
6 Deniers 1717	$1,250
12 Deniers 1717	2,000

Crowned arms on reverse

6 Deniers 1720	750.00

BILLON COINAGE

The piece of 30 deniers was called a *mousquetaire*, and was coined at Metz and Lyon. The 15 deniers was coined only at Metz. The sou marque and half were coined at almost every French mint, those of Paris being commonest. The half sou of 1740 is the only commonly available date. Specimens of the sou marque dated after 1760 were not used in North America.

FRENCH COLONIES
BILLON COINAGE

30 Deniers "Mousquetaire"   **Sou Marque (24 Deniers)**

	V. Good	Fine	V. Fine	E. Fine
15 Deniers 1711-1713AA	$120.00	$225.00	$375.00	$700.00
30 Deniers 1709-1713AA	80.00	140.00	235.00	425.00
30 Deniers 1709-1713D.................	80.00	140.00	235.00	425.00
Half sou marque 1738-1748.............	60.00	100.00	200.00	400.00
Sou marque 1738-1760, various mints	40.00	75.00	120.00	240.00

COINAGE OF 1721-1722

The copper coinage of 1721-1722 was authorized by an edict of Louis XV dated June 1721. The coins were struck on copper blanks imported from Sweden. Rouen and La Rochelle struck pieces of 9 deniers in 1721 and 1722. New France received 534,000 pieces, mostly from the mint of La Rochelle, but only 8,180 were successfully put into circulation as the colonists disliked copper. In 1726 the rest of the issue was sent back to France.

COPPER SOU OR NINE DENIERS

	V. Good	Fine
1721-B (Rouen) ...	$110.00	$250.00
1721-H		
(La Rochelle) ...	55.00	150.00
1722-H...........	55.00	150.00
1722-H, 2 over 1 ..	110.00	210.00

FRENCH COLONIES IN GENERAL

Coined for use in the French colonies and only unofficially circulated in Louisiana along with other foreign coins and tokens. Most were counterstamped RF (République Française) for use in the West Indies.

	V. Good	V. Fine	E. Fine
1767 French Colonies, Sou	$75.00	$200.00	$500.00
1767 French Colonies, Sou. Counterstamped RF	55.00	170.00	325.00

V. SPECULATIVE ISSUES, TOKENS & PATTERNS
THE CONTINENTAL CURRENCY

The Continental Currency pieces probably had some value at the time they were issued, but the exact nature of their monetary role is still unclear. They were the first silver dollar-sized coins ever proposed for the United States. One obverse die was engraved by someone whose initials were E.G. (possibly, Elisha Gallaudet), and is marked with his signature EG FECIT. Studies of the coinage show that there may have been two separate emissions made at different mints. The link design on the reverse was suggested by Benjamin Franklin.

Varieties result from differences in the spelling of the word CURRENCY and the addition of EG FECIT on the obverse. A unique variety is known with a cross after the date. These coins were struck in silver, pewter, and brass. The silver coins probably did service as a dollar, while the brass pieces may have substituted for a penny (although this is considered controversial). Pewter coins most likely had a token value only, if they were used in circulation. Pewter pieces in original bright Uncirculated condition are worth an additional premium.

Copies were struck in various metals for the 1876 Centennial Exposition in Philadelphia and also restruck from hubbed copy dies circa 1961.

★

"CURRENCY"   "CURENCY"

	Good	Fine	E. Fine	Unc.
1776 CURENCY — Pewter (2 varieties)	$1,000	$2,750	$6,500	$13,500
1776 CURENCY — Brass (2 varieties)......	6,000	12,000	17,000	—
1776 CURENCY — Silver — Garrett Sale, 1980	95,000			
1776 CURRENCY — Pewter...............	1,350	3,750	8,500	20,000
1776 CURRENCY — Pewter, EG FECIT......	1,000	2,900	7,500	17,000
1776 CURRENCY — Silver, EG FECIT.......	—	—	—	—
1776 CURRENCEY — Pewter..............	—	—	—	—

★Star throughout colonial section indicates that struck copies exist

NOVA CONSTELLATIO COPPERS

The Nova Constellatio pieces were struck supposedly by order of Gouverneur Morris who had been Assistant Financier of the Confederation. The tokens

NOVA CONSTELLATIO COPPERS

were turned out in fairly large quantities and dated 1783 and 1785. Evidence indicates that they were all struck in Birmingham in 1785 from dies made there by George Wyon, and imported for American circulation as a private business venture by Gouverneur Morris.

1783
"CONSTELLATIO"
Pointed Rays, Small U.S.

V. Good	$75.00
Fine.	125.00
V. Fine.	250.00
Ex. Fine	575.00

1783
"CONSTELLATIO"
Pointed Rays, Large U.S.

V. Good	$85.00
Fine.	175.00
V. Fine.	325.00
Ex. Fine	650.00

1783
"CONSTELLATIO"
Blunt Rays

V. Good	$75.00
Fine.	150.00
V. Fine.	300.00
Ex. Fine	625.00

1785
"CONSTELATIO"
Blunt Rays

V. Good	$85.00
Fine.	175.00
V. Fine.	350.00
Ex. Fine	725.00

1785
"CONSTELLATIO"
Pointed Rays

V. Good	$75.00
Fine.	150.00
V. Fine.	285.00
Ex. Fine	650.00

1786 (Similar). . . . . . . V. Rare

[33]

NOVA CONSTELLATIO PATTERNS (Silver)

These Nova Constellatio pieces undoubtedly represent the first patterns for a coinage of the United States. They were designed by Benjamin Dudley for Gouverneur Morris to carry out his ideas for a decimal coinage system. The 1000 unit designation he called a "mark," the 500 a "quint." These denominations, together with the small 100 unit piece, were designed to standardize the many different coin values among the several States. These pattern pieces represent the first attempt at a decimal ratio, and were the forerunners of our present system of money values. Neither the proposed denominations nor the coins advanced beyond the pattern stage. These unique pieces are all dated 1783. There are two types of the "quint." The enigmatic copper "five" was first brought to the attention of collectors in 1980.

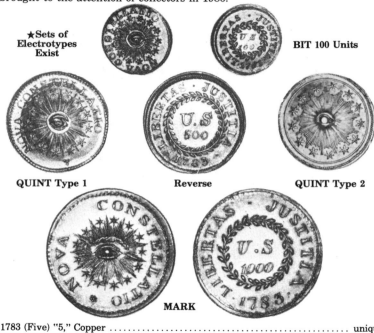

★Sets of Electrotypes Exist

BIT 100 Units

QUINT Type 1   Reverse   QUINT Type 2

MARK

1783 (Five) "5," Copper	unique
1783 (Bit) "100," Silver (2 varieties) — Garrett Sale, 1979	$97,500
1783 (Quint) "500," Silver — Type 1 — Garrett Sale, 1979	165,000
1783 (Quint) "500," Silver — Type 2 — Garrett Sale, 1979	55,000
1783 (Mark) "1000," Silver — Garrett Sale, 1979	190,000

IMMUNE COLUMBIA PIECES

These are considered experimental or pattern pieces. No laws describing them are known. There are several types with the seated figure of Justice device. These dies were possibly the work of George Wyon.

1785 Copper, 13 stars	$8,000
1785 Silver, 13 stars	13,500

IMMUNE COLUMBIA PIECES

1785 Ptd. Rays CONSTELLATIO
Copper. Extra star in legend $8,000
1785 Blunt Rays CONSTELATIO
Copper....... (*2 known*) $22,000
Gold .... (*Unique*)   ——
A gold specimen in the National Coin
Collection was acquired from Stickney
in exchange for an 1804 dollar.

1785
George III Obverse
Good....... $1,500   Fine...... $3,000

1785
Vermon Auctori Obverse
Good....... $1,750   Fine...... $3,500

1787
IMMUNIS COLUMBIA
Eagle Reverse
Dies by James Atlee

V. Good..............	$400.00
Fine.................	800.00
V. Fine	1,750
Ex. Fine	3,500

This piece is believed to be a pattern for Federal coinage submitted to Congress
by Matthias Ogden.

CONFEDERATIO COPPERS

The Confederatio Coppers are experimental or pattern pieces. This will explain
why the die with the CONFEDERATIO legend was combined with other designs
such as bust of George Washington, Libertas et Justitia of 1785, Immunis
Columbia of 1786, the New York "Excelsiors," Inimica Tyrannis Americana
and others. There were in all thirteen dies struck in fourteen combinations.
Some of the dies are believed to have been made by George Wyon of Birmingham, England.

There are two types of the Confederatio reverse. In one instance the stars are
contained in a small circle; in the other larger stars are in a larger circle.

Typical Obverse   **Small Circle Reverse**   **Large Circle Reverse**

	Fine
1785 Stars in small circle — various obverses........................	$11,000
1785 Stars in large circle — various obverses........................	11,000

SPECULATIVE PATTERNS

The motto and shield design used on some of these patterns was later adopted for use on the New Jersey copper coins.

1786 IMMUNIS COLUMBIA   **Eagle Reverse**   **Shield Reverse**

1786 IMMUNIS COLUMBIA, eagle rev....................................... $25,000
1786 IMMUNIS COLUMBIA, shield rev. — Garrett Sale, 1980.................... 17,000

1786 (No date) Washington obv., shield reverse — Garrett Sale, 1980......... 50,000
1786 Eagle obverse, shield reverse — Garrett Sale, 1980...................... 37,500
1786 Washington obverse, eagle reverse (*Unique*)............................ ——

VI. COINAGE OF THE STATES
NEW HAMPSHIRE

New Hampshire was the first of the states to consider the subject of coinage following the Declaration of Independence.

William Moulton was empowered to make a limited quantity of coins of pure copper authorized by the State House of Representatives in 1776. Although cast patterns were prepared, it is believed that they were not approved. Little of the proposed coinage was ever actually circulated.

Other purported patterns are of doubtful origin. These include a unique engraved piece and a rare struck piece with large initials WM on the reverse.

V. Good

1776 New Hampshire copper — Garrett Sale, 1980.................... $13,000

MASSACHUSETTS
MASSACHUSETTS UNOFFICIAL COPPERS

Nothing is known regarding the origin of the Pine Tree piece dated 1776. The obverse has a crude pine tree with the letters 1d LM at its base; Inscription, MASSACHUSETTS STATE. The reverse has a figure probably intended to represent the Goddess of Liberty, seated on a globe and holding a liberty cap and staff. A dog sits at her feet. The legend LIBERTY AND VIRTUE surrounds the figure.

1776 Pine Tree copper (*Unique*) .... —

A similar piece, probably from the same source, has an Indian with bow on the obverse, and seated figure on the reverse.

1776 Indian copper (*Unique*) .... —

This piece is sometimes called the "Janus Copper." There are three heads facing left, front and right on the obverse with the inscription STATE OF MASSA. ½ D. The reverse shows the Goddess of Liberty facing right, resting against a globe inscribed GODDESS LIBERTY 1776.

1776 Halfpenny, 3 heads on obverse (*Unique*) — Garrett Sale, 1979 .... $40,000

MASSACHUSETTS AUTHORIZED ISSUES

An "Act for establishing a mint for the coinage of gold, silver and copper" was passed by the Massachusetts General Court October 17, 1786. The next year the Council directed that the design should incorporate "the figure of an Indian with a bow and arrow and a star at one side, with the word 'Commonwealth,' the reverse, a spread eagle with the words 'of Massachusetts A.D. 1787'."

MASSACHUSETTS

The coinage of Massachusetts copper cents and half cents in 1787 and 1788 was under the direction of Joshua Witherle. These were the first coins bearing the denomination Cent as established by Congress. Many varieties exist, the most valuable being that with arrows in the eagle's right talon.

Most of the dies for these coppers were made by Joseph Callender. Jacob Perkins of Newburyport also engraved some of the dies.

The mint was abandoned early in 1789 in compliance with the newly ratified constitution.

1787 Half Cent	
Good	$75.00
Fine.................	175.00
V. Fine...............	325.00
Ex. Fine..............	800.00

Obverse	Arrows in Eagle's Right Talon	Arrows in Left Talon

	Good	Fine	V. Fine	E. Fine
1787 Cent, arrows in right talon—				
Garrett Sale, 1979	$2,500	$6,000	——	——
1787 Cent, arrows in left talon.............	60.00	150.00	$350.00	$725.00
1787 Cent, "horn" (die break) from				
eagle's head	60.00	150.00	350.00	850.00

1788 Half Cent	
Good	$75.00
Fine.............	200.00
Very Fine........	375.00
Ex. Fine	850.00

1788 Cent	
Period after Massachusetts	
Good	60.00
Fine.............	150.00
V. Fine	350.00
Ex. Fine	750.00
No period after	
Massachusetts	
Good	65.00
Fine.............	175.00
V. Fine	375.00
Ex. Fine	875.00

CONNECTICUT

Authority for establishing a mint near New Haven was granted by the State to Samuel Bishop, Joseph Hopkins, James Hillhouse and John Goodrich in 1785.

Available records indicate that most of the Connecticut coppers were coined under a sub-contract by Samuel Broome and Jeremiah Platt, former New York merchants. Abel Buel and James Atlee were the principal die-sinkers.

1785 Copper
Bust Facing Right
Good............ $50.00
V. Good......... 75.00
Fine 150.00
V. Fine.......... 400.00

1785 Copper
African Head
Good........... $60.00
V. Good....... 125.00
Fine 250.00
V. Fine........ 675.00

1785 Copper
Bust Facing Left
Good............ 150.00
V. Good......... 275.00
Fine 450.00
V. Fine.......... 850.00

1786 Copper
ETLIB INDE
Good 65.00
V. Good 125.00
Fine.............. 250.00
V. Fine............ 500.00

1786 Copper
Large Head Facing Right
Good............ 75.00
V. Good......... 175.00
Fine 400.00
V. Fine.......... 850.00

[39]

CONNECTICUT

1786 Copper
Mailed Bust Facing Left
Good $40.00
V. Good 70.00
Fine 150.00
V. Fine 350.00

1786 Copper
Mailed Bust Facing Left
Hercules Head
Good........... $100.00
V. Good........ 150.00
Fine 350.00
V. Fine........ 800.00

1786 Copper
Draped Bust
Good 75.00
V. Good 135.00
Fine........... 300.00
V. Fine......... 650.00

The Connecticut coppers, especially those dated 1787 and 1788, were usually crudely struck and on imperfect planchets.

1787 Copper
Mailed Bust Facing Left
IND ET LIB
1787 over 1788
Good $90.00
V. Good 150.00
Fine.............. 400.00
V. Fine 850.00

1787 Copper
Small Head Facing Right
ETLIB INDE
Good 100.00
V. Good 150.00
Fine.............. 325.00
V. Fine 775.00

1787 Copper
Mailed Bust Facing Right
INDE ET LIB
Good.................. 90.00
V. Good................ 175.00
Fine 375.00
V. Fine................ 1,100

1787 Muttonhead Variety
Good.................. 90.00
V. Good................ 140.00
Fine 300.00
V. Fine................ 600.00

CONNECTICUT

	Good	V. Good	Fine	V. Fine
1787 Mailed bust facing left	$40.00	$75.00	$140.00	$350.00
1787 Similar, laughing head variety	50.00	80.00	145.00	375.00
1787 Similar, Hercules head (see 1786)	250.00	400.00	725.00	1,250
1787 Similar, dated 1787 over 1877	65.00	135.00	275.00	675.00

	Good	V. Good	Fine	V. Fine
1787 Similar, horned bust variety	35.00	75.00	175.00	375.00
1787 Similar, CONNECT variety	55.00	100.00	225.00	500.00

	Good	V. Good	Fine	V. Fine
1787 Draped bust facing left (many varieties)	40.00	60.00	125.00	300.00
1787 Similar, AUCIORI variety	40.00	60.00	130.00	325.00
1787 Similar, AUCTOPI variety	45.00	75.00	150.00	350.00
1787 Similar, AUCTOBI variety	50.00	80.00	200.00	375.00
1787 Similar, CONNFC variety	45.00	75.00	140.00	300.00
1787 Similar, CONNLC variety	60.00	120.00	250.00	450.00
1787 Similar, FNDE variety	50.00	80.00	145.00	325.00
1787 Similar, ETLIR variety	45.00	70.00	135.00	325.00
1787 Similar, ETIIB variety	45.00	70.00	135.00	325.00

	Good	V. Good	Fine	V. Fine
1788 Mailed bust facing right	45.00	85.00	175.00	450.00
1788 Similar, small head (see picture page 40)	300.00	500.00	1,400	3,000

CONNECTICUT

	Good	V. Good	Fine	V. Fine
1788 Mailed bust facing left...............	$40.00	$65.00	$150.00	$375.00
1788 Mailed bust left CONNLC	45.00	80.00	200.00	425.00

1788 Draped bust facing left...............	45.00	75.00	200.00	350.00
1788 Similar, CONNLC variety..............	75.00	125.00	275.00	500.00
1788 Similar, INDL ET LIB variety	65.00	115.00	225.00	475.00

NEW YORK
THE BRASHER DOUBLOON

Perhaps the most famous pieces coined before the establishment of the U.S. Mint at Philadelphia were those produced by a well-known goldsmith and jeweler, Ephraim Brasher (pronounced BRAYzher), neighbor of George Washington, in New York.

Brasher produced a gold piece weighing about 408 grains, approximately equal in value to a Spanish doubloon (about $16.00).

The punch-mark EB appears in either of two positions as illustrated. This mark is found on some foreign gold coins as well, and probably was so used by Brasher as evidence of his testing of their value.

★

NEW YORK

1787 Doubloon, punch on breast. Gold *(Unique)* — Garrett Sale, 1981		$625,000
1787 Doubloon, punch on wing. Gold	Garrett Sale, 1979	725,000
	Auction '79 Sale, 1979	430,000
1787 Half Doubloon. Gold *(Unique)* — Smithsonian Collection		

The unique piece known as a "half doubloon", is undersized, but made from the normal doubloon dies. Its source is undetermined. A mystery also surrounds the origin and intent of the 1742 "Lima Style Doubloon", which includes an E.B. counterstamp and the name Brasher.

COPPER COINAGE

Several individuals petitioned the New York legislature in early 1787 for the right to coin copper for the state, but a coinage was never authorized. Instead a law was passed to regulate the copper coins already in use. Nevertheless, various unauthorized copper coins were issued within the state, principally by two private mints.

One firm, known as Machin's Mills, was located at the mills of Thomas Machin near Newburgh. Shortly after this mint was formed, on April 18, 1787, it was merged with the Rupert, Vermont mint operated by Reuben Harmon, Jr. Harmon held a coinage grant from the Republic of Vermont. The combined partnership agreed to conduct their business in New York, Vermont, Connecticut, or elsewhere if they could benefit by it.

The Operations at Machin's Mills were conducted in secret and were looked upon with suspicion by the local residents. They minted several varieties of imitation George III halfpence, and coppers of Connecticut, Vermont and New Jersey.

The other mint, located in or near New York City, was operated by John Bailey and Ephraim Brasher. They had petitioned the legislature on February 12, 1787 for a franchise to coin copper. The extent of their partnership and details of their operation are not known. Studies of the state coinages show that they produced primarily the EXCELSIOR and NOVA EBORAC pieces of New York, and the "running fox" New Jersey coppers.

★

	Good	Fine	V. Fine
1786 NON VI VIRTUTE VICI			
(Believed to be the bust of Washington.)	$2,300	$4,500	$8,500

NEW YORK

★

	Good	Fine	V. Fine
1787 EXCELSIOR copper, eagle on globe facing right....	$900.00	$2,300	$4,800
1787 EXCELSIOR copper, eagle on globe facing left	900.00	2,200	4,500

1787 Large Eagle on Reverse—Arrows and branch
   transposed —Garrett Sale, 1979 .... $20,000

★

1787 George Clinton
Good	$5,000
Fine............	10,000
V. Fine	17,000

1787
Indian and N.Y. Arms
Good	$2,500
Fine...........	5,500
V. Fine	8,500

★

NEW YORK

<table>
</table>

1787
Indian and Eagle
on Globe

Good............	4,750
Fine.............	8,500
V. Fine..........	13,500

1787 Indian and George III
Reverse (*3 known*) $8,500

IMITATION BRITISH HALFPENCE
(Machin's Mills Coinage, Etc. 1786-1789)

The most common coin used for small transactions in early America was the copper British halfpence. Wide acceptance and the non-legal tender status of these copper coins made them a prime choice for unauthorized reproduction by private individuals. Many such counterfeits were made in this country by casting or other crude methods. Some were made in England and imported to this country. Pieces dated 1781 and 1785 seem to have been made specifically for this purpose, while others were circulated in both countries.

During the American state coinage era, James F. Atlee engraved dies that were used to mint unauthorized lightweight imitation British halfpence. These American made British halfpence have the same devices, legends and in some cases the same dates as genuine regal halfpence. There are three distinct groups of Atlee halfpence, all linked to the regular state coinages. The first group was struck in New York City in affiliation with Walter Mould during 1786. Group two was minted in New York City in association with John Bailey and Ephraim Brasher during the first half of 1787. The third group was struck at Machin's Mills during the second half of 1787 and into 1788.

Dates used on these pieces were often evasive and are: 1771, 1772 and 1774-1776 for group one; 1747 and 1787 for group two; and 1776, 1778, 1787 and 1788 for group three. Atlee's halfpence can be identified by a single outline in the crosses (British Union) of Britannia's shield and large triangular denticles along the coin's circumference. These pieces are not to be confused with the similar English made George III counterfeits, some of which have identical dates, or genuine British halfpence, which were dated 1770 to 1775.

NEW YORK

	GROUP I	**GROUP II**		**GROUP III**	

	Good	V. Good	Fine	V. Fine
Machin's Mills Copper, various dates				
GEORGIUS III REX/BRITANNIA	$60.00	$125.00	$275.00	$450.00

THE NOVA EBORACS

1787
NOVA EBORAC
Reverse Seated
Figure Facing Right

Fair	$25.00
Good	100.00
Fine	325.00
V. Fine	650.00

1787
NOVA EBORAC
Reverse Seated
Figure Facing Left

Fair	$25.00
Good	100.00
Fine	300.00
V. Fine	550.00

NEW YORK

1787
NOVA EBORAC
Small Head

Fair	$500.00
Good...........	1,250
Fine	——
V. Fine........	——

1787
NOVA EBORAC
Large Head

Fair...............	$100.00
Good.............	275.00
Fine.............	800.00
V. Fine............	2,100

NEW JERSEY

On June 1, 1786, the New Jersey Colonial legislature granted to Thomas Goadsby, Albion Cox and Walter Mould authority to coin some three million coppers weighing six pennyweight and six grains apiece, not later than June 1788, on condition that they delivered to the Treasurer of the State, "one-tenth part of the full sum they shall strike and coin," in quarterly installments. These coppers were to pass current at 15 to the shilling.

In an operation of this kind the contractors purchased the metal and assumed all expenses of coining. The difference between these expenses and the total face value of the coins issued represented the profit.

Later Goadsby and Cox asked authority to coin two-thirds of the total independently. Their petition was granted November 22, 1786. Mould was known to have produced his coins at Morristown, while Cox (and probably Goadsby) operated in Rahway. Coins were also minted in Elizabethtown and Newburgh, New York.

The series offers many varieties. The obverse shows a horse's head with plow and the legend NOVA CAESAREA (New Jersey). The reverse has a United States shield and legend E PLURIBUS UNUM (One composed of many).

1786 Date Under Draw Bar

1786 No Coulter

	Good	Fine	V. Fine
1786 Date under draw bar			$30,000
1786 No coulter	$150.00	$600.00	1,200

NEW JERSEY

Narrow Shield   **Wide Shield**

		Good	Fine	V. Fine
1786	Narrow shield	$40.00	$150.00	$325.00
1786	Wide shield	50.00	175.00	350.00
1786	Similar, bridle variety	50.00	175.00	350.00

Pluribs Variety, Lg. Planchet   **Small Planchet**   **Outlined Shield**

1787	Pronounced outline to shield	40.00	150.00	300.00
1787	Small planchet, plain shield	40.00	150.00	300.00
1787	Large planchet, plain shield	40.00	150.00	300.00
1787	Similar, PLURIBS variety	75.00	175.00	625.00

Serpent Head   **Fox Variety**

1787	Serpent head variety	65.00	250.00	650.00
1788	Horse's head facing right	45.00	150.00	350.00
1788	Similar, running fox before legend	80.00	275.00	700.00
1788	Horse's head facing left	175.00	600.00	1,000

VERMONT

Reuben Harmon, Jr., of Rupert, Vermont, was granted permission to coin copper pieces for a period of two years beginning July 1, 1785. The well-known Vermont plow coppers were first produced in that year. The franchise was extended for eight years in 1786.

Harmon's mint was located in the northeast corner of Rupert near a stream known as Millbrook. Col. William Coley, a New York goldsmith, made the first dies.

Some of the late issues were made near Newburgh, N.Y. by the Machin's Mills coiners.

1785 IMMUNE COLUMBIA   **1785 VERMONTS**

	Good	Fine		Good	Fine
1785 IMMUNE COLUMBIA...	$1,750	$3,500	1785 VERMONTS ...	$200.00	$800.00

1785 VERMONTIS   **1786 VERMONTENSIUM**

1785 VERMONTIS ..	275.00	800.00	1786 VERMON-TENSIUM	150.00	600.00

1786 Baby Head   **1787 BRITANNIA**

1786 Baby head ..	250.00	800.00	1787 BRITANNIA ...	80.00	275.00

Reverse of this coin is always weak.

VERMONT

1786 Bust Left

	Good	Fine
1786 Bust left	$125.00	$550.00

1788 (Several Varieties)

	Good	Fine
1788 (Several var.)	$90.00	$300.00
1788 VERMON AUCTORI	—	—
1788 *ET LIB* *INDE	200.00	675.00

1787 Bust Left

| 1787 Bust left . . . | — | — |

1788 GEORGIVS III REX

| 1788 GEORGIVS III REX . . . . | 225.00 | 875.00 |

This piece should not be confused with the common English halfpence with similar design and reverse legend BRITANNIA.

1787 Bust Right

| 1787 Bust right (Several var.) | 100.00 | 350.00 |

Most Vermont coppers are struck on poor and defective planchets. Well struck coins on smooth full planchets command higher prices.

VII. PRIVATE TOKENS AFTER CONFEDERATION
NORTH AMERICAN TOKEN

This piece was struck in Dublin, Ireland. The obverse shows the seated figure of Hibernia facing left. The date of issue is believed to have been much later than that shown on the token.

Like many Irish tokens, this issue found its way to America in limited quantities and was accepted near the Canadian border.

Copper or Brass

	V. Good	Fine	V. Fine
1781..	$35.00	$70.00	$175.00

THE BAR "COPPER"

The Bar "Copper" is undated and of uncertain origin. It has thirteen parallel and unconnected bars on one side. On the other side is the large roman letter USA monogram. The design was supposedly copied from a Continental button.

The significance of the design is clearly defined by its extreme simplicity. The separate thirteen states (bars) unite into a single entity as symbolized by the interlocking letters (USA).

This coin is believed to have been issued at the same time as the Nova Constellatio coppers by Thomas Wyon at Birmingham, England, for America. It first circulated in New York during November, 1785.

On the less valuable struck copy made by J. A. Bolen c. 1862 the A passes under, instead of over, the S.

★

	V. Good	Fine	v. Fine	E. Fine
Undated (about 1785) Bar "Copper".......	$275.00	$550.00	$800.00	$1,650

AUCTORI PLEBIS TOKEN

This token is sometimes included with the coins of Connecticut as it greatly resembles issues of that state. It was struck in England by an unknown maker, possibly for use in America.

1787
AUCTORI PLEBIS

Good	$50.00
V. Good	100.00
Fine	150.00
V. Fine	300.00

THE MOTT TOKEN

This item has long been confused as an early token because of its date 1789. It most likely was produced c. 1839 as a commemorative of the founding of the Mott Company, and probably served as a business card. The firm was composed of William and John Mott, located at 240 Water Street, a fashionable section of New York at that time.

	V. Good	Fine	V. Fine	E. Fine
"1789" Mott Token, thick planchet............	$100.00	$210.00	$350.00	$650.00
"1789" Mott Token, thin planchet.............	130.00	300.00	450.00	900.00
"1789" Mott Token, entire edge engrailed	165.00	450.00	650.00	1,600

STANDISH BARRY, BALTIMORE, MARYLAND

Standish Barry, a Baltimore silversmith, circulated a silver threepence in 1790. He was a watch and clockmaker, engraver and later a silversmith. The tokens were believed to have been an advertising venture at a time when small change was scarce. The precise date, July 4, 90, on this piece may indicate that Barry intended to commemorate Independence Day, but there are no records to substantiate this belief. The head shown on the obverse is probably that of George Washington. The legend BALTIMORE TOWN JULY 4, 90 appears in the border. STANDISH BARRY THREE PENCE is on the reverse.

	Fine	V. Fine
1790 Threepence...	$3,750	$7,000

ALBANY CHURCH PENNY

The First Presbyterian Church of Albany, New York authorized an issue of one thousand copper uniface tokens in 1790. These passed at twelve to a shilling and were used to stop contributions of worn and counterfeit coppers. Two varieties were made, one with the addition of a large D above the word CHURCH.

	V. Good	Fine
(1790) Without D............	$2,200	$5,000
(1790) With D added........	2,100	4,500

KENTUCKY TOKEN

These tokens were struck in England about 1792-94. Each star in the triangle represents a state, identified by its initial letter. These pieces are usually called Kentucky Cents because the letter K (for Kentucky) happens to be at the top. Some of the edges are plain; others are engrailed with an oblique reeding, and some have the edge lettered: "PAYABLE IN LANCASTER LONDON OR BRISTOL," or "PAYABLE AT BEDWORTH NUNEATON OR HINKLEY."

	V. Good	V. Fine	E. Fine	Unc.
Cent, (1792-94) plain edge	$60.00	$150.00	$300.00	$725.00
Cent, engrailed edge		400.00	550.00	1,700
Cent, lettered edge PAYABLE AT BEDWORTH, etc.	——	——	——	——
Cent, lettered edge PAYABLE IN LANCASTER, etc.	80.00	200.00	350.00	950.00
Cent, lettered edge PAYABLE AT I. FIELDING, etc.	——	——	——	——

FRANKLIN PRESS

This piece is an English tradesman's token but, being associated with Benjamin Franklin, has accordingly been included in American collections.

1794 Franklin Press Token	65.00	150.00	350.00	775.00

TALBOT, ALLUM & LEE CENTS

Talbot, Allum & Lee, engaged in the India trade and located at 241 Pearl Street, New York, placed a large quantity of English-made coppers in circulation during 1794 and 1795. ONE CENT appears on the 1794 issue, and the legend PAYABLE AT THE STORE OF on the edge. The denomination is not found on the 1795 reverse but the edge legend was changed to read: WE PROMISE TO PAY THE

TALBOT, ALLUM & LEE CENTS

BEARER ONE CENT. Rare plain edge specimens of both dates exist. Exceptional pieces have edge ornamented or with lettering CAMBRIDGE BEDFORD AND HUNTINGDON.X.X.

1794 Cent with
NEW YORK

V. Good	$50.00
V. Fine	175.00
Unc.	900.00

1794 Cent Without
NEW YORK

V. Good	425.00
V. Fine	1,000
Unc.	5,000

1795 Cent

V. Good	$60.00
V. Fine	175.00
E. Fine	350.00
Unc.	850.00

MYDDELTON TOKENS

These tokens were struck at the Soho Mint of Boulton and Watt near Birmingham, England. They are unsurpassed in beauty and design by any piece of this period.

1796
Myddelton Token

	Proof
Copper	$7,000
Silver	6,000

COPPER COMPANY OF UPPER CANADA

The obverse of this piece is the same as the Myddleton token. The new reverse legend was apparently intended for Canadian circulation, or it was used to give the token credibility.

	Proof
1796 Copper	$4,000

THE CASTORLAND MEDAL

This medal is dated 1796 and alludes to a proposed French settlement known as Castorland in Carthage, New York, at the time of the French Revolution.

1796 Silver original. (Reeded edge).. $5,000
1796 Copper original. (Reeded edge, unbroken dies) 3,500

Copy dies are still available and have been used at the Paris Mint for restriking throughout the years. Restrikes are thinner and usually have more modern letters.

NEW YORK THEATRE TOKEN

Token penny issued by Skidmore illustrating the Park Theatre, New York c. 1797.

	E. Fine	Proof
Penny, THE • THEATRE • AT • NEW YORK • AMERICA	$3,200	$7,500

NEW SPAIN (TEXAS) JOLA

These tokens were authorized by the military governor of San Antonio in 1818. Eight thousand pieces were coined by Jose Antonio de la Garza (JAG). Large and small planchet varieties exist, and all are very rare.

1818 ½ Real..................... Fine $2,000

NORTH WEST COMPANY TOKEN

These tokens were probably valued at one beaver and struck in Birmingham in 1820 by John Walker & Co. All but two known specimens are holed, and most have been found in the region of the lower Columbia River valley in Oregon.

V. Good
1820 Copper or brass ... $700.00

VIII. WASHINGTON PIECES

An interesting series of coins and tokens dated from 1783 to 1795 bear the

WASHINGTON PIECES

portrait of George Washington. The likenesses in most instances were faithfully reproduced and were designed to honor Washington. Many of these pieces were of English origin and made later than the dates indicate.

The legends generally signify a strong unity among the states and a marked display of patriotism which pervaded the new nation during that period. We find among these tokens an employment of what were soon to become our official coin devices, namely, the American eagle, the United States shield and stars. The denomination One Cent is used in several instances, while on some of the English pieces Halfpenny will be found. Several of these pieces were private patterns for proposed coinage contracts.

GEORGIUS TRIUMPHO TOKEN

Although the head shown on this token bears a strong resemblance to that upon some coins of George III, many collectors consider the Georgius Triumpho (Triumphant George) a token intended to commemorate the successful termination of the Revolutionary War — a triumph justly claimed for Washington.

The reverse side shows the Goddess of Liberty behind a framework of thirteen bars and fleur de lis. She holds an olive branch in her right hand and staff of liberty in her left. VOCE POPOLI (By the Voice of the People) 1783.

 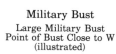

1783 GEORGIUS TRIUMPHO

V. Good	$65.00
Fine	200.00
V. Fine	500.00

Military Bust
Large Military Bust
Point of Bust Close to W
(illustrated)

	Fine	V. Fine	E. Fine
1783 Large military bust	$60.00	$125.00	$275.00
1783 Small military bust, plain edge	65.00	135.00	300.00
1783 Small military bust, engrailed edge	85.00	185.00	425.00

1783 Draped bust, no button (illustrated)	60.00	125.00	275.00
1783 Draped bust, with button on drapery at neck ..	110.00	185.00	400.00

WASHINGTON PIECES

	Proof
1783 Draped bust. Copper restrike, plain edge	$575.00
1783 Draped bust. Copper restrike, engrailed edge	375.00
1783 Draped bust. Silver restrike, engrailed edge	900.00

1783
UNITY STATES

V. Good	$60.00
V. Fine	150.00
E. Fine	300.00

Undated Double Head Cent

Fine	$65.00
V. Fine	150.00
E. Fine	300.00

Satirical Medal presumably of
American origin.
1784 Ugly head —
    Roper Sale, 1983 ..... $14,850

1791 Cent
Edge Lettered: UNITED STATES OF AMERICA

	Fine	*E. Fine*	*Unc.*
1791 Cent, small eagle	$250.00	$625.00	$1,750
1791 Cent, large eagle..........................	225.00	600.00	1,700

**1791 Liverpool
Halfpenny
Lettered Edge**

Fine	$500.00
Ex. Fine	900.00
Unc.	2,000

WASHINGTON PIECES

1792 Eagle with Stars
Copper..........   ——
Silver...........   ——
Gold (*Unique*)....   ——

Eagle reverse with "Washington Born Virginia" obverse (3 known)...   ——

	Fine		*Fine*
(1792) Undated Cent "WASHINGTON BORN VIRGINIA"		1792 Cent "WASHINGTON PRESIDENT"	
Copper..................	$1,900	Plain edge	$3,500
Silver....................	——	Lettered edge	——

Uniface restrike of Obverse exists, made by Albert Collis, 1959.

★

	V. Good	*Fine*
1792 Small eagle. Silver.................................	——	——
1792 Small eagle. Copper...............................	$2,750	$4,000
1792 Same. Ornamented edge (circles and squares)........	——	——
1792 Same. Silver.......................................	——	——
1792 Lg. eagle. Silver (unknown origin) — Garrett Sale, 1981 (Ex. F.)		$16,500

WASHINGTON PIECES

**1792 Cent
Roman Head**

Lettered Edge:
UNITED STATES OF
AMERICA
Proof $14,000

**1793 Ship
Halfpenny**

Lettered Edge
Fine $125.00
V. Fine............ 275.00
Ex. Fine.......... 450.00
Plain edge (Rare) .. ——

**1795 Halfpenny
Grate Token**
(Large coat buttons
variety illustrated.)

	V. Fine	E. Fine	Unc.
1795 Large buttons, lettered edge	$300.00	$625.00	$1,400
1795 Large buttons, reeded edge	125.00	250.00	650.00
1795 Small buttons, reeded edge	150.00	375.00	800.00

LIBERTY AND SECURITY TOKENS

	Fine	V. Fine	E. Fine
1795 Halfpenny, plain edge	$100.00	$200.00	$500.00
1795 Halfpenny, LONDON edge	85.00	150.00	400.00
1795 Halfpenny, BIRMINGHAM edge...............	100.00	175.00	475.00
1795 Halfpenny, ASYLUM edge	175.00	400.00	850.00
1795 Penny, ASYLUM edge	——	——	

WASHINGTON PIECES

Liberty and
Security Penny
Undated (1795)

Fine $150.00
V. Fine............ 275.00
E. Fine............ 500.00
Unc. 1,600

SUCCESS MEDALS

	Fine	*V. Fine*	*E. Fine*
SUCCESS medal, large. Plain or reeded edge	$150.00	$275.00	$500.00
SUCCESS medal, small. Plain or reeded edge	175.00	300.00	600.00

These pieces are struck in copper or brass and are believed to have been made in the mid nineteenth century. Specimens with full silvering are extremely rare and more valuable.

NORTH WALES HALFPENNY

	Good	*Fine*
1795 NORTH WALES		
Halfpenny .	$80.00	$200.00
Lettered edge	400.00	900.00
Two stars at each		
side of harp....	800.00	2,200

IX. THE FUGIO CENTS

The first coins issued by authority of the United States were the "Fugio" cents. Entries in the Journal of Congress supply interesting information about proceedings relating to this coinage.

"Saturday, April 21, 1787. . . .

"That the board of treasury be authorized to contract for three hundred tons of copper coin of the federal standard, agreeable to the proposition of Mr. James Jarvis, . . . That it be coined at the expense of the contractor, etc."

On Friday, July 6, 1787, there was "Resolved, that the board of treasury direct the contractor for the copper coinage to stamp on one side of each piece the following device, viz: thirteen circles linked together, a small circle in the middle, with the words 'United States,' around it; and in the centre, the words 'We are one'; on the other side of the same piece the following device, viz: a dial with the hours expressed on the face of it; a meridian sun above on one side of which is the word 'Fugio,' (The intended meaning is, 'time flies') and on the other the year in figures '1787', below the dial, the words 'Mind Your Business.' "

The legends have been credited to Benjamin Franklin, and the coin, as a consequence, has been referred to as the Franklin Cent.

These cents were coined in New Haven, Conn., and possibly elsewhere. Most of the copper used in this coinage came from military stores. It is believed to have been the copper bands which held together the powder kegs sent to us by the French. The dies were made by Abel Buel of New Haven.

1787 WITH POINTED RAYS

	V. Good	Fine	V. Fine	E. Fine	Unc.
Obv. no cinquefoils. Cross after date. Rev. label with raised rims	(Ex. Rare)				
Same obv., rev. STATES UNITED	$375.00	$550.00	$1,300	——	——
Same obv., rev. UNITED STATES	325.00	500.00	1,150	——	——

Note: The following types with pointed rays have regular obverses punctuated with four cinquefoils.

STATES UNITED at sides of circle.

	V. Good	Fine	V. Fine	E. Fine	Unc.
Cinquefoils (small, five-bladed clover design) on label	$135.00	$250.00	$425.00	$675.00	$1,475
STATES UNITED, 1 over horizontal 1	125.00	300.00	650.00	1,100	
UNITED STATES. at sides of circle	110.00	225.00	400.00	625.00	1,250

THE FUGIO CENTS

	V. Good	Fine	V. Fine	E. Fine	Unc.
STATES UNITED. Label with raised rims (simply two concentric circles). Large letters in WE ARE ONE	$250.00	$350.00	$1,000	$2,400	——
STATES UNITED. 8-pointed stars on label .	200.00	300.00	675.00	1,600	——
UNITED above, STATES below. (Rare)	——	——	——	——	——

1787 WITH CLUB RAYS

	V. Good	Fine	V. Fine
Club Rays. Rounded ends	$175.00	$375.00	$900.00
Club Rays. Concavce ends to rays:			
FUCIO (C instead of G). (Ex. Rare)......	1,500	4,200	6,000
Club Rays. Concave ends. FUGIO UNITED STATES ...	1,600	4,500	6,500
Club Rays. Similar, STATES UNITED Rev.	——	——	——

American Congress Pattern

New Haven "Restrike", note narrow rings

		E. Fine	Unc.
Reverse with rays and AMERICAN CONGRESS....... $65,000	Gold (2 known)	——	——
	Silver..............	$500.00	$1,000
	Copper or Brass	200.00	400.00

New Haven "restrikes" were supposedly struck from dies discovered by the fourteen-year-old C. Wyllys Betts in 1858 on the site of the Broome & Platt Store in New Haven, Conn., where the originals were made. Three pairs of dies were reportedly found and are still extant. Actually, the "restrikes" were made from copy dies c. 1860.

BIBLIOGRAPHY

Baker, W. S. *Medallic Portraits of Washington.* Philadelphia 1885 (reprinted 1965).
Crosby, S. S. *The Early Coins of America.* Boston 1875 (reprinted 1945, 1965, 1975).
Dickeson, M. W. *The American Numismatic Manual.* Philadelphia 1859, 1860, 1865.
Kessler, Alan. *The Fugio Cents.* Newtonville, Massachusetts 1976.
Maris, Edward. *A Historic Sketch of the Coins of New Jersey.* Philadelphia 1881 (reprinted 1925).
Miller, Henry C. and Hillyer Ryder. *The State Coinages of New England.* New York 1920.
Nelson, Philip. *The Coinage of William Wood 1722-1733.* London 1903 (reprinted 1959).
Newman, Eric P. *Coinage for Colonial Virginia.* New York 1957.
    Studies on Money in Early America. American Numismatic Society. New York, 1976.
Noe, Sydney P. *The New England and Willow Tree Coinage of Massachusetts.* New York 1943. *The Oak Tree Coinage of Massachusetts.* New York 1947, and *The Pine Tree Coinage of Massachusetts.* New York 1952. (all reprinted 1973).
Wurtzbach, Carl. *Massachusetts Colonial Silver Money.* 1937.

FIRST UNITED STATES MINT ISSUES

Many members of the House favored a representation of the President's head on the obverse of each coin. Others considered the idea a monarchical practice. Washington is believed to have expressed disapproval of the use of his portrait on our coins.

The majority considered a figure emblematic of Liberty more appropriate and the Senate finally concurred in this opinion. Robert Birch was an engraver employed at designing proposed devices for our coins. He, perhaps together with Adam Eckfeldt, engraved the dies for the disme and half disme. He has also been associated with a large copper cent of unusual design known as the Birch Cent.

1792 SILVER CENTER CENT

Cent. Silver Center — Garrett Sale, 1981 (Unc.)...................... $95,000
Cent. No silver center... 40,000

1792 BIRCH CENT

Copper — Garrett Sale, 1981 (Unc.) 200,000
G.W. PT. (George Washington President) below wreath, white metal —
    Garrett Sale, 1981 (*Unique*) 90,000

1792 HALF DISME

	Good	Fine	V. Fine
Silver...	$1,500	$4,500	$7,500
Copper (*Unique*).......................................			

FIRST UNITED STATES MINT ISSUES

1792 DISME

	E. Fine	Unc.
Silver (*3 known*)		
Copper	$30,000	$50,000

1792 PATTERN QUARTER DOLLAR

Copper....... (*2 known*)
White Metal..... (*Unique*)

MINTS AND MINT MARKS

Mint marks are small letters designating where coins were made. Coins struck at Philadelphia before 1979 (except 1942-1945 five-cent pieces) do not have a mint mark. Starting in 1979 a letter P was used on the dollar, and thereafter on all other denominations except the cent. Mint mark position is on the reverse of nearly all coins prior to 1965 (the cent is an exception), and on the obverse after 1967. Letters used are as follows:

      C — Charlotte, North Carolina (gold coins only). 1838-1861.
      CC — Carson City, Nevada. 1870-1893.
      D — Dahlonega, Georgia (gold coins only). 1838-1861.
      D — Denver, Colorado. 1906 to date.
      O — New Orleans, Louisiana. 1838-1909.
      P — Philadelphia, Pennsylvania. 1793 to date.
      S — San Francisco, California. 1854 to date.
      W — West Point. 1984 to date.

All dies for United States coins are made at the Philadelphia Mint. Dies for use at branch mints are stamped with the appropriate mint mark before they are shipped from Philadelphia. Because this was a hand operation prior to 1985, the exact positioning and size of the mint mark may vary slightly, depending on where and how deeply the punch was impressed. This also accounts for double-punched and superimposed mint marks such as the 1900 D over D, and D over S Buffalo nickels. Polishing of dies may also alter the apparent size of fine details. Occasionally the mint mark is inadvertently left off a die sent to a branch mint, as was the case with some of the recent proof dimes. Similarly, some 1982 dimes without mint mark were made as business strikes.

Prior to 1900, punches for mint marks varied greatly in size. This is particularly noticeable in the 1850 to 1880 period in which the letters range from very small to very large. An attempt to standardize sizes started in 1892 with the Barber series, but exceptions are seen in the 1892O half dollar and 1905 O dime, both of which have normal and "microscopic" mint marks. A more or less standard size small mint mark was used on all minor coins starting in 1909, and on all dimes, quarters and halves after the Barber series was replaced in 1916. Slight variations in mint mark size occur through 1940 with notable differences in 1928, when small and large S mint marks were used.

In recent years a single D or S punch has been used to mark all branch mint dies. The change to the larger D for Denver coins occurred in 1933. Dimes, half dollars and dollars of 1934 exist with either the old, smaller size mint mark or the new, larger size D. All other denominations of 1934 and after are standard. The San Francisco mint mark was changed to larger size during 1941 and, with the exception of the half dollar, all 1941 S coins are known with either small or large size mint mark. Halves were not changed until 1942, and the 1942 S and 1943 S pieces exist both ways. The 1945 S dime with "microscopic" S is an unexplained abnormality. In 1979 the punches were replaced. Varieties of some 1979 coins appear with either the old or new shaped S or D. The S punch was again replaced in 1982 with a more distinct letter.

Mint mark application technique for proof coins was changed in 1985 when the letter was applied directly to the production hub rather than being hand punched on each working die. At the same time all the mint mark letters were made much larger and clearer than those of previous years.

PROOF COINS

A "proof" is a specimen striking of coinage for presentation, souvenir, exhibition, or numismatic purposes. Pre-1968 proofs were made only at the Philadelphia Mint. Current proofs are made at San Francisco and West Point.

The term "proof" refers to the method of manufacture and not the condition of a coin. Regular production coins in mint state have coruscating, frosty luster, soft details, and minor imperfections. Proof coins can usually be distinguished by their sharpness of detail, high wire edge, and extremely brilliant, mirrorlike surface. All proofs are originally sold by the mint at a premium.

PROOF COINS

Very few proof coins were made prior to 1856. Because of their rarity and infrequent sales, they are not all listed in this catalog.

Frosted proofs were issued prior to 1936 and starting again in the late 1970's. These have a brilliant mirrorlike field with contrasting dull or frosted design.

Matte proofs have a granular "sandblast" surface instead of the mirror finish. Matte proof cents, nickels, and gold coins were issued from 1908 to 1916; a few 1921 and 1922 silver dollars were also struck this way.

Brilliant proofs have been issued from 1936 to date. These have a uniformly brilliant mirrorlike surface and sharp, high relief details.

"Prooflike" coins are occasionally seen. These are specimens from the first few impressions of regular coinage dies from any mint. They are not true proofs, but may have most of the characteristics of a proof coin and generally command a premium. Collectors should beware of coins that have been buffed to look like proofs; magnification will reveal polishing lines and lack of detail.

How A Proof Coin Is Made . . .

Selected dies are inspected for perfection and are highly polished and cleaned. They are again wiped clean or polished after every 15 to 25 impressions and are replaced frequently to avoid imperfections from worn dies. Coinage blanks are polished and cleaned to assure high quality in striking. They are then hand fed into the coinage press one at a time, each blank receiving two or more blows from the dies to bring up sharp, high relief details. The coinage operation is done at slow speed with extra pressure. Finished proofs are individually inspected and are handled by gloves or tongs. They also receive a final inspection by packers before being sonically sealed in special plastic cases.

After a lapse of twenty years, proof coins were struck at the Philadelphia Mint from 1936 to 1942 inclusive. In 1942, when the composition of the five-cent piece was changed, there were two types of this denomination available to collectors. The striking of proof coins was temporarily suspended from 1943 to 1949, and again from 1965 to 1967; during the latter period special mint sets were struck. Proof sets were resumed in 1968. They are available during the year of issue from: The United States Mint, P.O. Box 13576, Philadelphia, PA. 19162-0011. Sets from 1936 through 1972 include the cent, nickel, dime, quarter and half; from 1973 through 1981 the dollar was also included. Regular proof sets issued from 1982 to date contain the cent through half dollar. Special sets containing commemorative coins were sold at an additional premium.

Figures in parentheses represent the total number of full sets minted.

Year Minted	Sets Minted	Issue Price	Current Value
1936	(3,837)	$1.89	$5,100
1937	(5,542)	1.89	3,600
1938	(8,045)	1.89	1,900
1939	(8,795)	1.89	1,650
1940	(11,246)	1.89	1,450
1941	(15,287)	1.89	1,300
1942 both nickels	⎱ (21,120)	1.89	1,500
1942 one nickel	⎰	1.89	1,300
1950	(51,386)	2.10	625.00
1951	(57,500)	2.10	375.00
1952	(81,980)	2.10	240.00
1953	(128,800)	2.10	145.00
1954	(233,300)	2.10	90.00
1955 box pack	⎱ (378,200)	2.10	75.00
1955 flat pack	⎰	2.10	80.00
1956	(669,384)	2.10	45.00
1957	(1,247,952)	2.10	23.00
1958	(875,652)	2.10	30.00
1959	(1,149,291)	2.10	21.00
1960 with lg. date 1c	(1,691,602)	2.10	20.00
1960 with sm. date 1c	Incl. above	2.10	23.00
1961	(3,028,244)	2.10	16.00

PROOF SETS

Year Minted	Sets Minted	Issue Price	Current Value
1962	(3,218,019)	$2.10	$16.00
1963	(3,075,645)	2.10	16.00
1964	(3,950,762)	2.10	17.00
1968S	(3,041,506)	5.00	5.50
1968S 10c w/o mint mark	Incl. above	5.00	—
1969S	(2,934,631)	5.00	5.50
1970S	(2,632,810)	5.00	12.00
1970S with sm. date 1c	Incl. above	5.00	80.00
1970S 10c w/o mint mark (est 2,200)	Incl. above	5.00	675.00
1971S	(3,220,733)	5.00	5.00
1971S 5c w/o mint mark (est 1,655)	Incl. above	5.00	1,200
1972S	(3,260,996)	5.00	5.00
1973S	(2,760,339)	7.00	12.00
1974S	(2,612,568)	7.00	12.00
1975S	(2,845,450)	7.00	9.00
1975S 10c w/o mint mark	Incl. above	7.00	—
1976S	(4,149,730)	7.00	10.00
1976S three pc. set	(3,998,621)	15.00	18.00
1977S	(3,251,152)	9.00	8.00
1978S	(3,127,781)	9.00	8.00
1979S filled S	(3,677,175)	9.00	11.00
1979S clear S		9.00	100.00
1980S	(3,554,806)	10.00	7.00
1981S	(4,063,083)	11.00	7.00
1982S	(3,857,479)	11.00	6.00
1983S	(3,138,765)	11.00	10.00
1983S 10c w/o mint mark	Incl. above	11.00	1,400
1983S Prestige Set	(140,361)	59.00	100.00
1984S	(2,748,430)	11.00	25.00
1984S Prestige Set	(316,680)	59.00	60.00
1985S	(3,362,821)	11.00	18.00
1986S	(2,411,180)	11.00	24.00
1986S Prestige Set	(599,317)	48.50	50.00
1987S	(3,356,738)	11.00	12.00
1987S Prestige Set	(435,495)	45.00	40.00
1988S		11.00	17.00
1988S Prestige Set		45.00	60.00
1989S		11.00	12.00
1989S Prestige Set		49.00	75.00
1990S		11.00	12.00
1990S Prestige Set		46.00	60.00

UNCIRCULATED MINT SETS

Official Mint Sets are specially packaged by the government for sale to collectors. They contain uncirculated specimens of each year's coins for every denomination issued from each mint. Unlike the proof sets, these are normal coins intended for circulation and are not minted with any special consideration for quality. Coins struck only as proofs are not included.

Uncirculated sets sold by the Treasury from 1947 through 1958 contained two examples of each regular issue coin. These were packaged in cardboard holders that did not protect the coins from tarnish. Nicely preserved early sets generally command a 10 to 20 percent premium above listed values. No official mint sets were produced in 1950, 1982 or 1983.

Since 1959 sets have been sealed in a protective plastic envelope. In 1965, 1966 and 1967, Special Mint Sets of higher than normal quality were packaged in hard plastic holders as a substitute for proof sets which were not made during that period.

UNCIRCULATED MINT SETS

Privately assembled mint sets, and souvenir sets produced for sale at the Philadelphia or Denver mints, or for special occasions, are valued according to the individual pieces they contain. Only the official government sealed full sets are included in the following list.

Current year sets may be ordered from The United States Mint, P.O. Box 13576, Philadelphia, PA. 19162-0011.

Year Minted	Sets Sold	Issue Price	Face Value	Current Value
1947 P-D-S		$4.87	$4.46	$825.00
1948 P-D-S		4.92	4.46	250.00
1949 P-D-S		5.45	4.96	750.00
1951 P-D-S	8,654	6.75	5.46	400.00
1952 P-D-S	11,499	6.14	5.46	300.00
1953 P-D-S	15,538	6.14	5.46	235.00
1954 P-D-S	25,599	6.19	5.46	135.00
1955 P-D-S	49,656	3.57	2.86	85.00
1956 P-D	45,475	3.34	2.64	65.00
1957 P-D	34,324	4.40	3.64	90.00
1958 P-D	50,314	4.43	3.64	80.00
1959 P-D	187,000	2.40	1.82	31.00
1960 P-D	260,485	2.40	1.82	20.00
1961 P-D	223,704	2.40	1.82	18.00
1962 P-D	385,285	2.40	1.82	22.00
1963 P-D	606,612	2.40	1.82	20.00
1964 P-D	1,008,108	2.40	1.82	15.00
1968 P-D-S	2,105,128	2.50	1.33	5.50
1969 P-D-S	1,817,392	2.50	1.33	7.50
1970 P-D-S Lg. Date	2,038,134	2.50	1.33	20.00
1970 P-D-S Sm. Date	Incl. above	2.50	1.33	40.00
1971 P-D-S†	2,193,396	3.50	1.83	6.00
1972 P-D-S†	2,750,000	3.50	1.83	5.75
1973 P-D-S	1,767,691	6.00	3.83	11.00
1974 P-D-S	1,975,981	6.00	3.83	10.00
1975 P-D	1,921,488	6.00	3.82	7.00
1776-1976 (3 pieces)	4,908,319	9.00	1.75	14.00
1976 P-D	1,892,513	6.00	3.82	9.00
1977 P-D	2,006,869	7.00	3.82	9.00
1978 P-D	2,162,609	7.00	3.82	8.00
1979 P-D*	2,526,000	8.00	3.82	6.50
1980 P-D-S	2,815,066	9.00	4.82	6.50
1981 P-D-S	2,908,145	11.00	4.82	11.00
1984 P-D	1,832,857	7.00	1.82	21.00
1985 P-D	1,710,571	7.00	1.82	23.00
1986 P-D	1,153,536	7.00	1.82	38.00
1987 P-D	2,890,758	7.00	1.82	8.00
1988 P-D	1,447,100	7.00	1.82	21.00
1989 P-D		7.00	1.82	9.00
1990 P-D		7.00	1.82	9.00

† Dollar not included. *S mint dollar not included.

SPECIAL MINT SETS

1965 (2,360,000) .... $9.00 1966 (2,261,583) ..... $8.00 1967 (1,863,344) $12.00

UNITED STATES REGULAR ISSUES
HALF CENTS — 1793-1857

From the standpoint of face value the half cent is the smallest coin struck by the United States. All half cents are scarce, but the series has never enjoyed the popularity of some of the other series, hence the more common dates and varieties are reasonably priced.

There were various intermissions in coinage, and during most of the period 1836 to 1849 the coinage was very small, causing a very noticeable lapse in the series for the average collector. While 1796 is the most valuable date, the originals and restrikes of 1831, 1836 and 1840 through 1849, and rare varieties are all difficult to obtain.

The half cent was authorized to be coined April 2, 1792. Originally the weight was to have been 132 grains, but this was changed to 104 grains by the Act of January 14, 1793, before coinage commenced. The weight was again changed to 84 grains January 26, 1796 by presidential proclamation in conformity with the Act of March 3, 1795. Coinage was discontinued by the Act of February 21, 1857. All were coined at the Philadelphia Mint.

+ or − indicates change from previous year	TYPE COIN VALUES									
	G-4	F-12	EF-40	AU-50	MS-60	MS-63	MS-65	PF-60	PF-63	PF-65
Flowing Hair 1793	$1,400+	$3,000+	$7,750+	$14,000+	$22,500	$30,000	$50,000+			
Liberty Cap 1794-1797	200.00+	500.00	2,100+	3,000	5,700	12,000+	20,000+			
Draped Bust 1800-1808	23.00	45.00	200.00	400.00	750.00	1,700	7,500+			
Classic Head 1809-1835	19.00	30.00	60.00	115.00	275.00	550.00	3,500+	$2,250	$3,300	$8,000+
Braided Hair 1840-1857	25.00	40.00+	75.00	125.00	275.00	550.00−	3,500+	2,250	3,300	8,000+

LIBERTY CAP TYPE 1793-1797

AG-3 ABOUT GOOD—*Clear enough to identify.*
G-4 GOOD—*Outline of bust clear, no details. Date readable. Reverse lettering incomplete.*
VG-8 VERY GOOD—*Some hair details. Reverse lettering complete.*
F-12 FINE—*Most of hair detail shows. Leaves worn but all visible.*
VF-20 VERY FINE—*Hair near ear and forehead worn, other areas distinct. Some details in leaves show.*
EF-40 EXTREMELY FINE—*Light wear on highest parts of head and wreath.*

Head Facing Left 1793

Designer, possibly Adam Eckfeldt; weight 6.74 grams; composition: copper; approx. diameter 22 mm; edge: TWO HUNDRED FOR A DOLLAR.

Quan. Minted	AG-3	G-4	VG-8	F-12	VF-20	EF-40
1793 35,334	$600.00	$1,400	$2,000	$3,000	$4,500	$7,750

HALF CENTS
Head Facing Right 1794-1797

1794 — Designer Robert Scot; weight 6.74 grams; composition: copper; approx. diameter 23.5 mm; edge: TWO HUNDRED FOR A DOLLAR.

1795 — Designer John Smith Gardner; weight 6.74 grams; composition: copper; approx. diameter 23.5 mm; edge: TWO HUNDRED FOR A DOLLAR.

1795-1797 (thin planchet) — Weight 5.44 grams; composition: copper; approx. diameter 23.5 mm; edge: plain (some 1797 are either lettered or gripped).

	Quan. Minted	AG-3	G-4	VG-8	F-12	VF-20	EF-40
1794	81,600	$90.00	$250.00	$350.00	$625.00	$1,250	$2,375

Pole to Cap	**Punctuated Date**	**No Pole to Cap**

1795 All kinds	139,690						
1795 Lettered edge, with pole		75.00	200.00	300.00	500.00	1,000	2,100
1795 Lettered edge, punctuated date		75.00	200.00	300.00	500.00	1,000	2,100
1795 Plain edge, punctuated date		75.00	200.00	300.00	500.00	1,000	2,100
1795 Plain edge, no pole		75.00	200.00	300.00	500.00	1,000	2,100
1796 With pole*		2,000	4,200	6,500	9,000	15,000	22,000
1796 No pole	1,390	4,500	8,500	15,000	24,000	32,000	——

*The deceptive "Dr. Edwards" struck copy of this coin has a different head and larger letters.

1797 Plain Edge	**1797, 1 above 1, Plain Edge**

1797 All kinds	127,840						
1797 Lettered edge		250.00	450.00	750.00	1,500	3,750	8,000
1797 Plain edge		75.00	200.00	300.00	500.00	1,000	2,000
1797 Gripped edge		1,000	1,750	5,000	——	——	——
1797, 1 above 1, plain edge		75.00	200.00	300.00	500.00	1,000	2,000

HALF CENTS
DRAPED BUST TYPE 1800-1808

A modified reverse design was introduced during 1802, and used through 1808.

Designer Robert Scot: weight 5.44 grams; composition: copper; diameter 23.5 mm; plain edge.

AG-3 ABOUT GOOD—*Clear enough to identify.*
G-4 GOOD—*Bust outline clear, few details, date readable. Reverse lettering worn and incomplete.*
VG-8 VERY GOOD—*Some drapery shows. Date and legends complete.*
F-12 FINE—*Shoulder drapery and hair over brow worn smooth.*
VF-20 VERY FINE—*Only slight wear in above areas. Slight wear on reverse.*
EF-40 EXTREMELY FINE—*Light wear on highest parts of head and wreath.*

	Quan. Minted	AG-3	G-4	VG-8	F-12	VF-20	EF-40
1800	202,908	$17.00	$25.00	$35.00	$55.00	$100.00	$275.00
1802, 2 over 0, rev. of 1800	20,266	2,000	4,500	9,000	20,000		
1802, 2 over 0, 2nd rev.		100.00	200.00	400.00	900.00	2,500	6,000
1803	92,000	16.50	25.00	35.00	55.00	100.00	325.00

Plain 4	**Crosslet 4**	**Stemless Wreath**	**Stems to Wreath**

1804 Plain 4, stems . .		16.50	25.00	35.00	50.00	85.00	250.00
1804 Pl. 4, stemless .		15.00	23.00	32.00	45.00	70.00	200.00
1804 Cr. 4, stems . . .	1,055,312	15.00	23.00	32.00	45.00	70.00	200.00
1804 Cr. 4, stemless . .		15.00	23.00	32.00	45.00	70.00	200.00
1804 "Spiked chin" . .		17.50	25.00	35.00	50.00	90.00	275.00

1804 "Spiked Chin"	**Small 5**	**Medium 5**	**Large 5**

1805 Med. 5, stemless		15.00	23.00	32.00	45.00	70.00	200.00
1805 Small 5, stems .	814,464	55.00	150.00	200.00	600.00	850.00	——
1805 Large 5, stems . .		15.00	23.00	32.00	45.00	70.00	200.00

HALF CENTS

Small 6 **Large 6** **1808, 8 over 7** **Normal Date**

	Quan. Minted	AG-3	G-4	VG-8	F-12	VF-20	EF-40
1806 Small 6, stems . ⎫		$25.00	$60.00	$100.00	$200.00	$300.00	$800.00
1806 Sm. 6, stemless . ⎬	356,000	15.00	23.00	32.00	45.00	70.00	200.00
1806 Large 6, stems.. ⎭		15.00	23.00	32.00	45.00	70.00	200.00
1807..................	476,000	15.00	23.00	32.00	45.00	70.00	200.00
1808, 8 over 7 ...... ⎫	400,000	45.00	60.00	100.00	175.00	550.00	1,000
1808 Normal date.... ⎭		15.00	23.00	32.00	45.00	85.00	250.00

CLASSIC HEAD TYPE 1809-1836

Designer John Reich. Standards same as previous issue.

G-4 GOOD—*LIBERTY only partly visible on hair band. Lettering, date, stars, worn but visible.*
VG-8 VERY GOOD—*LIBERTY entirely visible on hair band. Lower curls worn.*
F-12 FINE—*Only part wear on LIBERTY and hair at top worn in spots.*
VF-20 VERY FINE—*Lettering clear-cut. Hair only slightly worn.*
EF-40 EXTREMELY FINE—*Light wear on highest points of hair and leaves*
MS-60 UNCIRCULATED—*Typical brown to red surface. No trace of wear.*

1809 Normal Date **1809, 9 over 6** **1809 Circle Inside 0**

	Quan. Minted	G-4	VG-8	F-12	VF-20	EF-40	MS-60
1809 Circle inside 0. ⎫		$20.00	$25.00	$35.00	$60.00	$100.00	$500.00
1809 9 over 6....... ⎬	1,154,572	20.00	25.00	35.00	60.00	100.00	450.00
1809 Normal date ... ⎭		20.00	25.00	35.00	60.00	100.00	450.00
1810	215,000	25.00	35.00	50.00	90.00	200.00	1,400
1811	63,140	75.00	125.00	250.00	750.00	1,500	3,500
1811 Rev. of 1802. Unofficial restrike. (*Extremely Rare.*)							——
1825	63,000	23.00	30.00	40.00	60.00	100.00	400.00
1826	234,000	19.00	23.00	33.00	50.00	75.00	375.00

HALF CENTS

13 Stars

12 Stars

	Quan. Minted	G-4	VG-8	F-12	VF-20	EF-40	MS-60
1828, 13 Stars ......⎱		$19.00	$23.00	$33.00	$45.00	$60.00	$375.00
1828, 12 Stars ....⎰	606,000	22.00	28.00	38.00	60.00	100.00	650.00
1829	487,000	19.00	23.00	33.00	45.00	60.00	375.00

Reverse
1831-1836

Reverse
1840-1857

Beginning in 1831 new coinage equipment and modified dies produced a raised rim on each side of these coins. Proofs and restrikes were made at the mint for sale to collectors. Restrikes are believed to have been struck c. 1858-59.

	Quan. Minted	EF-40	MS-60	Proof-63
1831 Original. (Beware of altered date)............	2,200	$6,000	——	$11,000
1831 Restrike. Lg. berries (Rev. of 1836)				8,000
1831 Restrike. Sm. berries (Rev. of 1840-1857)				15,000

	Quan. Minted	VG-8	F-12	VF-20	EF-40	MS-60	Proof-63
1832	154,000*	$25.00	$30.00	$40.00	$65.00	$275.00	$3,300
1833	120,000*	25.00	30.00	40.00	65.00	275.00	3,300
1834	141,000*	25.00	30.00	40.00	65.00	275.00	3,300
1835	398,000*	25.00	30.00	40.00	65.00	275.00	3,300
1836 Original...................							5,650
1836 Restrike. (Rev. of 1840-1857)							7,200

*The figures given here are thought to be correct, although official mint records report these quantities for 1833-36 rather than 1832-35.

No half cents were struck in 1837. Because of the great need for small change, however, a large number of tokens similar in size to current half cents and large cents were issued privately by businessmen who needed them in commerce. One of the most popular pieces is listed and illustrated below.

	G-4	VG-8	F-12	VF-20	EF-40	MS-60
1837 Token (not a coin)	$20.00	$27.50	$40.00	$85.00	$120.00	$400.00

HALF CENTS
CORONET TYPE 1840-1857

Brilliant red uncirculated half cents are worth more than prices shown.

Designer Christian Gobrecht; weight 5.44 grams; composition: copper; diameter 23 mm; plain edge.

VG-8 VERY GOOD—*Beads uniformly distinct. Hairlines show in spots.*
F-12 FINE—*Hairlines above ear worn. Beads sharp.*
VF-20 VERY FINE—*Lowest curl shows wear, hair otherwise distinct.*
EF-40 EXTREMELY FINE—*Light wear on highest points of hair and leaves.*
MS-60 UNCIRCULATED—*No trace of wear, light blemishes.*

Both originals and restrikes use reverse of 1840-1857. Originals have large berries, restrikes have small berries in wreath.

	Proof-63		Proof-63
1840 Original...............	$3,400	1845 Original...............	$4,600
1840 Restrike	3,300	1845 Restrike	4,100
1841 Original...............	3,400	1846 Original...............	4,200
1841 Restrike	3,300	1846 Restrike	3,400
1842 Original...............	3,600	1847 Original...............	3,400
1842 Restrike	3,300	1847 Restrike	3,400
1843 Original...............	3,500	1848 Original...............	3,400
1843 Restrike	3,400	1848 Restrike	3,400
1844 Original...............	4,600	1849 Original. Small date ...	4,000
1844 Restrike	3,400	1849 Restrike. Small date ...	4,000

Small Date　　　　**Large Date**

Brilliant or red uncirculated half cents are worth more than prices shown.

	Quan. Minted	VG-8	F-12	VF-20	EF-40	MS-60	Proof-63
1849 Large date	39,864	$35.00	$45.00	$60.00	$85.00	$400.00	——
1850	39,812	35.00	45.00	60.00	85.00	400.00	——
1851	147,672	30.00	40.00	50.00	75.00	275.00	——
1852 restrike							$3,900
1853	129,694	30.00	40.00	50.00	75.00	275.00	
1854	55,358	30.00	40.00	50.00	75.00	275.00	4,100
1855	56,500	30.00	40.00	50.00	75.00	275.00	4,100
1856	40,430	35.00	45.00	55.00	85.00	300.00	4,100
1857	35,180	37.50	47.50	65.00	100.00	350.00	4,100

BIBLIOGRAPHY

Breen, Walter, *Walter Breen's Encyclopedia of United States Half Cents 1793-1857.* South Gate, California, 1983.
Cohen, Roger S., Jr. *American Half Cents—The "Little Half Sisters".* 2nd Edition, 1982.
Crosby, S. S. *United States Coinage of 1793—Cents and Half Cents.* Boston, 1897.
Frossard, Edward. *United States Cents and Half Cents 1793-1857.* Irvington, New York, 1879.
Gilbert, Ebenezer, *United States Half Cents.* New York, 1916. Hewitt Reprint, Chicago.

LARGE CENTS — 1793-1857

Cents and half cents were the first coins struck under the authority of the United States Government. Coinage began in 1793 with laws specifying that the cent should weigh exactly twice as much as the half cent. Large cents were coined every year from 1793 to 1857 with the exception of 1815, when a lack of copper prevented production. All were coined at the Philadelphia Mint. Mintage records in some cases may be inaccurate, as many of the early pieces were struck later than the dates shown on the coins. Varieties listed are those most significant to collectors. Numerous other die varieties may be found because each of the early dies was individually made. Values of varieties not listed in this guide depend on collector interest, rarity and demand. Proof large cents were first made in 1817; all proofs are rare, as they were not made available to the general public before the mid-1850's.

+ or − indicates change from previous year	G-4	F-12	EF-40	AU-50	MS-60	MS-63	MS-65	PF-60	PF-63	PF-65
TYPE COIN VALUES										
Chain 1793	2,200+	4,750+	16,000+	25,000	45,000	—	—			
Wreath 1793	900.00+	1,750+	6,500+	10,000	20,000+	30,000+	50,000+			
Liberty Cap 1793-1796	100.00	275.00	1,400	2,500	5,000−	11,000	20,000+			
Draped Bust 1796-1807	20.00	70.00	550.00	1,000	2,400	4,500	13,000			
Classic Head 1808-1814	22.50	75.00	675.00	1,500+	2,500−	7,500+	20,000+			
Coronet Head 1816-1839	8.00	18.00	85.00	175.00	500.00	575.00	2,100−	—		
Braided Hair 1840-1857	7.00	11.00	50.00	110.00	210.00	450.00−	1,800−	2,500−	4,500	8,000+

FLOWING HAIR, CHAIN TYPE REVERSE 1793

Designer Henry Voigt; weight 13.48 grams; composition: copper; approx. diameter 26-27 mm; edge: bars and slender vine with leaves.

AG-3 ABOUT GOOD—*Date and devices clear enough to identify.*

G-4 GOOD—*Lettering worn but readable. Bust has no detail.*

VG-8 VERY GOOD—*Date and lettering distinct, some details of head visible.*

F-12 FINE—*About half of hair, etc. details show.*

VF-20 VERY FINE—*Ear visible. Most of details can be seen.*

EF-40 EXTREMELY FINE—*Highest points of hair and back of temple show wear.*

Values shown for Fine and better copper coins are for those with attractive surfaces and color that are consistent with the amount of normal wear. Coins that are porous, corroded, or similarly defective are worth significantly lower prices.

	Obverse	AMERI. Reverse		AMERICA Reverse		
	Quan. Minted	AG-3	G-4	VG-8	F-12	VF-20	EF-40
1793 Chain	36,103						
1793 AMERI. in legend		$1,000	$2,400	$3,500	$5,000	$8,500	$18,000
1793 AMERICA*		900.00	2,200	3,200	4,750	7,500	16,000

*Varieties with or without periods after date and LIBERTY.

FLOWING HAIR, WREATH TYPE REVERSE 1793

The reverse of this type bears a "single-bow" wreath, as distinguished from the wreath tied with a double bow on the following type. A three-leaf sprig appears above the date on the obverse, and both sides have borders of small beads.

LARGE CENTS

Introduction of this reverse answered criticism of the chain design, but the stronger modeling of the face and hair still failed to gain acceptance as representative of Liberty. After three months' production the design was abandoned in favor of the Liberty Cap type.

Instead of the normal sprig above the date, the rare "strawberry leaf" variety has a spray of trefoil leaves and a small blossom. The trefoils match those found on the normal wreath reverse. It is not clear why this variety was created. All known specimens are badly worn.

Designer Adam Eckfeldt; weight 13.48 grams; composition: copper; approx. diameter 26-28 mm; edge: vine and bars, or lettered ONE HUNDRED FOR A DOLLAR followed by either a single or double leaf.

Wreath Type   **Strawberry Leaf Var.**

Quan. Minted	AG-3	G-4	VG-8	F-12	VF-20	EF-40
1793 Wreath ... 63,353						
1793 Vine/bars edge ..	$400.00	$900.00	$1,200	$1,750	$3,000	$6,500
1793 Lettered Edge ...	500.00	1,000	1,400	1,900	3,200	7,000
1793 Strawberry leaf..			*(4 known)*			

LIBERTY CAP TYPE 1793-1796

Another major change was made in 1793 to satisfy continuing objections to the obverse portrait. This version appears to have been more successful, as it was continued into 1796. The 1793 pieces had beaded borders, but a border of denticles or "teeth" was adopted in 1794. A famous 1794 variety is the probably whimsical "starred" reverse, with a border of 94 tiny 5-pointed stars under the denticles.

Portrait variations listed below for 1794 are the result of several changes of die engravers. The so-called "Jefferson head" of 1795 is now thought to be a sample for a proposed coinage contract by a private manufacturer, John Harper.

Planchets became too thin for edge lettering after the weight reduction ordered late in 1795. The variety with reeded edge was probably an experimental substitute, rejected in favor of a plain edge.

1793-1795 (thick planchet) — Designer Joseph Wright; weight 13.48 grams; composition: copper; approx. diameter 29 mm; edge: ONE HUNDRED FOR A DOLLAR followed by a single leaf.
1795-1796 (thin planchet) — Designer John Smith Gardner; weight 10.89 grams; composition: copper; approx. diameter 29 mm; plain edge.

1793 Vine and Bars edge   **Lettered edge 1793-1795**
Chain and Wreath type only   ONE HUNDRED FOR A DOLLAR

LARGE CENTS

1793-1794

Beaded Border, 1793 Only

"Head of 1793"
Head is in high
rounded relief

1794 Only

1794-1796

"Head of 1794"
Well defined hair,
hook on lowest curl

"Head of 1795"
Head in low relief,
no hook on lowest curl

1794 Starred Reverse

	Quan. Minted	AG-3	G-4	VG-8	F-12	VF-20	EF-40
1793 Lib. Cap ..	11,056	$650.00	$1,500	$2,500	$3,750	$7,000	$24,000
1794 All kinds.	918,521						
1794 "Head of 1793"..		150.00	250.00	450.00	1,100	3,000	8,500
1794 "Head of 1794"..		50.00	100.00	160.00	350.00	700.00	2,000
1794 "Head of 1795"..		50.00	100.00	160.00	350.00	700.00	2,000
1794 Starred rev......		3,000	5,000	9,500	15,000	30,000	——
1795 Ltd. ed....	37,000	50.00	100.00	200.00	350.00	700.00	1,800
1795 Plain ed..	501,500	35.00	100.00	140.00	275.00	550.00	1,400

1796-1807

Reeded Edge

"Jefferson Head"

This head was modified
slightly in 1798. See
page 79 for details.

		AG-3	G-4	VG-8	F-12	VF-20	EF-40
1795 Reeded edge				*(6 known)*			
1795 Jefferson Head (not a regular mint issue)							
Plain edge.......		1,200	2,000	3,600	6,500	20,000	
Lettered edge....				*(3 known)*			
1796 Lib. Cap .	109,825	45.00	100.00	160.00	300.00	700.00	1,800

LARGE CENTS
DRAPED BUST TYPE 1796-1807

Designer Robert Scot; weight 10.89 grams; composition: copper; approx. diameter 29 mm; plain edge.

AG-3 ABOUT GOOD—*Clear enough to identify.*

G-4 GOOD—*Lettering worn, but clear; date clear. Bust lacks details.*

VG-8 VERY GOOD—*Drapery partly visible. Less wear in date and lettering.*

F-12 FINE—*Hair over brow is smooth, some detail showing in other parts of hair.*

VF-20 VERY FINE—*Hairlines slightly worn. Hair over brow better defined.*

EF-40 EXTREMELY FINE—*Hair above forehead and left of eye outlined and detailed. Only slight wear on olive leaves.*

1794-1796	1795-1798	1796-1807

"Reverse of 1794" Note double leaf at top right; 14-16 leaves left, 16 - 18 leaves right.	"Reverse of 1796" Note single leaf at top right; 17-21 leaves left, 16-20 leaves right.	"Reverse of 1797" Note double leaf at top right; 16 leaves left, 19 leaves right.

LIHERTY error

Quan. Minted	AG-3	G-4	VG-8	F-12	VF-20	EF-40
1796 Dr. Bust... 363,375						
1796 reverse of 1794 ...	$35.00	$70.00	$125.00	$200.00	$600.00	$1,500
1796 reverse of 1796 ...	37.50	75.00	150.00	250.00	650.00	1,800
1796 reverse of 1797 ...	40.00	80.00	160.00	275.00	700.00	2,000
1796 LIHERTY error.....	50.00	90.00	185.00	375.00	1,000	3,500

Gripped Edge

		Stems		Stemless	
1797 All kinds .. 897,510					
1797 Gr. Ed., '96 rev....	21.00	37.50	90.00	200.00	450.00	1,000
1797 Pl. edge, '96 rev...	21.00	40.00	100.00	225.00	500.00	1,100
1797, '97 rev., Stems ...	17.00	35.00	70.00	125.00	300.00	800.00
1797, '97 rev., Stemless.	28.00	55.00	125.00	250.00	600.00	2,000

LARGE CENTS

Style 1 Hair

Style 2 Hair

1798, 8 over 7

Style 1 hair appears on all 1796-97, many 1798 varieties and 1800 over 1798. Style 2 hair, used 1798-1807, is most easily recognized by the extra curl near the shoulder.

	Quan. Minted	AG-3	G-4	VG-8	F-12	VF-20	EF-40
1798 All kinds	1,841,745						
1798, 8 over 7		$25.00	$40.00	$100.00	$225.00	$600.00	$1,600
1798, reverse of 1796		22.50	37.50	80.00	175.00	500.00	1,500
1798, 1st hair style		12.50	25.00	45.00	100.00	275.00	750.00
1798, 2nd hair style		12.50	25.00	45.00	100.00	275.00	700.00

1799, 9 over 8

1800 over 1798

1800, 80 over 79

1799, 9 over 8*	375.00	700.00	1,500	3,000	6,250	——
1799 Nor. date .. 42,540	350.00	700.00	1,500	3,000	6,000	——
1800 All kds... 2,822,175						
1800 over 1798,						
Style 1 hair	10.00	23.00	32.50	75.00	250.00	800.00
1800, 80 over 79,						
Style 2 hair	9.00	20.00	30.00	70.00	225.00	600.00
1800 Normal date	9.00	20.00	30.00	70.00	225.00	600.00

*Mintage for 1799, 9 over 8 variety is included with the 1798 figure.

Fraction 1/000

Corrected Fraction

1801 Reverse, 3 Errors

Error-fraction dies appear on cents of 1801, 1802, and 1803, but all of these dies originated in 1801, possibly all by the same blunderer.

LARGE CENTS

Quan. Minted	AG-3	G-4	VG-8	F-12	VF-20	EF-40
1801 All kds. . . 1,362,837						
1801 Normal rev.	$9.00	$20.00	$30.00	$70.00	$225.00	$600.00
1801, 3 errors: 1/000, one						
stem & IINITED.	17.50	45.00	85.00	200.00	450.00	1,650
1801 Fraction 1/000. . . .	11.00	22.00	40.00	90.00	250.00	750.00
1801, 1/100 over 1/000 .	11.00	25.00	65.00	120.00	350.00	950.00
1802 All kds. . . 3,435,100						
1802 Normal rev.	9.00	20.00	30.00	70.00	200.00	550.00
1802 Fraction 1/000. . . .	11.00	23.00	40.00	90.00	275.00	700.00
1802 Stemless wreath . .	9.00	20.00	30.00	70.00	200.00	600.00

1803 Small Date Blunt 1	1803 Large Date Pointed 1	Small Fraction	Large Fraction

All small date varieties have a blunt 1 in date. Large dates have pointed 1 and noticeably larger 3.

1803 All kds. . 3,131,691						
1803 Sm. dt., sm. fract .	9.00	20.00	30.00	70.00	200.00	550.00
1803 Sm. dt., lg. fract . .	9.00	20.00	30.00	70.00	200.00	550.00
1803 Lg. dt., sm. fract. .	500.00	1,000	2,200	3,500	5,500	
1803 Lg. dt., lg. fract. . .	25.00	45.00	80.00	160.00	325.00	1,200
1803, 1/100 over 1/000.	11.00	24.00	50.00	90.00	250.00	700.00
1803 Stemless wreath. .	10.00	22.00	45.00	80.00	235.00	675.00

1804 With Normal or Broken Dies
(Broken die variety is illustrated)

Broken Dies

All genuine 1804 Cents have a crosslet 4 in the date and a large fraction. The 0 in the date is in line with the O in OF on the reverse of the coin.

1804 96,500	185.00	325.00	650.00	1,100	2,200	5,250

LARGE CENTS
Restrike of 1804 Cent

1804 Unofficial restrike of 1860 (Uncirculated) $350.00

A fake 1804 was manufactured from discarded mint dies. An altered 1803 die was used for the obverse and a die of the 1820 cent used for the reverse. They were struck about the year 1860 to satisfy the demand for this rare date. Known as the "restrike," it was a patchwork job and is easily distinguished from a genuine 1804 cent.

	Quan. Minted	AG-3	G-4	VG-8	F-12	VF-20	EF-40
1805	 941,116	$9.00	$20.00	$30.00	$75.00	$225.00	$600.00
1806	 348,000	11.00	25.00	55.00	125.00	300.00	850.00

Small 1807, 7 over 6, blunt 1   **Lg. 1807, 7 over 6, pointed 1**   **"Comet" Variety**

1807 All kinds.. 829,221						
1807 Small 7 over 6, Blunt 1...........	500.00	800.00	1,750	3,000	5,500	——
1807 Large 7 over 6 ...	9.00	20.00	30.00	75.00	225.00	600.00
1807 Small fraction	10.00	22.00	45.00	100.00	250.00	700.00
1807 Large fraction....	9.00	20.00	30.00	75.00	225.00	600.00
1807 "Comet" variety (die break behind head)	10.00	22.00	45.00	100.00	250.00	750.00

CLASSIC HEAD TYPE 1808-1814

1808 to 1814 — This group does not compare in sharpness and quality to those struck before (1793-1807), nor to those struck after (1816 on). The copper used was "softer," having less metallic impurity. This impaired the wearing quality of the series. For this reason collectors find greater difficulty in obtaining these dates in choice condition.

Designer John Reich. Standards same as previous issue.

LARGE CENTS

AG-3 ABOUT GOOD—*Details clear enough to identify.*
G-4 GOOD—*Legends, stars, date worn, but plain.*
VG-8 VERY GOOD—*LIBERTY all readable. Ear shows. Details worn but plain.*
F-12 FINE—*Hair on forehead and before ear nearly smooth. Ear and hair under ear sharp.*
VF-20 VERY FINE—*All hairlines show some detail. Leaves on reverse show slight wear.*
EF-40 EXTREMELY FINE—*All hairlines sharp. Very slight wear on high points.*

	Quan. Minted	AG-3	G-4	VG-8	F-12	VF-20	EF-40
1808	1,007,000	$12.00	$25.00	$50.00	$100.00	$275.00	$800.00
1809	222,867	32.50	65.00	110.00	225.00	525.00	1,300

1810, 10 over 09   **Normal Date**   **1811, last 1 over 0**   **Normal Date**

1810 All kds. . . 1,458,500						
1810, 10 over 09	11.00	22.50	40.00	75.00	225.00	675.00
1810 Normal date	11.00	22.50	40.00	75.00	225.00	675.00
1811 All kds. 218,025						
1811 Last 1 over 0	27.50	45.00	85.00	200.00	500.00	1,400
1811 Normal date	25.00	42.50	80.00	175.00	450.00	1,200

1812 Small date   **1812 Large date**   **1814 Plain 4**   **1814 Crosslet 4**

1812 Sm. dt. . . } 1,075,500	11.00	22.50	40.00	75.00	225.00	675.00
1812 Lg. dt. . . }	11.00	22.50	40.00	75.00	225.00	675.00
1813 418,000	15.00	32.00	60.00	110.00	275.00	850.00
1814 Plain 4 . . . . } 357,830	11.00	22.50	40.00	75.00	225.00	675.00
1814 Crosslet 4 . }	11.00	22.50	40.00	95.00	275.00	750.00

LARGE CENTS

CORONET TYPE 1816-1857

Designer Robert Scot; weight 10.89 grams; composition: copper; approx. diameter 28-29 mm; plain edge.

G-4 GOOD—*Head details partly visible. Even wear in date and legends.*
VG-8 VERY GOOD—*LIBERTY, date, stars, legends clear. Part of hair cord visible.*
F-12 FINE—*All hairlines show. Hair cords show uniformly.*
VF-20 VERY FINE—*Hair cords only slightly worn. Hairlines only partly worn, all well defined.*
EF-40 EXTREMELY FINE—*Both hair cords stand out sharply. All hairlines sharp.*
MS-60 UNCIRCULATED—*Typical brown to red surface. No trace of wear.*

MATRON HEAD 1816-1835

13 Stars **15 Stars**

	Quan. Minted	G-4	VG-8	F-12	VF-20	EF-40	MS-60*
1816	2,820,982	$8.00	$10.00	$19.00	$37.50	$85.00	$325.00
1817, 13 stars		8.00	10.00	18.00	35.00	85.00	300.00
1817, 15 stars	} 3,948,400	12.00	15.00	25.00	50.00	140.00	800.00
1818	3,167,000	8.00	10.00	18.00	35.00	85.00	300.00

1819, 9 over 8 **1819 Large Date** **1819 Small Date**

1819, 9 over 8	}		10.00	13.00	22.00	45.00	95.00	450.00
1819 Large date	} 2,671,000	8.00	10.00	18.00	37.50	85.00	300.00
1819 Small date	}	8.00	10.00	18.00	37.50	85.00	300.00

1820, 20 over 19
note 1 under 2

1820 Large Date
note plain-topped 2

1820 Small Date
note curl-topped 2

*Values shown are for average condition. Red to bright red uncirculated large cents with attractive surface (not cleaned) command higher prices. Beware of slightly worn copper coins which have been cleaned and recolored to simulate uncirculated luster. Cents in VF or better condition with attractive surface and tone may also command higher prices than listed here.

LARGE CENTS

	Quan. Minted	G-4	VG-8	F-12	VF-20	EF-40	MS-60*
1820, 20 over 19 ...		$10.00	$12.00	$23.00	$45.00	$95.00	$375.00
1820 Large date ...	4,407,550	8.00	10.00	18.00	37.50	85.00	300.00
1820 Small date ...		8.00	10.00	18.00	40.00	100.00	425.00
1821	389,000	18.00	29.00	45.00	95.00	350.00	2,000
1822	2,072,339	8.00	10.00	18.00	37.50	100.00	500.00

1823, 3 over 2   **1823 Restrike**

		G-4	VG-8	F-12	VF-20	EF-40	MS-60*
1823, 3 over 2	Included	25.00	37.50	75.00	150.00	500.00	——
1823 Normal date..	with 1824	27.50	40.00	85.00	175.00	700.00	——
1823 Unofficial restrike, from broken obverse die						200.00	525.00

The 1823 unofficial restrike was made at the same time and by the same people as the 1804 restrike copy (qv), using a discarded 1823 obverse and an 1813 reverse die. The dies are heavily rusted (lumps on coin) and most examples have both dies cracked across.

1824, 4 over 2   **1826, 6 over 5**

		G-4	VG-8	F-12	VF-20	EF-40	MS-60*
1824, 4 over 2		15.00	23.00	45.00	100.00	400.00	——
1824 Normal date	1,262,000	8.00	10.00	18.00	40.00	175.00	1,200
1825	1,461,100	8.00	10.00	18.00	40.00	100.00	500.00
1826, 6 over 5		14.00	22.00	40.00	85.00	200.00	1,200
1826 Normal date	1,517,425	8.00	10.00	18.00	37.50	95.00	475.00
1827	2,357,732	8.00	10.00	18.00	37.50	85.00	325.00

This date-size appears on cents before 1828

This date-size appears on cents after 1828

		G-4	VG-8	F-12	VF-20	EF-40	MS-60*
1828 Lg. nar. date ..	2,260,624	8.00	10.00	18.00	37.50	85.00	350.00
1828 Sm. wide date		10.00	12.00	20.00	40.00	90.00	425.00

*See footnote page 83.

LARGE CENTS

This letter-size appears on cents of 1808-1834.

This letter size appears on cents of 1829-1837.

Note individual letter size and proximity.

Note isolation of letters, esp. STATES.

	Quan. Minted	G-4	VG-8	F-12	VF-20	EF-40	MS-60*
1829 Large letters . . .		$8.00	$10.00	$18.00	$37.50	$85.00	$325.00
1829 Med. letters	1,414,500	10.00	15.00	25.00	60.00	125.00	——
1830 Large letters . . .		8.00	10.00	18.00	37.50	85.00	325.00
1830 Med. letters	1,711,500	18.00	30.00	60.00	135.00	270.00	——
1831 Large letters . . .		8.00	10.00	18.00	37.50	85.00	325.00
1831 Med. letters	3,359,260	8.00	10.00	18.00	37.50	85.00	325.00
1832 Large letters . . . .⎫		8.00	10.00	18.00	37.50	85.00	325.00
1832 Med. letters . . . . .⎭	2,362,000	8.00	10.00	18.00	37.50	85.00	325.00
1833	2,739,000	8.00	10.00	18.00	37.50	85.00	325.00

Large 8 and Stars   **Large 8, Small Stars**   **Small 8, Large Stars**

		G-4	VG-8	F-12	VF-20	EF-40	MS-60*
1834 All kinds	1,855,100						
1834 Lg. 8, stars & rev. letters . . .		10.00	14.00	22.00	45.00	125.00	425.00
1834 Lg. 8 & stars, med. letters . .		20.00	35.00	50.00	90.00	190.00	——
1834 Lg. 8, sm. stars, med. let. . . .		8.00	10.00	18.00	37.50	90.00	350.00
1834 Sm. 8, lg. stars, med. let. . . .		8.00	10.00	18.00	37.50	90.00	350.00

Large 8 and Stars, Matron Head   **Small 8 and Stars, Matron Head**   **"Head of 1836" 1835-1837 Slim Bust**

		G-4	VG-8	F-12	VF-20	EF-40	MS-60*
1835 Lg. 8 & stars . . . .⎫		9.00	12.00	19.00	40.00	100.00	375.00
1835 Sm. 8 & stars. . . .⎭	3,878,400	9.00	12.00	19.00	40.00	100.00	375.00
1835 "Head of 1836" . .		8.00	10.00	18.00	37.50	85.00	375.00
1836	2,111,000	8.00	10.00	18.00	37.50	85.00	375.00

*See footnote page 83.

LARGE CENTS

YOUNG HEAD 1835-1857

Designer Christian Gobrecht; weight 10.89 grams; composition: copper; diameter 27.5 mm; plain edge.

G-4 GOOD—*Considerably worn. LIBERTY readable.*

VG-8 VERY GOOD—*Hairlines smooth but visible, outline of ear clearly defined.*

F-12 FINE—*Hairlines at top of head and behind ear worn but visible. Braid over brow plain, ear clear.*

VF-20 VERY FINE—*All details more sharp. Hair over brow shows only slight wear.*

EF-40 EXTREMELY FINE—*Hair above ear detailed, but slightly worn.*

MS-60 UNCIRCULATED—*Typical brown to red surface. No trace of wear.*

1829-1837
Medium letters
note isolation
of letters.

"Head of 1838"
Beaded Cords,
note slim bust
with beaded cords.

1837-1839
Small letters
note separation
of letters.

	Quan. Minted	G-4	VG-8	F-12	VF-20	EF-40	MS-60*
1837 Pl. crd., med. let .		$8.00	$10.00	$18.00	$37.50	$85.00	$325.00
1837 Pl. crd., sm. let ..	5,558,300	9.50	12.00	20.00	40.00	95.00	350.00
1837 Head of 1838		8.00	10.00	18.00	37.50	85.00	325.00
1838	6,370,200	8.00	10.00	18.00	37.50	85.00	325.00

1839 over 1836
Note closed 9,
plain cords.

Silly Head
Note browlock
at forehead

Booby Head
Note back tip of
shoulder exposed.

1839 All kinds 3,128,661						
1839, 9 over 6, plain cords	95.00	175.00	300.00	600.00	1,800	——
1839 Head of 1838, beaded cords.	8.00	12.00	18.00	35.00	85.00	375.00
1839 Silly Head.................	10.00	15.00	25.00	50.00	115.00	550.00
1839 Booby Head...............	9.00	13.00	22.00	43.00	95.00	475.00
1839 Petite head...............	8.00	12.00	18.00	35.00	85.00	375.00

The last two 1839 heads use a modified reverse which omits the line under CENT (see illustration of 1849).

*See footnote page 83.

LARGE CENTS

1840 Large Date

1840 Small Date

**Small Date
over Large 18**

	Quan. Minted	G-4	VG-8	F-12	VF-20	EF-40	MS-60*
1840 Large date .... ⎫		$8.00	$10.00	$12.00	$20.00	$60.00	$250.00
1840 Small date .... ⎬	2,462,700	8.00	10.00	12.00	20.00	60.00	250.00
1840 Sm. dt., lg. 18.. ⎭		9.00	11.00	15.00	25.00	65.00	300.00
1841 Small date	1,597,367	8.00	10.00	12.00	20.00	60.00	275.00

1842 Small Date

1842 Large Date

**Small Letters
1839-1843**

1842 Small date ... ⎫		8.00	10.00	12.00	20.00	60.00	250.00
1842 Large date . ⎬	2,383,390	8.00	10.00	12.00	20.00	60.00	250.00

**"Head of 1840"
Petite Head
1839-1843**

**"Head of 1844"
Mature Head
1843-1857**

**Large Letters
1843-1857**

1843 Petite, sm. let.. ⎫		8.00	10.00	12.00	20.00	60.00	250.00
1843 Petite, lg. let .. ⎬	2,425,342	10.00	18.00	34.00	55.00	90.00	500.00
1843 Mature, lg. let . ⎭		9.00	12.00	19.00	35.00	70.00	250.00
1844 Normal date.. ⎫		8.00	10.00	12.00	20.00	60.00	250.00
1844 over 81 (error) ⎬	2,398,752	10.00	15.00	23.00	50.00	150.00	595.00
1845	3,894,804	7.00	9.00	11.00	16.00	50.00	225.00

*See footnote page 83.

LARGE CENTS

1846 Small Date note squat date with closed 6	**1846 Medium Date** note medium height with ball-top 6	**1846 Tall Date** note vertically-stretched date with open-mouthed 6

	Quan. Minted	G-4	VG-8	F-12	VF-20	EF-40	MS-60*
1846 Small date		$7.00	$9.00	$11.00	$16.00	$50.00	$225.00
1846 Medium date	4,120,800	8.00	10.00	12.00	20.00	60.00	225.00
1846 Tall date		8.00	10.00	12.00	20.00	50.00	225.00
1847		7.00	9.00	11.00	16.00	50.00	225.00
1847, 7 over "sm." 7	6,183,669	10.00	12.00	22.00	40.00	85.00	300.00

1848	6,415,799	7.00	9.00	11.00	16.00	60.00	225.00
1849	4,178,500	7.00	9.00	11.00	16.00	70.00	225.00
1850	4,426,844	7.00	9.00	11.00	16.00	60.00	225.00

1844, 44 over 81	**1851, 51 over 81**	**1847, 7 over "Small" 7**

These are not true overdates, but are some of the more spectacular of several date-punch blunders of the 1844-1854 period. The so-called "overdates" of 1844 and 1851 each have the date punched upside-down, then corrected normally.

1851 Normal date.	9,889,707	7.00	9.00	11.00	16.00	50.00	210.00
1851 over 81 (error). . .		10.00	12.00	19.00	43.00	85.00	350.00
1852	5,063,094	7.00	9.00	11.00	16.00	50.00	210.00
1853	6,641,131	7.00	9.00	11.00	16.00	50.00	210.00
1854	4,236,156	7.00	9.00	11.00	16.00	50.00	210.00

*See footnote page 83.

LARGE CENTS

1855 Upright 5's   1855 Slanting 5's   1855 Knob on ear

Original sketches of engraver James B. Longacre's work reveal that slanting 5's were a peculiarity of his work. The figure punch for an upright 5 was probably the work of an apprentice.

	Quan. Minted	G-4	VG-8	F-12	VF-20	EF-40	MS-60*
1855 All kinds	1,574,829						
1855 Upright 5's		$7.00	$9.00	$11.00	$16.00	$50.00	$210.00
1855 Slanting 5's		7.00	9.00	11.00	16.00	50.00	210.00
1855 Slanting 5's, knob on ear		8.00	10.00	14.00	30.00	60.00	250.00
1856 Upright 5		7.00	9.00	11.00	16.00	50.00	210.00
1856 Slanting 5	2,690,463	7.00	9.00	11.00	16.00	50.00	210.00

1857 Large Date   1857 Small date

1857 Large date		22.50	30.00	40.00	50.00	70.00	300.00
1857 Small date	333,456	25.00	35.00	45.00	55.00	80.00	325.00

*See footnote page 83.

Passing of the Large Cent and Half Cent

By 1857 the cost of making and distributing copper coins had risen. Mint Director Snowden reported that they "barely paid expenses." Both cents and half cents had become unpopular, in fact, they hardly circulated outside of the larger cities. The practice of issuing subsidiary silver coins which began in 1853, brought about a reform of the copper coinage. The half cent was abandoned and a smaller cent was introduced late in 1857.

The law of 1857 brought important benefits to the citizens. By its terms Spanish coins were redeemed and melted at the mint in exchange for new small cents. The decimal system became popular and official thereafter, and the old method of reckoning in reals, medios, shillings, etc., was gradually given up, although the terms, "two bits" and "penny" are still commonly used. The new, convenient small cent won popular favor and soon became a useful instrument of retail trade and a boon to society generally.

BIBLIOGRAPHY
Sheldon, Wm. H. Penny Whimsy (1793-1814). New York, 1958.
Newcomb, H.R. United States Copper Cents 1816-1857. New York, 1944.
PENNY-WISE, official publication of Early American Coppers, Inc. (EAC)

SMALL CENTS — 1856 to Date

+ or − indicates change from previous year	TYPE COIN VALUES									
	G-4	F-12	EF-40	AU-50	MS-60	MS-63	MS-65	PF-60	PF-63	PF-65
Flying Eagle 1857-1858	10.00+	15.00+	70.00+	150.00+	235.00+	500.00	3,500	1,400	3,000+	15,000+
Indian CN 1859	5.00+	15.00+	75.00+	175.00+	200.00+	550.00+	3,000+	750.00−	1,300+	4,000
Indian CN 1860-1864	4.00+	6.00+	20.00+	40.00+	100.00	200.00−	1,100	325.00−	700.00−	2,250−
Indian 1864-1909	.75	1.30	7.00	12.00	30.00	60.00−	275.00−	125.00	250.00−	600.00−
Lincoln 1909-V.D.B.	2.25	3.00	4.00	5.50	13.00	27.50	65.00	650.00−	1,750+	2,400

FLYING EAGLE TYPE 1856-1858

The Act of February 21, 1857 provided for the coinage of the small cent, and made uncurrent the coins of other countries, particularly the Spanish and Mexican dollars. The new cents weighed 72 grains. Composition, 88% copper, 12% nickel.

The 1856 Eagle cent was not an authorized mint issue, as the law governing the new size coin was enacted after the date of issue. It is believed that about 1,000 of these pieces were struck. They are properly referred to as patterns.

Collectors are advised to inspect any 1856 Flying Eagle cent carefully.

A few tests will aid in establishing genuineness of this cent, as follows: If the lower half of the 6 is thick it is probably an altered 1858. A magnifying glass will often reveal poor workmanship.

The figure 5 slants slightly to the right on a genuine 1856. The vertical bar points to the center of the ball just beneath. On the 1858, this bar points *outside* the ball.

The 1858 cent is found in two minor varieties. The A and M in the word AMERICA are joined in the large letter variety and separated in the small letter variety. The reverse design of the eagle cents is dominated by a wreath of corn, wheat, cotton and tobacco.

Designer James B. Longacre; weight 4.67 grams; composition: .880 copper, .120 nickel; diameter 19 mm; plain edge. All coined at Philadelphia Mint.

G-4 GOOD—*All details worn, but readable.*

VG-8 VERY GOOD—*Feather details and eye of eagle are evident, but worn.*

F-12 FINE—*Eagle head details and feather tips sharp.*

VF-20 VERY FINE—*Feathers in right wing and tail show considerable detail.*

EF-40 EXTREMELY FINE—*Slight wear, all details sharp.*

MS-60 UNCIRCULATED—*No trace of wear. Light blemishes.*

1858, 8 over 7

Large Letters

Small Letters

	Quan. Minted	G-4	VG-8	F-12	VF-20	EF-40	MS-60	Proof-63
1856	est. 1,000	$1,800	$2,100	$2,500	$2,750	$3,200	$4,100	$4,800
1857	(485) 17,450,000	10.00	12.00	15.00	30.00	70.00	235.00	3,000
1858 Lg. let .	(80)	10.00	12.00	15.00	30.00	70.00	235.00	3,000
1858 Sm. let .	(200) } 24,600,00	10.00	12.00	15.00	30.00	70.00	235.00	3,000
1858, 8 over 7			55.00	125.00	275.00	500.00	1,100	

SMALL CENTS
INDIAN HEAD TYPE 1859-1909

The small cent was redesigned in 1859, and a representation of an Indian princess was adopted as the obverse device. The 1859 reverse was also changed to represent a laurel wreath. In 1860 the reverse was modified to display an oak wreath with a small shield at the top. The weight and composition of the coin were not changed.

Designer James B. Longacre; weight 4.67 grams; composition: .880 copper, .120 nickel; diameter 19 mm; plain edge. All coined at Philadelphia Mint.

G-4 GOOD—*No LIBERTY visible.*

VG-8 VERY GOOD—*At least three letters of LIBERTY readable on head band.*

F-12 FINE—*LIBERTY completely visible.*

VF-20 VERY FINE—*Slight but even wear on LIBERTY.*

EF-40 EXTREMELY FINE—*LIBERTY sharp. All other details sharp. Only slight wear on ribbon end.*

MS-60 UNCIRCULATED—*No trace of wear. Light blemishes.*

Without Shield at Top of Wreath
1859 Only

With Shield on Reverse
1860 to 1909

Variety 1 — Copper-nickel, Laurel Wreath Reverse 1859

Spotted, cleaned or discolored pieces are worth less than values shown.

	Quan. Minted	G-4	VG-8	F-12	VF-20	EF-40	MS-60	Proof-63
1859 .... *(800)*	36,400,000	$5.00	$8.00	$15.00	$30.00	$75.00	$200.00	$1,300

Variety 2 — Copper-nickel, Oak Wreath with Shield 1860-1864

	Quan. Minted	G-4	VG-8	F-12	VF-20	EF-40	MS-60	Proof-63
1860 .. *(1,000)*	20,566,000	4.00	6.00	11.00	20.00	35.00	125.00	800.00
1861 .. *(1,000)*	10,100,000	11.00	17.00	25.00	30.00	40.00	200.00	900.00
1862 .... *(550)*	28,075,000	4.00	6.00	8.00	10.00	20.00	100.00	700.00
1863 .... *(460)*	49,840,000	4.00	6.00	8.00	10.00	20.00	100.00	700.00
1864 .... *(370)*	13,740,000	8.00	10.00	16.00	22.00	35.00	140.00	1,100

Variety 3 — Bronze 1864-1909

During the year 1864 the alloy of the cent was changed to 95% copper and 5% tin and zinc. The weight was reduced to 48 grains, resulting in a thinner coin than the so-called "white" cents of 1856-1864. The design remained unchanged. Before 1864 cents did not have the designer's initial L on the bonnet ribbon; late in that year the letter appeared on only a small quantity. The initial appeared on all dates of Indian cents thereafter. Consult the illustration details.

Indian Head Cent with "L"

If the coin is turned slightly (so Indian faces observer) the highlighted details of the "L" will appear to better advantage. The point of the bust is pointed on the variety with "L"; rounded without "L." The "L" is the initial of the engraver, Longacre.

SMALL CENTS

On coins 1859-1886 the last feather of the headdress points between I and C of AMERICA; from mid-1886 to 1909 it points between C and A.

Designer James B. Longacre; weight 3.11 grams; composition: .950 copper, .050 tin and zinc; diameter 19 mm; plain edge; mints: Philadelphia, San Francisco.

Choice brilliant Unc. and Proof small cents command higher prices. Spotted, cleaned or discolored pieces are worth less.

	Quan. Minted	G-4	VG-8	F-12	VF-20	EF-40	MS-60	Proof-63
1864 All kinds . .	39,233,714							
1864 No L. . . . . *(150)*		$3.50	$5.50	$8.50	$17.50	$27.50	$80.00	$1,100
1864 L must show . . . . . *(20)*		25.00	35.00	55.00	90.00	130.00	340.00	10,000
1865* . *(500+)*	35,429,286	3.25	4.50	7.50	15.00	25.00	60.00	550.00
1866 . . *(725+)*	9,826,500	20.00	25.00	33.00	55.00	85.00	175.00	550.00
1867 . . *(625+)*	9,821,000	20.00	25.00	33.00	50.00	75.00	175.00	550.00
1868 . . *(600+)*	10,266,500	20.00	25.00	33.00	50.00	75.00	175.00	550.00
1869 over 9*		75.00	125.00	175.00	300.00	450.00	925.00	
1869 . . *(600+)*	6,420,000	30.00	37.00	65.00	110.00	165.00	350.00	750.00
1870 *(1,000+)*	5,275,000	23.00	30.00	50.00	85.00	125.00	250.00	550.00
1871 . . *(960+)*	3,929,500	30.00	40.00	70.00	115.00	150.00	300.00	650.00
1872 . . *(950+)*	4,042,000	43.00	50.00	80.00	150.00	200.00	375.00	675.00

*One variety of 1865 appears to show traces of a 4 under the 5 in the date. The 9 is doubled on some varieties of the 1869; on others it appears to be over an 8, although it is actually a doubled 9.

Closed 3  **Open 3**

1873 All Kinds. .	11,676,500							
1873 Closed 3 *(1,100+)*		9.00	11.00	20.00	30.00	50.00	125.00	475.00
1873 Doubled LIBERTY				175.00	350.00	600.00	1,500	
1873 Open 3		9.00	11.00	20.00	30.00	50.00	125.00	
1874 . . *(700+)*	14,187,500	9.00	11.00	20.00	30.00	50.00	115.00	450.00
1875 . . *(700+)*	13,528,000	9.00	11.00	20.00	30.00	50.00	115.00	450.00
1876 *(1,150+)*	7,944,000	12.00	15.00	30.00	50.00	75.00	140.00	450.00
1877 . . *(900+)*	852,500	200.00	250.00	350.00	525.00	750.00	1,500	2,750
1878 . . *(2,350)*	5,799,850	14.00	17.00	30.00	45.00	75.00	135.00	400.00
1879 . . *(3,200)*	16,231,200	3.50	4.25	7.00	13.00	21.00	50.00	325.00
1880 . . *(3,955)*	38,964,955	1.50	2.25	3.50	5.75	14.00	42.00	300.00
1881 . . *(3,575)*	39,211,575	1.50	2.25	3.50	5.75	14.00	42.00	300.00
1882 . . *(3,100)*	38,581,100	1.50	2.25	3.50	5.75	14.00	42.00	300.00
1883 . . *(6,609)*	45,598,109	1.50	2.25	3.50	5.75	14.00	42.00	300.00
1884 . . *(3,942)*	23,261,742	1.75	2.75	5.00	8.00	15.00	50.00	325.00
1885 . . *(3,790)*	11,765,384	3.75	6.00	9.00	15.00	27.50	70.00	350.00
1886 . . *(4,290)*	17,654,290	2.10	3.25	6.00	10.00	20.00	55.00	300.00
1887 . . *(2,960)*	45,226,483	1.00	1.25	2.00	3.50	10.00	36.00	300.00

1888, last 8 over 7

1888 over 7					—	—	—	—
1888 . . *(4,582)*	37,494,414	1.00	1.25	2.00	3.50	10.00	36.00	300.00
1889 . . *(3,336)*	48,869,361	1.00	1.25	2.00	3.50	8.00	36.00	275.00

SMALL CENTS

	Quan. Minted	G-4	VG-8	F-12	VF-20	EF-40	MS-60	Proof-63
1890 .. (2,740)	57,182,854	$1.00	$1.25	$2.00	$3.50	$8.00	$36.00	$275.00
1891 .. (2,350)	47,072,350	1.00	1.25	2.00	3.50	8.00	36.00	275.00
1892 .. (2,745)	37,649,832	1.00	1.25	2.00	3.50	8.00	36.00	275.00
1893 .. (2,195)	46,642,195	1.00	1.25	2.00	3.50	8.00	36.00	275.00
1894 .. (2,632)	16,752,132	1.50	3.00	5.00	9.00	15.00	45.00	300.00
1895 .. (2,062)	38,343,636	.75	1.00	1.60	2.75	7.00	35.00	250.00
1896 .. (1,862)	39,057,293	.75	1.00	1.60	2.75	7.00	35.00	250.00
1897 .. (1,938)	50,466,330	.75	1.00	1.60	2.75	7.00	32.00	250.00
1898 .. (1,795)	49,823,079	.75	1.00	1.60	2.75	7.00	32.00	250.00
1899 .. (2,031)	53,600,031	.75	1.00	1.60	2.75	7.00	32.00	250.00
1900 .. (2,262)	66,833,764	.75	.90	1.30	2.30	7.00	30.00	250.00
1901 .. (1,985)	79,611,143	.75	.90	1.30	2.30	7.00	30.00	250.00
1902 .. (2,018)	87,376,722	.75	.90	1.30	2.30	7.00	30.00	250.00
1903 .. (1,790)	85,094,493	.75	.90	1.30	2.30	7.00	30.00	250.00
1904 .. (1,817)	61,328,015	.75	.90	1.30	2.30	7.00	30.00	250.00
1905 .. (2,152)	80,719,163	.75	.90	1.30	2.30	7.00	30.00	250.00
1906 .. (1,725)	96,022,255	.75	.90	1.30	2.30	7.00	30.00	250.00
1907 .. (1,475)	108,138,618	.75	.90	1.30	2.30	7.00	30.00	250.00

**Location of mint mark S
on reverse of Indian cent
(1908 and 1909 only).**

1908 .. (1,620)	32,327,987	.75	.90	1.30	2.30	7.00	35.00	275.00
1908S	1,115,000	18.00	22.00	25.00	32.00	45.00	155.00	
1909 .. (2,175)	14,370,645	.85	1.25	2.00	3.00	8.00	45.00	325.00
1909S	309,000	95.00	115.00	135.00	160.00	225.00	400.00	

LINCOLN TYPE, WHEAT EARS REVERSE 1909-1958

Victor D. Brenner designed this cent which was issued to commemorate the
hundredth anniversary of Lincoln's birth. The designer's initials VDB appear
on the reverse of a limited quantity of cents of 1909. The initials were restored,
in 1918, to the obverse side as illustrated below. The Lincoln type was the first
cent to have the motto IN GOD WE TRUST.

Matte proof coins were made for collectors from 1909 through 1916, and an
exceptional specimen dated 1917 is also known to exist.

Designer Victor D. Brenner; weight 3.11 grams; composition: 950 copper, 050 tin and zinc; diameter
19 mm; plain edge; mints: Philadelphia, Denver, San Francisco, West Point.

G-4 GOOD—*Date worn but apparent. Lines in wheat ears missing. Full rims.*

VG-8 VERY GOOD—*Half of lines show in upper wheat ears.*

F-12 FINE—*Wheat lines worn but visible.*

VF-20 VERY FINE—*Cheek and jaw bones worn but separated. No worn spots on wheat ears.*

EF-40 EXTREMELY FINE—*Slight wear. All details sharp.*

MS-60 UNCIRCULATED—*No trace of wear. Light blemishes or discoloration.*

MS-63 SELECT UNCIRCULATED—*No trace of wear. Slight blemishes.*

MS-65 CHOICE UNCIRCULATED—*No trace of wear. Barely noticeable blemishes.*

SMALL CENTS

Location of designer's initials V.D.B. on 1909 only.   **No V.D.B. on reverse 1909-1958**   **Location of mint mark.**

Variety 1 — Bronze 1909-1942

Choice brilliant uncirculated cents command higher prices. Discolored or weakly struck pieces are worth less.

Quan. Minted	G-4	VG-8	F-12	VF-20	EF-40	MS-60	MS-63
1909 V.D.B. 27,995,000	$2.25	$2.65	$3.00	$3.25	$4.00	$13.00	$27.50
1909 V.D.B. Matte prf. (420)							1,750
1909S, V.D.B...... 484,000	250.00	270.00	300.00	325.00	375.00	475.00	650.00
1909 72,702,618	.50	.60	.75	1.00	1.75	12.00	25.00
1909 Matte proof ... (2,198)							300.00
1909S 1,825,000	40.00	43.00	50.00	55.00	85.00	175.00	250.00
1909S, S over horiz. S.....	40.00	43.00	50.00	60.00	90.00	185.00	275.00
1910 146,801,218	.20	.30	.45	.80	1.75	13.00	23.00
1910 Matte proof ... (2,405)							300.00
1910S 6,045,000	8.00	9.00	10.00	11.00	18.00	95.00	150.00
1911 101,177,787	.20	.30	.60	1.25	3.75	18.00	30.00
1911 Matte proof ... (1,733)							300.00
1911D......... 12,672,000	3.50	4.25	6.00	10.00	25.00	100.00	170.00
1911S 4,026,000	13.00	15.00	17.00	20.00	30.00	115.00	240.00
1912 68,153,060	.25	.40	1.35	3.50	6.50	25.00	45.00
1912 Matte proof ... (2,145)							300.00
1912D......... 10,411,000	4.00	5.00	6.00	12.00	31.00	110.00	175.00
1912S 4,431,000	10.00	11.00	13.00	17.00	35.00	110.00	200.00
1913 76,532,352	.20	.35	1.00	2.25	8.00	20.00	35.00
1913 Matte proof ... (2,848)							300.00
1913D......... 15,804,000	2.00	2.50	4.50	7.00	17.50	70.00	145.00
1913S 6,101,000	8.00	9.00	10.00	13.00	23.00	100.00	225.00
1914 75,238,432	.20	.40	1.25	2.50	6.00	65.00	90.00
1914 Matte proof ... (1,365)							475.00
1914D*........ 1,193,000	65.00	80.00	85.00	145.00	375.00	800.00	1,400
1914S 4,137,000	9.00	10.00	12.00	18.00	31.00	165.00	425.00
1915 29,092,120	.80	1.50	3.25	6.00	22.00	110.00	175.00
1915 Matte proof ... (1,150)							700.00
1915D......... 22,050,000	.60	1.00	1.50	3.00	10.00	45.00	110.00
1915S 4,833,000	7.75	8.50	9.00	12.00	22.00	100.00	200.00
1916 131,833,677	.20	.25	.35	.75	1.50	12.00	25.00
1916 Matte proof ... (1,050)							900.00
1916D......... 35,956,000	.20	.35	.75	1.85	6.00	50.00	125.00
1916S 22,510,000	.75	1.25	1.75	2.25	7.50	60.00	125.00
1917 196,429,785	.20	.25	.30	.85	1.50	12.00	25.00
1917 Matte proof							—
1917D......... 55,120,000	.25	.35	.65	1.50	5.00	50.00	100.00
1917S 32,620,000	.25	.35	.65	1.50	5.00	55.00	125.00

*Beware of altered date or mint mark. No VDB on shoulder of genuine 1914D cent.

SMALL CENTS

Designer's initials restored starting 1918.

	Quan. Minted	G-4	VG-8	F-12	VF-20	EF-40	MS-60	MS-63
1918	288,104,634	$ .20	$ .25	$ .40	$ .80	$ 1.50	$13.00	$25.00
1918D	47,830,000	.25	.35	.65	1.50	5.00	50.00	105.00
1918S	34,680,000	.25	.35	.65	1.50	5.00	55.00	120.00
1919	392,021,000	.15	.25	.40	.60	1.50	11.00	20.00
1919D	57,154,000	.25	.30	.45	1.30	4.00	40.00	80.00
1919S	139,760,000	.15	.25	.40	.80	2.50	30.00	65.00
1920	310,165,000	.15	.25	.35	.40	1.50	10.00	20.00
1920D	49,280,000	.25	.35	.60	1.00	4.00	50.00	90.00
1920S	46,220,000	.25	.35	.60	1.00	4.00	65.00	120.00
1921	39,157,000	.20	.35	.60	1.00	3.00	40.00	70.00
1921S	} 15,274,000	.60	.85	1.50	3.00	10.00	125.00	300.00
1922D		4.75	6.00	7.00	9.50	19.00	80.00	150.00
1922 Plain†	7,160,000	150.00	200.00	275.00	400.00	800.00	3,000	—
1923	74,723,000	.15	.20	.35	.50	1.50	10.00	20.00
1923S	8,700,000	1.50	2.00	3.00	4.75	13.00	175.00	350.00
1924	75,178,000	.15	.20	.35	.50	2.00	22.00	40.00
1924D	2,520,000	8.00	10.00	12.00	18.00	40.00	235.00	375.00
1924S	11,696,000	.60	.80	1.25	2.50	6.00	110.00	185.00
1925	139,949,000	.15	.25	.35	.50	1.50	10.00	22.50
1925D	22,580,000	.20	.30	.40	1.00	4.00	50.00	80.00
1925S	26,380,000	.20	.25	.35	.75	4.00	60.00	120.00
1926	157,088,000	.15	.20	.30	.45	1.25	8.00	16.00
1926D	28,020,000	.25	.35	.60	1.30	5.00	50.00	85.00
1926S	4,550,000	3.00	3.60	5.00	6.00	12.00	100.00	170.00
1927	144,440,000	.15	.20	.30	.55	1.25	8.00	16.00
1927D	27,170,000	.25	.35	.50	.85	2.75	26.00	60.00
1927S	14,276,000	.40	.55	.90	1.65	4.00	65.00	135.00
1928	134,116,000	.15	.20	.30	.55	1.25	8.00	16.00
1928D	31,170,000	.20	.30	.40	.80	2.00	22.00	50.00
1928S*	17,266,000	.25	.35	.60	1.25	3.50	45.00	100.00
1929	185,262,000	.15	.20	.30	.60	1.35	7.50	13.00
1929D	41,730,000	.15	.25	.35	.65	1.35	18.00	40.00
1929S	50,148,000	.15	.25	.35	.60	1.25	9.00	18.00
1930	157,415,000	.10	.15	.25	.40	.90	5.50	11.00
1930D	40,100,000	.15	.20	.30	.45	1.50	12.00	26.00
1930S	24,286,000	.15	.20	.30	.50	1.00	9.00	16.00
1931	19,396,000	.25	.35	.45	.85	1.80	17.00	40.00
1931D	4,480,000	2.25	2.50	3.50	4.25	7.50	55.00	100.00
1931S	866,000	30.00	35.00	40.00	45.00	50.00	75.00	110.00
1932	9,062,000	1.50	1.75	2.00	2.50	3.00	18.00	40.00
1932D	10,500,000	.60	.80	1.20	1.75	2.50	16.00	33.00
1933	14,360,000	.75	.90	1.25	1.50	2.75	18.50	40.00
1933D	6,200,000	1.75	2.00	2.25	3.00	4.00	25.00	50.00
1934	219,080,000	.....	.10	.15	.30	.60	4.00	7.00
1934D	28,446,000	.15	.25	.30	.45	1.00	23.00	40.00
1935	245,388,000	.....	.10	.15	.20	.40	2.00	3.50
1935D	47,000,000	.....	.10	.15	.25	.40	4.00	8.00
1935S	38,702,000	.....	.10	.20	.30	.60	12.00	25.00

†The 1922 without D caused by defective die. Beware removed mint mark.
*Large and small mint mark varieties, see page 65.

SMALL CENTS

	Quan. Minted	G-4	VG-8	F-12	VF-20	EF-40	MS-65	Proof-63
1936 .. (5,569)	309,637,569		$ .10	$ .15	$ .20	$ .30	$4.00	$125.00
1936D.........	40,620,000		.10	.20	.30	.45	7.00	
1936S.........	29,130,000		.10	.25	.40	.55	8.00	
1937 .. (9,320)	309,179,320			.10	.15	.30	4.00	60.00
1937D.........	50,430,000		.10	.15	.25	.35	5.50	
1937S.........	34,500,000		.10	.20	.30	.40	8.00	
1938 . (14,734)	156,696,734			.10	.15	.20	.30	5.00	40.00
1938D.........	20,010,000	$ .15	.20	.30	.45	.65	6.50	
1938S.........	15,180,000	.25	.35	.45	.55	.75	8.00	
1939 . (13,520)	316,479,520			.10	.15	.25	2.00	35.00
1939D.........	15,160,000	.35	.45	.55	.65	.85	9.00	
1939S.........	52,070,000	.10	.15	.20	.30	.40	6.00	
1940. (15,872)	586,825,872				.10	.20	2.00	30.00
1940D.........	81,390,000			.10	.15	.25	3.50	
1940S*........	112,940,000			.10	.15	.25	4.00	
1941 . (21,100)	887,039,100				.10	.20	2.00	27.50
1941D.........	128,700,000				.10	.25	6.50	
1941S*........	92,360,000			.10	.15	.30	9.00	
1942 . (32,600)	657,828,600				.10	.20	1.75	27.50
1942D.........	206,698,000				.10	.20	2.00	
1942S.........	85,590,000	.10	.15	.25	.30	.45	14.00	

*Large and small mint mark varieties, see page 65.

Variety 2 — Zinc-coated Steel 1943, Only

Owing to a shortage of copper during the critical war year 1943, the Treasury Department resorted to the use of zinc-coated steel for our cents. No bronze cents were officially issued in 1943. A few specimens struck on bronze planchets by error are known to exist. Through a similar error, a few of the 1944 cents were struck on steel planchets.

1943 — Weight 2.70 grams; composition: steel, coated with zinc; diameter 19 mm; plain edge.

	Quan. Minted.	F-12	VF-20	EF-40	MS-65
1943	684,628,670	$ .15	$ .25	$ .30	$3.00
1943D....................	217,660,000	.15	.25	.30	4.50
1943S....................	191,550,000	.30	.45	.55	8.00

Variety 1 Resumed 1944-1958

1944D, D over S

Cartridge cases were salvaged for coinage of 1944 through 1946. Although the color was slightly different for uncirculated specimens, the coins proved satisfactory in every respect. The original alloy of 1864-1942 was resumed in 1947.

1944-1946 — Weight 3.11 grams; composition: .950 copper, .050 zinc; diameter 19 mm; plain edge.

	Quan. Minted	VF-20	EF-40	MS-65
1944	1,435,400,000	$ .10	$ .20	$ .75
1944D................... }		.10	.15	1.25
1944D, D over S .... }	430,578,000	110.00	160.00	*700.00
1944S.........................	282,760,000	.10	.20	.65
1945	1,040,515,000	.10	.15	.40
1945D.........................	266,268,000	.10	.20	1.00
1945S.........................	181,770,000	.10	.20	.75

*Value for MS-60 is $300.00. Two varieties exist, but only the one illustrated above is valued at the prices shown here, the other being less obvious and less desirable.

SMALL CENTS

	Quan. minted	VF-20	EF-40	MS-65	Proof-65
1946	991,655,000	$ .10	$ .15	$ .40	
1946D	315,690,000	.10	.20	.50	
1946S	198,100,000	.10	.20	.90	
1947	190,555,000	.10	.20	1.25	
1947D	194,750,000	.10	.20	.60	
1947S	99,000,000	.15	.25	1.10	
1948	317,570,000	.10	.20	1.00	
1948D	172,637,500	.10	.20	1.00	
1948S	81,735,000	.15	.30	1.50	
1949	217,775,000	.10	.20	1.75	
1949D	153,132,500	.10	.20	1.35	
1949S	64,290,000	.20	.30	4.00	
1950 .... (51,386)	272,686,386	.10	.20	1.50	$65.00
1950D	334,950,000	.10	.20	.50	
1950S	118,505,000	.10	.25	1.25	
1951 .... (57,500)	284,633,500	.10	.25	1.50	65.00
1951D	625,355,000	.10	.15	.60	
1951S	136,010,000	.15	.25	2.25	
1952 .... (81,980)	186,856,980		.15	.75	50.00
1952D	746,130,000		.15	1.00	
1952S	137,800,004		.20	1.25	
1953 .... (128,800)	256,883,800		.10	.50	40.00
1953D	700,515,000		.10	.70	
1953S	181,835,000		.15	.80	
1954 .... (233,300)	71,873,350	.25	.35	1.00	15.00
1954D	251,552,500		.10	.40	
1954S	96,190,000		.20	.45	

1955 Doubled Die Error

The 1955 doubled die error coins were made from improperly prepared dies
that show full-doubled outline of date and legend. Do not confuse with less
valuable pieces showing only minor traces of doubling.

	Quan. minted	VF-20	EF-40	MS-65	Proof-65
1955 Doubled die obv.		350.00	450.00	*3,000	
1955 .... (378,200)	330,958,200		.10	.25	10.00
1955D	563,257,500		.10	.25	
1955S	44,610,000	.30	.40	.70	
1956 .... (669,384)	421,414,384			.35	3.00
1956D	1,098,201,100			.20	
1957 .... (1,247,952)	283,787,952			.20	2.25
1957D	1,051,342,000			.15	
1958 .... (875,652)	253,400,652			.15	2.50
1958D	800,953,300			.15	

*Value for MS-60 Uncirculated is $675.00; MS-63 is $1,200.

SMALL CENTS
LINCOLN TYPE, MEMORIAL REVERSE 1959 TO DATE

Frank Gasparro designed the Lincoln Memorial reverse which was introduced in 1959 on the 150th anniversary of Lincoln's birth.

1959-1962 — Designer: Obv. V. D. Brenner, Rev. Frank Gasparro; weight 3.11 grams; composition: .950 copper, .050 tin and zinc; diameter 19 mm; plain edge; mints: Philadelphia, Denver, San Francisco. 1962-1982-composition changed to: .950 copper, .050 zinc. 1982-composition changed to: copper plated zinc. Core is 99.2% zinc, 0.8% copper, with a plating of pure copper. Total content is 97.5% zinc, 2.5% copper. Weight 2.5 grams. Both types issued in 1982.

	Quan. Minted	MS-65	Proof-65
1959 . . . . (1,149,291)	610,864,291	$ .10	$1.50
1959D.	1,279,760,000	.10	

Small Date **Large Date**

			MS-65	Proof-65
1960 Large date . . ⎱ (1,691,602)		. . . .	.10	1.10
1960 Sm. date . . . . ⎰	588,096,602		3.00	13.00
1960D Large date. . . . . ⎱ 1,580,884,000		. . . .	.10	
1960D Small date. . . . . ⎰		. . . .	.25	
1961 . . . . (3,028,244)	756,373,244	.10	1.00
1961D.	1,753,266,700	.10	
1962 . . . . (3,218,019)	609,263,019	.10	1.00
1962D.	1,793,148,400	.10	
1963 . . . . (3,075,645)	757,185,645	.10	1.00
1963D.	1,774,020,400	.10	
1964 . . . . (3,950,762)	2,652,525,762	.10	1.00
1964D.	3,799,071,500	.10	
1965	1,497,224,900	.10	
1966	2,188,147,783	.10	
1967	3,048,667,100	.10	
1968	1,707,880,970	.15	
1968D.	2,886,269,600	.10	
1968S . . . . (3,041,506)	261,311,507	.10	1.00

In 1969, the dies were modified to strengthen the design, and Lincoln's head was made slightly smaller. In 1973, dies were further modified and engraver's initials FG made larger. The initials were reduced slightly in 1974. During 1982 the dies were again modified and the bust, lettering and date made slightly smaller. One variety of the 1984 cent shows Lincoln's ear doubled.

SMALL CENTS

1969S Double Die Error

Small Date   **Large Date**

	Quan. Minted	MS-65	Proof-65
1969.........	1,136,910,000	$ .60	
1969D	4,002,832,200	.15	
1969S Doubled die obv....		——	
1969S (2,934,631)			
......	547,309,631	.15	$1.50
1970.........	1,898,315,000	.50	
1970D	2,891,438,900	.10	
1970S (2,632,810)			
......	693,192,814		
1970S Sm. date...........		20.00	85.00
1970S Lg. date (low 7)		.15	1.00
1971.........	1,919,490,000	.30	
1971D	2,911,045,600	.15	
1971S (3,220,733)			
......	528,354,192	.35	1.50

1972 Doubled Die Error

	Quan. Minted	MS-65	Proof-65
1972 Doubled die obv.* ...		310.00	
1972.........	2,933,255,000	.10	
1972D	2,665,071,400	.15	
1972S (3,260,996)			
......	380,200,104	.10	1.50
1973.........	3,728,245,000	.10	
1973D	3,549,576,588	.10	
1973S (2,760,339)			
......	319,937,634	.10	1.50
1974.........	4,232,140,523	.10	

	Quan. Minted	MS-65	Proof-65
1974D	4,235,098,000	$ .10	
1974S (2,612,568)			
......	412,039,228	.15	$ 1.50
1975.........	5,451,476,142	.10	
1975D	4,505,275,300	.10	
1975S Proof....	(2,845,450)		10.00
1976.........	4,674,292,426	.10	
1976D	4,221,592,455	.10	
1976S Proof	(4,149,730)		3.00
1977.........	4,469,930,000	.10	
1977D	4,194,062,300	.10	
1977S Proof....	(3,251,152)		3.00
1978.........	5,558,605,000	.10	
1978D	4,280,233,400	.10	
1978S Proof....	(3,127,781)		3.25
1979.........	6,018,515,000	.10	
1979D	4,139,357,254	.10	
1979S Proof....	(3,677,175)		
Filled S................			3.50
Clear S			5.50
1980.........	7,414,705,000	.10	
1980D	5,140,098,660	.10	
1980S Proof....	(3,554,806)		2.25
1981.........	7,491,750,000	.10	
1981D	5,373,235,677	.10	
1981S Proof....	(4,063,083)		2.25
1982	10,712,525,000		
Lg. Date................		.10	
Sm. Date		.15	
1982D	6,012,979,368		
Lg. date		.10	
1982S Proof....	(3,857,479)		3.00

Copper Plated Zinc

Large Date

Small Date

1982 Lg. Date .. } inc. above	.10
1982 Sm. Date . }	.10

1982D Lg. Date } inc. above	.25
1982D Sm. Date }	.10

*Other slightly doubled varieties exist, but are worth far less.

SMALL CENTS

1983 Double Die Rev.

1984 Double Die Obv.

	Quan. Minted	MS-65	Proof-65
1983 Doubled die rev......	$175.00		
1983.........	7,752,355,000	.10	
1983D	6,467,199,428	.10	
1983S Proof....	(3,279,126)		$8.50
1984.........	8,151,079,000	.10	
1984 Doubled die obv.		90.00	
1984D	5,569,238,906	.10	
1984S Proof....	(3,065,110)		10.00
1985........	*5,648,489,887	.10	
1985D	5,287,399,926	.10	
1985S Proof.....	3,362,821		8.00
1986.........	4,491,395,493	.10	
1986D	4,442,866,698	.10	
1986S Proof....	(3,010,497)		$8.00
1987.........	4,682,466,931	$.10	
1987D	4,879,389,514	.10	
1987S Proof....	(3,792,233)		6.50
1988.........	6,092,810,000	.10	
1988D	5,253,740,443	.10	
1988S Proof..............			6.00
1989.........	7,261,535,000	.10	
1989D	5,345,467,111	.10	
1989S Proof..............			6.00
1990.....................		.10	
1990D		.10	
1990S Proof..............			6.00

*696,585,000 of these were manufactured at West Point

TWO-CENT PIECES — 1864-1873

+ or − indicates change from previous year 1864-1873	**TYPE COIN VALUES**									
	G-4	F-12	EF-40	AU-50	MS-60	MS-63	MS-65	PF-60	PF-63	PF-65
	5.00+	7.00+	30.00	60.00	135.00	300.00+	800.00−	350.00−	675.00	1,800

The Act of April 22, 1864, which changed the weight and composition of the cent, included a provision for the bronze two cent piece. The weight was specified as 96 grains, the alloy being the same as for the cent.

The two cent piece is one of the short-lived issues of United States coinage. The motto "In God We Trust" appeared for the first time on the new coin due largely to the increased religious sentiment during the Civil War Crisis.

There are two varieties for the first year of issue, 1864: the small motto which is scarce and the large motto. See illustrations below.

1864 Small Motto   **1864 Large Motto**

On the obverse the D in GOD is narrow on the large motto. The stem to the leaf shows plainly on the small motto variety. There is no stem on the large motto.

The first T in TRUST touches ribbon crease at left on the small motto variety; there is a 1mm gap on the large motto variety.

It will be noted that the shield device is very similar to the nickel five cent piece introduced in 1866. Proof mintage totals are unknown.

Designer James B. Longacre; weight 6.22 grams; composition: .950 copper, .050 tin and zinc; diameter 23 mm; plain edge. All coined at Philadelphia Mint.

G-4 GOOD—At least IN GOD visible.

VG-8 VERY GOOD—WE weakly visible.

F-12 FINE—Complete motto visible. WE weak.

EF-40 EXTREMELY FINE—WE is bold.

MS-60 UNCIRCULATED—No trace of wear. Light blemishes.

MS-63 SELECT UNCIRCULATED—No trace of wear. Nice color, few blemishes.

Brilliant red choice uncirculated and proof coins command higher prices. Spotted, cleaned or discolored pieces are worth less.

	Quan. Minted	G-4	F-12	EF-40	MS-60	MS-63	Proof-63
1864 Sm. motto.....	19,847,500	$60.00	$90.00	$250.00	$550.00	$1,200	——
1864 Lg. motto (100+)		5.00	7.00	30.00	135.00	300.00	$775.00
1865* ....(500+)	13,640,000	5.00	7.00	30.00	135.00	300.00	775.00
1866 ....(725+)	3,177,000	5.00	7.00	30.00	135.00	300.00	675.00
1867 ....(625+)	2,938,750	5.00	7.00	30.00	140.00	300.00	675.00
1867 Doubled die		——	——	175.00	325.00	650.00	
1868 ....(600+)	2,803,750	5.00	7.00	30.00	150.00	300.00	675.00
1869, 9 over 8	1,546,500	150.00	225.00	600.00	1,100		
1869 ....(600+)		7.00	12.00	40.00	200.00	400.00	775.00
1870 .... (1,000+)	861,250	9.00	18.00	65.00	300.00	475.00	1,000
1871 ....(960+)	721,250	10.00	21.00	80.00	325.00	600.00	1,100
1872 ....(950+)	65,000	75.00	145.00	325.00	775.00	1,700	1,800
1873 Closed 3. Proofs only (Est. 600). (See illustration on page 92)..............							2,400
1873 Open 3. Restrike (Est. 500)							2,600

*One variety appears to show traces of a 4 under the 5 in the date.

BIBLIOGRAPHY

Kliman, Myron M. *The Two Cent Piece and Varieties.* 1977.

SILVER THREE-CENT PIECES 1851-1873

+ or − indicates change from previous year				TYPE COIN VALUES							
	G-4	F-12	EF-40	AU-50	MS-60	MS-63	MS-65	PF-60	PF-63	PF-65	
Variety I 1851-1853	11.00+	15.00	52.00+	110.00	200.00	450.00	3,000+				
Variety II 1854-1858	10.00	18.00	80.00	200.00	325.00	800.00	8,000+	800.00−	2,300+	12,000+	
Variety III 1859-1873	11.00+	20.00+	55.00−	120.00	200.00−	500.00	3,000+	400.00−	900.00+	3,500+	

This smallest of United States silver coins was authorized by Congress March 3, 1851. The first three-cent silver pieces had no lines bordering the six-pointed star. From 1854 through 1858 there were three lines, while issues of the last fifteen years show only two lines. Issues from 1854 through 1873 have an olive sprig over the III and a bundle of three arrows beneath. Nearly the entire production of non-proof coins from 1863 to 1872 was melted in 1873.

1851-1853 — Designer James B. Longacre; weight .80 gram; composition: .750 silver, .250 copper; diameter 14 mm; plain edge; mints: Philadelphia, New Orleans.

1854-1873 — Weight .75 gram; composition: .900 silver, .100 copper; diameter 14 mm; plain edge. All coined at Philadelphia Mint.

mint mark
o
◄

G-4 GOOD—*Star worn smooth. Legend and date readable.*
VG-8 VERY GOOD—*Outline of shield defined. Legend and date clear.*
F-12 FINE—*Only star points worn smooth.*
VF-20 VERY FINE—*Only partial wear on star ridges.*
EF-40 EXTREMELY FINE—*Ridges on star points show.*
MS-60 UNCIRCULATED—*No trace of wear. Light blemishes.*

Variety 1 — 1851-1853

	Quan. Minted	G-4	VG-8	F-12	VF-20	EF-40	MS-60	Proof-63
1851	5,447,400	$11.00	$12.00	$18.00	$30.00	$54.00	$225.00	——
1851O..........	720,000	18.00	22.00	31.00	60.00	125.00	475.00	
1852	18,663,500	11.00	12.00	15.00	27.50	52.00	200.00	——
1853	11,400,000	11.00	12.00	15.00	27.50	52.00	200.00	

Variety 2
1854-1858

Well struck specimens command higher prices.

1854	671,000	13.50	17.50	24.00	40.00	85.00	325.00	——
1855	139,000	18.00	25.00	40.00	70.00	150.00	650.00	$2,800
1856	1,458,000	11.00	15.00	20.00	35.00	80.00	325.00	2,700
1857	1,042,000	11.00	15.00	20.00	40.00	85.00	325.00	2,700
1858	1,604,000	11.00	15.00	20.00	40.00	85.00	325.00	2,300

Variety 3
1859-1873

**1862,
2 over 1**

1859 .... (800)	365,000	11.00	15.00	20.00	33.00	55.00	200.00	900.00
1860 .. (1,000)	287,000	11.00	15.00	20.00	33.00	55.00	200.00	900.00
1861 .. (1,000)	498,000	11.00	15.00	20.00	33.00	55.00	200.00	900.00
1862, 2 over 1	} 343,550	15.00	18.00	25.00	50.00	75.00	275.00	
1862 .... (550)		11.00	15.00	20.00	33.00	55.00	200.00	900.00
1863, 3 over 2	} 21,460	....						1,300
1863 .... (460)							550.00	875.00
1864 .... (470)	12,470	....					600.00	875.00

SILVER THREE-CENT PIECES

	Quan. Minted		MS-60	Proof-63
1865 .... (500)	8,500		$650.00	$950.00
1866 .... (725)	22,725		650.00	950.00
1867 .... (625)	4,625		650.00	950.00
1868 .... (600)	4,100		650.00	950.00
1869, 9 over 8			—	—
1869 .... (600)	5,100		650.00	1,000
1870 .. (1,000)	4,000		650.00	1,000
1871 .... (960)	4,360		650.00	1,000
1872 .... (950)	1,950		750.00	1,000
1873 .... (600)	600 (Closed 3, proof only)			2,000

NICKEL THREE-CENT PIECES 1865-1889

+ or − indicates change from previous year			TYPE COIN VALUES							
	G-4	F-12	EF-40	AU-50	MS-60	MS-63	MS-65	PF-60	PF-63	PF-65
1865-1889	5.00+	7.00+	17.00+	37.50	85.00−	250.00	2,000+	225.00−	450.00−	1,600

The three cent pieces struck in nickel composition were designed to replace the silver three cent coins. Composition is 75% copper and 25% nickel. All were coined at Philadelphia and have plain edges.

Designer James B. Longacre; weight 1.94 grams; composition: .750 copper, .250 nickel; diameter 17.9 mm; plain edge. All coined at Philadelphia Mint.

G-4 GOOD—*Date and legends complete though worn. III smooth.*

VG-8 VERY GOOD—*III is half worn. Rims complete.*

F-12 FINE—*Hair curls well defined.*

EF-40 EXTREMELY FINE—*Slight, even wear.*

MS-60 UNCIRCULATED—*No trace of wear. Light blemishes.*

	Quan. Minted	G-4	VG-8	F-12	EF-40	MS-60	Proof-63
1865 .... (500+)	11,382,000	$5.00	$6.00	$7.00	$17.00	$85.00	$1,200
1866 .... (725+)	4,801,000	5.00	6.00	7.00	17.00	85.00	450.00
1867 .... (625+)	3,915,000	5.00	6.00	7.00	17.00	85.00	450.00
1868 .... (600+)	3,252,000	5.00	6.00	7.00	17.00	85.00	450.00
1869 .... (600+)	1,604,000	5.00	6.00	7.00	17.00	85.00	450.00
1870 .... (1,000+)	1,335,000	6.00	7.00	8.00	20.00	110.00	450.00
1871 .... (960+)	604,000	6.00	7.00	9.00	20.00	110.00	450.00
1872 .... (950+)	862,000	6.00	7.00	9.00	20.00	125.00	450.00
1873 Closed 3 (1,100 ।)	390,000	6.00	7.00	9.00	20.00	125.00	450.00
1873 Open 3	783,000	6.00	7.00	9.00	20.00	120.00	
1874 .... (700+)	790,000	6.00	7.00	9.00	20.00	120.00	450.00
1875 .... (700+)	228,000	9.00	11.00	13.00	26.00	160.00	450.00
1876 .... (1,150+)	162,000	9.00	11.00	14.00	30.00	165.00	450.00
1877 (Prfs. only) (510+)	510			800.00	1,250		1,700
1878 (Prfs. only) (2,350)	2,350			500.00	650.00		950.00
1879 .... (3,200)	41,200	48.00	52.00	60.00	80.00	235.00	500.00
1880 .... (3,955)	24,955	60.00	70.00	80.00	110.00	270.00	500.00
1881 .... (3,575)	1,080,575	5.00	6.00	7.00	18.00	90.00	500.00
1882 .... (3,100)	25,300	60.00	70.00	80.00	110.00	250.00	625.00
1883 .... (6,609)	10,609	115.00	135.00	175.00	250.00	400.00	700.00
1884 .... (3,942)	5,642	250.00	300.00	325.00	375.00	500.00	800.00
1885 .... (3,790)	4,790	350.00	400.00	450.00	600.00	875.00	1,000
1886 (Prfs. only) (4,290)	4,290			350.00	600.00		775.00
1887 All kinds		225.00	275.00	325.00	450.00	575.00	800.00
1887, 7 over 6 (2,960)	7,961			425.00	600.00		800.00
1888 .... (4,582)	41,083	40.00	45.00	55.00	75.00	275.00	450.00
1889 .... (3,436)	21,561	60.00	70.00	80.00	115.00	325.00	450.00

NICKEL FIVE-CENT PIECES — 1866 to Date

SHIELD TYPE 1866-1883

The shield type nickel was made possible by the Act of May 16, 1866. Its weight was set at 77-16/100 grains with the same composition as the nickel three-cent piece which was authorized in 1865. In 1866 the coin was designed with rays between the stars on the reverse. Some of the pieces minted in 1867 have the same details, but later the rays were eliminated creating two varieties for that year. There was no further change in the type until it was replaced by the Liberty head device in 1883. Only proof pieces were struck in 1877 and 1878.

Designer James B. Longacre; weight 5 grams; composition: .750 copper, .250 nickel; diameter 20.5 mm; plain edge. All coined at Philadelphia Mint.

G-4 GOOD—*All letters in motto readable.*

VG-8 VERY GOOD—*Motto stands out clearly. Rims worn slightly but even. Part of shield lines visible.*

F-12 FINE—*Half of each olive leaf is smooth.*

EF-40 EXTREMELY FINE—*Leaf tips show slight wear. Cross over shield slightly worn.*

MS-60 UNCIRCULATED—*No trace of wear. Light blemishes.*

Rays Between Stars 1866-1867

Sharply struck uncirculated coins are valued higher than the prices shown here.

	Quan. Minted	G-4	VG-8	F-12	EF-40	MS-60	Proof-63
1866 Rays..... *(125+)*	14,742,500	$11.25	$14.50	$20.00	$85.00	$300.00	$2,500
1867 Rays...... *(25+)*	2,019,000	13.50	18.00	30.00	95.00	425.00	8,000

Without Rays 1867-1883

Typical example of 1883, 3 over 2. Other varieties exist, as well as pieces with recut 3.

1867 No rays.. *(600+)*	28,890,500	7.00	9.00	11.00	30.00	110.00	500.00
1868 .... *(600+)*	28,817,000	7.00	9.00	11.00	30.00	110.00	500.00
1869 .... *(600+)*	16,395,000	7.00	9.00	11.00	30.00	175.00	500.00
1870 ....*(1,000+)*	4,806,000	7.00	10.00	12.00	35.00	200.00	500.00
1871 .... *(960+)*	561,000	30.00	40.00	50.00	95.00	300.00	750.00
1872 .... *(950+)*	6,036,000	7.00	10.00	12.00	35.00	200.00	500.00
1873 Closed 3 *(1,100+)*	436,050	10.00	15.00	20.00	50.00	300.00	500.00
1873 Open 3 .... 1873, lg. over sm. 3 ... }	4,113,950	8.00	10.00	12.00	35.00	200.00	
1874 .... *(700+)*	3,538,000	10.00	12.00	15.00	40.00	200.00	500.00
1875 .... *(700+)*	2,097,000	11.00	13.50	20.00	50.00	250.00	650.00

NICKEL FIVE-CENT PIECES

	Quan. Minted	G-4	VG-8	F-12	EF-40	MS-60	Proof-63
1876 . . . . (1,150+)	2,530,000	$11.00	$13.50	$20.00	$50.00	$225.00	$650.00
1877 (Prfs. only) (510+)	510				1,500		2,200
1878 (Prfs. only) (2,350)	2,350				750.00		1,500
1879 . . . . (3,200)	29,100	210.00	265.00	325.00	475.00	625.00	1,000
1879, 9 over 8							—
1880 . . . . (3,955)	19,955	225.00	300.00	350.00	500.00	700.00	1,100
1881 . . . . (3,575)	72,375	175.00	210.00	275.00	375.00	550.00	1,000
1882 . . . . (3,100)	11,476,000	7.00	9.00	12.00	27.50	110.00	500.00
1883 . . . . (5,419)	1,456,919	7.00	9.00	12.00	27.50	110.00	500.00
1883, 3 over 2				45.00	65.00	150.00	400.00

LIBERTY HEAD TYPE 1883-1913

In 1883 the type was changed to the familiar "Liberty head." This type first appeared without the word CENTS on the coin, merely a large letter "V." These "centless" coins were gold-plated and passed for five dollars. Later in that year the word CENTS was added.

Five 1913 Liberty head nickels were originally owned by Col. E. H. R. Green (son of the famous Hetty Green). These have since been dispersed and are now held in individuals' collections. These were not a regular issue and were never placed in circulation.

Designer Charles E. Barber; weight 5 grams; composition: .750 copper, .250 nickel; diameter 21.2 mm; plain edge; mints: Philadelphia, Denver, San Francisco.

Sharply struck uncirculated coins are valued higher than the prices shown; dull or weakly struck pieces are worth less.

Variety 1 — Without CENTS 1883 Only

G-4 GOOD—No details in head. LIBERTY obliterated.

VG-8 VERY GOOD—At least 3 letters in LIBERTY readable.

F-12 FINE—All letters in LIBERTY show.

VF-20 VERY FINE—LIBERTY bold, including letter I.

EF-40 EXTREMELY FINE—LIBERTY sharp. Corn grains at bottom of wreath show, on reverse.

MS-60 UNCIRCULATED—No trace of wear. Light blemishes.

	Quan. Minted	G-4	VG-8	F-12	VF-20	EF-40	MS-60	Proof-63
1883 without CENTS								
(5,219)	5,479,519	$2.50	$3.00	$4.00	$6.00	$8.00	$40.00	$500.00

Variety 2 — With CENTS 1883-1913

Location of mint mark.

1883 with CENTS								
(6,783)	16,032,983	5.50	8.00	12.00	20.00	30.00	150.00	500.00
1884 (3,942)	11,273,942	6.75	9.50	15.00	24.00	35.00	200.00	500.00
1885 (3,790)	1,476,490	225.00	275.00	375.00	525.00	700.00	1,100	1,500
1886 (4,290)	3,330,290	50.00	60.00	100.00	140.00	225.00	475.00	750.00
1887 (2,960)	15,263,652	4.50	6.00	15.00	20.00	30.00	160.00	400.00
1888 (4,582)	10,720,483	6.00	9.00	17.00	25.00	37.50	150.00	400.00
1889 (3,336)	15,881,361	4.00	5.00	14.00	20.00	30.00	140.00	400.00

NICKEL FIVE-CENT PIECES

	Quan. Minted	G-4	VG-8	F-12	VF-20	EF-40	MS-60	Proof-63
1890 (2,740)	16,259,272	$4.00	$5.00	$14.00	$20.00	$30.00	$150.00	$400.00
1891 (2,350)	16,834,350	3.50	5.00	14.00	20.00	30.00	140.00	400.00
1892 (2,745)	11,699,642	3.50	5.00	14.00	20.00	30.00	150.00	400.00
1893 (2,195)	13,370,195	3.50	5.00	14.00	20.00	30.00	140.00	400.00
1894 (2,632)	5,413,132	5.50	8.00	17.00	25.00	40.00	200.00	400.00
1895 (2,062)	9,979,884	3.00	4.50	14.00	17.50	25.00	125.00	400.00
1896 (1,862)	8,842,920	3.50	5.00	15.00	20.00	30.00	125.00	400.00
1897 (1,938)	20,428,735	1.00	2.00	5.00	7.50	20.00	110.00	400.00
1898 (1,795)	12,532,087	1.00	2.00	5.00	7.50	20.00	110.00	400.00
1899 (2,031)	26,029,031	1.00	2.00	5.00	7.50	20.00	110.00	400.00
1900 (2,262)	27,255,995	.60	1.00	3.00	6.00	18.00	90.00	375.00
1901 (1,985)	26,480,213	.60	1.00	3.00	6.00	18.00	90.00	375.00
1902 (2,018)	31,489,579	.60	1.00	3.00	6.00	18.00	90.00	375.00
1903 (1,790)	28,006,725	.60	1.00	3.00	6.00	18.00	90.00	375.00
1904 (1,817)	21,404,984	.60	1.00	3.00	6.00	18.00	90.00	375.00
1905 (2,152)	29,827,276	.60	1.00	3.00	6.00	18.00	90.00	375.00
1906 (1,725)	38,613,725	.60	1.00	3.00	6.00	18.00	90.00	375.00
1907 (1,475)	39,214,800	.60	1.00	3.00	6.00	18.00	90.00	375.00
1908 (1,620)	22,686,177	.60	1.00	3.00	6.00	18.00	90.00	375.00
1909 (4,763)	11,590,526	.75	1.25	3.25	7.00	19.00	100.00	375.00
1910 (2,405)	30,169,353	.60	1.00	3.00	6.00	18.00	90.00	375.00
1911 (1,733)	39,559,372	.60	1.00	3.00	6.00	18.00	90.00	375.00
1912 (2,145)	26,236,714	.60	1.00	3.00	6.00	18.00	90.00	375.00
1912D........	8,474,000	1.00	1.50	4.00	10.00	45.00	250.00	
1912S..........	238,000	40.00	50.00	65.00	175.00	375.00	625.00	

1913 Liberty Head (*5 known*) .... 1985 Buss Sale $385,000

INDIAN HEAD or BUFFALO TYPE 1913-1938

These pieces are known as Buffalo, Bison or Indian Head nickels. In the first
year of issue, 1913, there were two distinct varieties, the first showing the bison
on a mound, and the second with the base redesigned to a thinner, straight line.

James E. Fraser designed this nickel employing three different Indians as
models. His initial F is beneath the date. The bison was modeled after "Black
Diamond" in the New York Zoological Gardens.

Matte proof coins were made for collectors from 1913 to 1917.

Designer James Earle Fraser; weight 5 grams; composition: .750 copper, .250 nickel; diameter 21.2 mm;
plain edge; mints: Philadelphia, Denver, San Francisco.

G-4 GOOD—*Legends and date readable. Horn worn off.*
VG-8 VERY GOOD—*Half horn shows.*
F-12 FINE—*Three-quarters of horn shows. Obv. rim intact.*
VF-20 VERY FINE—*Full horn shows. Indian's cheekbone worn.*
EF-40 EXTREMELY FINE—*Full horn. Slight wear on Indian's hair ribbon.*
MS-63 SELECT UNCIRCULATED—*No trace of wear. Light blemishes. Attractive mint luster.*

Variety 1 — FIVE CENTS on Raised Ground

NICKEL FIVE-CENT PIECES

	Quan. Minted	G-4	VG-8	F-12	VF-20	EF-40	MS-63	Matte Proof-63
1913 Var. 1								
(1,520)	30,993,520	$3.25	$3.75	$4.50	$7.00	$12.00	$80.00	$2,000
1913D Var. 1 ...	5,337,000	6.25	7.25	8.75	13.00	22.50	125.00	
1913S Var. 1 ...	2,105,000	9.50	12.00	16.00	25.00	40.00	175.00	

Variety 2 — FIVE CENTS in Recess

Mint mark below FIVE CENTS.

1916 Doubled Die obverse

1918D, 8 over 7

	Quan. Minted	G-4	VG-8	F-12	VF-20	EF-40	MS-63	Matte Proof-63
1913 Var. 2								
(1,514)	29,858,700	3.00	3.50	4.25	6.75	13.00	80.00	1,300
1913D Var. 2 ...	4,156,000	40.00	45.00	55.00	65.00	100.00	325.00	
1913S Var. 2 ...	1,209,000	65.00	80.00	115.00	135.00	200.00	550.00	
1914 .. (1,275)	20,665,738	3.75	4.50	5.75	7.25	15.00	130.00	1,200
1914D..........	3,912,000	30.00	34.00	45.00	60.00	100.00	425.00	
1914S..........	3,470,000	4.50	6.00	9.00	16.00	37.50	250.00	
1915 .. (1,050)	20,987,270	1.75	2.50	3.75	6.50	12.50	125.00	1,500
1915D..........	7,569,000	6.50	8.00	15.00	35.00	55.00	275.00	
1915S..........	1,505,000	10.00	12.00	20.00	55.00	100.00	600.00	
1916 .... (600)	63,498,066	.75	1.00	1.75	2.50	5.00	90.00	2,500
1916 Doubled die obv.....	800.00	1,000	1,750	2,500	3,750	——		
1916D.........	13,333,000	4.50	5.50	8.00	25.00	45.00	275.00	
1916S........	11,860,000	3.00	4.00	6.00	17.50	42.50	260.00	
1917	51,424,019	.85	1.25	1.90	3.00	8.00	110.00	——
1917D.........	9,910,000	4.50	6.00	11.00	37.50	85.00	365.00	
1917S.........	4,193,000	3.50	5.50	10.00	35.00	70.00	390.00	
1918	32,086,314	.85	1.35	2.50	5.50	15.00	180.00	
1918D, 8 over 7 }	8,362,000	415.00	525.00	725.00	1,500	2,750	16,000	
1918D......... }		4.50	6.00	12.00	60.00	85.00	550.00	
1918S.........	4,882,000	3.50	5.00	9.50	37.50	75.00	475.00	
1919	60,868,000	.65	.85	1.50	3.00	7.50	85.00	
1919D†.........	8,006,000	4.00	6.00	11.50	70.00	100.00	650.00	
1919S†.........	7,521,000	2.50	4.50	9.00	45.00	80.00	525.00	
1920	63,093,000	.65	.85	1.50	3.00	7.50	90.00	
1920D†.........	9,418,000	3.00	4.50	8.75	55.00	100.00	700.00	
1920S.........	9,689,000	1.75	2.75	6.25	26.00	75.00	500.00	
1921	10,663,000	.85	1.25	3.00	6.75	17.00	190.00	
1921S†.........	1,557,000	13.00	18.00	40.00	145.00	325.00	1,000	
1923	35,715,000	.45	.65	1.25	2.75	7.00	90.00	
1923S†.........	6,142,000	1.50	2.50	5.50	22.50	60.00	400.00	
1924	21,620,000	.45	.65	1.25	3.50	8.00	135.00	
1924D.........	5,258,000	2.25	3.00	8.00	45.00	85.00	450.00	
1924S.........	1,437,000	4.50	6.50	14.50	200.00	475.00	1,450	
1925	35,565,100	.45	.65	1.25	2.75	7.00	90.00	
1925D†.........	4,450,000	3.50	5.50	11.00	55.00	90.00	550.00	
1925S.........	6,256,000	2.25	3.50	6.75	20.00	55.00	450.00	
1926	44,693,000	.40	.60	.95	1.50	5.00	80.00	
1926D†.........	5,638,000	2.00	3.75	9.00	50.00	90.00	425.00	

†Uncirculated pieces with full sharp details are worth considerably more.

NICKEL FIVE-CENT PIECES

	Quan. Minted	G-4	VG-8	F-12	VF-20	EF-40	MS-63	Proof-65
1926S	970,000	$5.50	$8.50	$14.00	$65.00	$300.00	$1,300	
1927	37,981,000	.40	.60	.95	1.50	5.00	75.00	
1927D.	5,730,000	1.00	1.75	3.00	10.00	35.00	250.00	
1927S	3,430,000	1.00	1.75	3.00	13.00	60.00	325.00	
1928	23,411,000	.40	.60	.95	1.50	4.50	75.00	
1928D.	6,436,000	.75	1.00	2.25	4.50	11.00	110.00	
1928S	6,936,000	.75	1.00	1.50	3.00	10.00	175.00	
1929	36,446,000	.40	.50	.85	1.50	4.00	65.00	
1929D.	8,370,000	.60	.80	1.40	3.50	10.00	125.00	
1929S	7,754,000	.55	.75	1.00	2.25	7.00	90.00	
1930	22,849,000	.40	.50	.85	1.50	4.00	65.00	
1930S	5,435,000	.50	.75	1.00	2.00	6.75	125.00	
1931S	1,200,000	3.50	4.50	5.50	6.50	10.00	125.00	
1934	20,213,003	.30	.45	.60	1.50	3.50	60.00	
1934D.	7,480,000	.45	.60	.85	1.50	5.00	115.00	
1935	58,264,000	.30	.35	.45	.75	2.25	35.00	
1935D.	12,092,000	.35	.45	.60	1.75	3.50	110.00	
1935S	10,300,000	.35	.40	.50	1.00	2.50	50.00	
1936 . . (4,420)	119,001,420	.30	.35	.40	.75	2.25	25.00	$2,000
1936D.	24,814,000	.30	.40	.50	1.00	2.25	35.00	
1936S	14,930,000	.30	.40	.50	1.00	2.25	37.50	
1937 . . (5,769)	79,485,769	.30	.35	.45	.75	2.25	23.00	1,500

1937D "3-Legged" Variety

1938 D over S

1937D All Kinds

	Quan. Minted	G-4	VG-8	F-12	VF-20	EF-40	MS-63
. . . .	17,826,00	.30	.40	.55	1.00	2.25	25.00
1937D 3-Legged. .		80.00	100.00	140.00	175.00	250.00	1,800
1937S	5,635,000	.40	.45	.55	1.00	2.25	25.00
1938D.	} 7,020,000	.40	.45	.55	1.00	2.25	23.00
1938D, D over S‡				6.00	7.50	11.00	45.00

‡Varieties exist.

JEFFERSON TYPE 1938 to Date

This nickel was designed by Felix Schlag. He won an award of $1,000 in a competition with some 390 artists. It established the definite public approval of portrait and pictorial rather than symbolic devices on our coinage.

Designer Felix Schlag; weight 5 grams; composition: 1938-1942, 1946- , .750 copper, .250 nickel; 1942-1945, .560 copper, .350 silver, .090 manganese; diameter 21.2 mm; plain edge; mints: Philadelphia, Denver, San Francisco. Net weight 1942-1945: .05626 oz. pure silver.

VG-8 VERY GOOD—*Second porch pillar from right nearly gone, other three still visible but weak.*

F-12 FINE—*Cheekbone worn flat. Hairlines and eyebrow faint. Second pillar weak, especially at bottom.*

VF-20 VERY FINE—*Second pillar plain and complete on both sides.*

EF-40 EXTREMELY FINE—*Cheekbone, hairlines, eyebrow slightly worn but well defined. Base of triangle above pillars visible but weak.*

MS-65 CHOICE UNCIRCULATED—*No trace of wear. Barely noticeable blemishes.*

NICKEL FIVE-CENT PIECES

Uncirculated pieces with fully struck steps are valued higher.

	Quan. Minted	VG-8	F-12	VF-20	EF-40	MS-65	Proof-65
1938 .... (19,365)	19,515,365	$ .15	$ .25	$ .40	$ .55	$3.00	$100.00
1938D...............	5,376,000	1.10	1.45	1.65	2.25	8.00	
1938S...............	4,105,000	2.00	2.25	3.00	3.50	10.00	
1939 .... (12,535)	120,627,535	.15	.25	.35	.50	1.75	130.00
1939 Doubled MONTICELLO and FIVE CENTS		9.00	12.00	27.50	60.00	——	
1939D...............	3,514,000	4.00	4.50	5.50	9.00	55.00	
1939S...............	6,630,000	.70	.90	1.25	2.30	40.00	
1940 .... (14,158)	176,499,158			.20	.35	1.50	85.00
1940D...............	43,540,000			.25	.40	3.50	
1940S...............	39,690,000			.30	.60	3.50	
1941 .... (18,720)	203,283,720			.15	.30	1.25	75.00
1941D...............	53,432,000			.20	.35	4.25	
1941S†..............	43,445,000			.25	.45	5.75	
1942 .... (29,600)	49,818,600			.25	.40	2.00	75.00
1942D............... }	13,938,000	.40	.75	1.00	2.00	35.00	
1942D over horiz. D .. }					35.00		

†Large and small mint mark varieties, see page 65.

Wartime Alloy Variety 1942-1945

On October 8, 1942, the wartime five-cent piece composed of copper (56%), silver (35%) and manganese (9%) was introduced to eliminate nickel, a critical war material. A larger mint mark was placed above the dome. Letter P (Philadelphia) was used for the first time, indicating the change of alloy.

Location of mint mark

1943 3 over 2

1942P....... (27,600)	57,900,600			.50	.80	1.25	17.00	325.00
1942S...............	32,900,000			.50	.85	1.50	16.00	
1943P, 3 over 2......}				65.00	100.00	150.00	850.00	
1943P............ }	271,165,000			.50	.80	1.00	7.00	
1943D...............	15,294,000			.50	.80	1.00	8.00	
1943S...............	104,060,000			.50	.80	1.10	7.50	
1944P*..............	119,150,000			.50	.80	1.00	7.50	
1944D...............	32,309,000			.50	.80	1.25	12.00	
1944S...............	21,640,000			.50	.80	1.25	13.00	
1945P...............	119,408,100			.50	.80	1.00	8.00	
1945D...............	37,158,000			.50	.80	1.15	8.00	
1945S...............	58,939,000			.50	.80	1.10	7.00	

*1944 nickels without mint marks are counterfeits. Genuine pieces of other dates struck in nickel by error are known to exist.

Prewar composition and mint mark style resumed 1946-1964

	Quan. Minted	VF-20	EF-40	MS-65	Proof-65
1946	161,116,000		$.20	$.85	
1946D.........................	45,292,200	$.20	.30	.90	
1946S.........................	13,560,000	.25	.35	1.00	
1947	95,000,000		.20	.50	
1947D.........................	37,822,000		.25	1.00	
1947S.........................	24,720,000	.25	.35	.80	

NICKEL FIVE-CENT PIECES

	Quan. Minted	VF-20	EF-40	MS-65	Proof-65
1948	89,348,000		$ .20	$ .70	
1948D	44,734,000	$ .25	.40	1.25	
1948S	11,300,000	.35	.40	1.25	
1949	60,652,000	.15	.25	1.35	
1949D	} 36,498,000		.30	1.25	
1949D, D over S		35.00	65.00	400.00	
1949S	9,716,000	.40	.75	2.25	
1950 .... (51,386)	9,847,386	.40	.70	2.00	$60.00
1950D	2,630,030	7.00	8.00	12.00	
1951 .... (57,500)	28,609,500	.20	.30	1.25	50.00
1951D	20,460,000	.20	.30	1.25	
1951S	7,776,000	.50	.90	3.25	
1952 .... (81,980)	64,069,980		.20	.80	35.00
1952D	30,638,000	.30	.65	2.00	
1952S	20,572,000	.20	.30	.75	
1953 .... (128,800)	46,772,800		.20	.30	30.00
1953D	59,878,600		.20	.30	
1953S	19,210,900	.20	.30	.50	

**1954S,
S over D**

**1955D,
D over S***

1954 .... (233,300)	47,917,350		.15	.30	12.00
1954D	117,183,060		.15	.30	
1954S	} 29,384,000	.15	.20	.30	
1954S, S over D		6.00	12.00	40.00	
1955 .... (378,200)	8,266,200	.50	.60	1.00	10.00
1955D	} 74,464,100		.15	.25	
1955D, D over S*		7.00	15.00	70.00	
1956 .... (669,384)	35,885,384		.15	.25	2.50
1956D	67,222,940		.15	.25	
1957 .... (1,247,952)	39,655,952		.15	.25	2.00
1957D	136,828,900		.15	.20	
1958 .... (875,652)	17,963,652		.20	.35	2.50
1958D	168,249,120		.15	.20	
1959 .... (1,149,291)	28,397,291		.15	.30	1.25
1959D	160,738,240			.15	
1960 .... (1,691,602)	57,107,602			.15	1.00
1960D	192,582,180			.15	
1961 .... (3,028,144)	76,668,244			.15	1.00
1961D	229,342,760			.15	
1962 .... (3,218,019)	100,602,019			.15	1.00
1962D	280,195,720			.15	
1963 .... (3,075,645)	178,851,645			.15	1.00
1963D	276,829,460			.15	
1964 .... (3,950,762)	1,028,622,762			.15	1.00
1964D	1,787,297,160			.15	
1965	136,131,380			.15	

*Varieties exist. Value is for that illustrated.

NICKEL FIVE-CENT PIECES

The designer's initials FS were added below the bust starting in 1966, and dies were further remodeled to strengthen the design in 1971, 1972, 1977 and 1982. Mint mark position was moved to the obverse starting in 1968.

Quan. Minted	MS-65	Proof-65	Quan. Minted	MS-65	Proof-65
1966 156,208,283	$ .15	——†	1979D 325,867,672	$ .10	
1967 107,325,800	.15		1979S Proof (3,677,175)		
1968D 91,227,880	.15		Filled S		$1.00
1968S (3,041,506)			Clear S		2.50
. 103,437,510	.15	$.75	1980P 593,004,000	.10	
1969D 202,807,500	.15		1980D 502,323,448	.10	
1969S (2,934,631)			1980S Proof (3,554,806)		1.00
. 123,009,631	.15	.75	1981P 657,504,000	.10	
1970D 515,485,380	.15		1981D 364,801,843	.10	
1970S (2,632,810)			1981S Proof (4,063,083)		1.00
. 241,464,814	.15	.75	1982P 292,355,000	.10	
1971 106,884,000	.40		1982D 373,726,544	.10	
1971D 316,144,800	.15		1982S Proof (3,857,479)		1.25
1971S Proof*			1983P 561,615,000	.10	
. . . . . . (3,220,733)		1.50	1983D 536,726,276	.10	
1972 202,036,000	.10		1983S Proof (3,279,126)		2.00
1972D 351,694,600	.10		1984P 746,769,000	.10	
1972S Proof (3,260,996)		1.50	1984D 517,675,146	.10	
1973 384,396,000	.10		1984S Proof (3,065,110)		4.50
1973D 261,405,000	.10		1985P 647,114,962	.10	
1973S Proof (2,760,339)		1.50	1985D 459,747,446	.10	
1974 601,752,000	.10		1985S Proof (3,362,821)		3.50
1974D 277,373,000	.20		1986P 536,883,483	.10	
1974S Proof (2,612,568)		1.75	1986D 361,819,140	.10	
1975 181,772,000	.20		1986S Proof (3,010,497)		3.50
1975D 401,875,300	.20		1987P 371,499,481	.10	
1975S Proof (2,845,450)		1.75	1987D 410,590,604	.10	
1976 367,124,000	.10		1987S Proof (3,792,233)		3.50
1976D 563,964,147	.10		1988P 771,360,000	.10	
1976S Proof (4,149,730)		1.25	1988D 663,771,652	.10	
1977 585,376,000	.10		1988S Proof		3.00
1977D 297,313,422	.20		1989P 898,812,000	.10	
1977S Proof (3,251,152)		1.15	1989D 570,842,474	.10	
1978 391,308,000	.10		1989S Proof		1.50
1978D 313,092,780	.10		1990P	.10	
1978S Proof (3,127,781)		1.15	1990D	.10	
1979 463,188,000	.10		1990S Proof		1.50

*1971 proof nickels without mint mark were made in error. See pages 65.
†Two presentation pieces were struck in proof.

HALF DIMES 1794-1873

The half dime types present the same general characteristics as larger United States silver coins. Authorized by the Act of April 2, 1792, they were not coined until February, 1795, although dated 1794. At first the weight was 20.8 grains, and fineness 892.4. By the Act of January 18, 1837, the weight was slightly reduced to 20 5/8 grains and the fineness changed to .900. Finally the weight was reduced to 19.2 grains by the Act of February 21, 1853. Both half dimes and dimes offer many varieties in the early dates.

+ or − indicates change from previous year	TYPE COIN VALUES									
	G-4	F-12	EF-40	AU-50	MS-60	MS-63	MS-65	PF-60	PF-63	PF-65
Flowing Hair 1794-1795	575.00	1,000	2,500	3,500	6,750	10,000−	35,000			
Drpd Bust, SE 1796-1797	700.00	1,100	2,800	4,250	7,500	15,000	50,000+			
Drpd Bust, HE 1800-1805	575.00	900	2,250	3,000	7,000	13,000	45,000+			
Cap Bust 1829-1837	12.50	23.00	100.00	225.00	400.00+	1,100+	8,000+			
Lib Seated-NS 1837-1838	25.00	45.00	200.00	325.00	600.00	1,400+	9,000+			
Lib. Seat-Stars 1838-1859	5.00	9.00	40.00	90.00	225.00	600.00	6,000+	800+	1,750+	8,000+
Lib. Seat-Arr. 1853-1855	4.50	8.00	40.00	90.00	250.00	850.00+	7,000+	2,800	4,500+	15,000+
Lib. Seat-Leg. 1860-1873	4.50	7.00	30.00	65.00	175.00	500.00+	3,500+	300.00−	750.00+	4,000+

FLOWING HAIR TYPE 1794-1795

Designer Robert Scot; weight 1.35 grams; composition: .8924 silver, .1076 copper; approx. diameter 16.5 mm; reeded edge. All coined at Philadelphia Mint.

AG-3 ABOUT GOOD—*Details clear enough to identify.*

G-4 GOOD—*Eagle, wreath, bust outlined but lack details.*

VG-8 VERY GOOD—*Some details remain on face. All lettering readable.*

F-12 FINE—*Hair ends show. Hair at top smooth.*

VF-20 VERY FINE—*Hairlines at top show. Hair about ear defined.*

EF-40 EXTREMELY FINE—*Hair above forehead and at neck well defined but shows some wear.*

MS-60 UNCIRCULATED—*No trace of wear. Light blemishes.*

	Quan. Minted	AG-3	G-4	VG-8	F-12	VF-20	EF-40	MS-60
1794 ...	} 86,416	$350.00	$800.00	$1,000	$1,500	$2,400	$4,000	$8,500
1795 ...		300.00	575.00	700.00	1,000	1,700	2,500	6,750

DRAPED BUST TYPE, SMALL EAGLE REVERSE 1796-1797

Designer Robert Scot; weight 1.35 grams; composition: .8924 silver, .1076 copper; approx. diameter 16.5 mm; reeded edge. All coined at Philadelphia Mint.

AG-3 ABOUT GOOD—*Details clear enough to identify.*

G-4 GOOD—*Date, stars, LIBERTY readable. Bust outlined but no details.*

VG-8 VERY GOOD—*Some details show.*

F-12 FINE—*Hair and drapery lines worn, but visible.*

VF-20 VERY FINE—*Only left of drapery indistinct.*

EF-40 EXTREMELY FINE—*All hairlines show details.*

MS-60 UNCIRCULATED—*No trace of wear. Light blemishes.*

	Quan. Minted	AG-3	G-4	VG-8	F-12	VF-20	EF-40	MS-60
1796, 6 over 5	}	$450.00	$750.00	$1,000	$1,300	$2,250	$3,250	$9,000
1796 Nor. dt.	} 10,230	425.00	725.00	900.00	1,200	2,000	3,000	8,500
1796 LIKERTY	}	425.00	725.00	900.00	1,200	2,000	3,200	10,000
1797, 15 Stars	}	350.00	700.00	800.00	1,100	1,800	2,800	7,500
1797, 16 stars	} 44,527	350.00	700.00	800.00	1,100	1,800	2,800	7,500
1797, 13 stars	}	350.00	700.00	800.00	1,100	1,800	3,000	9,000

HALF DIMES
DRAPED BUST TYPE, HERALDIC EAGLE REVERSE 1800-1805

1800 LIBEKTY

	Quan. Minted	AG-3	G-4	VG-8	F-12	VF-20	EF-40	MS-60
1800	24,000	$180.00	$575.00	$675.00	$900.00	$1,300	$2,250	$7,000
1800 LIBEKTY ...	16,000	180.00	575.00	675.00	900.00	1,300	2,250	7,500
1801	27,760	180.00	575.00	675.00	900.00	1,500	2,500	8,000
1802	3,060	3,500	9,000	12,000	20,000	27,500	45,000	——
1803 Large 8 .. ⎱ 37,850		180.00	575.00	675.00	900.00	1,300	2,250	7,000
1803 Small 8 .. ⎰		180.00	575.00	675.00	900.00	1,400	2,500	8,000
1805	15,600	250.00	700.00	850.00	1150.00	1,900	3,250	——

CAPPED BUST TYPE 1829-1837

Designer William Kneass; weight 1.35 grams; composition: .8924 silver, .1076 copper; approx. diameter 15.5 mm; reeded edge. All coined at Philadelphia Mint.

G-4 GOOD—*Bust outlined, no detail. Date and legend readable.*

VG-8 VERY GOOD—*Complete legend and date plain. At least 3 letters of LIBERTY show clearly.*

F-12 FINE—*All letters in LIBERTY show.*

VF-20 VERY FINE—*Full rims. Ear and shoulder clasp show plainly.*

EF-40 EXTREMELY FINE—*Ear very distinct, eyebrow and hair well defined.*

MS-60 UNCIRCULATED—*No trace of wear. Light blemishes.*

	Quan. Minted	G-4	VG-8	F-12	VF-20	EF-40	MS-60
1829	1,230,000	$12.50	$17.00	$23.00	$46.00	$100.00	$400.00
1830	1,240,000	12.50	17.00	23.00	46.00	100.00	400.00
1831	1,242,700	12.50	17.00	23.00	46.00	100.00	400.00
1832	965,000	13.00	18.00	25.00	47.00	115.00	425.00
1833	1,370,000	12.50	17.00	23.00	46.00	100.00	400.00
1834	1,480,000	12.50	17.00	23.00	46.00	100.00	400.00
1835 All kinds	2,760,000						
1835 Lg. date and 5c		12.50	17.00	23.00	46.00	100.00	400.00
1835 Lg. date, sm. 5c		12.50	17.00	23.00	46.00	100.00	400.00
1835 Sm. date, lg. 5c		12.50	17.00	23.00	46.00	100.00	400.00
1835 Sm. date and 5c		12.50	17.00	23.00	46.00	100.00	400.00
1836 Small 5c. ⎱ 1,900,000		12.50	17.00	23.00	46.00	100.00	400.00
1836 Large 5c ⎰		12.50	17.00	23.00	46.00	100.00	400.00
1837 Small 5c. ⎱ 871,000		17.00	25.00	35.00	75.00	150.00	1,250
1837 Large 5c ⎰		12.50	17.00	23.00	46.00	100.00	400.00

LIBERTY SEATED TYPE 1837-1873
Variety 1 — No Stars on Obverse 1837-1838

Designer Christian Gobrecht; weight 1.34 grams; composition: .900 silver, .100 copper; diameter 15.5 mm; reeded edge; mints: Philadelphia, New Orleans.

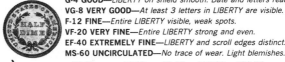

G-4 GOOD—*LIBERTY on shield smooth. Date and letters readable.*

VG-8 VERY GOOD—*At least 3 letters in LIBERTY are visible.*

F-12 FINE—*Entire LIBERTY visible, weak spots.*

VF-20 VERY FINE—*Entire LIBERTY strong and even.*

EF-40 EXTREMELY FINE—*LIBERTY and scroll edges distinct.*

MS-60 UNCIRCULATED—*No trace of wear. Light blemishes.*

1837 Sm. date ... ⎱ 1,405,000	27.50	40.00	55.00	100.00	225.00	750.00
1837 Lg. date . ⎰	25.00	35.00	45.00	90.00	200.00	600.00
1838O No stars 70,000	75.00	110.00	200.00	400.00	750.00	3,500

HALF DIMES

From 1838 through 1859 mint mark is located above bow on reverse. Large, medium or small mint mark varieties occur for several dates.

Variety 2 — Stars on Obverse 1838-1853

	Quan. Minted	G-4	VG-8	F-12	VF-20	EF-40	MS-60
1838 No drpy...	} 2,225,000	$7.00	$8.25	$12.50	$27.50	$55.00	$425.00
1838 Small stars		15.00	25.00	50.00	75.00	150.00	900.00
1839 No drpy.....	1,069,150	7.00	8.25	12.50	27.50	55.00	450.00
1839O No drpy ...	1,034,039	9.00	12.50	17.50	30.00	60.00	500.00
1840 No drapery..	1,034,000	7.00	8.25	12.50	27.50	55.00	400.00
1840O No drapery .	695,000	8.00	11.00	17.50	40.00	80.00	525.00
1840 Drapery......	310,085	10.00	20.00	40.00	70.00	150.00	650.00
1840O Drapery	240,000	25.00	40.00	75.00	150.00	300.00	——
1841	1,150,000	5.00	6.00	9.00	17.50	40.00	250.00
1841O............	815,000	10.00	13.00	20.00	35.00	80.00	550.00
1842	815,000	5.00	6.00	9.00	17.50	40.00	250.00
1842O............	350,000	20.00	30.00	50.00	100.00	200.00	——
1843	1,165,000	5.00	6.00	9.00	17.50	40.00	250.00
1844	430,000	5.00	6.00	9.00	17.50	40.00	250.00
1844O............	220,000	55.00	85.00	140.00	325.00	800.00	——
1845	1,564,000	5.00	6.00	9.00	17.50	40.00	250.00
1846	27,000	125.00	175.00	250.00	475.00	900.00	——
1847	1,274,000	5.00	6.00	9.00	17.50	40.00	250.00
1848 Med. date ⎫		5.00	6.00	9.00	17.50	40.00	250.00
1848 Lg. date ⎬	668,000	10.00	15.00	20.00	40.00	100.00	475.00
1848O............	600,000	12.00	20.00	27.50	60.00	100.00	475.00
1849, 9 over 6 .. ⎫		8.00	12.00	20.00	30.00	75.00	475.00
1849, 9 over 8 .. ⎬	1,309,000	9.00	14.00	22.00	35.00	80.00	500.00
1849 Nor. date.. ⎭		5.00	6.00	9.00	17.50	40.00	250.00
1849O............	140,000	30.00	45.00	85.00	225.00	450.00	——
1850	955,000	5.00	6.00	9.00	17.50	40.00	250.00
1850O............	690,000	12.00	20.00	27.50	60.00	110.00	800.00
1851	781,000	5.00	6.00	9.00	17.50	40.00	250.00
1851O............	860,000	12.00	17.00	25.00	40.00	80.00	700.00
1852	1,000,500	5.00	6.00	9.00	17.50	40.00	250.00
1852O............	260,000	26.00	35.00	65.00	125.00	250.00	——
1853 No arrows....	135,000	24.00	32.50	60.00	100.00	175.00	700.00
1853O No arrows ..	160,000	125.00	175.00	250.00	400.00	750.00	——

Variety 3 — Arrows at Date 1853-1855

Weight 1.24 grams; composition: .900 silver, .100 copper; diameter 15.5 mm; reeded edge; mints: Philadelphia, New Orleans, San Francisco.

As on the dimes, quarters and halves, arrows were placed at the sides of the date for a short period starting in 1853. They were placed there to denote the reduction of weight under the terms of the Act of February 21, 1853.

	Quan. Minted	G-4	VG-8	F-12	VF-20	EF-40	MS-60	Proof-63
1853	13,210,020	$4.50	$6.00	$8.00	$17.00	$40.00	$250.00	
1853O........	2,200,000	7.00	10.00	14.00	25.00	75.00	400.00	
1854	5,740,000	4.50	6.00	8.00	17.00	40.00	275.00	
1854O........	1,560,000	6.50	8.50	11.00	23.00	50.00	700.00	

HALF DIMES

	Quan. Minted	G-4	VG-8	F-12	VF-20	EF-40	MS-60	Proof-63
1855	1,750,000	$5.00	$6.00	$8.00	$17.00	$40.00	$325.00	$4,200
1855O	600,000	12.00	15.00	25.00	40.00	100.00	800.00	

Variety 2 Resumed 1856-1859

1858 over Inverted Date

1856	4,880,000	5.00	6.00	8.00	17.50	40.00	225.00	2,750
1856O	1,100,000	6.50	8.50	11.00	22.00	45.00	650.00	
1857	7,280,000	5.00	6.00	8.00	17.50	40.00	225.00	2,400
1857O	1,380,000	6.50	8.50	11.00	22.00	45.00	650.00	
1858 . . . . ⎫		5.00	6.00	8.00	17.50	40.00	225.00	1,750
1858 over inverted ⎬	3,500,000							
date . . . . . . ⎭		30.00	35.00	67.50	110.00	200.00	750.00	
1858O	1,660,000	6.50	8.50	11.00	22.00	45.00	575.00	
1859O	560,000	10.00	17.50	25.00	40.00	75.00	650.00	
1859	340,000	10.00	17.50	25.00	40.00	75.00	300.00	1,750

New die 1859 Philadelphia Mint. Stars hollow in center. Arms slimmer.

In the years 1859 and 1860 interesting half dime patterns were made which do not bear our nation's identity. These are transitional pieces, not made for circulation, but struck at the time the inscription UNITED STATES OF AMERICA was being transferred from the reverse to the obverse.

1859 Obv. of 59, rev. of 60		10,000
1860 Obv. of 59, rev. of 60 (With stars) 100	2,750	

Variety 4 — Legend on Obverse 1860-1873

 **Mint mark below bow 1860-1869, 1872-1873.**

Mint mark above bow 1870-1872.

1860 Legend (1,000)	799,000	5.00	6.00	7.00	14.00	30.00	225.00	950.00
1860O	1,060,000	5.00	6.00	8.00	15.00	32.50	375.00	
1861 . (1,000)	3,361,000	5.00	6.00	7.00	12.00	30.00	175.00	750.00
1861, 1 over 0		—	—	—	—	—	—	
1862 . . . (550)	1,492,550	5.00	6.00	7.00	12.00	30.00	175.00	750.00
1863 . . . (460)	18,460	100.00	150.00	200.00	250.00	350.00	700.00	950.00
1863S	100,000	12.50	17.50	25.00	50.00	110.00	675.00	
1864 . . . (470)	48,470	200.00	300.00	350.00	450.00	650.00	1,400	1,900
1864S	90,000	22.50	30.00	65.00	100.00	200.00	825.00	
1865 . . . (500)	13,500	200.00	250.00	300.00	400.00	500.00	1,000	1,200
1865S	120,000	12.50	17.50	25.00	50.00	110.00	675.00	

HALF DIMES

	Quan. Minted	G-4	VG-8	F-12	VF-20	EF-40	MS-60	Proof-63
1866 ... (725)	10,725	$150.00	$200.00	$275.00	$325.00	$450.00	$700.00	$950.00
1866S......	120,000	12.50	17.50	25.00	50.00	110.00	650.00	
1867 ... (625)	8,625	200.00	300.00	400.00	500.00	600.00	900.00	950.00
1867S......	120,000	12.50	17.50	25.00	50.00	110.00	650.00	
1868 ... (600)	89,200	30.00	45.00	70.00	110.00	225.00	525.00	750.00
1868S......	280,000	8.00	11.50	15.00	25.00	50.00	200.00	
1869 ... (600)	208,600	6.00	8.00	12.00	17.50	35.00	175.00	750.00
1869S......	230,000	8.00	11.50	15.00	25.00	50.00	225.00	
1870 . (1,000)	536,000	5.00	6.00	7.00	12.00	30.00	175.00	750.00
1870S......	Unique				Auction sale 1986		253,000.	
1871 ... (960)	1,873,960	5.00	6.00	7.00	12.00	30.00	175.00	750.00
1871S......	161,000	10.00	15.00	30.00	50.00	90.00	425.00	
1872 ... (950)	2,947,950	5.00	6.00	7.00	12.00	30.00	175.00	750.00
1872S All kinds.	837,000							
1872S mm. above bow..		5.00	6.00	7.00	12.00	30.00	175.00	
1872S mm. below bow..		5.00	6.00	7.00	12.00	30.00	175.00	
1873 (Closed 3 only)								
...... (600)	712,600	5.00	6.00	7.00	12.00	30.00	175.00	750.00
1873S (Closed 3 only)								
....	324,000	5.00	6.00	7.00	12.00	30.00	175.00	

BIBLIOGRAPHY

Ahwash, Kamal M. *Encyclopedia of United States Liberty Seated Dimes 1837-1891.* Kamal Press, 1977.
Breen, Walter. *United States Half Dimes: A Supplement.* New York, 1958.
Davis, David. et al. *Early United States Dimes 1796-1837.* Ypsilanti, Michigan, 1984.
Kosoff, A. *United States Dimes from 1796.* New York, 1945.
Nagengast, Bernard. *The Jefferson Nickel Analyst.* Sidney, Ohio, 1979.
Newlin, H. P. *The Early Half-Dimes of the United States.* Philadelphia, 1883 (reprinted 1933).
Valentine, D. W. *The United States Half Dimes.* New York, 1931

DIMES — 1796 to Date

The designs of the dimes, first coined in 1796, follow closely those of the half dimes up through the Liberty seated type. The dimes in each instance weigh twice as much as the half dimes.

+ or – indicates change from previous year	G-4	F-12	EF-40	AU-50	MS-60	MS-63	MS-65	PF-60	PF-63	PF-65
				TYPE COIN VALUES						
Drpd Bust, SE 1796-1797	850.00	1,500+	3,400+	5,000+	10,000+	15,000	70,000+			
Drpd Bust, HE 1798-1807	475.00	850	1,600+	3,000+	4,500	10,000	40,000+			
Cap Bust lg. 1809-1828	13.00	30.00	275.00	675.00	1,250	2,750+	18,000+			
Cap Bust sm. 1828-1837	9.00	20.00	175.00	425.00+	800.00+	1,800+	13,000+			
Lib Seated-NS 1837-1838	24.00	50.00	325.00+	600.00	900.00	2,000+	14,000+			
Lib. Seat-Stars 1838-1860	4.00	7.50	40.00	90.00	325.00	750.00	6,000+	850	2,000	10,000+
Lib. Seat-Arr. 1853-1855	4.50	7.50	40.00	115.00	350.00	800.00	7,000+	3,000	5,750	13,000+
Lib. Seat-Leg. 1860-1891	3.50	6.00	20.00	50.00	200.00	475.00	3,500+	350.00	750.00	3,500
Lib. Seat-Arr. 1873-1874	7.00	16.00	100.00	275.00	700.00	1,800+	9,000+	650.00	2,000+	10,000+
Barber 1892-1916	1.25	3.00	18.00	37.50	150.00	350.00–	2,300+	350.00	950.00+	3,500+
Mercury 1916-1945	1.00	1.00	3.00	4.00	10.00	16.00	45.00	175.00	250.00	700.00
Roosevelt 1946-1964	.70	.80	1.00	1.10	1.15	1.25	2.00	1.50	1.75	2.00

DRAPED BUST TYPE, SMALL EAGLE REVERSE 1796-1797

Designer Robert Scot; weight 2.70 grams; composition: .8924 silver, .1076 copper; approx. diameter 19 mm; reeded edge. All coined at Philadelphia Mint.

AG-3 ABOUT GOOD—*Details clear enough to identify.*

G-4 GOOD—*Date readable. Bust outlined, but no detail.*

VG-8 VERY GOOD—*All but deepest drapery folds worn smooth. Hairlines nearly gone and curls lack detail.*

F-12 FINE—*All drapery lines visible. Hair partly worn.*

VF-20 VERY FINE—*Only left side of drapery is indistinct.*

EF-40 EXTREMELY FINE—*Hair well outlined and shows details.*

MS-60 UNCIRCULATED—*No trace of wear. Light blemishes.*

DIMES

1797, 16 Stars   **1797, 13 Stars**

	Quan. Minted	AG-3	G-4	VG-8	F-12	VF-20	EF-40	MS-60
1796	22,135	$550.00	$950.00	$1,250	$1,750	$2,500	$3,500	$10,000
1797 16 stars	} 25,261	500.00	850.00	1,200	1,500	2,400	3,500	10,000
1797 13 stars		500.00	850.00	1,200	1,500	2,400	3,400	10,000

DRAPED BUST TYPE, HERALDIC EAGLE REVERSE 1798-1807

		AG-3	G-4	VG-8	F-12	VF-20	EF-40	MS-60
1798 All kinds 27,550								
1798 over 97, 16 stars on rev.		200.00	500.00	650.00	900.00	1,400	1,700	6,750
1798 over 97, 13 stars				1,200	1,700	3,200	——	
1798		200.00	500.00	650.00	900.00	1,400	1,700	6,750
1798 Small 8		250.00	625.00	800.00	1,400	2,000	2,600	
1800	21,760	200.00	500.00	650.00	900.00	1,400	1,700	6,200
1801	34,640	200.00	500.00	650.00	900.00	1,400	1,700	6,200
1802	10,975	200.00	500.00	700.00	1,000	1,800	2,200	10,000
1803	33,040	200.00	500.00	650.00	900.00	1,400	1,700	6,200
1804 All kinds . 8,265								
1804 13 stars on rev.		450.00	900.00	1,500	2,000	3,250	6,000	——
1804 14 stars on rev.		450.00	900.00	1,500	2,000	3,250	6,000	10,000
1805 4 ber.	} 120,780	200.00	475.00	600.00	850.00	1,300	1,600	4,500
1805 5 ber.		200.00	475.00	600.00	900.00	1,500	3,000	9,000
1807	165,000	200.00	475.00	600.00	850.00	1,300	1,600	4,500

CAPPED BUST TYPE 1809-1837

Designer John Reich; weight 2.70 grams; composition: .8924 silver, .1076 copper; approx. diameter 18.8 mm; reeded edge. All coined at Philadelphia Mint. Diameter c. 18.5 mm from 1828 to 1837.

AG-3 ABOUT GOOD—*Details clear enough to identify.*

G-4 GOOD—*Date, letters and stars discernible. Bust outlined, no details.*

VG-8 VERY GOOD—*Legends and date plain. Minimum of 3 letters in LIBERTY.*

F-12 FINE—*Full LIBERTY. Ear and shoulder clasp visible. Part of rim shows both sides.*

VF-20 VERY FINE—*LIBERTY distinct. Full rim. Ear and clasp plain and distinct.*

EF-40 EXTREMELY FINE—*LIBERTY sharp. Ear distinct. Hair above eye well defined.*

MS-60 UNCIRCULATED—*No trace of wear. Light blemishes.*

Variety 1 — Wide Border 1809-1828

		AG-3	G-4	VG-8	F-12	VF-20	EF-40	MS-60
1809	51,065	35.00	70.00	100.00	150.00	250.00	400.00	3,750
1811 over 9...	65,180	25.00	50.00	75.00	90.00	150.00	300.00	3,500

DIMES

1814 Small Date   **1814 Large Date**

	Quan. Minted	G-4	VG-8	F-12	VF-20	EF-40	MS-60
1814 Sm. date	⎱ 421,500	$50.00	$75.00	$90.00	$175.00	$325.00	$3,500
1814 Lg. date	⎰	25.00	30.00	45.00	125.00	300.00	1,750
1814 STATESOFAMERICA		25.00	30.00	45.00	125.00	300.00	2,000
1820 STATESOFAMERICA		25.00	30.00	45.00	125.00	300.00	2,000

1820 Large 0   **1821 Small Date**   **1821 Large Date**

1820 Lg. 0.....	⎱ 942,587	13.00	18.00	30.00	90.00	275.00	1,250
1820 Sm. 0 ..	⎰	13.00	18.00	30.00	90.00	275.00	1,250
1821 Sm. date	⎱ 1,186,512	13.00	18.00	30.00	90.00	275.00	1,250
1821 Lg. date	⎰	13.00	18.00	30.00	90.00	275.00	1,250
1822 100,000		100.00	225.00	500.00	800.00	1,500	6,000

1823, 3 over 2   **Small E's**   **Large E's**

1823, 3 over 2, All kinds 440,000							
1823, 3 over 2, sm. E's	13.00	18.00	25.00	90.00	275.00	1,750
1823, 3 over 2, lg. E's	13.00	18.00	25.00	90.00	275.00	1,750

1824, 4 over 2   **Large Date**   **Small Date**

1824, 4 over 2 .	⎱ 510,000	25.00	30.00	45.00	125.00	300.00	1,750
1825........	⎰	13.00	18.00	30.00	90.00	275.00	1,250
1827............. 1,215,000		13.00	18.00	30.00	90.00	275.00	1,250
1827, 7 over 5 .... (rare)							
1828 Both vars 125,000							
1828 Lg. date, curl base 2 ..	30.00	40.00	70.00	150.00	325.00	2,250

DIMES

Variety 2 — Modified Design 1828-1837

New mint equipment was used to make the small date 1828 dimes and subsequent issues. Unlike earlier coinage, these have beaded borders and a uniform diameter. Large date has curl base knob 2; small date has square base knob 2.

| 1829 Small 10c | Large 10c | 1829 Curl base 2 | 1830, 30 over 29 |

	Quan. Minted	G-4	F-12	VF-20	EF-40	MS-60
1828 Small date, sq. base 2		$25.00	$50.00	$85.00	$250.00	$1,200
1829 Curl base 2....		900.00	1,600	4,500		
1829 Small 10c	770,000	9.00	20.00	50.00	175.00	850.00
1829 Medium 10c ...		9.00	20.00	50.00	175.00	800.00
1829 Large 10c		12.00	25.00	60.00	200.00	850.00
1830, 30 over 29	510,000	——	125.00	200.00	425.00	2,100
1830 Large 10c		9.00	20.00	50.00	175.00	800.00
1830 Small 10c		9.00	20.00	50.00	175.00	800.00
1831	771,350	9.00	20.00	50.00	175.00	800.00
1832	522,500	9.00	20.00	50.00	175.00	800.00
1833	485,000	9.00	20.00	50.00	175.00	800.00
1833 Last 3 high......		9.00	20.00	50.00	175.00	850.00
1834 Small 4	635,000	9.00	20.00	50.00	175.00	975.00
1834 Large 4		9.00	20.00	50.00	175.00	850.00
1835	1,410,000	9.00	20.00	50.00	175.00	800.00
1836	1,190,000	9.00	20.00	50.00	175.00	800.00
1837	359,500	9.00	20.00	50.00	175.00	800.00

LIBERTY SEATED TYPE 1837-1891

Variety 1 — No Stars on Obverse 1837-1838

Designer Christian Gobrecht; weight 2.67 grams; composition: .900 silver, .100 copper; diameter 17.9 mm; reeded edge; mints: Philadelphia, New Orleans.

G-4 GOOD—*LIBERTY on shield smooth. Date and letters readable.*

F-12 FINE—*Entire LIBERTY visible, weak spots.*

VF-20 VERY FINE—*Entire LIBERTY strong and even.*

EF-40 EXTREMELY FINE—*LIBERTY and scroll edges distinct.*

MS-60 UNCIRCULATED—*No trace of wear. Light blemishes.*

No Drapery from Elbow
No Stars on Obverse

Mint marks on Liberty seated dimes are placed on the reverse within, or below, the wreath. Size of mint mark varies on many dates.

1837 Large date	682,500	24.00	50.00	150.00	325.00	900.00
1837 Small date		24.00	50.00	150.00	350.00	1,000
1838O.................	406,034	30.00	90.00	200.00	400.00	2,500

DIMES
Variety 2 — Stars on Obverse 1838-1853

**No Drapery from Elbow
Tilted Shield**

1838 Small Stars

1838 Large Stars

	Quan. Minted	G-4	F-12	VF-20	EF-40	MS-60
1838 Small stars	⎫	$15.00	$35.00	$60.00	$150.00	$1,600
1838 Large stars	⎬ 1,992,500	8.00	12.50	20.00	50.00	475.00
1838 Partial drapery	⎭	15.00	32.50	55.00	110.00	1,400
1839	1,053,115	5.50	10.00	18.00	50.00	400.00
1839O	1,323,000	6.50	14.00	27.50	65.00	475.00
1840	981,500	5.50	10.00	18.00	40.00	400.00
1840O	1,175,000	7.00	15.00	30.00	65.00	1,200
1841 Proof, see below.						

**Drapery from Elbow
Upright Shield**

	Quan. Minted	G-4	F-12	VF-20	EF-40	MS-60	Proof-63
1840	377,500	$25.00	$65.00	$120.00	$400.00	——	
1841	1,622,500	4.75	9.00	18.00	40.00	$350.00	——*
1841O	2,007,500	7.00	15.00	25.00	65.00	1,200	
1842	1,887,500	4.75	9.00	18.00	40.00	350.00	
1842O	2,020,000	4.75	10.00	20.00	75.00	——	
1843	1,370,000	4.75	9.00	18.00	40.00	350.00	
1843O	150,000	35.00	90.00	235.00	625.00	——	
1844	72,500	30.00	80.00	160.00	375.00	2,000	
1845	1,755,000	4.75	9.00	18.00	40.00	350.00	
1845O	230,000	15.00	40.00	150.00	600.00	——	
1846	31,300	75.00	125.00	300.00	700.00	——	
1847	245,000	10.00	30.00	55.00	150.00	1,000	
1848	451,500	8.00	20.00	40.00	90.00	375.00	
1849	839,000	4.75	9.00	18.00	40.00	350.00	
1849O	300,000	10.00	20.00	85.00	250.00	——	
1850	1,931,500	4.75	9.00	18.00	40.00	350.00	
1850O	510,000	8.00	15.00	60.00	150.00	1,500	
1851	1,026,500	4.75	9.00	18.00	45.00	350.00	
1851O	400,000	10.00	20.00	60.00	150.00	1,400	
1852	1,535,500	4.75	9.00	17.00	45.00	350.00	
1852O	430,000	13.00	30.00	90.00	200.00	1,600	
1853 No arrows	95,000	35.00	60.00	110.00	250.00	1,000	

*Termed "no drapery" because excessive polishing of the proof die removed most of the drapery and reduced the size of the stars. Unique. 1973 M.A.N.A. sale $52,000.

DIMES
Variety 3 — Arrows at Date 1853-1855

Weight 2.49 grams; composition: .900 silver, .100 copper; diameter 17.9 mm, reeded edge; mints: Philadelphia, New Orleans. Also San Francisco and Carson City after 1855.

1853-1855
Arrows at Date

1856-1860
Small Date, Arrows Removed

	Quan. Minted	G-4	F-12	VF-20	EF-40	MS-60	Proof-63
1853 With arrows...	12,078,010	$4.50	$7.50	$16.00	$40.00	$350.00	
1853O	1,100,000	6.00	9.00	25.00	85.00	650.00	
1854	4,470,000	4.50	7.50	16.00	40.00	400.00	$10,000
1854O	1,770,000	6.00	9.00	22.50	80.00	650.00	
1855	2,075,000	4.50	7.50	16.00	40.00	350.00	5,750

Variety 2 Resumed 1856-1860

	Quan. Minted	G-4	F-12	VF-20	EF-40	MS-60	Proof-63
1856 Lg. date....	}	4.25	8.00	15.00	40.00	350.00	
1856 Sm. date ... }	5,780,000	4.25	8.00	15.00	40.00	325.00	2,600
1856O	1,180,000	4.25	8.00	18.00	45.00	350.00	
1856S	70,000	45.00	90.00	200.00	400.00	——	
1857	5,580,000	4.00	7.50	14.00	40.00	325.00	2,400
1857O	1,540,000	4.00	7.75	15.00	45.00	350.00	
1858	1,540,000	4.00	7.50	14.00	40.00	325.00	2,300
1858O	290,000	10.00	30.00	75.00	165.00	800.00	
1858S	60,000	45.00	100.00	200.00	450.00	——	
1859 .... (800)	430,000	5.00	9.00	20.00	50.00	325.00	2,000
1859O	480,000	5.00	15.00	40.00	80.00	350.00	
1859S	60,000	60.00	125.00	225.00	450.00	2,000	
1860S	140,000	13.00	40.00	80.00	185.00	——	

In 1859 an interesting dime pattern was made which does not bear our nation's identity. It is a "transitional" piece, not made for circulation, but struck at the time the inscription UNITED STATES OF AMERICA was being transferred from the reverse to the obverse.

1859 15,000

Variety 4 — Legend on Obverse 1860-1873

		Quan. Minted	G-4	F-12	VF-20	EF-40	MS-60	Proof-63
1860 .... (1,000)		607,000	3.50	7.50	12.50	25.00	225.00	825.00
1860O		40,000	325.00	650.00	1,000	2,000	——	
1861* ...... (1,000)		1,884,000	3.50	7.50	12.50	25.00	225.00	825.00
1861S		172,500	15.00	35.00	80.00	175.00	1,100	
1862 .... (550)		847,550	3.50	7.50	12.50	25.00	225.00	825.00
1862S		180,750	15.00	30.00	70.00	150.00	1,000	
1863 .... (460)		14,460	100.00	150.00	275.00	400.00	1,000	1,000
1863S		157,500	18.00	40.00	75.00	175.00	1,000	

*Dies modified slightly during 1861. First variety with only five vertical lines in top of shield is scarcer than the later variety.

DIMES

	Quan. Minted	G-4	F-12	VF-20	EF-40	MS-60	Proof-63
1864 . . . . (470)	11,470	$125.00	$250.00	$350.00	$450.00	$900.00	$1,000
1864S	230,000	12.00	30.00	60.00	140.00	850.00	
1865 . . . . (500)	10,500	100.00	150.00	250.00	400.00	1,000	1,000
1865S	175,000	12.00	30.00	60.00	140.00	1,000	
1866 . . . . (725)	8,725	125.00	300.00	450.00	650.00	1,100	1,000
1866S	135,000	15.00	30.00	60.00	150.00	1,250	
1867 . . . . (625)	6,625	200.00	350.00	500.00	750.00	1,500	1,100
1867S	140,000	12.50	27.50	55.00	125.00	1,100	
1868 . . . . (600)	464,600	5.00	10.00	30.00	70.00	375.00	750.00
1868S	260,000	10.00	20.00	60.00	125.00	300.00	
1869 . . . . (600)	256,600	5.00	10.00	30.00	70.00	300.00	750.00
1869S	450,000	8.00	15.00	33.00	80.00	325.00	
1870 . . . . (1,000)	471,500	3.50	7.50	17.50	35.00	225.00	750.00
1870S	50,000	50.00	100.00	200.00	425.00	2,750	
1871 . . . . (960)	907,710	3.50	7.50	12.50	25.00	225.00	750.00
1871CC	20,100	350.00	850.00	1,300	2,500	——	
1871S	320,000	11.00	30.00	50.00	110.00	750.00	
1872 . . . . (950)	2,396,450	3.50	7.50	12.50	25.00	200.00	750.00
1872CC	35,480	200.00	500.00	900.00	1,800	——	
1872S	190,000	20.00	50.00	100.00	200.00	800.00	
1873 Closed 3 (1,100) .	1,508,000	3.50	7.50	12.50	25.00	300.00	750.00
1873 Open 3	60,000	23.00	45.00	85.00	160.00	325.00	
1873CC (*Unique*)	12,400					——	

Variety 5 — Arrows at Date 1873-1874

In 1873 the dime was increased in weight to 2.50 grams. Arrows at date in 1873
and 1874 indicate this change.

Weight 2.50 grams; composition: .900 silver, .100 copper; diameter 17.9 mm; reeded edge; mints: Philadelphia, New Orleans, San Francisco, Carson City.

1873 . . . . (800)	2,378,500	7.00	16.00	45.00	100.00	700.00	2,000
1873CC	18,791	450.00	900.00	1,350	2,750	——	
1873S	455,000	16.00	32.50	60.00	140.00	900.00	
1874 . . . . (700)	2,940,000	7.00	16.00	45.00	125.00	700.00	2,000
1874CC	10,817	750.00	1,600	2,300	4,000	——	
1874S	240,000	25.00	60.00	100.00	175.00	1,000	

Variety 4 Resumed 1875-1891

1875 . . . . (700)	10,350,700	3.50	6.00	12.00	20.00	200.00	750.00
1875CC Below bow							
All kinds	4,645,000	4.50	8.50	16.00	35.00	375.00	
1875CC Above bow		3.50	6.00	12.00	25.00	275.00	
1875S Below bow							
All kinds	9,070,000	3.50	6.00	12.00	20.00	200.00	
1875S Above bow		3.50	6.00	12.00	30.00	275.00	
1876 . . (1,150)	11,461,150	3.50	6.00	12.00	20.00	200.00	750.00
1876CC	8,270,000	3.50	6.00	12.00	20.00	225.00	
1876S	10,420,000	3.50	6.00	12.00	20.00	200.00	
1877 . . . . (510)	7,310,510	3.50	6.00	12.00	20.00	200.00	800.00

DIMES

	Quan. Minted	G-4	F-12	VF-20	EF-40	MS-60	Proof-63
1877CC	7,700,000	$3.50	$6.00	$12.00	$20.00	$225.00	
1877S	2,340,000	3.50	6.00	12.00	20.00	225.00	
1878 .... (800)	1,678,000	3.50	6.00	12.00	20.00	200.00	$750.00
1878CC	200,000	30.00	80.00	115.00	200.00	650.00	
1879 ...... (1,100)	15,100	125.00	250.00	300.00	400.00	650.00	800.00
1880 .... (1,355)	37,355	60.00	125.00	200.00	300.00	500.00	800.00
1881 .... (975)	24,975	75.00	175.00	250.00	350.00	550.00	800.00
1882 .... (1,100)	3,911,100	3.50	6.00	12.00	20.00	200.00	750.00
1883 .... (1,039)	7,675,712	3.50	6.00	12.00	20.00	200.00	750.00
1884 .... (875)	3,366,380	3.50	6.00	12.00	20.00	200.00	750.00
1884S	564,969	11.00	20.00	40.00	60.00	450.00	
1885 .... (930)	2,533,427	3.50	6.00	12.00	20.00	200.00	750.00
1885S	43,690	125.00	225.00	325.00	500.00	2,200	
1886 .... (886)	6,377,570	3.50	6.00	12.00	20.00	200.00	750.00
1886S	206,524	11.00	20.00	40.00	75.00	500.00	
1887 .... (710)	11,283,939	3.50	6.00	12.00	20.00	200.00	750.00
1887S	4,454,450	3.50	6.00	12.00	20.00	200.00	
1888 .... (832)	5,496,487	3.50	6.00	12.00	20.00	200.00	750.00
1888S	1,720,000	3.50	6.00	12.00	20.00	200.00	
1889 .... (711)	7,380,711	3.50	6.00	12.00	20.00	200.00	750.00
1889S	972,678	11.00	20.00	45.00	80.00	375.00	
1890 .... (590)	9,911,541	4.75	6.00	12.00	20.00	200.00	750.00
1890S	1,423,076	3.50	9.00	18.00	30.00	250.00	
1891 .... (600)	15,310,600	3.50	6.00	12.00	20.00	200.00	750.00
1891O............	4,540,000	3.50	6.00	20.00	35.00	250.00	
1891S	3,196,116	3.50	6.00	12.00	20.00	225.00	

BARBER or LIBERTY HEAD TYPE 1892-1916

Designed by Charles E. Barber, Chief Engraver of the Mint. He also designed
the 25 and 50-cent pieces. His initial B is at the truncation of the neck.

Designer Charles E. Barber; weight 2.50 grams; composition: .900 silver, .100 copper; diameter 17.9 mm;
reeded edge; mints: Philadelphia, Denver, New Orleans, San Francisco. Net weight: .07234 oz. pure
silver.

G-4 GOOD—*Date and letters plain. LIBERTY is obliterated.*

VG-8 VERY GOOD—*At least 3 letters visible in LIBERTY.*

F-12 FINE—*All letters in LIBERTY visible, though some are weak.*

VF-20 VERY FINE—*All letters of LIBERTY evenly plain.*

EF-40 EXTREMELY FINE—*All letters in LIBERTY are sharp, distinct. Headband edges are distinct.*

MS-60 UNCIRCULATED—*No trace of wear. Light blemishes.*

Mint mark location is on the reverse below the wreath.

	Quan. Minted	G-4	VG-8	F-12	VF-20	EF-40	MS-60	Proof-63
1892 . (1,245)	12,121,245	$2.35	$4.00	$5.50	$8.50	$25.00	$160.00	$975.00
1892O..........	3,841,700	4.50	6.00	8.00	13.00	28.00	180.00	
1892S	990,710	25.00	35.00	45.00	65.00	85.00	250.00	
1893, 3 over 2 ⎫					——	150.00	400.00	1,000
1893 ... (792) ⎬	3,340,792	4.50	5.50	7.50	11.00	25.00	160.00	950.00
1893O........	1,760,000	13.00	18.00	35.00	45.00	55.00	225.00	
1893S..........	2,491,401	6.00	8.00	12.00	19.00	32.00	200.00	

DIMES

	Quan. Minted	G-4	VG-8	F-12	VF-20	EF-40	MS-60	Proof-63
1894 ... (972)	1,330,972	$10.00	$15.00	$40.00	$50.00	$75.00	$220.00	$950.00
1894O	720,000	32.00	37.50	75.00	125.00	250.00	1,000	
1894S	24			Stack Auction, 1990			275,000	
1895 ... (880)	690,880	55.00	62.50	100.00	150.00	225.00	550.00	950.00
1895O	440,000	150.00	175.00	225.00	300.00	425.00	1,000	
1895S	1,120,000	14.00	18.00	30.00	40.00	65.00	225.00	
1896 ... (762)	2,000,762	5.00	6.00	15.00	25.00	40.00	170.00	950.00
1896O	610,000	42.50	48.00	100.00	140.00	200.00	575.00	
1896S	575,056	35.00	45.00	65.00	85.00	135.00	400.00	
1897 ... (731)	10,869,264	1.25	1.50	3.00	6.00	18.00	150.00	950.00
1897O	666,000	35.00	40.00	70.00	100.00	200.00	650.00	
1897S	1,342,844	7.00	9.00	20.00	35.00	60.00	225.00	
1898 ... (735)	16,320,735	1.25	1.50	3.00	6.00	18.00	150.00	950.00
1898O	2,130,000	3.25	6.00	15.00	35.00	60.00	300.00	
1898S	1,702,507	3.25	5.00	9.00	16.00	30.00	175.00	
1899 ... (846)	19,580,846	1.25	1.50	3.00	6.00	18.00	150.00	950.00
1899O	2,650,000	3.25	5.00	12.00	25.00	50.00	300.00	
1899S	1,867,493	3.25	5.00	8.00	15.00	30.00	175.00	
1900 ... (912)	17,600,912	1.25	1.50	3.00	6.00	18.00	150.00	950.00
1900O	2,010,000	4.50	8.00	15.00	30.00	65.00	325.00	
1900S	5,168,270	2.00	3.00	5.00	9.00	25.00	175.00	
1901 ... (813)	18,860,478	1.25	1.50	3.00	6.00	18.00	150.00	950.00
1901O	5,620,000	2.00	3.00	5.00	14.00	42.00	300.00	
1901S	593,022	32.50	50.00	80.00	130.00	200.00	800.00	
1902 ... (777)	21,380,777	1.25	1.50	3.00	6.00	18.00	150.00	950.00
1902O	4,500,000	2.00	3.00	5.00	10.00	27.50	225.00	
1902S	2,070,000	3.00	5.00	12.00	22.50	52.50	260.00	
1903 ... (755)	19,500,755	1.25	1.50	3.00	6.00	18.00	150.00	950.00
1903O	8,180,000	2.00	3.00	4.00	8.00	25.00	225.00	
1903S	613,300	25.00	35.00	60.00	100.00	200.00	600.00	
1904 ... (670)	14,601,027	1.25	1.50	3.00	6.00	18.00	150.00	950.00
1904S	800,000	18.00	25.00	50.00	85.00	160.00	550.00	
1905 ... (727)	14,552,350	1.25	1.50	3.00	6.00	18.00	150.00	950.00
1905O*	3,400,000	1.75	3.00	6.00	12.00	25.00	200.00	
1905S	6,855,199	1.75	3.00	5.00	9.00	24.00	210.00	
1906 ... (675)	19,958,406	1.25	1.50	3.00	6.00	18.00	150.00	950.00
1906D	4,060,000	2.00	3.00	5.00	9.00	23.00	190.00	
1906O	2,610,000	2.00	4.50	8.50	15.00	30.00	200.00	
1906S	3,136,640	2.00	3.25	7.50	12.00	30.00	200.00	
1907 ... (575)	22,220,575	1.25	1.50	3.00	6.00	18.00	150.00	950.00
1907D	4,080,000	1.75	2.75	5.00	8.50	24.00	200.00	
1907O	5,058,000	1.75	2.75	5.00	8.50	23.00	160.00	
1907S	3,178,470	2.00	3.00	5.00	10.00	28.00	210.00	
1908 ... (545)	10,600,545	1.25	1.50	3.00	6.00	18.00	150.00	950.00
1908D	7,490,000	1.75	2.75	4.50	6.50	19.00	160.00	
1908O	1,789,000	2.25	4.00	12.00	20.00	40.00	220.00	
1908S	3,220,000	1.75	3.00	4.50	9.00	25.00	200.00	
1909 ... (650)	10,240,650	1.25	1.50	3.00	6.00	18.00	150.00	950.00
1909D	954,000	2.75	5.00	11.00	20.00	35.00	300.00	
1909O	2,287,000	2.25	3.00	5.50	12.00	27.50	175.00	
1909S	1,000,000	2.75	5.00	14.00	35.00	50.00	225.00	
1910 ... (551)	11,520,551	1.25	1.50	3.00	6.00	18.00	150.00	950.00
1910D	3,490,000	1.75	2.75	4.50	9.00	28.00	300.00	
1910S	1,240,000	1.75	2.75	6.75	13.00	28.00	200.00	
1911 ... (543)	18,870,543	1.25	1.50	3.00	6.00	18.00	150.00	950.00
1911D	11,209,000	1.25	1.50	3.00	6.00	18.00	150.00	
1911S	3,520,000	1.75	2.75	5.00	8.00	20.00	175.00	

*Normal and "microscopic" mint mark varieties, see page 65.

DIMES

	Quan. Minted	G-4	VG-8	F-12	VF-20	EF-40	MS-63	Proof-63
1912 ... (700)	19,350,000	$1.25	$1.50	$3.00	$6.00	$18.00	$150.00	$950.00
1912D	11,760,000	1.25	1.50	3.00	6.00	18.00	150.00	
1912S	3,420,000	1.75	2.75	5.00	8.00	20.00	175.00	
1913 ... (622)	19,760,622	1.25	1.50	3.00	6.00	18.00	150.00	950.00
1913S	510,000	6.50	10.00	24.00	60.00	135.00	325.00	
1914 ... (425)	17,360,655	1.25	1.50	3.00	6.00	18.00	150.00	950.00
1914D	11,908,000	1.25	1.50	3.00	6.00	18.00	150.00	
1914S	2,100,000	1.75	2.50	4.50	8.00	22.00	175.00	
1915 ... (450)	5,620,450	1.25	1.50	3.00	6.00	18.00	160.00	950.00
1915S	960,000	2.00	3.00	6.00	12.00	35.00	200.00	
1916	18,490,000	1.25	1.50	3.00	6.00	18.00	150.00	
1916S	5,820,000	1.25	1.50	3.00	6.00	18.00	150.00	

WINGED LIBERTY HEAD or "MERCURY" TYPE 1916-1945

Although this coin is commonly called the "Mercury Dime," the main device is in fact a representation of Liberty. The wings crowning her cap are intended to symbolize liberty of thought. The designer's monogram AW is right of neck.

Designer Adolph A. Weinman; weight 2.50 grams; composition: .900 silver, .100 copper; diameter 17.9 mm; reeded edge; mints: Philadelphia, Denver, San Francisco. Net weight: .07234 oz. pure silver.

G-4 GOOD—*Letters and date clear. Lines and bands in fasces are obliterated.*

VG-8 VERY GOOD—*One-half of sticks discernible in fasces.*

F-12 FINE—*All sticks in fasces are defined. Diagonal bands worn nearly flat.*

VF-20 VERY FINE—*The two crossing diagonal bands must show.*

EF-40 EXTREMELY FINE—*Diagonal bands show only slight wear. Braids and hair before ear show clearly.*

MS-63 SELECT UNCIRCULATED—*No trace of wear. Light blemishes. Attractive mint luster.*

MS-65—**CHOICE UNCIRCULATED**—*No trace of wear. Barely noticeable blemishes.*

Mint mark location is on reverse, left of fasces.

Uncirculated values shown are for average pieces with minimum blemishes, those with sharp strikes and split bands on reverse are worth much more.

	Quan. Minted	G-4	VG-8	F-12	VF-20	EF-40	MS-63
1916	22,180,080	$2.00	$2.50	$3.75	$6.00	$8.50	$60.00
1916D	264,000	325.00	425.00	800.00	1,200	1,750	3,500
1916S	10,450,000	2.75	3.25	6.00	8.00	14.00	65.00
1917	55,230,000	1.25	1.50	2.00	4.25	6.00	30.00
1917D	9,402,000	2.75	4.00	7.00	13.00	32.00	190.00
1917S	27,330,000	1.50	2.00	4.00	5.50	8.00	75.00
1918	26,680,000	1.50	2.00	4.00	9.00	21.00	95.00
1918D	22,674,800	1.50	2.25	4.00	8.00	20.00	125.00
1918S	19,300,000	1.50	2.25	3.50	6.50	13.00	85.00
1919	35,740,000	1.25	1.50	3.00	4.75	7.50	50.00
1919D	9,939,000	2.50	3.25	5.50	14.00	30.00	200.00
1919S	8,850,000	2.25	3.00	5.00	12.00	28.00	240.00
1920	59,030,000	1.25	1.50	2.50	4.75	6.50	30.00
1920D	19,171,000	1.35	2.00	3.50	6.00	14.00	125.00
1920S	13,820,000	1.35	2.00	3.25	5.50	12.00	100.00

Note: Prices in italic are based on silver bullion value.

DIMES

	Quan. Minted	G-4	VG-8	F-12	VF-20	EF-40	MS-63
1921	1,230,000	$20.00	$30.00	$60.00	$125.00	$325.00	$1,000
1921D	1,080,000	30.00	40.00	85.00	160.00	335.00	1,100
1923*	50,130,000	1.25	1.50	2.50	4.00	6.00	27.50
1923S	6,440,000	1.50	2.25	4.00	6.75	18.00	150.00
1924	24,010,000	1.25	1.50	2.50	4.50	7.00	65.00
1924D	6,810,000	1.35	2.25	4.00	7.00	17.50	190.00
1924S	7,120,000	1.35	2.25	4.00	6.00	16.00	200.00
1925	25,610,000	1.25	1.50	2.50	4.00	6.50	60.00
1925D	5,117,000	4.00	5.00	8.00	21.00	60.00	300.00
1925S	5,850,000	1.35	2.25	4.00	7.00	17.00	260.00
1926	32,160,000	1.15	1.35	3.00	4.00	5.00	27.00
1926D	6,828,000	1.25	1.50	3.00	5.00	15.00	125.00
1926S	1,520,000	6.50	8.00	15.00	27.50	85.00	900.00
1927	28,080,000	1.15	1.25	2.25	3.75	5.50	26.00
1927D	4,812,000	2.50	3.00	5.00	14.00	30.00	300.00
1927S	4,770,000	1.75	2.25	3.50	5.50	13.50	150.00
1928	19,480,000	1.15	1.25	2.25	3.75	5.00	25.00
1928D	4,161,000	1.75	2.75	6.00	14.00	30.00	210.00
1928S†	7,400,000	1.25	2.00	3.00	4.50	12.00	100.00
1929	25,970,000	1.15	1.25	2.25	3.75	4.50	21.00
1929D	5,034,000	1.75	2.25	3.75	6.75	9.00	75.00
1929S	4,730,000	1.15	2.00	3.00	4.00	6.00	80.00
1930*	6,770,000	1.15	1.35	2.50	4.00	5.25	35.00
1930S	1,843,000	3.00	3.50	4.50	6.00	12.00	140.00
1931	3,150,000	1.25	1.50	3.00	4.50	9.00	52.00
1931D	1,260,000	6.00	7.00	10.00	16.00	27.50	150.00
1931S	1,800,000	2.75	3.50	5.00	6.50	11.00	135.00

*Dimes dated 1923D and 1930D are counterfeit.

	Quan. Minted	F-12	VF-20	EF-40	MS-63	MS-65	Proof-65
1934	24,080,000	$1.25	$2.50	$3.00	$37.50	$75.00	
1934D†	6,772,000	1.50	3.00	6.00	45.00	115.00	
1935	58,830,000	1.25	2.50	3.00	25.00	75.00	
1935D	10,477,000	1.25	2.50	7.00	85.00	165.00	
1935S	15,840,000	1.25	2.50	5.00	37.50	100.00	
1936 .... (4,130)	87,504,130	1.25	2.50	3.00	24.00	70.00	$2,000
1936D	16,132,000	1.25	2.50	5.00	50.00	115.00	
1936S	9,210,000	1.25	2.50	3.00	30.00	75.00	
1937 .... (5,756)	56,865,756	1.25	2.50	3.00	22.00	60.00	1,000
1937D	14,146,000	1.25	2.75	3.50	37.50	125.00	
1937S	9,740,000	1.25	2.50	3.00	27.50	85.00	
1938 ... (8,728)	22,198,728	1.00	1.25	3.00	25.00	65.00	900.00
1938D	5,537,000	1.00	1.25	3.00	35.00	110.00	
1938S	8,090,000	1.00	1.25	3.00	30.00	75.00	
1939 .... (9,321)	67,749,321	1.00	1.25	3.00	20.00	60.00	900.00
1939D	24,394,000	1.00	1.25	3.00	21.00	65.00	
1939S	10,540,000	1.00	1.25	3.00	40.00	80.00	
1940 ... (11,827)	65,361,827	1.00	1.25	3.00	19.00	45.00	800.00
1940D	21,198,000	1.00	1.25	3.00	25.00	55.00	
1940S	21,560,000	1.00	1.25	3.00	18.00	55.00	
1941 ... (16,557)	175,106,557	1.00	1.25	3.00	16.00	45.00	750.00
1941D	45,634,000	1.00	1.25	3.00	25.00	50.00	
1941S†	43,090,000	1.00	1.25	3.00	20.00	50.00	

†Large and small mint marks. See pg. 65.

Note: Prices in italic are based on silver bullion value.

DIMES

	1942, 2 over 1			1942D, 2 over 1		

	Quan. Minted	F-12	VF-20	EF-40	MS-63	MS-65	Proof-65
1942, 2 over 1	} 205,432,329	$210.00	$235.00	$300.00	$1,750	$2,500	
1942 . . . . . . (22,329)		1.00	1.25	3.00	16.00	48.00	$700.00
1942D, 2 over 1...	} 60,740,000	225.00	250.00	325.00	1,900	2,750	
1942D.		1.00	1.25	3.00	20.00	48.00	
1942S	49,300,000	1.00	1.25	3.00	25.00	65.00	
1943	191,710,000	1.00	1.25	3.00	16.00	45.00	
1943D.	71,949,000	1.00	1.25	3.00	19.00	45.00	
1943S	60,400,000	1.00	1.25	3.00	19.00	45.00	
1944	231,410,000	1.00	1.25	3.00	16.00	65.00	
1944D.	62,224,000	1.00	1.25	3.00	16.00	45.00	
1944S	49,490,000	1.00	1.25	3.00	16.00	45.00	
1945	159,130,000	1.00	1.25	3.00	16.00	65.00	
1945D.	40,245,000	1.00	1.25	3.00	16.00	45.00	
1945S Normal S . .	} 41,920,000	1.00	1.25	3.00	16.00	45.00	
1945S Micro S* . . .		1.75	2.25	4.75	24.00	70.00	

*Large and small mint mark varieties, see page 65.

ROOSEVELT TYPE 1946 to Date

John R. Sinnock (whose initials JS are at the truncation of the neck) designed this dime showing a portrait of Franklin D. Roosevelt. The design has heavier lettering and a more modernistic character than preceding types.

Mint mark on
reverse 1946-1964.

Mint mark on
obverse starting 1968.

Silver Coinage — 1946-1964

Designer John R. Sinnock; weight 2.50 grams; composition: .900 silver, .100 copper; diameter 17.9 mm; reeded edge; mints: Philadelphia, Denver, San Francisco. Net weight: .07234 oz. pure silver.

VF-20 VERY FINE—*Hair above ear slightly worn. All vertical lines on torch plain.*
EF-40 EXTREMELY FINE—*All lines of torch, flame and hair very plain.*
MS-60 UNCIRCULATED—*No trace of wear. Light blemishes.*
MS-63 SELECT UNCIRCULATED—*No trace of wear. Very light blemishes. Attractive mint luster.*
MS-65 CHOICE UNCIRCULATED—*No trace of wear. Barely noticeable blemishes.*

	Quan. Minted	EF-40	MS-63	MS-65	Proof-65
1946	255,250,000	$1.00	$2.00	$3.00	
1946D.	61,043,500	1.00	3.50	5.00	
1946S	27,900,000	1.00	4.00	6.00	

Note: Prices in italic are based on silver bullion value.

DIMES

	Quan. Minted	EF-40	MS-63	MS-65	Proof-65
1947	121,520,000	$1.00	$3.00	$4.25	
1947D	46,835,000	1.00	5.00	7.50	
1947S	34,840,000	1.00	5.00	7.50	
1948	74,950,000	1.00	8.50	13.00	
1948D	52,841,000	1.00	6.50	10.00	
1948S	35,520,000	1.00	8.00	12.00	
1949	30,940,000	1.25	20.00	28.00	
1949D	26,034,000	1.00	9.00	13.50	
1949S	13,510,000	3.75	45.00	60.00	
1950 .... (51,386)	50,181,500	1.00	4.50	6.00	$60.00
1950D	46,803,000	1.00	4.50	6.00	
1950S	20,440,000	1.75	20.00	28.00	
1951 .... (57,500)	103,937,602	1.00	2.75	3.50	55.00
1951D	56,529,000	1.00	2.50	3.75	
1951S	31,630,000	1.50	13.00	20.00	
1952 .... (81,980)	99,122,073	1.00	3.00	4.00	33.00
1952D	122,100,000	1.00	3.00	4.00	
1952S	44,419,500	1.25	5.50	7.50	
1953 .... (128,800)	53,618,920	1.25	2.00	3.00	25.00
1953D	136,433,000	1.00	2.00	3.00	
1953S	39,180,000	1.00	2.00	2.75	
1954 .... (233,300)	114,243,503	1.00	2.00	2.75	9.00
1954D	106,397,000	1.00	2.00	2.50	
1954S	22,860,000	1.00	2.00	3.00	
1955 .... (378,200)	12,828,381	1.00	3.00	4.00	9.00
1955D	13,959,000	1.00	2.00	3.00	
1955S	18,510,000	1.00	1.75	2.75	
1956 .... (669,384)	109,309,384	1.00	1.50	2.00	3.00
1956D	108,015,100	1.00	1.50	2.00	
1957 .... (1,247,952)	161,407,952	1.00	1.50	2.00	2.50
1957D	113,354,330	1.00	1.75	2.50	
1958 .... (875,652)	32,785,652	1.00	1.75	2.50	3.00
1958D	136,564,600	1.00	1.50	2.00	
1959 .... (1,149,291)	86,929,291	1.00	1.50	2.00	2.25
1959D	164,919,790	1.00	1.50	2.00	
1960 .... (1,691,602)	72,081,602	1.00	1.25	2.00	2.25
1960D	200,160,400	1.00	1.25	2.00	
1961 .... (3,028,244)	96,758,244	1.00	1.25	2.00	2.00
1961D	209,146,550	1.00	1.25	2.00	
1962 .... (3,218,019)	75,668,019	1.00	1.25	2.00	2.00
1962D	334,948,380	1.00	1.25	2.00	
1963 .... (3,075,645)	126,725,645	1.00	1.25	2.00	2.00
1963D	421,476,530	1.00	1.25	2.00	
1964* .... (3,950,762)	933,310,762	1.00	1.25	2.00	2.00
1964D*	1,357,517,180	1.00	1.25	2.00	

*Variations of 9 in date have either pointed or straight tail.

Clad Coinage — 1965 to date

Weight 2.27 grams; composition: outer layers of copper-nickel (.750 copper, .250 nickel) bonded to inner core of pure copper; diameter 17.9 mm; reeded edge.

	Quan. Minted	MS-65	Proof-65		Quan. Minted	MS-65	Proof-65
1965	1,652,140,570	$ .35		1969	145,790,000	$.50	
1966	1,382,734,540	.35		1969D	563,323,870	.25	
1967	2,244,007,320	.30		1969S Proof... (2,934,631)			$.85
1968	424,470,400	.25		1970	345,570,000	.25	
1968D	480,748,280	.25		1970D	754,942,100	.25	
1968S Proof* .. (3,041,506)			$ .85	1970S Proof* .. (2,632,810)			.85

*1968 and 1970 proof dimes without mint mark were made in error. See page 67.

DIMES

	Quan. Minted	MS-65	Proof-65
1971	162,690,000	$.30	
1971D	377,914,240	.30	
1971S Proof . . .	(3,220,733)		$.85
1972	431,540,000	.25	
1972D	330,290,000	.25	
1972S Proof . . .	(3,260,996)		.85
1973	315,670,000	.25	
1973D	455,032,426	.25	
1973S Proof . . .	(2,760,339)		.85
1974	470,248,000	.25	
1974D	571,083,000	.25	
1974S Proof . . .	(2,612,568)		.85
1975	585,673,900	.30	
1975D	313,705,300	.25	
1975S Proof* . .	(2,845,450)		1.25
1976	568,760,000	.25	
1976D	695,222,774	.25	
1976S Proof . . .	(4,149,730)		.85
1977	796,930,000	.25	
1977D	376,607,228	.25	
1977S Proof . . .	(3,251,152)		.85
1978	663,980,000	.25	
1978D	282,847,540	.25	
1978S Proof . . .	(3,127,781)		.85
1979	315,440,000	.25	
1979D	390,921,184	.25	
1979S Proof . . .	(3,677,175)		
Filled S			1.00
Clear S			2.00
1980P	735,170,000	.20	
1980D	719,354,321	.20	
1980S Proof . . .	(3,554,806)		1.00
1981P	676,650,000	$.20	
1981D	712,284,143	.20	
1981S Proof . . .	(4,063,083)		$1.00
1982 (no mint mark)		175.00	
1982P*	519,475,000	.30	
1982D	542,713,584	.20	
1982S Proof . . .	(3,857,479)		1.00
1983P	647,025,000	.20	
1983D	730,129,224	.20	
1983S Proof* . .	(3,279,126)		1.75
1984P	856,669,000	.20	
1984D	704,803,976	.20	
1984S Proof . . .	(3,065,110)		2.25
1985P	705,200,962	.20	
1985D	587,979,970	.20	
1985S Proof . . .	(3,362,821)		2.25
1986P	682,649,693	.20	
1986D	473,326,970	.20	
1986S Proof . . .	(3,010,497)		1.75
1987P	762,709,481	.20	
1987D	653,203,402	.20	
1987S Proof . . .	(3,792,233)		1.50
1988P	1,030,550,000	.20	
1988D	962,385,489	.20	
1988S Proof			1.25
1989P	1,298,400,000	.20	
1989D	896,535,597	.20	
1989S Proof			1.25
1990P		.20	
1990D		.20	
1990S Proof			1.25

*1975 and 1983 proof dimes without S mint mark were made in error. Some of the 1982 business strike dimes were also made without a mint mark. See page 67.

TWENTY-CENT PIECES — 1875-1878

This short-lived coin was authorized by the Act of March 3, 1875. Soon after the appearance of the first twenty-cent pieces, the people complained about the similarity in design and size to the quarter dollar. The eagle is very similar to that used on the Trade Dollar. The edge of the coin is plain. Most of the 1876CC coins were melted at the mint and never released. Mint mark is on the reverse below the eagle.

+ or − indicates change from previous year	TYPE COIN VALUES									
	G-4	F-12	EF-40	AU-50	MS-60	MS-63	MS-65	PF-60	PF-63	PF-65
1875-1878	35.00	60.00	190.00	400.00	800.00	2,000+	12,000+	1,000	2,500	12,000

Designer William Barber; weight 5 grams; composition: .900 silver, .100 copper; diameter 22 mm; plain edge; mints: Philadelphia, Carson City, San Francisco.

G-4 GOOD—*LIBERTY on shield obliterated. Letters and date legible.*

VG-8 VERY GOOD—*One or two letters in LIBERTY may show. Other details will be bold.*

F-12 FINE—*At least 3 letters of LIBERTY show.*

VF-20 VERY FINE—*LIBERTY completely readable, but partly weak.*

EF-40 EXTREMELY FINE—*LIBERTY sharp. Only slight wear on high points of coin.*

MS-60 UNCIRCULATED—*No trace of wear. Light blemishes.*

Quan. Minted		G-4	VG-8	F-12	VF-20	EF-40	MS-60	Proof-63
1875 ... (2,790)	39,700	$50.00	$60.00	$85.00	$135.00	$250.00	$1,000	$2,500
1875CC	133,290	45.00	55.00	75.00	120.00	230.00	1,000	
1875S	1,155,000	35.00	45.00	60.00	90.00	190.00	800.00	——
1876 ... (1,260)	15,900	75.00	100.00	135.00	200.00	300.00	1,200	2,700
1876CC	10,000	....					60,000	
1877 ..... (350)	350	....						3,700
1878 ..... (600)	600	....						3,600

QUARTER DOLLARS — 1796 to Date

Authorized in 1792, this denomination was not issued until four years later. The first coinage, dated 1796, follows the pattern of the early half-dimes and dimes by the absence of a mark of value. In 1804 the value "25c" was added to the reverse. Figures were used until 1838 when the term "QUAR. DOL." appeared. It was not until 1892 that the value was spelled out entirely.

The first type weighed 104 grains which remained standard until modified to 103⅛ grains by the Act of January 18, 1837. As with the dime and half dime, the weight was reduced and arrows placed at the date in 1853. Rays were placed in the field of the reverse during that year only.

The law of 1873 also affected the quarter, for the weight was slightly increased and arrows again placed at the date.

Proofs of some dates prior to 1856 are known to exist, and all are rare.

+ or − indicates change from previous year	TYPE COIN VALUES									
	G-4	F-12	EF-40	AU-50	MS-60	MS-63	MS-65	PF-60	PF-63	PF-65
Drpd Bust-SE 1796	$3,500	$5,500	$17,000	$20,000	$30,000	$35,000	$85,000+			
Drpd Bust-HE 1804-1807	250.00	500.00	1,600	2,600	7,000	12,000	50,000+			
Lg. Bust 1815-1828	40.00	80.00	550.00	1,200	2,300+	5,000+	25,000+			
Sm. Bust 1831-1838	30.00	50.00	225.00	650.00	1,100+	3,200+	25,000+			
Lib Seated-NM 1838-1865	8.00	18.00	50.00	125.00	400.00−	1,200+	12,000+	500.00	1,300+	9,500+
Lib. Seat-A&R 1853	8.00	20.00	115.00	325.00	1,100	2,800+	25,000+			
Lib. Seat-Arr. 1854-1855	8.00	19.00	70.00	225.00	750.00	1,500	12,000+			
Lib. Seat-WM 1866-1891	7.00	17.00	45.00	115.00	375.00	850.00	5,000+	450.00	1,000	5,000+
Lib. Seat-Arr. 1873-1874	10.00	22.00	150.00	350.00	900.00	2,300+	7,500+	850.00	2,300+	15,000+
Barber 1892-1916	2.75	9.00	50.00	100.00	250.00	600.00−	4,000+	475.00	1,200+	4,500
Stand Lib. I 1916-1917	9.00	15.00	60.00	100.00	200.00	500.00−	2,500			
Stand Lib. II 1917-1930	2.75	7.00	25.00	55.00	125.00+	340.00+	1,500+			
Washington 1932-1964	2.00	2.00	2.25	2.25	2.50	2.75	3.25	4.00	5.00	6.00

QUARTER DOLLARS
DRAPED BUST TYPE, SMALL EAGLE REVERSE 1796

Designer Robert Scot; weight 6.74 grams; composition: .8924 silver, .1076 copper; approx. diameter 27.5 mm; reeded edge. All coined at Philadelphia.

AG-3 ABOUT GOOD—*Details clear enough to identify.*
G-4 GOOD—*Date readable. Bust outlined, but no detail.*
VG-8 VERY GOOD—*All but deepest drapery folds worn smooth. Hairlines nearly gone and curls lack detail.*
F-12 FINE—*All drapery lines visible. Hair partly worn.*
VF-20 VERY FINE—*Only left side of drapery is indistinct.*
EF-40 EXTREMELY FINE—*Hair well outlined and detailed.*
MS-60 UNCIRCULATED—*No trace of wear. Light blemishes.*

	Quan. Minted	AG-3	G-4	VG-8	F-12	VF-20	EF-40	MS-60
1796	6,146	$1,600	$3,500	$4,000	$5,500	$12,000	$17,000	$30,000

DRAPED BUST TYPE, HERALDIC EAGLE REVERSE 1804-1807

		AG-3	G-4	VG-8	F-12	VF-20	EF-40	MS-60
1804	6,738	450.00	850.00	1,200	2,500	5,000	8,500	
1805	121,394	125.00	250.00	325.00	500.00	1,000	1,600	7,000
1806 6 over 5	206,124	125.00	250.00	325.00	500.00	1,000	1,600	7,000
1806		125.00	250.00	325.00	500.00	1,000	1,600	7,000
1807	220,643	125.00	250.00	325.00	500.00	1,000	1,600	7,000

CAPPED BUST TYPE 1815-1838
Variety 1 — Large Size 1815-1828

Designer John Reich; weight 6.74 grams; composition: .8924 silver, .1076 copper; approx. diameter 27 mm; reeded edge. All coined at Philadelphia.

AG-3 ABOUT GOOD—*Details clear enough to identify.*
G-4 GOOD—*Date, letters and stars readable. Hair under headband smooth. Cap lines worn smooth.*
VG-8 VERY GOOD—*Rim well defined. Main details visible. Full LIBERTY on cap. Hair above eye nearly smooth.*
F-12 FINE—*All hairlines show but drapery has only part details. Shoulder clasp distinct.*
VF-20 VERY FINE—*All details show, but some wear. Clasp and ear sharp.*
EF-40 EXTREMELY FINE—*All details show distinctly. Hair well outlined.*
MS-60 UNCIRCULATED—*No trace of wear. Light blemishes.*

QUARTER DOLLARS

	Quan. Minted	AG-3	G-4	VG-8	F-12	VF-20	EF-40	MS-60
1815	89,235	$25.00	$50.00	$70.00	$100.00	$250.00	$700.00	$3,200
1818 8 over 5		25.00	50.00	70.00	100.00	275.00	725.00	3,000
1818 Normal date .	} 361,174	25.00	45.00	65.00	95.00	225.00	600.00	2,300
1819 Small 9		25.00	45.00	65.00	95.00	225.00	600.00	2,300
1819 Large 9	} 144,000	25.00	45.00	65.00	95.00	225.00	600.00	2,300

1820 Small 0   **1820 Large 0**   **1822, 25 over 50c**

		AG-3	G-4	VG-8	F-12	VF-20	EF-40	MS-60
1820 Small 0	} 127,444	25.00	45.00	65.00	95.00	225.00	600.00	2,300
1820 Large 0		25.00	45.00	65.00	95.00	225.00	600.00	2,300
1821	216,851	25.00	45.00	65.00	95.00	225.00	600.00	2,300
1822 All kinds . .	64,080	25.00	45.00	65.00	95.00	225.00	625.00	2,750
1822, 25 over 50c		150.00	200.00	300.00	450.00	900.00	1,600	5,250
1823, 3 over 2 . .	17,800	1,500	3,500	7,500	9,000	13,000	20,000	——

1825, 5 over 2 (wide date)   **1825, 5 over 3 or 4 (close date)**

		AG-3	G-4	VG-8	F-12	VF-20	EF-40	MS-60
1824 4 over 2		30.00	50.00	70.00	100.00	275.00	650.00	3,250
1825 5 over 2	{ 168,000	25.00	45.00	60.00	90.00	225.00	600.00	3,000
1825 5 over 3		25.00	45.00	60.00	90.00	225.00	550.00	2,300
1825 5 over 4		25.00	45.00	60.00	90.00	225.00	550.00	2,750
1827 Original (Curled base 2 in 25c) 4,000 Minted								60,000
1827 Restrike (Square base 2 in 25c)								25,000
1828 All kds . . .	102,000	22.00	40.00	55.00	80.00	200.00	550.00	2,300
1828, 25 over 50c		50.00	90.00	125.00	225.00	500.00	750.00	4,000

Variety 2 — Reduced Size, No Motto on Reverse 1831-1838

Designer William Kneass; weight 6.74 grams; composition: .8924 silver, .1076 copper; diameter 24.3 mm; reeded edge. All coined at Philadelphia.

G-4 GOOD—*Bust well defined. Hair under headband smooth. Date, letters, stars readable. Scant rims.*

VG-8 VERY GOOD—*Details apparent but worn on high spots. Rims strong. Full LIBERTY.*

F-12 FINE—*All hairlines visible. Drapery partly worn. Shoulder clasp distinct.*

VF-20 VERY FINE—*Only top spots worn. Clasp sharp. Ear distinct.*

EF-40 EXTREMELY FINE—*Hair details and clasp are bold and clear.*

MS-60 UNCIRCULATED—*No trace of wear. Light blemishes.*

QUARTER DOLLARS

Small Letters (1831)　　　Large Letters

	Quan. Minted	G-4	VG-8	F-12	VF-20	EF-40	MS-60
1831 Small letters	⎱ 398,000	$30.00	$40.00	$50.00	$100.00	$225.00	$1,100
1831 Large letters	⎰	30.00	40.00	50.00	100.00	225.00	1,100
1832	320,000	30.00	40.00	50.00	100.00	225.00	1,100
1833	156,000	35.00	45.00	65.00	125.00	275.00	1,700
1834	286,000	30.00	40.00	50.00	100.00	225.00	1,100
1835	1,952,000	30.00	40.00	50.00	100.00	225.00	1,100
1836	472,000	30.00	40.00	50.00	100.00	225.00	1,100
1837	252,400	30.00	40.00	50.00	100.00	225.00	1,100
1838	366,000	30.00	40.00	50.00	100.00	225.00	1,100

LIBERTY SEATED TYPE 1838-1891
Variety 1 — No Motto Above Eagle 1838-1853

Designer Christian Gobrecht; weight 6.68 grams; composition: .900 silver, .100 copper; diameter 24.3 mm; reeded edge; mints: Philadelphia, New Orleans.

G-4 GOOD—*Scant rim. LIBERTY on shield worn off. Date and letters readable.*

VG-8 VERY GOOD—*Rim fairly defined, at least 3 letters in LIBERTY evident.*

F-12 FINE—*LIBERTY complete, but partly weak.*

VF-20 VERY FINE—*LIBERTY strong.*

EF-40 EXTREMELY FINE—*Complete LIBERTY and edges of scroll. Clasp shows plainly.*

MS-60 UNCIRCULATED—*No trace of wear. Light blemishes.*

No Drapery from Elbow　　　Drapery from Elbow

Mint mark location is on the reverse below the eagle.

1838 No drapery	466,000	10.00	15.00	25.00	50.00	160.00	1,800
1839 No drapery	491,146	10.00	15.00	25.00	50.00	160.00	1,800
1840O No drapery	382,200	10.00	15.00	25.00	50.00	160.00	2,000
1840 Drapery	188,127	15.00	20.00	30.00	75.00	175.00	1,500
1840O Drapery	43,000	12.00	18.00	30.00	60.00	135.00	1,500
1841	120,000	30.00	40.00	100.00	160.00	250.00	1,000
1841O	452,000	12.00	18.00	30.00	60.00	150.00	1,000

Small date 　　　 **Large date**

1842 Small Date Proofs Only							25,000
1842 Large date	88,000	60.00	80.00	125.00	250.00	400.00	1,600

QUARTER DOLLARS

	Quan. Minted	G-4	VG-8	F-12	VF-20	EF-40	MS-60
1842O Small date..	769,000	$200.00	$350.00	$700.00	$1,000	$2,000	——
1842O Large date..		15.00	20.00	30.00	50.00	100.00	$1,200
1843	645,600	12.00	16.00	20.00	40.00	80.00	800.00
1843O.	968,000	15.00	25.00	40.00	70.00	200.00	——
1844	421,200	12.00	16.00	25.00	40.00	85.00	600.00
1844O.	740,000	15.00	20.00	30.00	60.00	110.00	1,200
1845	922,000	12.00	16.00	20.00	35.00	75.00	600.00
1846	510,000	12.00	16.00	25.00	40.00	85.00	600.00
1847	734,000	12.00	16.00	20.00	35.00	75.00	600.00
1847O.	368,000	20.00	30.00	50.00	90.00	190.00	1,000
1848	146,000	20.00	30.00	50.00	90.00	150.00	950.00
1849	340,000	15.00	20.00	35.00	50.00	125.00	750.00
1849O.	†incl. below	350.00	450.00	850.00	1,650	3,000	——
1850	190,800	15.00	25.00	35.00	60.00	100.00	900.00
1850O.	412,000	25.00	35.00	50.00	70.00	125.00	1,000
1851	160,000	15.00	25.00	35.00	60.00	110.00	850.00
1851O.	88,000	150.00	225.00	400.00	600.00	1,200	2,000
1852	177,060	20.00	30.00	45.00	65.00	110.00	900.00
1852O.	96,000	210.00	300.00	450.00	750.00	1,200	2,500
1853* Recut date, no arrows or rays.	44,200	150.00	200.00	300.00	425.00	600.00	3,000

†Coinage for 1849O included with 1850O.
*Beware of altered 1858.

Variety 2 — Arrows at Date, Rays Around Eagle 1853 Only

The reduction in weight is indicated by the arrows at the date. Rays were added on the reverse side in the field around the eagle. The arrows were retained through 1855, but the rays were omitted after 1853.

Weight 6.22 grams; composition: .900 silver, .100 copper; diameter 24.3 mm; reeded edge; mints: Philadelphia, New Orleans, San Francisco, Carson City.

1853, 3 over 4

1853	15,210,020	8.00	12.00	20.00	35.00	115.00	1,100
1853, 3 over 4		70.00	125.00	300.00	400.00	800.00	2,500
1853O.	1,332,000	10.00	13.00	25.00	50.00	140.00	1,350

Variety 3 — Arrows at Date, No Rays 1854-1855

1854	12,380,000	8.00	10.00	19.00	30.00	70.00	750.00
1854O.		8.00	11.00	20.00	32.00	75.00	900.00
1854O Huge O..	1,484,000	60.00	80.00	150.00	250.00	500.00	——
1855	2,857,000	8.00	11.00	20.00	32.00	75.00	800.00
1855O.	176,000	45.00	65.00	95.00	175.00	325.00	1,850
1855S.	396,400	45.00	65.00	95.00	160.00	300.00	1,750

QUARTER DOLLARS
Variety 1 Resumed 1856-1865

	Quan. Minted	G-4	VG-8	F-12	VF-20	EF-40	MS-60	Proof-63
1856	7,264,000	$8.00	$10.00	$14.00	$20.00	$50.00	$450.00	$3,000
1856O	968,000	10.00	15.00	25.00	35.00	75.00	800.00	
1856S	286,000	21.00	30.00	45.00	100.00	200.00	1,100	
1856S, S over S		25.00	50.00	100.00	250.00	400.00	——	
1857	9,644,000	8.00	10.00	18.00	25.00	50.00	400.00	2,500
1857O	1,180,000	9.00	11.50	18.00	25.00	50.00	800.00	
1857S	82,000	45.00	70.00	100.00	235.00	500.00	1,500	
1858	7,368,000	8.00	10.00	18.00	25.00	50.00	400.00	2,000
1858O	520,000	9.00	12.00	20.00	30.00	70.00	1,100	
1858S	121,000	35.00	40.00	65.00	175.00	300.00	——	
1859 . . . . (800)	1,344,000	8.00	10.00	18.00	25.00	50.00	425.00	1,300
1859O	260,000	15.00	25.00	40.00	65.00	95.00	1,000	
1859S	80,000	55.00	90.00	150.00	250.00	450.00	——	
1860 . . (1,000)	805,400	8.00	10.00	18.00	25.00	50.00	425.00	1,300
1860O	388,000	10.00	14.00	20.00	30.00	60.00	1,000	
1860S	56,000	80.00	135.00	225.00	400.00	800.00	2,500	
1861 . . (1,000)	4,854,600	8.00	10.00	18.00	25.00	50.00	400.00	1,300
1861S	96,000	25.00	35.00	75.00	200.00	300.00	2,000	
1862 . . . . (550)	932,550	8.00	10.00	18.00	25.00	50.00	425.00	1,300
1862S	67,000	25.00	35.00	75.00	200.00	300.00	2,000	
1863 . . . . (460)	192,060	16.00	20.00	30.00	45.00	85.00	750.00	1,400
1864 . . . . (470)	94,070	25.00	35.00	65.00	100.00	175.00	900.00	1,400
1864S	20,000	100.00	175.00	275.00	450.00	1,000	——	
1865 . . . . (500)	59,300	35.00	50.00	75.00	110.00	200.00	900.00	1,400
1865S	41,000	35.00	50.00	100.00	225.00	325.00	2,500	
1866 . . . . (Unique)								——

The 1866 proof quarter, half and dollar without motto are not mentioned in the Director's Report, and were not issued for circulation.

Variety 4 — Motto Above Eagle 1866-1873

The motto IN GOD WE TRUST was added to the reverse side in 1866. As on the half dollar and silver dollar the motto has been retained since that time.

	Quan. Minted	G-4	VG-8	F-12	VF-20	EF-40	MS-60	Proof-63
1866 . . . . (725)	17,525	175.00	225.00	325.00	450.00	650.00	1,550	1,500
1866S	28,000	80.00	120.00	200.00	325.00	550.00	1,900	
1867 . . . . (625)	20,625	80.00	120.00	180.00	300.00	475.00	1,200	1,500
1867S	48,000	45.00	65.00	120.00	175.00	275.00	2,000	
1868 . . . . (600)	30,000	50.00	75.00	150.00	200.00	300.00	900.00	1,500
1868S	96,000	30.00	50.00	90.00	125.00	200.00	1,750	
1869 . . . . (600)	16,600	80.00	120.00	200.00	300.00	500.00	1,200	1,500
1869S	76,000	30.00	50.00	90.00	125.00	200.00	1,500	
1870 . . (1,000)	87,400	25.00	35.00	50.00	90.00	140.00	750.00	1,500
1870CC	8,340	1,000	1,500	2,500	3,500	4,750	——	
1871 . . . . (960)	119,160	12.00	15.00	30.00	50.00	85.00	600.00	1,300
1871CC	10,890	450.00	700.00	1,100	1,900	3,000	——	
1871S	30,900	125.00	250.00	400.00	550.00	850.00	2,250	
1872 . . . . (950)	182,950	10.00	20.00	27.50	50.00	75.00	500.00	1,300

QUARTER DOLLARS

	Quan. Minted	G-4	VG-8	F-12	VF-20	EF-40	MS-60	Proof-63
1872CC	22,850	$225.00	$350.00	$475.00	$750.00	$1,800	$5,000	
1872S...........	83,000	125.00	225.00	350.00	450.00	700.00	3,750	
1873 Cl. 3 (600) ...	40,600	30.00	50.00	90.00	175.00	275.00	900.00	$1,300
1873 Open 3.....	172,000	10.00	20.00	30.00	50.00	115.00	500.00	
1873CC	4,000						150,000	

Variety 5 — Arrows at Date 1873-1874

Arrows were placed at the date in the years 1873 and 1874 to denote the change of weight from 6.22 to 6.25 grams.

Weight 6.25 grams; composition: .900 silver, .100 copper; diameter 24.3 mm; reeded edge; mints: Philadelphia, San Francisco, Carson City.

1873 .. (540)	1,271,700	10.00	16.00	22.00	55.00	150.00	900.00	2,300
1873CC	12,462	500.00	650.00	900.00	1,250	2,500	7,800	
1873S...........	156,000	18.00	21.00	40.00	80.00	200.00	1,200	
1874 .. (700)	471,900	10.00	16.00	22.00	55.00	150.00	1,000	2,300
1874S...........	392,000	18.00	21.00	40.00	80.00	200.00	1,200	

Variety 4 Resumed 1875-1891

  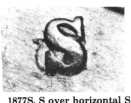

1877S, S over horizontal S

1875 .. (700)	4,293,500	7.00	9.00	17.00	23.00	40.00	375.00	1,000
1875CC	140,000	35.00	45.00	95.00	135.00	300.00	1,400	
1875S...........	680,000	8.00	12.00	20.00	35.00	65.00	600.00	
1876 (1,150)	17,817,150	7.00	9.00	17.00	20.00	45.00	375.00	1,000
1876CC*	4,944,000	8.00	11.00	20.00	30.00	60.00	500.00	
1876S.........	8,596,000	7.00	9.00	17.00	23.00	45.00	425.00	
1877 .. (510)	10,911,710	7.00	9.00	17.00	23.00	45.00	375.00	1,000
1877CC	4,192,000	8.00	11.00	20.00	30.00	60.00	500.00	
1877S.........	8,996,000	7.00	9.00	17.00	23.00	45.00	375.00	
1877S over horizontal S .		——	——	100.00	135.00	225.00	1,000	
1878 .. (800)	2,260,800	7.00	9.00	17.00	23.00	45.00	375.00	1,000
1878CC	996,000	9.00	12.00	21.00	30.00	60.00	500.00	
1878S...........	140,000	50.00	75.00	125.00	175.00	275.00	1,750	
1879 (1,100)	14,700	70.00	80.00	110.00	145.00	225.00	650.00	1,200
1880 (1,355)	14,955	70.00	80.00	110.00	145.00	225.00	650.00	1,200
1881 .. (975)	12,975	70.00	80.00	110.00	145.00	225.00	650.00	1,200

*Variety with fine edge reeding is scarcer than normal.

QUARTER DOLLARS

	Quan. Minted	G-4	VG-8	F-12	VF-20	EF-40	MS-60	Proof-63
1882 (1,100)	16,300	$70.00	$80.00	$110.00	$145.00	$225.00	$650.00	$1,200
1883 (1,039)	15,439	70.00	80.00	110.00	145.00	225.00	650.00	1,200
1884 .. (875)	8,875	80.00	95.00	125.00	165.00	275.00	725.00	1,200
1885 .. (930)	14,530	70.00	80.00	110.00	145.00	250.00	700.00	1,200
1886 .. (886)	5,886	90.00	110.00	140.00	190.00	350.00	725.00	1,200
1887 .. (710)	10,710	70.00	80.00	110.00	145.00	250.00	700.00	1,200
1888 .. (832)	10,833	70.00	80.00	110.00	145.00	250.00	700.00	1,200
1888S	1,216,000	10.00	12.00	20.00	25.00	40.00	375.00	
1889 .. (711)	12,711	65.00	75.00	100.00	125.00	175.00	700.00	1,200
1890 .. (590)	80,590	40.00	50.00	65.00	90.00	125.00	650.00	1,100
1891 .. (600)	3,920,600	7.00	9.00	17.00	23.00	45.00	425.00	1,000
1891O............	68,000	110.00	125.00	200.00	325.00	550.00	2,100	
1891S	2,216,000	7.00	10.00	20.00	27.50	50.00	400.00	

BARBER or LIBERTY HEAD TYPE 1892-1916

Like other silver coins of this type the quarter dollars minted from 1892 to 1916 were designed by Charles E. Barber. His initial B is found at the truncation of the neck of Liberty. There are two varieties of the 1892 reverse: 1) Eagle's wing covers only half of E in UNITED. 2) Eagle's wing covers most of E.

Designer Charles E. Barber; weight 6.25 grams; composition: .900 silver, .100 copper; diameter 24.3 mm; reeded edge; mints: Philadelphia, Denver, New Orleans, San Francisco. Net weight: .18084 oz. pure silver.

G-4 GOOD—*Date and legends readable. LIBERTY worn off headband.*

VG-8 VERY GOOD—*Minimum of 3 letters in LIBERTY readable.*

F-12 FINE—*LIBERTY completely readable but not sharp.*

VF-20 VERY FINE—*All letters in LIBERTY evenly plain.*

EF-40 EXTREMELY FINE—*LIBERTY bold, and its ribbon distinct.*

MS-60 UNCIRCULATED—*No trace of wear. Light blemishes.*

Mint mark location is on the reverse below the eagle.

	Quan. Minted	G-4	VG-8	F-12	VF-20	EF-40	MS-60	Proof-63
1892 (1,245)	8,237,245	$3.00	$3.75	$11.00	$17.00	$50.00	$300.00	$1,200
1892O.........	2,640,000	5.00	7.00	13.00	24.00	55.00	340.00	
1892S	964,079	15.00	18.00	30.00	50.00	90.00	425.00	
1893 .. (792)	5,444,815	2.85	3.75	10.00	17.00	50.00	275.00	1,200
1893O.........	3,396,000	4.00	6.00	14.00	27.50	60.00	350.00	
1893S	1,454,535	5.50	7.00	20.00	35.00	80.00	350.00	
1894 .. (972)	3,432,972	2.75	3.50	10.00	20.00	50.00	275.00	1,200
1894O.........	2,852,000	3.00	4.00	12.00	25.00	55.00	350.00	
1894S	2,648,821	3.00	4.00	12.00	25.00	55.00	350.00	
1895 .. (880)	4,440,880	2.75	3.50	10.00	18.00	50.00	275.00	1,200
1895O.........	2,816,000	3.00	4.00	12.00	25.00	65.00	425.00	
1895S	1,764,681	3.00	4.50	20.00	35.00	65.00	425.00	
1896 .. (762)	3,874,762	2.75	3.50	10.00	20.00	52.50	300.00	1,200
1896O.........	1,484,000	3.50	6.50	20.00	40.00	125.00	825.00	
1896S	188,039	235.00	265.00	550.00	900.00	1,400	3,500	
1897 .. (731)	8,140,731	2.75	3.50	9.00	16.00	50.00	275.00	1,200
1897O.........	1,414,800	6.00	9.00	25.00	45.00	125.00	825.00	

QUARTER DOLLARS

	Quan. Minted	G-4	VG-8	F-12	VF-20	EF-40	MS-60	Proof-63
1897S	542,229	$10.00	$14.00	$25.00	$42.00	$90.00	$425.00	
1898 . . (735)	11,100,735	2.75	3.50	9.00	16.00	50.00	275.00	$1,200
1898O	1,868,000	3.00	5.00	20.00	50.00	100.00	550.00	
1898S	1,020,592	3.00	4.50	15.00	25.00	55.00	375.00	
1899 . . (846)	12,624,846	2.75	3.50	9.00	16.00	50.00	275.00	1,200
1899O	2,644,000	4.00	6.00	15.00	27.50	65.00	375.00	
1899S	708,000	7.50	11.00	18.00	32.00	62.50	400.00	
1900 . . (912)	10,016,912	2.75	3.50	9.00	18.00	50.00	275.00	1,200
1900O	3,416,000	5.00	7.00	20.00	35.00	75.00	400.00	
1900S	1,858,585	3.50	5.00	12.00	25.00	52.50	325.00	
1901 . . (813)	8,892,813	2.75	3.50	9.00	16.00	50.00	275.00	1,200
1901O	1,612,000	10.00	16.00	32.00	65.00	175.00	775.00	
1901S	72,664	950.00	1,250	2,000	2,800	3,750	10,000	
1902 . . (777)	12,197,744	2.75	3.50	9.00	16.00	50.00	275.00	1,200
1902O	4,748,000	3.00	4.00	10.00	17.00	55.00	425.00	
1902S	1,524,612	6.00	10.00	14.00	30.00	75.00	400.00	
1903 . . (755)	9,670,064	2.75	3.50	9.00	16.00	50.00	250.00	1,200
1903O	3,500,000	3.00	4.00	10.00	25.00	60.00	350.00	
1903S	1,036,000	7.00	10.00	14.00	35.00	80.00	425.00	
1904 . . (670)	9,588,813	2.75	3.50	9.00	16.00	50.00	250.00	1,200
1904O	2,456,000	3.50	7.00	15.00	32.50	85.00	725.00	
1905 . . (727)	4,968,250	2.75	3.50	9.00	16.00	50.00	250.00	1,200
1905O	1,230,000	5.00	7.00	15.00	30.00	60.00	375.00	
1905S	1,884,000	5.00	3.50	9.00	23.00	55.00	350.00	
1906 . . (675)	3,656,435	2.75	3.50	9.00	16.00	50.00	250.00	1,200
1906D	3,280,000	2.75	3.50	9.00	20.00	50.00	325.00	
1906O	2,056,000	2.75	3.50	9.00	23.00	50.00	325.00	
1907 . . (575)	7,192,575	2.75	3.50	9.00	16.00	50.00	250.00	1,200
1907D	2,484,000	2.75	3.50	9.00	20.00	50.00	325.00	
1907O	4,560,000	2.75	3.50	9.00	19.00	50.00	300.00	
1907S	1,360,000	3.00	3.75	10.00	21.00	55.00	375.00	
1908 . . (545)	4,232,545	2.75	3.50	9.00	16.00	50.00	250.00	1,200
1908D	5,788,000	2.75	3.50	9.00	16.00	50.00	300.00	
1908O	6,244,000	2.75	3.50	9.00	16.00	50.00	300.00	
1908S	784,000	6.00	9.00	17.50	35.00	80.00	450.00	
1909 . . (650)	9,268,650	2.75	3.50	9.00	16.00	50.00	250.00	1,200
1909D	5,114,000	2.75	3.50	9.00	16.00	50.00	300.00	
1909O	712,000	9.00	13.00	30.00	55.00	130.00	625.00	
1909S	1,348,000	2.75	3.50	9.00	16.00	50.00	375.00	
1910 . . (551)	2,244,551	2.75	3.50	9.00	16.00	50.00	250.00	1,200
1910D	1,500,000	2.75	3.50	9.00	16.00	50.00	325.00	
1911 . . (543)	3,720,543	2.75	3.50	9.00	16.00	50.00	250.00	1,200
1911D	933,600	2.75	3.50	10.00	20.00	50.00	325.00	
1911S	988,000	2.75	3.50	10.00	20.00	50.00	375.00	
1912 . . (700)	4,400,700	2.75	3.50	9.00	16.00	50.00	250.00	1,200
1912S	708,000	2.75	3.50	10.00	20.00	52.50	350.00	
1913 . . (613)	484,613	10.00	14.00	45.00	110.00	375.00	1,400	1,400
1913D	1,450,800	2.75	3.50	9.00	16.00	50.00	300.00	
1913S	40,000	300.00	350.00	700.00	1,200	1,800	3,200	
1914 . . (380)	6,244,610	2.75	3.50	9.00	16.00	50.00	250.00	1,200
1914D	3,046,000	2.75	3.50	9.00	16.00	50.00	250.00	
1914S	264,000	13.00	18.00	45.00	95.00	235.00	700.00	
1915 . . (450)	3,480,450	2.75	3.50	9.00	16.00	50.00	250.00	1,200
1915D	3,694,000	2.75	3.50	9.00	16.00	50.00	250.00	
1915S	704,000	3.50	6.00	13.00	23.00	50.00	300.00	
1916	1,788,000	2.75	3.50	9.00	16.00	50.00	250.00	
1916D	6,540,800	2.75	3.50	9.00	16.00	50.00	250.00	

QUARTER DOLLARS

STANDING LIBERTY TYPE 1916-1930

This type quarter was designed by Hermon A. MacNeil. The left arm of Liberty is upraised bearing a shield in the attitude of protection, from which the cover is being drawn. The right hand bears the olive branch of peace. The designer's initial M is located above and to the right of the date.

There was a modification in 1917 because of public resentment to Liberty's exposed breast. The reverse has a new arrangement of the stars and the eagle is higher.

In 1925 a depression was made in the pedestal on which Liberty stands and which bears the date. On the first issues the dates wore off easily because they were too high and were not protected by other features of the coin. The new "recessed" dates proved more durable as a result of this change.

No proof coins of this type were officially issued, but specimens of the first variety, dated 1917, are known to exist.

Designer Hermon A. MacNeil. Standards same as previous issue; mints: Philadelphia, Denver, San Francisco.

G-4 GOOD—*Date and lettering readable. Top of date worn. Liberty's right leg and toes worn off. Left leg and drapery lines show much wear.*

VG-8 VERY GOOD—*Distinct date. Toes show faintly. Drapery lines visible above her left leg.*

F-12 FINE—*High curve of right leg flat from thigh to ankle. Left leg shows only slight wear. Drapery lines over right thigh seen only at sides of leg.*

VF-20 VERY FINE—*Garment line across right leg will be worn but show at sides.*

EF-40 EXTREMELY FINE—*Flattened only at high spots. Her toes are sharp. Drapery lines across right leg are evident.*

MS-63 SELECT UNCIRCULATED—*No trace of wear. Light blemishes. Attractive mint luster.*

(Some modifications must be made for grading variety 2.)

Uncirculated pieces with fully struck head of Liberty are worth more than double the prices listed below.

Variety 1

	Quan. Minted	G-4	VG-8	F-12	VF-20	EF-40	MS-63
1916	52,000	$1,000	$1,200	$1,500	$1,800	$2,200	$4,500
1917 Variety 1	8,740,000	9.00	12.00	15.00	30.00	60.00	500.00
1917D Variety 1	1,509,200	13.00	17.00	24.00	55.00	100.00	500.00
1917S Variety 1	1,952,000	12.00	16.00	23.00	50.00	90.00	525.00

Variety 2

1918S, 8 over 7

Mint mark location is on obverse at left of date.

	Quan. Minted	G-4	VG-8	F-12	VF-20	EF-40	MS-63
1917 Variety 2	13,880,000	10.00	14.00	18.00	25.00	40.00	375.00
1917D Variety 2	6,224,400	20.00	25.00	45.00	65.00	100.00	425.00
1917S Variety 2	5,552,000	18.00	23.00	32.00	50.00	80.00	415.00
1918	14,240,000	13.00	17.00	25.00	35.00	55.00	425.00

QUARTER DOLLARS

	Quan. Minted	G-4	VG-8	F-12	VF-20	EF-40	MS-63
1918D	7,380,000	$22.00	$26.00	$40.00	$60.00	$95.00	$475.00
1918S Norm. date		13.00	17.00	22.50	30.00	50.00	450.00
1918S 8 over 7.	11,072,000	1,000	1,200	1,600	2,200	3,250	15,000
1919	11,324,000	27.00	32.00	40.00	50.00	75.00	425.00
1919D	1,944,000	45.00	70.00	100.00	140.00	240.00	975.00
1919S	1,836,000	45.00	65.00	95.00	130.00	220.00	925.00
1920	27,860,000	12.00	15.00	18.00	22.50	37.50	400.00
1920D	3,586,400	25.00	35.00	50.00	75.00	125.00	475.00
1920S	6,380,000	13.00	18.00	24.00	30.00	50.00	425.00
1921	1,916,000	50.00	80.00	125.00	160.00	250.00	775.00
1923	9,716,000	12.00	15.00	19.00	25.00	40.00	400.00
1923S	1,360,000	100.00	150.00	210.00	275.00	400.00	850.00
1924	10,920,000	11.00	15.00	19.00	25.00	40.00	400.00
1924D	3,112,000	25.00	30.00	40.00	60.00	90.00	400.00
1924S	2,860,000	15.00	18.00	25.00	30.00	45.00	450.00

Recessed Date Style 1925-1930

	Quan. Minted	G-4	VG-8	F-12	VF-20	EF-40	MS-63
1925	12,280,000	2.75	3.50	7.00	15.00	25.00	350.00
1926	11,316,000	2.75	3.50	7.00	15.00	25.00	350.00
1926D	1,716,000	7.00	7.50	12.00	19.00	40.00	350.00
1926S	2,700,000	2.75	3.50	11.00	19.00	55.00	500.00
1927	11,912,000	2.75	3.50	7.00	15.00	25.00	350.00
1927D	976,000	8.00	10.00	15.00	30.00	60.00	400.00
1927S	396,000	12.00	18.00	50.00	140.00	600.00	3,500
1928	6,336,000	2.75	3.50	7.00	15.00	25.00	350.00
1928D	1,627,600	5.00	8.00	12.00	18.00	38.00	360.00
1928S*	2,644,000	4.00	6.00	10.00	16.00	30.00	375.00
1929	11,140,000	2.75	3.50	7.00	15.00	25.00	350.00
1929D	1,358,000	5.00	8.00	10.00	16.00	32.00	360.00
1929S	1,764,000	4.00	6.00	8.00	16.00	30.00	350.00
1930	5,632,000	2.75	3.50	7.00	15.00	25.00	340.00
1930S	1,556,000	2.75	3.50	7.00	15.00	28.00	340.00

*Large and small mint mark varieties, see page 65.

WASHINGTON TYPE 1932 to Date

This type was intended to be a commemorative issue marking the two-hundredth anniversary of Washington's birth. John Flanagan, a New York sculptor, was the designer. The initials JF are found at the base of the neck. Mint mark is on reverse below wreath, 1932 to 1964.

Weight 6.25 grams; composition: .900 silver, .100 copper; diameter 24.3 mm; reeded edge. Net weight: .18084 oz. pure silver.

VG-8 VERY GOOD—*Wing tips outlined. Rims are fine and even. Tops of letters at rim are flattened.*

F-12 FINE—*Hairlines about ear are visible. Tiny feathers on eagle's breast are faintly visible.*

VF-20 VERY FINE—*Most hair details show. Wing feathers are clear.*

EF-40 EXTREMELY FINE—*Hairlines sharp. Wear spots confined to top of eagle's legs and center of breast.*

MS-63 SELECT UNCIRCULATED—*No trace of wear. Light blemishes. Attractive mint luster.*

MS-65 CHOICE UNCIRCULATED—*No trace of wear. Barely noticeable blemishes.*

1934 Doubled Die

[140]

QUARTER DOLLARS
Silver Coinage — 1932-1964

	Quan. Minted	VG-8	F-12	VF-20	EF-40	MS-63	MS-65
1932	5,404,000	$2.75	$3.00	$8.00	$11.00	$60.00	$450.00
1932D	436,800	40.00	55.00	80.00	150.00	900.00	5,500
1932S	408,000	38.00	42.50	55.00	70.00	425.00	5,000
1934 Light motto .		2.75	3.00	7.00	11.00	55.00	300.00
1934 Hvy. motto . .	31,912,052	2.75	3.00	6.50	10.00	45.00	275.00
1934 Doubled die .				60.00	175.00	400.00	750.00
1934D	3,527,200	2.75	3.00	11.00	15.00	125.00	900.00
1935	32,484,000	2.25	2.50	6.50	9.00	40.00	200.00
1935D	5,780,000	2.25	2.50	10.00	18.00	125.00	600.00
1935S	5,660,000	2.25	2.50	8.00	12.00	100.00	400.00

	Quan. Minted	VF-20	EF-40	MS-63	MS-65	Proof-65
1936 . . . . . (3,837)	41,303,837	$2.25	$7.00	$35.00	$225.00	$3,000
1936D	5,374,000	14.00	30.00	350.00	1,500	
1936S	3,828,000	8.00	12.00	100.00	300.00	
1937 . . . . . (5,542)	19,701,542	2.25	7.00	35.00	215.00	600.00
1937D	7,189,600	7.00	10.00	50.00	275.00	
1937S	1,652,000	13.00	20.00	140.00	550.00	
1938 . . . . . (8,045)	9,480,045	10.00	14.00	65.00	275.00	550.00
1938S	2,832,000	8.00	12.00	65.00	350.00	
1939 . . . . . (8,795)	33,548,795	2.25	6.00	23.00	125.00	350.00
1939D	7,092,000	6.00	8.00	35.00	150.00	
1939S	2,628,000	9.00	12.00	70.00	325.00	
1940 . . . . (11,246)	35,715,246	2.00	6.00	20.00	50.00	275.00
1940D	2,797,600	10.00	14.00	85.00	350.00	
1940S	8,244,000	2.00	6.00	25.00	100.00	
1941 . . . . (15,287)	79,047,287	2.00	4.00	10.00	50.00	250.00
1941D	16,714,800	2.00	5.00	25.00	60.00	
1941S*	16,080,000	2.00	5.00	23.00	85.00	
1942 . . . . (21,123)	102,117,123	2.00	4.00	10.00	50.00	250.00
1942D	17,487,200	2.00	5.00	15.00	60.00	
1942S	19,384,000	2.00	7.00	90.00	250.00	
1943	99,700,000	2.00	4.00	8.00	35.00	
1943D	16,095,600	2.00	5.00	18.00	40.00	
1943S	21,700,000	2.00	6.00	50.00	135.00	
1943S Doubled die obverse . .		165.00	200.00	600.00	1,200	
1944	104,956,000	2.00	2.50	6.00	18.00	
1944D	14,600,800	2.00	2.50	12.00	35.00	
1944S	12,560,000	2.00	2.50	13.00	30.00	
1945	74,372,000	2.00	2.50	5.00	20.00	
1945D	12,341,600	2.00	2.50	10.00	35.00	
1945S	17,004,001	2.00	2.50	8.00	18.00	
1946	53,436,000	2.00	2.50	6.00	12.00	
1946D	9,072,800	2.00	2.50	7.00	11.00	
1946S	4,204,000	2.00	2.50	8.00	22.00	
1947	22,556,000	2.00	2.50	7.00	10.00	
1947D	15,338,400	2.00	2.50	8.00	12.00	
1947S	5,532,000	2.00	2.50	6.00	11.00	
1948	35,196,000	2.00	2.50	4.00	8.00	
1948D	16,766,800	2.00	2.50	6.00	10.00	
1948S	15,960,000	2.00	2.50	6.00	12.00	
1949	9,312,000	2.00	2.50	27.50	40.00	
1949D	10,068,400	2.00	2.50	10.00	22.00	
1950 . . . . (51,386)	24,971,512	2.00	2.50	5.00	9.00	125.00
1950D		2.00	2.50	5.00	10.00	
1950D, D over S	21,075,600	60.00	150.00	350.00	500.00	

*Large and small mint mark varieties, see page 65.

[141]

QUARTER DOLLARS

	Quan. Minted	VF-20	EF-40	MS-63	MS-65	Proof-65
1950S.........	} 10,284,004	$2.00	$2.50	$8.00	$14.00	
1950S, S over D		60.00	165.00	475.00	600.00	
1951 .... (57,500)	43,505,602	2.00	2.25	4.00	6.00	$85.00
1951D............	35,354,800	2.00	2.25	4.00	6.50	
1951S.............	9,048,000	2.00	2.25	9.00	16.00	
1952 .... (81,980)	38,862,073	2.00	2.25	4.00	7.00	55.00
1952D............	49,795,200	2.00	2.25	5.00	7.50	
1952S............	13,707,800	2.00	2.25	7.00	12.00	
1953 ... (128,800)	18,664,920	2.00	2.25	5.00	7.50	35.00
1953D............	56,112,400	2.00	2.25	3.75	5.00	
1953S............	14,016,000	2.00	2.25	5.00	7.50	
1954 ... (233,300)	54,645,503	2.00	2.25	3.50	5.00	17.00
1954D............	42,305,500	2.00	2.25	3.50	5.00	
1954S............	11,834,722	2.00	2.25	3.75	5.50	
1955 ... (378,200)	18,558,381	2.00	2.25	3.50	5.25	13.00
1955D............	3,182,400	2.00	2.25	4.00	7.00	
1956 ... (669,384)	44,813,384	2.00	2.25	2.75	3.25	6.00
1956D............	32,334,500	2.00	2.25	2.75	3.25	
1957 .. (1,247,952)	47,779,952	2.00	2.25	2.75	3.25	5.00
1957D............	77,924,160	2.00	2.25	2.75	3.25	
1958 ... (875,652)	7,235,652	2.00	2.25	2.75	5.50	7.00
1958D............	78,124,900	2.00	2.25	2.75	3.25	
1959 .. (1,149,291)	25,533,291	2.00	2.25	2.75	3.25	6.00
1959D............	62,054,232	2.00	2.25	2.75	3.25	
1960 .. (1,691,602)	30,855,602	2.00	2.25	2.75	3.25	5.00
1960D............	63,000,324	2.00	2.25	2.75	3.25	
1961 .. (3,028,244)	40,064,244	2.00	2.25	2.75	3.25	5.00
1961D............	83,656,928	2.00	2.25	2.75	3.25	
1962 .. (3,218,019)	39,374,019	2.00	2.25	2.75	3.25	5.00
1962D............	127,554,756	2.00	2.25	2.75	3.25	
1963 .. (3,075,645)	77,391,645	2.00	2.25	2.75	3.25	5.00
1963D............	135,288,184	2.00	2.25	2.75	3.25	
1964 .. (3,950,762)	564,341,347	2.00	2.25	2.75	3.25	5.00
1964D............	704,135,528	2.00	2.25	2.75	3.25	

Note: Prices in italic are based on silver bullion value.

Clad Coinage — 1965 to Date

Proof coins from 1937 through 1972 were made from special dies with high relief and minor detail differences. Some of the circulation coins of 1956-1964 and 1969D-1972D were also made from reverse dies with these same features. A variety of the 1964D quarter occurs with the modified reverse normally found only on the clad coins.

Weight 5.67 grams; composition: outer layers of copper-nickel (.750 copper, .250 nickel) bonded to inner core of pure copper; diameter 24.3 mm; reeded edge.

Starting in 1968 mint mark is on obverse at right of ribbon.

QUARTER DOLLARS

	Quan. Minted	MS-65	Proof-65		Quan. Minted	MS-65	Proof-65
1965	1,819,717,540	$ .75		1971	109,284,000	$ .50	
1966	821,101,500	.75		1971D	258,634,428	.50	
1967	1,524,031,848	.75		1971S Proof	(3,220,733)		$1.00
1968	220,731,500	.75		1972	215,048,000	.50	
1968D	101,534,000	1.00		1972D	311,067,732	.50	
1968S Proof	(3,041,506)		$1.00	1972S Proof	(3,260,996)		1.00
1969	176,212,000	.50		1973	346,924,000	.50	
1969D	114,372,000	1.00		1973D	232,977,400	.50	
1969S Proof	(2,934,631)		1.00	1973S Proof	(2,760,339)		1.00
1970	136,420,000	.50		1974	801,456,000	.50	
1970D	417,341,364	.50		1974D	353,160,300	.50	
1970S Proof	(2,632,810)		1.00	1974S Proof	(2,612,568)		1.00

BICENTENNIAL COINAGE DATED 1776-1976

In October of 1973, the Treasury announced an open contest for the selection of suitable designs for the Bicentennial reverses of the quarter, half dollar and dollar, with $5,000 to be awarded to each winner. Twelve semifinalists were chosen, and from these the symbolic entry of Jack L. Ahr was selected for the quarter reverse. It features a Colonial drummer facing left, with a victory torch encircled by thirteen stars at the upper left. Except for a dual dating, 1776-1976, the obverse remained unchanged. Only pieces with this dual dating were coined during 1975 and 1976. They were struck for general circulation and included in all the Mint's offerings of proof and uncirculated sets.

Designers John Flanagan and Jack L. Ahr. Silver issue: weight 5.75 grams; composition: outer layers of .800 silver, .200 copper bonded to inner core of .209 silver, .791 copper. Copper-nickel issue: weight 5.67 grams; composition: outer layers of .750 copper, .250 nickel bonded to inner core of pure copper. Diameter 24.3 mm; reeded edge. Net weight of silver issues: .0739 oz. pure silver.

	Quan. Minted	MS 65	Proof 65
1776-1976 Copper-nickel clad	809,784,016	$ .50	
1776-1976D Copper-nickel clad	860,118,839	.50	
1776-1976S Copper-nickel clad	(7,059,099)		$1.75
1776-1976S Silver clad	*11,000,000	2.50	
1776-1976S Silver clad	(*4,000,000)		4.00

*Approximate mintage.

Eagle Reverse Resumed (Dies slightly modified to lower relief)

	Quan. Minted	MS-65	Proof-65		Quan. Minted	MS-60	Proof-65
1977	468,556,000	$ .50		1979S Proof	(3,677,175)		
1977D	256,524,978	.50		Filled S			$1.00
1977S Proof	(3,251,152)		$1.00	Clear S			3.00
1978	521,452,000	.50		1980P	635,832,000	$ .50	
1978D	287,373,152	.50		1980D	518,327,487	.50	
1978S Proof	(3,127,781)		1.00	1980S Proof	(3,554,806)		1.00
1979	515,708,000	.50		1981P	601,716,000	.50	
1979D	489,789,780	.50		1981D	575,722,833	.50	

QUARTER DOLLARS

	Quan. Minted	MS-65	Proof-65
1981S Proof..	(4,063,083)		$1.00
1982P.......	500,931,000	$ .75	
1982D	480,042,788	.50	
1982S Proof..	(3,857,479)		1.00
1983P.......	673,535,000	.50	
1983D	617,806,446	.50	
1983S Proof..	(3,279,126)		1.25
1984P.......	676,545,000	.50	
1984D	546,483,064	.50	
1984S Proof..	(3,065,110)		1.75
1985P.......	775,818,962	.50	
1985D	519,962,888	.50	
1985S Proof..	(3,362,821)		2.00
1986P.......	551,199,333	.50	
1986D	504,298,660	$.50	
1986S Proof..	(3,010,497)		$1.25
1987P.......	582,499,481	.50	
1987D	655,594,696	.50	
1987S Proof..	(3,792,233)		1.10
1988P.......	562,052,000	.50	
1988D	596,810,688	.50	
1988S Proof...........			1.00
1989P.......	512,868,000	.50	
1989D	896,535,597	.50	
1989S Proof...........			1.00
1990P................		.50	
1990D		.50	
1990S Proof...........			1.00

BIBLIOGRAPHY

Browning, A. W. *The Early Quarter Dollars of the United States 1796-1838.* New York, 1925.
Cline, J. H. *Standing Liberty Quarters.* 1976.
Duphorne, R. *The Early Quarter Dollars of The United States.* 1975.
Haseltine, J. W. *Type Table of United States Dollars, Half Dollars and Quarter Dollars.* Philadelphia, 1881 (reprinted 1927, 1968).
Kelman, Keith N. *Standing Liberty Quarters,* N.H., 1976.

HALF DOLLARS — 1794 to Date

The half dollar, authorized by the Act of April 2, 1792, was not minted until December, 1794. The early types of this series have been extensively collected by die varieties, of which many exist for most dates. Valuations given below are in each case for the most common variety, scarcer ones as listed by Beistle and Overton (see bibliography) generally command higher prices.

The weight of the half dollar was 208 grains and its fineness .8924 when first issued. This standard was not changed until 1837 when the law of January 18, 1837 specified 206¼ grains, .900 fine. This fineness continued in use until 1965.

Arrows at the date in 1853 indicate the reduction of weight to 192 grains, in conformity with the Act of February 21, 1853. During that year only, rays were added to the field on the reverse side. Arrows remained in 1854 and 1855.

The 1866 proof quarter, half and dollar without motto are not mentioned in the Director's Report, and were not issued for circulation.

In 1873 the weight was raised by law to 192.9 grains and arrows were again placed at the date, to be removed in 1875.

+ or − indicates change from previous year	TYPE COIN VALUES									
	G-4	F-12	EF-40	AU-50	MS-60	MS-63	MS-65	PF-60	PF-63	PF-65
Flowing Hair 1794-1795	425.00	700.00	2,800+	5,500+	11,000	32,000+	80,000+			
Drpd Bust, SE 1796-1797	10,000	17,000+	40,000+	47,000						
Drpd Bust, HE 1801-1807	70.00	150.00	700.00	2,000+	4,750	11,000	50,000+			
Cap Bust Type 1807-1836	27.00	37.50	100.00	300.00+	900.00+	2,500+	12,000+			
Cap Bust, RE 1836-1839	35.00	45.00	150.00	400.00	1,100+	3,500+	32,000+			
Lib Seated-NM 1839-1866	14.00	27.00	70.00	140.00	450.00	1,800+	13,500+	500.00−	1,500+	11,000+
Lib. Seat-A&R 1853	15.00	38.00	225.00	500.00	2,000	5,000	31,000+			
Lib. Seat-Arr. 1854-1855	14.00	35.00	95.00	250.00	850.00	2,200+	15,000+			
Lib. Seated-WM 1866-1891	12.00	30.00	60.00	125.00	400.00	1,100	6,500+	500.00	1,300+	6,000
Lib. Seat-Arr. 1873-1874	20.00	38.00	175.00	400.00	900.00	4,000+	25,000+	850.00	2,300+	18,500+
Barber 1892-1915	5.50	23.00	130.00	250.00	500.00−	1,300	5,500	550.00	1,500−	6,500
Lib Walking 1916-1947	4.50	4.50	9.00	16.00	50.00	135.00	400.00	350.00	600.00	1,350+
Franklin 1948-1963	4.50	4.50	4.50	5.00	6.00	8.00	100.00+	12.00	18.00	40.00

FLOWING HAIR TYPE 1794-1795

Designer Robert Scot; weight 13.48 grams; composition: .8924 silver, .1076 copper; approx. diameter 32.5 mm; edge: FIFTY CENTS OR HALF A DOLLAR with decorations between words.

AG-3 ABOUT GOOD—*Clear enough to identify.*

G-4 GOOD—*Date and letters sufficient to be readable. Main devices outlined, but lack details.*

VG-8 VERY GOOD—*Major details discernible. Letters well formed but worn.*

F-12 FINE—*Hair ends distinguishable. Top hairlines show, but otherwise worn smooth.*

VF-20 VERY FINE—*Hair in center shows some detail. Other details more bold.*

EF-40 EXTREMELY FINE—*Hair above head and down neck detailed, with slight wear.*

2 Leaves under Wings   **3 Leaves under Wings**

	Quan. Minted	AG-3	G-4	VG-8	F-12	VF-20	EF-40
1794	23,464	$475.00	$1,000	$1,600	$2,750	$4,000	$7,000
1795 All kinds	299,680	250.00	425.00	500.00	700.00	1,400	2,800
1795 Recut date		250.00	450.00	550.00	725.00	1,500	3,000
1795 3 leaves under each wing.		325.00	675.00	1,100	1,800	3,400	6,500

Varieties of 1795 are known with final S in STATES over D, with A in STATES over E, and with Y in LIBERTY over a star.

HALF DOLLARS
DRAPED BUST TYPE, SMALL EAGLE REVERSE 1796-1797

Designer Robert Scot; weight 13.48 grams; composition: .8924 silver, .1076 copper; approx. diameter 32.5 mm; edge: FIFTY CENTS OR HALF A DOLLAR with decorations between words.

AG-3 ABOUT GOOD—*Clear enough to identify.*

G-4 GOOD—*Date and letters sufficient to be readable. Main devices outlined, but lack details.*

VG-8 VERY GOOD—*Major details discernible. Letters well formed but worn.*

F-15 FINE—*Hair ends distinguishable. Top hairlines show, but otherwise worn smooth.*

VF-20 VERY FINE—*Right side of drapery slightly worn. Left side to curls is smooth.*

EF-40 EXTREMELY FINE—*All lines in drapery on bust will show distinctly around to hair curls.*

1796, 15 Stars　　　　　　　　　　　　　　**1796, 16 Stars**

	Quan. Minted	AG-3	G-4	VG-8	F-12	VF-20	EF-40
1796, 15 stars.........	⎫	$6,200	$10,000	$12,500	$17,000	$28,000	$40,000
1796, 16 stars.........	⎬ 3,918	6,200	10,000	12,500	17,000	28,000	40,000
1797, 15 stars........	⎭	6,200	10,000	12,500	17,000	28,000	40,000

DRAPED BUST TYPE, HERALDIC EAGLE REVERSE
1801-1807

	Quan. Minted	G-4	VG-8	F-12	VF-20	EF-40	MS-60
1801	30,289	$150.00	$250.00	$450.00	$850.00	$1,400	$9,500
1802	29,890	125.00	225.00	375.00	650.00	1,100	8,500
1803 Small 3	⎫ 188,234	115.00	160.00	250.00	575.00	1,000	7,000
1803 Large 3	⎭	90.00	120.00	200.00	475.00	850.00	6,500

HALF DOLLARS

1805, 5 over 4

1806, 6 over 5

	Quan. Minted	G-4	VG-8	F-12	VF-20	EF-40	MS-60
1805, 5 over 4 .... } 211,722		$100.00	$130.00	$225.00	$550.00	$1,200	$6,500
1805 Normal date.....		80.00	95.00	150.00	400.00	725.00	5,500

Knobbed Top 6, Small Stars

Branch Stem through Claw

Pointed Top 6

Branch Stem Not through Claw

	G-4	VG-8	F-12	VF-20	EF-40	MS-60
1806 All kinds......... 839,576						
1806, 6 over 5.................	85.00	100.00	185.00	425.00	800.00	5,500
1806, 6 over inverted 6........	90.00	115.00	200.00	500.00	900.00	6,000
1806 Knobbed 6, large stars (traces of overdate)	70.00	85.00	150.00	400.00	700.00	4,750
1806 Knobbed 6, small stars ...	70.00	85.00	150.00	400.00	700.00	4,750
1806 Knobbed 6, stem not through claw	Rare					
1806 Pointed 6, stem through claw*	70.00	85.00	150.00	400.00	700.00	4,750
1806 Pointed 6, stem not through claw	70.00	85.00	150.00	400.00	700.00	4,750
1807 301,076	70.00	85.00	150.00	400.00	700.00	4,750

*One variety shows E in STATES over A.

CAPPED BUST TYPE, Lettered Edge 1807-1836

John Reich designed this Capped Head concept of Liberty. The head of Liberty facing left was used on all U.S. coin denominations for the next thirty years. Reich was the first artist to consistently include the denomination on our gold and silver coins. He was from Germany and a bondman freed from servitude by a mint official.

Designer John Reich; weight 13.48 grams; composition: .8924 silver, .1076 copper; approx. diameter 32.5 mm; edge varieties, 1807-1814: FIFTY CENTS OR HALF A DOLLAR; 1814-1831: star added between DOLLAR and FIFTY; 1832-1836: vertical lines added between words.

G-4 GOOD—*Date and letters readable. Bust worn smooth with outline distinct.*

VG-8 VERY GOOD—*LIBERTY visible but faint. Legends distinguishable. Clasp at shoulder visible. Curl above it nearly smooth.*

F-12 FINE—*Clasp and adjacent curl clearly outlined with slight details.*

VF-20 VERY FINE—*Clasp at shoulder clear. Curl has wear only on highest point. Hair over brow distinguishable.*

EF-40 EXTREMELY FINE—*Clasp and adjacent curl fairly sharp. Brow and hair above distinct. Curls well defined.*

MS-60 UNCIRCULATED—*No trace of wear. Light blemishes.*

[147]

HALF DOLLARS
First style (Variety 1) 1807-1808

1807 Small Stars   1807 Large Stars   1807, 50 over 20

	Quan. Minted	G-4	VG-8	F-12	VF-20	EF-40	MS-60
1807 Small stars...		$45.00	$60.00	$125.00	$250.00	$550.00	$2,500
1807 Large stars...	750,500	40.00	50.00	100.00	175.00	400.00	2,200
1807 Same, 50 over 20....		35.00	45.00	75.00	150.00	300.00	2,300
1808, 8 over 7.......	1,368,600	35.00	45.00	70.00	110.00	200.00	1,500
1808		30.00	42.50	50.00	80.00	150.00	1,200

Remodeled Portrait and Eagle 1809-1834

1809 Experimental edge,
xxxx between words.

1809 Experimental edge,
IIIII between words.

HALF DOLLARS

	Quan. Minted	G-4	VG-8	F-12	VF-20	EF-40	MS-60
1809 Normal	} 1,405,810	$30.00	$38.00	$45.00	$75.00	$125.00	$1,200
1809 xxxx edge.....		30.00	40.00	47.50	80.00	150.00	1,300
1809 ıııııı edge....		30.00	38.00	45.00	75.00	125.00	1,200
1810	1,276,276	27.00	33.00	40.00	65.00	125.00	1,200

"Punctuated" Date 18.11

1811 Small 8

1811 Large 8

1812, 2 over 1, Small 8

1812, 2 over 1, Large 8

1811 (18.11)							
11 over 10....	} 1,203,644	30.00	35.00	60.00	100.00	200.00	1,100
1811 Small 8		27.00	32.00	37.50	60.00	135.00	1,100
1811 Large 8		27.00	32.00	37.50	60.00	135.00	1,000
1812, 2 over 1							
small 8.......	} 1,628,059	30.00	35.00	60.00	100.00	200.00	1,000
1812, 2 over 1							
large 8.......		85.00	125.00	250.00	400.00	850.00	——
1812 Normal		27.00	32.00	37.50	60.00	125.00	950.00

1813, 50 C. over UNI

1814, 4 over 3

1814 E over A in STATES

1813	} 1,241,903	27.00	32.00	37.50	60.00	110.00	950.00
1813, 50C over							
UNI		30.00	40.00	65.00	100.00	200.00	1,200
1814, 4 over 3......		27.00	35.00	45.00	70.00	125.00	950.00
1814 E over A in							
STATES	} 1,039,075	27.00	32.00	37.50	75.00	150.00	1,000
1814 Normal		27.00	32.00	37.50	75.00	150.00	950.00

HALF DOLLARS

1817, 7 over 3	1817, 7 over 4	1817 Punctuated Date

	Quan. Minted	G-4	VG-8	F-12	VF-20	EF-40	MS-60
1815, 5 over 2	47,150	$650.00	$850.00	$1,300	$1,750	$2,200	$6,000
1817, 7 over 3		50.00	75.00	200.00	300.00	650.00	1,900
1817, 7 over 4		V. Rare		4,500	9,500	——	
1817 dated 181.7	1,215,567	27.00	35.00	50.00	75.00	150.00	1,000
1817 Normal		27.00	32.00	37.50	60.00	125.00	900.00

1818, 1st 8 Small, 2nd 8 over 7

1819 Small 9 over 8

1818, 1st 8 Large, 2nd 8 over 7

1819 Large 9 over 8

1818, 8 over 7 small 8	1,960,322	27.00	32.00	37.50	60.00	125.00	1,100
1818, 8 over 7 large 8		27.00	32.00	37.50	60.00	125.00	1,000
1818 Normal		27.00	32.00	37.50	60.00	125.00	900.00
1819 Sm. 9 over 8	2,208,000	27.00	32.00	37.50	60.00	110.00	900.00
1819 Lg. 9 over 8		27.00	32.00	37.50	60.00	110.00	900.00
1819 Normal		27.00	32.00	37.50	60.00	110.00	900.00

1820, 20 over 19
Square Base 2

1820, 20 over 19
Curl Base 2

Curl Base, No Knob 2,
Small Date

1820 All kinds	751,122						
1820 20 over 19 square 2		27.00	32.00	37.50	60.00	100.00	1,000
1820, 20 over 19 curl 2		27.00	32.00	37.50	60.00	100.00	1,000
1820 Curl base 2 small date		27.00	32.00	37.50	60.00	100.00	1,000

HALF DOLLARS

Square Base, Knob 2,   **Square Base, No Knob 2,**   **1822, 2 over 1**
Large Date   **Large Date**

	Quan. Minted	G-4	VG-8	F-12	VF-20	EF-40	MS-60
1820 Sq. base knob 2, large date.....		$27.00	$32.00	$37.50	$60.00	$100.00	$1,000
1820 Sq. base no knob 2, lg. date		27.00	32.00	37.50	60.00	100.00	1,000
1821	1,305,797	27.00	32.00	37.50	60.00	100.00	900.00
1822, 2 over 1......	} 1,559,573	45.00	60.00	90.00	110.00	180.00	1,350
1822		27.00	32.00	37.50	60.00	100.00	900.00

1823 Broken 3   **1823 Patched 3**   **1823 Ugly 3**

1823 Broken 3.....		42.00	55.00	80.00	100.00	175.00	1,000
1823 Patched 3....	} 1,694,200	42.00	55.00	80.00	100.00	175.00	1,000
1823 Ugly 3.......		27.00	32.00	37.50	60.00	100.00	900.00
1823 Normal......		27.00	32.00	37.50	60.00	100.00	900.00

"Various Dates"   **1824, 4 over 1**   **1824, 4 over 4**   **1824, 4 over 4**
(probably 4 over
2 over 0)

1824 over various dates		27.00	32.00	37.50	60.00	100.00	900.00
1824, 4 over 1......	} 3,504,954	27.00	32.00	37.50	60.00	100.00	900.00
1824, 4 over 4 (2 var.).......		27.00	32.00	37.50	60.00	100.00	1,000
1824 Normal......		27.00	32.00	37.50	60.00	100.00	900.00
1825	2,943,166	27.00	32.00	37.50	60.00	100.00	900.00
1826	4,004,180	27.00	32.00	37.50	60.00	100.00	900.00
1827, 7 over 6......		27.00	32.00	37.50	60.00	100.00	900.00
1827 Sq. base 2....	} 5,493,400	27.00	32.00	37.50	60.00	100.00	900.00
1827 Curl base 2...		27.00	32.00	37.50	60.00	100.00	900.00

HALF DOLLARS

1828 Curl Base, Knob 2

1828 Square Base 2,
Large 8's

1828 Square Base 2,
Small 8's

1828 Large Letters

1828 Small Letters

	Quan. Minted	G-4	VG-8	F-12	VF-20	EF-40	MS-60
1828 All kinds....	3,075,200						
1828 Curl base no knob 2		$27.00	$32.00	$37.50	$60.00	$100.00	$900.00
1828 Curl base knob 2		35.00	45.00	60.00	85.00	125.00	1,000
1828 Sq. base 2, lg. 8's		27.00	32.00	37.50	60.00	100.00	900.00
1828 Sq. base 2, sm. 8's, lg. let.		27.00	32.00	37.50	60.00	100.00	900.00
1828 Sq. base 2, sm. 8's & let ..		27.00	35.00	40.00	75.00	125.00	1,000
1829, 9 over 7.....	3,712,156	27.00	32.00	37.50	60.00	100.00	900.00
1829		27.00	32.00	37.50	60.00	100.00	900.00

1830 Small 0

1832 Large Letters Reverse

Raised segment lines to right, 1830.

Raised segment lines to left, 1830-1831.

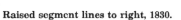

Adopted edge 1830-1836.

1830 Small 0	4,764,800	27.00	32.00	37.50	60.00	100.00	900.00
1830 Large 0		27.00	32.00	37.50	60.00	100.00	900.00
1831	5,873,660	27.00	32.00	37.50	60.00	100.00	900.00
1832 Normal	4,797,000	27.00	32.00	37.50	60.00	100.00	900.00
1832 Large letters		27.00	32.00	37.50	60.00	100.00	900.00
1833	5,206,000	27.00	32.00	37.50	60.00	100.00	900.00

HALF DOLLARS

| 1834 Large Date | 1834 Small Date |

1834 Lg. Letters Reverse   1834 Sm. Letters Reverse   1836, 50 over 00

Portrait Modified Slightly 1834-1836

	Quan. Minted	G-4	VG-8	F-12	VF-20	EF-40	MS-60
1834 Lg. date & let		$27.00	$32.00	$37.50	$60.00	$100.00	$900.00
1834 Large date, small letters	6,412,004	27.00	32.00	37.50	60.00	100.00	900.00
1834 Small date, stars, letters		27.00	32.00	37.50	60.00	100.00	900.00
1835	5,352,006	27.00	32.00	37.50	60.00	100.00	900.00
1836	6,545,000	27.00	32.00	37.50	60.00	100.00	900.00
1836, 50 over 00...		35.00	50.00	65.00	100.00	175.00	1,250

Variety 2 — Reeded Edge, Reverse "50 CENTS" 1836-1837

Designer Christian Gobrecht; weight 13.36 grams; composition: .900 silver, .100 copper; diameter 30 mm; reeded edge; mints: Philadelphia, New Orleans.

G-4 GOOD—*LIBERTY discernible on headband.*
VG-8 VERY GOOD—*Minimum of 3 letters in LIBERTY must be clear.*
F-12 FINE—*LIBERTY complete.*
VF-20 VERY FINE—*LIBERTY is sharp. Shoulder clasp is clear.*
EF-40 EXTREMELY FINE—*LIBERTY sharp and strong. Hair details show.*
MS-60 UNCIRCULATED—*No trace of wear. Light blemishes.*

	Quan. Minted	G-4	VG-8	F-12	VF-20	EF-40	MS-60
1836	1,200	$350.00	$475.00	$600.00	$1,100	$2,000	$5,500
1837	3,629,820	35.00	40.00	45.00	70.00	150.00	1,100

HALF DOLLARS

Variety 3 — Reeded Edge, Reverse "HALF DOL." 1838-1839

The 1838O was the first branch mint half dollar, though not mentioned in the Director's report. The New Orleans chief coiner stated that only 20 were struck. In 1838-39 the mint mark appears on the obverse; thereafter it is on the reverse through 1915.

	Quan. Minted	G-4	VG-8	F-12	VF-20	EF-40	MS-60
1838	3,546,000	$40.00	$45.00	$50.00	$85.00	$175.00	$1,100
1838O	(20)						50,000
1839	1,392,976	40.00	45.00	50.00	85.00	175.00	1,100
1839 Small letters reverse					——	——	
1839O	178,976	100.00	150.00	225.00	375.00	650.00	3,750

LIBERTY SEATED TYPE 1839-1891

Variety 1 — No Motto Above Eagle 1839-1853

Designer Christian Gobrecht; weight 13.36 grams; composition: .900 silver, .100 copper; diameter 30.6 mm; reeded edge; mints: Philadelphia, New Orleans.

G-4 GOOD—*Scant rim. LIBERTY on shield worn off. Date and letters readable.*

VG-8 VERY GOOD—*Rim fairly defined. At least 3 letters in LIBERTY are evident.*

F-12 FINE—*LIBERTY complete, but weak.*

VF-20 VERY FINE—*LIBERTY mostly sharp.*

EF-40 EXTREMELY FINE—*LIBERTY entirely sharp. Scroll edges and clasp distinct.*

MS-60 UNCIRCULATED—*No trace of wear. Light blemishes.*

1839 No drapery from elbow	30.00	50.00	80.00	225.00	650.00	6,250

HALF DOLLARS

Modified obverse, drapery from elbow. Small letters in legend 1839-1842.

		Drapery from Elbow Starting 1839	Small Letters in Legend 1839-41		1840 (only) with Medium Letters and Large Eagle		
	Quan. Minted	G-4	VG-8	F-12	VF-20	EF-40	MS-60
1839	1,972,400	$22.50	$27.50	$35.00	$50.00	$90.00	$575.00
1840 Sm. letters ...	1,435,008	20.00	30.00	40.00	75.00	125.00	600.00
1840 Med. letters*	} 855,100	35.00	45.00	75.00	150.00	300.00	——
1840O		20.00	27.50	35.00	50.00	90.00	650.00
1841	310,000	23.00	30.00	60.00	90.00	175.00	1,000
1841O	401,000	17.00	25.00	35.00	50.00	90.00	850.00
1842O Small date	203,000	350.00	700.00	1,000	2,000	3,500	——

*Struck at the New Orleans Mint from a reverse die of the previous style without mint mark.

Modified reverse with large letters in legend 1842-1853.

	Small Date	Medium Date		Large Letter Reverse		
1842 Sm. date ...... } 2,012,764	20.00	30.00	40.00	60.00	125.00	900.00
1842 Med. date	16.00	26.00	35.00	50.00	100.00	700.00
1842O Med. date....... 754,000	16.00	23.00	30.00	45.00	80.00	575.00
1843 3,844,000	16.00	23.00	30.00	42.00	75.00	550.00
1843O............... 2,268,000	16.00	23.00	30.00	42.00	75.00	550.00
1844 1,766,000	16.00	23.00	30.00	42.00	75.00	550.00
1844O............. } 2,005,000	16.00	23.00	30.00	42.00	75.00	550.00
1844O Double date..	30.00	45.00	60.00	125.00	325.00	1,000
1845 589,000	18.00	23.00	30.00	42.00	75.00	575.00
1845O............. } 2,094,000	16.00	23.00	30.00	42.00	75.00	600.00
1845O No drapery†	30.00	45.00	60.00	80.00	200.00	750.00

†Drapery missing because of excessive die polishing

HALF DOLLARS

In 1846 the date size was again enlarged. The 1846 medium date is approximately the size of the 1842 medium date shown. Tall date is similar to 1853.

	Quan. Minted	G-4	VG-8	F-12	VF-20	EF-40	MS-60
1846 Med. dt. All	2,210,000	$16.00	$23.00	$30.00	$42.00	$75.00	$550.00
1846 Tall date		18.00	23.00	30.00	42.00	75.00	600.00
1846 over horizontal 6 (error)..		40.00	60.00	90.00	150.00	300.00	1,200
1846O Med. date...	2,304,000	18.00	25.00	35.00	45.00	80.00	600.00
1846O Tall date....		45.00	70.00	100.00	225.00	375.00	1,400
1847, 7 over 6		2,000	3,000	4,500	8,000	——	——
1847 Normal date	1,156,000	16.00	23.00	30.00	40.00	75.00	550.00
1847O.............	2,584,000	16.00	23.00	30.00	40.00	75.00	550.00
1848.................	580,000	30.00	40.00	60.00	90.00	150.00	900.00
1848O.............	3,180,000	18.00	23.00	30.00	40.00	75.00	600.00
1849	1,252,000	18.00	23.00	30.00	40.00	75.00	600.00
1849O.............	2,310,000	18.00	23.00	30.00	40.00	75.00	600.00
1850	227,000	50.00	75.00	100.00	175.00	300.00	1,100
1850O.............	2,456,000	18.00	23.00	30.00	40.00	75.00	600.00
1851	200,750	50.00	80.00	125.00	200.00	325.00	1,250
1851O.............	402,000	18.00	23.00	30.00	40.00	75.00	600.00
1852	77,130	80.00	135.00	225.00	375.00	525.00	1,500
1852O.............	144,000	40.00	60.00	95.00	150.00	250.00	1,100
1853O.............		——		24,000	40,000		

Variety 2 — Arrows at Date, Rays Around Eagle 1853 Only

Weight 12.44 grams; composition: .900 silver, .100 copper; diameter 30.6 mm; reeded edge; mints: Philadelphia, New Orleans, San Francisco.

1853	3,532,708	15.00	20.00	38.00	85.00	225.00	2,000
1853O All kinds	1,328,000	16.00	22.00	42.00	100.00	250.00	2,300

Variety 3 — Arrows at Date, No Rays 1854-1855

1854	2,982,000	14.00	19.00	35.00	45.00	90.00	850.00
1854O.............	5,240,000	14.00	19.00	35.00	45.00	90.00	850.00
1855 over 1854			75.00	125.00	275.00	500.00	1,400
1855 Normal date	759,500	14.00	19.00	35.00	45.00	90.00	850.00
1855O.............	3,688,000	14.00	19.00	35.00	45.00	90.00	850.00
1855S..............	129,950	275.00	375.00	600.00	1,000	2,500	——

Variety 1 Design Resumed 1856-1866

1856	938,000	14.00	19.00	27.00	35.00	65.00	450.00
1856O.............	2,658,000	14.00	19.00	27.00	35.00	65.00	450.00
1856S..............	211,000	22.00	25.00	35.00	85.00	200.00	1,300
1857	1,988,000	14.00	19.00	27.00	35.00	65.00	450.00
1857O.............	818,000	18.00	22.00	30.00	40.00	75.00	650.00
1857S..............	158,000	25.00	33.00	45.00	90.00	250.00	1,400

HALF DOLLARS

	Quan. Minted	G-4	VG-8	F-12	VF-20	EF-40	MS-60	Proof-63
1858	4,226,000	$14.00	$19.00	$27.00	$35.00	$65.00	$450.00	$2,750
1858O	7,294,000	14.00	19.00	27.00	35.00	65.00	450.00	
1858S	476,000	21.00	25.00	30.00	55.00	125.00	900.00	
1859 .. (800)	748,000	16.00	19.00	27.00	35.00	75.00	500.00	1,800
1859O	2,834,000	14.00	19.00	27.00	35.00	65.00	450.00	
1859S	566,000	21.00	25.00	30.00	55.00	125.00	900.00	
1860 (1,000)	303,700	21.00	25.00	30.00	45.00	90.00	850.00	1,500
1860O	1,290,000	14.00	19.00	27.00	35.00	65.00	450.00	
1860S	472,000	21.00	24.00	30.00	40.00	75.00	625.00	
1861 (1,000)	2,888,400	14.00	19.00	27.00	35.00	65.00	450.00	1,500
1861O	2,532,633	14.00	19.00	27.00	35.00	65.00	450.00	

The 1861O quantity includes 330,000 struck under the United States government; 1,240,000 for the State of Louisiana after it seceded from the Union; and 962,633 after Louisiana joined the Confederate States of America. As all these 1861O coins were struck from U.S. dies. It is impossible to distinguish one from another. They should not be confused with the very rare Confederate half dollar of 1861 (see pgs. 273-274) which has a distinctive reverse.

	Quan. Minted	G-4	VG-8	F-12	VF-20	EF-40	MS-60	Proof-63
1861S	939,500	14.00	19.00	27.00	35.00	65.00	450.00	
1862 .. (550)	253,550	22.50	30.00	35.00	70.00	100.00	800.00	1,500
1862S	1,352,000	14.00	19.00	27.00	35.00	65.00	450.00	
1863 .. (460)	503,660	21.00	24.00	30.00	45.00	75.00	700.00	1,500
1863S	916,000	14.00	19.00	27.00	35.00	65.00	450.00	
1864 .. (470)	379,570	21.00	24.00	30.00	45.00	75.00	700.00	1,500
1864S	658,000	14.00	19.00	27.00	35.00	70.00	450.00	
1865 .. (500)	511,900	21.00	24.00	30.00	45.00	75.00	700.00	1,500
1865S	675,000	14.00	19.00	27.00	35.00	70.00	550.00	
1866S No motto	60,000	45.00	75.00	135.00	225.00	350.00	4,500	
1866		*(Unique*—see similar quarter and dollar)						——

**Variety 4 —
Motto "In God We Trust"
Added Above Eagle
1866-1873**

	Quan. Minted	G-4	VG-8	F-12	VF-20	EF-40	MS-60	Proof-63
1866 .. (725)	745,625	13.00	18.00	30.00	40.00	60.00	425.00	1,400
1866S	994,000	13.00	18.00	30.00	40.00	60.00	450.00	
1867 .. (625)	449,925	17.00	20.00	35.00	50.00	80.00	700.00	1,400
1867S	1,196,000	13.00	18.00	30.00	40.00	60.00	450.00	
1868 .. (600)	418,200	16.00	20.00	35.00	45.00	75.00	475.00	1,400
1868S	1,160,000	13.00	18.00	30.00	40.00	60.00	450.00	
1869 .. (600)	795,900	13.00	18.00	30.00	40.00	60.00	425.00	1,400
1869S	656,000	13.00	18.00	30.00	40.00	60.00	450.00	
1870 (1,000)	634,900	13.00	18.00	30.00	40.00	60.00	425.00	1,300
1870CC	54,617	300.00	500.00	1,000	2,000	3,000	——	
1870S	1,004,000	13.00	18.00	30.00	40.00	75.00	475.00	
1871 .. (960)	1,204,560	13.00	18.00	30.00	40.00	65.00	450.00	1,300
1871CC	153,950	75.00	125.00	150.00	325.00	675.00	3,200	
1871S	2,178,000	13.00	21.00	40.00	50.00	75.00	450.00	

HALF DOLLARS

	Quan. Minted	G-4	VG-8	F-12	VF-20	EF-40	MS-60	Proof-63
1872 .. (950)	881,550	$20.00	$22.00	$40.00	$50.00	$80.00	$750.00	$1,300
1872CC	257,000	45.00	75.00	100.00	225.00	350.00	2,400	
1872S.........	580,000	13.00	20.00	30.00	40.00	75.00	750.00	
1873 Closed 3								
...... (600)	587,600	13.00	18.00	30.00	40.00	70.00	700.00	1,300
1873 Open 3	214,200			—	—	—		
1873CC	122,500	50.00	75.00	135.00	235.00	400.00	2,500	
1873S No arrows	5,000			Unknown in any collection.				

**Variety 5 —
Arrows at Date
1873-1874**

Arrows were placed at the date to denote a change in weight from 12.44 to 12.50 grams.

Weight 12.50 grams; composition: .900 silver, .100 copper; diameter 30.6 mm; reeded edge; mints: Philadelphia, Carson City, San Francisco.

	Quan. Minted	G-4	VG-8	F-12	VF-20	EF-40	MS-60	Proof-63
1873 .. (550)	1,815,700	20.00	25.00	38.00	80.00	175.00	900.00	2,300
1873CC	214,560	35.00	60.00	125.00	185.00	300.00	1,750	
1873S.........	228,000	30.00	35.00	60.00	100.00	200.00	1,200	
1874 .. (700)	2,360,300	20.00	25.00	38.00	80.00	175.00	900.00	2,300
1874CC	59,000	100.00	175.00	350.00	500.00	900.00	4,000	
1874S.........	394,000	30.00	35.00	60.00	100.00	200.00	1,400	

Variety 4 Resumed 1875-1891

	Quan. Minted	G-4	VG-8	F-12	VF-20	EF-40	MS-60	Proof-63
1875 .. (700)	6,027,500	12.00	18.00	30.00	40.00	60.00	400.00	1,300
1875CC	1,008,000	17.00	20.00	35.00	45.00	75.00	600.00	
1875S.......	3,200,000	12.00	18.00	30.00	40.00	60.00	400.00	
1876 (1,150)	8,419,150	12.00	18.00	30.00	40.00	60.00	400.00	1,300
1876CC	1,956,000	17.00	20.00	35.00	45.00	75.00	600.00	
1876S.......	4,528,000	12.00	18.00	30.00	40.00	60.00	400.00	
1877 .. (510)	8,304,510	12.00	18.00	30.00	40.00	60.00	400.00	1,300
1877CC	1,420,000	17.00	20.00	35.00	45.00	75.00	600.00	
1877S.......	5,356,000	12.00	18.00	30.00	40.00	60.00	400.00	
1878 .. (800)	1,378,400	12.00	18.00	30.00	40.00	60.00	400.00	1,300
1878CC	62,000	150.00	225.00	350.00	600.00	950.00	2,400	
1878S..........	12,000	4,000	5,000	7,000	9,000	12,000	25,000	
1879 (1,100)	5,900	125.00	150.00	200.00	250.00	375.00	950.00	1,500
1880 (1,355)	9,755	110.00	135.00	180.00	225.00	325.00	850.00	1,500
1881 .. (975)	10,975	110.00	135.00	180.00	225.00	325.00	850.00	1,500
1882 (1,100)	5,500	125.00	150.00	200.00	250.00	375.00	950.00	1,500
1883 (1,039)	9,039	110.00	135.00	180.00	225.00	325.00	850.00	1,500
1884 .. (875)	5,275	125.00	150.00	200.00	250.00	375.00	1,000	1,500
1885 .. (930)	6,130	110.00	135.00	180.00	225.00	325.00	1,000	1,500
1886 .. (886)	5,886	110.00	135.00	180.00	225.00	325.00	1,000	1,500
1887 .. (710)	5,710	110.00	135.00	180.00	225.00	325.00	1,000	1,500
1888 .. (832)	12,833	100.00	125.00	150.00	200.00	300.00	850.00	1,500
1889 .. (711)	12,711	100.00	125.00	150.00	200.00	300.00	850.00	1,500
1890 .. (590)	12,590	100.00	125.00	150.00	200.00	300.00	850.00	1,500
1891 .. (600)	200,600	20.00	27.50	40.00	60.00	100.00	500.00	1,500

HALF DOLLARS
BARBER or LIBERTY HEAD TYPE 1892-1915

Like the dime and quarter dollar, this type was designed by Charles E. Barber, whose initial B is at the truncation of the neck.

Designer Charles E. Barber; weight 12.50 grams; composition: .900 silver, .100 copper; diameter 30.6 mm; reeded edge; mints: Philadelphia, Denver, New Orleans, San Francisco.

G-4 GOOD—*Date and legends readable. LIBERTY worn off headband.*
VG-8 VERY GOOD—*Minimum of 3 letters readable in LIBERTY.*
F-12 FINE—*LIBERTY completely readable, but not sharp.*
VF-20 VERY FINE—*All letters in LIBERTY evenly plain.*
EF-40 EXTREMELY FINE—*LIBERTY bold, and its ribbon distinct.*
MS-60 UNCIRCULATED—*No trace of wear. Light blemishes.*

Mint mark location on reverse below eagle.

	Quan. Minted	G-4	VG-8	F-12	VF-20	EF-40	MS-60	Proof-63
1892 (1,245)	935,245	$13.00	$20.00	$30.00	$50.00	$165.00	$500.00	$1,500
1892O*	390,000	100.00	125.00	150.00	250.00	375.00	900.00	
1892S	1,029,028	100.00	125.00	150.00	250.00	375.00	1,000	
1893 .. (792)	1,826,792	10.00	16.00	25.00	45.00	175.00	500.00	1,500
1893O	1,389,000	16.00	23.00	40.00	85.00	235.00	675.00	
1893S	740,000	50.00	65.00	110.00	200.00	350.00	900.00	
1894 .. (972)	1,148,972	10.00	16.00	25.00	60.00	175.00	500.00	1,500
1894O	2,138,000	9.00	15.00	30.00	60.00	210.00	600.00	
1894S	4,048,690	8.00	11.00	25.00	55.00	195.00	525.00	
1895 .. (880)	1,835,218	8.00	11.00	25.00	52.00	175.00	500.00	1,500
1895O	1,766,000	9.00	14.00	30.00	60.00	180.00	600.00	
1895S	1,108,086	16.00	22.50	37.50	70.00	180.00	525.00	
1896 .. (762)	950,762	9.00	14.00	30.00	55.00	175.00	525.00	1,500
1896O	924,000	16.00	25.00	40.00	100.00	250.00	900.00	
1896S	1,140,948	50.00	60.00	80.00	175.00	325.00	1,050	
1897 .. (731)	2,480,731	5.50	7.00	23.00	40.00	130.00	500.00	1,500
1897O	632,000	50.00	60.00	80.00	200.00	450.00	1,250	
1897S	933,900	85.00	100.00	140.00	210.00	400.00	1,100	
1898 .. (735)	2,956,735	5.50	7.00	23.00	40.00	130.00	500.00	1,500
1898O	874,000	15.00	24.00	37.50	80.00	235.00	675.00	
1898S	2,358,550	8.00	11.00	25.00	55.00	165.00	550.00	
1899 .. (846)	5,538,846	5.50	7.00	23.00	40.00	130.00	500.00	1,500
1899O	1,724,000	8.00	11.00	25.00	55.00	200.00	600.00	
1899S	1,686,411	9.00	15.00	25.00	55.00	165.00	525.00	
1900 .. (912)	4,762,912	5.50	7.00	23.00	40.00	130.00	500.00	1,500
1900O	2,744,000	8.00	11.00	25.00	55.00	200.00	675.00	
1900S	2,560,322	8.00	11.00	24.00	45.00	165.00	525.00	
1901 .. (813)	4,268,813	5.50	7.00	24.00	50.00	140.00	500.00	1,500
1901O	1,124,000	8.50	13.00	30.00	60.00	350.00	1,100	
1901S	847,044	13.00	19.00	45.00	150.00	450.00	1,400	
1902 .. (777)	4,922,777	5.50	7.00	23.00	40.00	130.00	500.00	1,500
1902O	2,526,000	8.00	11.00	25.00	45.00	170.00	675.00	

*Normal and "microscopic" mint mark varieties, see page 65.

HALF DOLLARS

	Quan. Minted	G-4	VG-8	F-12	VF-20	EF-40	MS-60	Proof-63
1902S	1,460,670	$8.00	$10.00	$25.00	$50.00	$175.00	$600.00	
1903 .. (755)	2,278,755	5.50	7.00	23.00	40.00	150.00	500.00	$1,500
1903O	2,100,000	8.00	10.00	25.00	45.00	165.00	600.00	
1903S	1,920,772	8.00	10.00	25.00	45.00	175.00	600.00	
1904 .. (670)	2,992,670	5.50	7.00	23.00	40.00	130.00	500.00	1,500
1904O	1,117,600	10.00	13.00	35.00	75.00	275.00	1,100	
1904S	553,038	13.00	18.00	50.00	150.00	350.00	1,100	
1905 .. (727)	662,727	10.00	12.00	30.00	75.00	200.00	650.00	1,500
1905O	505,000	11.00	13.00	40.00	100.00	235.00	700.00	
1905S	2,494,000	8.00	10.00	25.00	45.00	170.00	600.00	
1906 .. (675)	2,638,675	5.50	7.00	23.00	40.00	130.00	500.00	1,500
1906D	4,028,000	5.50	8.50	24.00	40.00	140.00	500.00	
1906O	2,446,000	5.50	8.50	24.00	40.00	150.00	600.00	
1906S	1,740,154	5.50	8.50	24.00	50.00	185.00	600.00	
1907 .. (575)	2,598,575	5.50	7.00	23.00	40.00	130.00	500.00	1,500
1907D	3,856,000	5.50	8.50	24.00	40.00	140.00	500.00	
1907O	3,946,600	5.50	8.50	24.00	40.00	140.00	525.00	
1907S	1,250,000	8.00	11.00	25.00	45.00	180.00	600.00	
1908 .. (545)	1,354,545	5.50	7.00	23.00	40.00	130.00	500.00	1,500
1908D	3,280,000	5.50	7.00	23.00	40.00	130.00	500.00	
1908O	5,360,000	5.50	7.00	23.00	40.00	130.00	500.00	
1908S	1,644,828	5.50	9.00	24.00	45.00	175.00	550.00	
1909 .. (650)	2,368,650	5.50	7.00	23.00	40.00	130.00	500.00	1,500
1909O	925,400	5.50	10.00	25.00	60.00	225.00	750.00	
1909S	1,764,000	5.50	7.00	23.00	40.00	160.00	625.00	
1910 .. (551)	418,551	9.00	13.00	30.00	60.00	225.00	600.00	1,500
1910S	1,948,000	5.50	7.00	23.00	40.00	160.00	550.00	
1911 .. (543)	1,406,543	5.50	7.00	23.00	40.00	130.00	500.00	1,500
1911D	695,080	8.00	11.00	25.00	45.00	145.00	550.00	
1911S	1,272,000	5.50	7.00	23.00	40.00	150.00	550.00	
1912 .. (700)	1,550,700	5.50	7.00	23.00	40.00	130.00	500.00	1,500
1912D	2,300,800	5.50	7.00	23.00	40.00	130.00	500.00	
1912S	1,370,000	5.50	7.00	23.00	40.00	150.00	525.00	
1913 .. (627)	188,627	18.00	22.50	40.00	120.00	250.00	900.00	1,800
1913D	534,000	5.50	10.00	25.00	50.00	150.00	525.00	
1913S	604,000	5.50	10.00	25.00	60.00	175.00	625.00	
1914 .. (380)	124,610	25.00	27.50	100.00	175.00	350.00	900.00	2,000
1914S	992,000	5.50	9.00	25.00	45.00	165.00	550.00	
1915 .. (450)	138,450	18.00	25.00	60.00	140.00	275.00	850.00	1,900
1915D	1,170,400	5.50	7.00	23.00	40.00	130.00	500.00	
1915S	1,604,000	5.50	7.00	23.00	40.00	140.00	500.00	

LIBERTY WALKING TYPE 1916-1947

This type was designed by A. A. Weinman. The designer's monogram AAW appears under the tip of the wing feathers. On the 1916 coins and some of the 1917 coins the mint mark is located on the obverse below the motto.

Designer Adolph A. Weinman; weight 12.50 grams; composition: .900 silver, .100 copper; diameter 30.6 mm; reeded edge; mints: Philadelphia, Denver, San Francisco. Net weight: .36169 oz. pure silver.

G-4 GOOD—*Rims are defined. Motto IN GOD WE TRUST readable.*

VG-8 VERY GOOD—*Motto is distinct. About half of skirt lines at left are clear.*

F-12 FINE—*All skirt lines evident, but worn in spots. Details in sandal below motto are clear.*

VF-20 VERY FINE—*Skirt lines sharp including leg area. Little wear on breast and right arm.*

EF-40 EXTREMELY FINE—*All skirt lines bold.*

MS-60 UNCIRCULATED—*No trace of wear. Light blemishes.*

MS-65 CHOICE UNCIRCULATED—*No trace of wear. Barely noticeable blemishes.*

HALF DOLLARS

Location of mint mark.

Choice uncirculated, well struck specimens are worth more than values listed.
See pg. 6 for information on investment grade coins.

	Quan. Minted	G-4	VG-8	F-12	VF-20	EF-40	MS-60	Proof-65
1916	608,000	$18.00	$25.00	$50.00	$90.00	$175.00	$375.00	
1916D (Obv.)	1,014,400	15.00	20.00	25.00	60.00	150.00	350.00	
1916S (Obv.)	508,000	27.00	40.00	100.00	200.00	400.00	700.00	
1917	12,292,000	5.50	7.50	9.00	20.00	35.00	150.00	
1917D (Obv.)	765,400	14.00	20.00	30.00	85.00	175.00	400.00	
1917D. (Rev.)	1,940,000	9.00	12.00	25.00	50.00	150.00	450.00	
1917S (Obv.)	952,000	15.00	20.00	40.00	175.00	350.00	1,000	
1917S . (Rev.)	5,554,000	5.50	7.50	9.00	30.00	45.00	200.00	
1918	6,634,000	5.50	7.50	9.00	40.00	110.00	350.00	
1918D.......	3,853,040	5.50	7.50	9.00	50.00	115.00	650.00	
1918S	10,282,000	5.50	7.50	9.00	30.00	40.00	300.00	
1919	962,000	10.00	15.00	30.00	100.00	325.00	1,000	
1919D.......	1,165,000	10.00	11.00	30.00	150.00	375.00	1,800	
1919S	1,552,000	8.00	9.00	20.00	100.00	325.00	1,600	
1920	6,372,000	5.50	7.50	9.00	20.00	50.00	200.00	
1920D.......	1,551,000	5.50	7.50	25.00	115.00	250.00	1,000	
1920S	4,624,000	5.50	7.50	20.00	40.00	125.00	800.00	
1921	246,000	55.00	85.00	160.00	425.00	1,000	2,000	
1921D........	208,000	80.00	110.00	250.00	525.00	1,400	2,200	
1921S	548,000	17.50	25.00	45.00	300.00	1,500	6,500	
1923S	2,178,000	*5.00*	*6.00*	*9.00*	40.00	125.00	850.00	
1927S	2,392,000	*5.00*	*6.00*	*9.00*	25.00	70.00	600.00	
1928S†	1,940,000	*5.00*	*6.00*	*9.00*	30.00	90.00	700.00	
1929D.......	1,001,200	*5.00*	*6.00*	*9.00*	20.00	60.00	300.00	
1929S	1,902,000	*5.00*	*6.00*	*9.00*	20.00	65.00	275.00	
1933S	1,786,000	*5.00*	*6.00*	*9.00*	20.00	40.00	300.00	
1934	6,964,000	*4.50*	*4.50*	*5.00*	12.00	20.00	75.00	
1934D†	2,361,400	*4.50*	*4.50*	*5.00*	12.00	40.00	120.00	
1934S	3,652,000	*4.50*	*4.50*	*5.00*	12.00	25.00	275.00	
1935	9,162,000	*4.50*	*4.50*	*5.00*	12.00	16.00	65.00	
1935D.......	3,003,800	*4.50*	*4.50*	*5.00*	12.00	40.00	125.00	
1935S	3,854,000	*4.50*	*4.50*	*5.00*	10.00	35.00	150.00	
1936 . (3,901)	12,617,901	*4.50*	*4.50*	*5.00*	10.00	16.00	60.00	$5,000
1936D.......	4,252,400	*4.50*	*4.50*	*5.00*	10.00	30.00	100.00	
1936S	3,884,000	*4.50*	*4.50*	*5.00*	10.00	30.00	125.00	
1937 . (5,728)	9,527,728	*4.50*	*4.50*	*5.00*	10.00	16.00	65.00	2,200
1937D.......	1,676,000	*4.50*	*4.50*	*5.00*	10.00	40.00	200.00	
1937S	2,090,000	*4.50*	*4.50*	*5.00*	10.00	35.00	125.00	
1938 . (8,152)	4,118,152	*4.50*	*4.50*	*5.00*	10.00	17.00	90.00	1,800
1938D........	491,600	24.00	27.00	30.00	40.00	90.00	400.00	

†Large and small mint mark varieties, see page 65. Pieces dated 1928D are counterfeit.

HALF DOLLARS

	Quan. Minted	F-12	VF-20	EF-40	MS-60	MS-65	Proof-65
1939 . . . . (8,808)	6,820,808	$5.00	$10.00	$16.00	$90.00	$525.00	$1,500
1939D.	4,267,800	5.00	10.00	17.00	85.00	500.00	
1939S	2,552,000	5.00	10.00	20.00	125.00	600.00	
1940 . . . . . . (11,279)	9,167,279	4.50	6.00	12.00	70.00	400.00	1,400
1940S	4,550,000	4.50	6.00	15.00	100.00	900.00	
1941* . . . . . (15,412)	24,207,412	4.50	5.00	9.00	50.00	400.00	*1,350
1941D.	11,248,400	4.50	5.00	9.00	65.00	475.00	
1941S†	8,098,000	4.50	5.00	9.00	200.00	1,800	
1942 . . . . . . (21,120)	47,839,120	4.50	5.00	9.00	50.00	400.00	1,350
1942D. . . . . ⎫		4.50	5.00	9.00	70.00	500.00	
1942D, D over S. ⎬	10,973,800			——			
1942S†	12,708,000	4.50	5.00	9.00	110.00	900.00	
1943	53,190,000	4.50	5.00	9.00	50.00	400.00	
1943D.	11,346,000	4.50	5.00	9.00	75.00	500.00	
1943S	13,450,000	4.50	5.00	9.00	115.00	800.00	
1944	28,206,000	4.50	5.00	9.00	50.00	400.00	
1944D.	9,769,000	4.50	5.00	9.00	60.00	450.00	
1944S	8,904,000	4.50	5.00	9.00	75.00	1,400	
1945	31,502,000	4.50	5.00	9.00	50.00	400.00	
1945D.	9,966,800	4.50	5.00	9.00	60.00	475.00	
1945S	10,156,000	4.50	5.00	9.00	75.00	525.00	
1946	12,118,000	4.50	5.00	9.00	50.00	450.00	
1946D.	2,151,000	4.50	5.00	9.00	50.00	425.00	
1946S	3,724,000	4.50	5.00	9.00	75.00	450.00	
1947	4,094,000	4.50	5.00	9.00	75.00	450.00	
1947D.	3,900,600	4.50	5.00	9.00	75.00	450.00	

*Proofs struck with or without designer's initials.
†Large and small mint mark varieties, see page 65.

FRANKLIN-LIBERTY BELL TYPE 1948-1963

The Benjamin Franklin half dollar and the Roosevelt dime were both designed by John R. Sinnock. His initials appear below the shoulder. The Liberty Bell is similar to that used by Sinnock on the 1926 Sesquicentennial commemorative half dollar modeled from a sketch by John Frederick Lewis.

Designer John R. Sinnock; weight 12.50 grams; composition: .900 silver, .100 copper; diameter 30.6 mm; reeded edge; mints: Philadelphia, Denver, San Francisco. Net weight: .36169 oz. pure silver.

VF-20 VERY FINE—*At least half of the lower and upper incused lines on the rim of the bell must show.*

EF-40 EXTREMELY FINE—*Wear spots appear at top of end curls and hair back of ears. On reverse, Liberty Bell will show wear at top and on lettering.*

MS-63 SELECT UNCIRCULATED—*No trace of wear. Light blemishes. Attractive mint luster.*

MS-65 CHOICE UNCIRCULATED—*No trace of wear. Barely noticeable blemishes.*

Values shown for MS-65 grade are based on averages of prices charged by dealers for premium quality investment-graded coins.

Mint mark location.

Choice, well struck uncirculated halves command higher prices.

	Quan. Minted	VF-20	EF-40	MS-63	MS-65	Proof-65
1948	3,006,814	$4.50	$5.00	$25.00	$175.00	
1948D.	4,028,600	4.50	5.00	23.00	300.00	

HALF DOLLARS

	Quan. Minted	VF-20	EF-40	MS-63	MS-65	Proof-65
1949	5,614,000	$4.50	$5.00	$70.00	$200.00	
1949D	4,120,600	4.50	5.00	70.00	1,200	
1949S	3,744,000	4.50	10.00	150.00	225.00	
1950 .... (51,386)	7,793,509	4.50	5.00	50.00	190.00	$700.00
1950D	8,031,600	4.50	5.00	35.00	1,000	
1951 .... (57,500)	16,859,602	4.50	5.00	20.00	150.00	420.00
1951D	9,475,200	4.50	5.00	50.00	350.00	
1951S	13,696,000	4.50	5.00	50.00	125.00	
1952 .... (81,980)	21,274,073	4.50	5.00	20.00	125.00	250.00
1952D	25,395,600	4.50	5.00	20.00	335.00	
1952S	5,526,000	4.50	5.00	45.00	175.00	
1953 ...... (128,800)	2,796,920	4.50	6.00	40.00	250.00	175.00
1953D	20,900,400	4.50	5.00	18.00	300.00	
1953S	4,148,000	4.50	5.00	30.00	125.00	
1954 ...... (233,300)	13,421,503	4.50	5.00	15.00	150.00	80.00
1954D	25,445,580	4.50	5.00	14.00	250.00	
1954S	4,993,400	4.50	5.00	20.00	100.00	
1955 .... (378,200)	2,876,381	4.50	6.00	17.00	100.00	80.00
1956 ...... (669,384)	4,701,384	4.50	5.00	17.00	100.00	60.00
1957 ...... (1,247,952)	6,361,952	4.50	5.00	16.00	100.00	55.00
1957D	19,966,850	4.50	5.00	12.00	100.00	
1958 ...... (875,652)	4,917,652	4.50	5.00	13.00	100.00	60.00
1958D	23,962,412	4.50	5.00	13.00	100.00	
1959 ...... (1,149,291)	7,349,291	4.50	5.00	13.00	225.00	55.00
1959D	13,053,750	4.50	5.00	14.00	275.00	
1960 ...... (1,691,602)	7,715,602	4.50	5.00	11.00	275.00	50.00
1960D	18,215,812	4.50	4.50	10.00	600.00	

**1961 Proof
Double Die**

1961 ...... (3,028,244)	11,318,244	4.50	4.50	10.00	250.00	40.00
1961 Double Die Proof	....					—
1961D	20,276,442	4.50	4.50	9.50	500.00	
1962 ...... (3,218,019)	12,932,019	4.50	4.50	9.50	250.00	40.00
1962D	35,473,281	4.50	4.50	9.50	600.00	
1963 ...... (3,075,645)	25,239,645	4.50	4.50	8.00	175.00	40.00
1963D	67,069,292	4.50	4.50	8.00	175.00	

Note: Prices in italic are based on silver bullion value.

KENNEDY TYPE 1964 to Date

Gilroy Roberts, former Chief Engraver of the Mint, designed the obverse of this coin. His stylized initials are on the truncation of the forceful bust of President John F. Kennedy. The reverse, which uses the presidential coat of arms for the motif, is the work of Chief Engraver Frank Gasparro. A few of the pieces dated 1971D and 1977D were struck in silver clad by error.

Designers Gilroy Roberts and Frank Gasparro. 1964: Standards same as previous issue; 1965-1970: weight 11.50 grams; composition: outer layers of .800 silver, .200 copper bonded to inner core of .209 silver, .791 copper; 1971: weight 11.34 grams; composition: outer layers of copper-nickel (.750 copper, .250 nickel) bonded to inner core of pure copper; diameter 30.6 mm; reeded edge. Net same as previous issue; 1965-1970: weight 11.50 grams; composition: silver.

HALF DOLLARS

1964
Mint
mark
location

1968
Mint
mark
location

Silver Coinage 1964

	Quan. Minted	MS-65	Proof-65		Quan Minted	MS-65	Proof-65
1964	(3,950,762)		$16.00	1964D	156,205,446	$6.00	
	277,254,766	$6.00					

Silver Clad Coinage 1965-1970

	Quan. Minted	MS-65			Quan. Minted	MS-65	
1965	65,879,366	2.50		1969D	129,881,800	2.50	
1966	108,984,932	2.50		1969S Proof	(2,934,631)		$4.00
1967	295,046,978	2.50		1970D (Issued only in			
1968D	246,951,930	2.50		mint sets)	2,150,000	25.00	
1968S Proof	(3,041,506)		4.00	1970S Proof	(2,632,810)		10.00

Copper-Nickel Clad Coinage — Modified Design 1971-

	Quan. Minted	MS-65	Proof-65		Quan. Minted	MS-65	Proof-65
1971	155,164,000	$1.00		1973	64,964,000	$1.00	
1971D	302,097,424	1.00		1973D	83,171,400	1.00	
1971S Proof	(3,220,733)		$3.00	1973S Proof	(2,760,339)		$3.00
1972	153,180,000	1.00		1974	201,596,000	1.00	
1972D	141,890,000	1.00		1974D	79,066,300	1.00	
1972S Proof	(3,260,996)		3.00	1974S Proof	(2,612,568)		3.50

BICENTENNIAL COINAGE DATED 1776—1976

In an open contest for the selection of suitable designs for the special Bicentennial reverses of the quarter, half dollar and dollar, Seth G. Huntington's winning entry was featured on the half dollar. It shows Independence Hall in
Philadelphia as the center device. The obverse was unchanged except for the
dual dating 1776-1976. They were the only coins struck during 1975 and 1976
and were used for general circulation as well as being included in proof and
uncirculated sets.

Designers Gilroy Roberts and Seth Huntington. Silver clad: weight 11.50 grams; composition: outer
layers of .800 silver, .200 copper bonded to inner core of .209 silver, .791 copper; copper-nickel clad:
weight 11.34 grams; composition: outer layers of copper-nickel (.750 copper, .250 nickel) bonded to inner
core of pure copper; diameter 30.6 mm; reeded edge. Net weight: silver clad coinage .14792 oz. pure
silver.

HALF DOLLARS

	Quan. Minted	MS-65	Proof-65
1776-1976 Copper-nickel clad........................	234,308,000	$1.00	
1776-1976D Copper-nickel clad......................	287,565,248	1.00	
1776-1976S Copper-nickel clad	(7,059,099)		$1.50
1776-1976S Silver clad.............................	*11,000,000	3.00	
1776-1976S Silver clad.............................	*(4,000,000)		5.50

*Approximate mintage.

Eagle Reverse Resumed

Quan. Minted	MS-65	Proof-65	Quan. Minted	MS-65	Proof-65
1977 43,598,000	$1.00		1983S Proof.. (3,279,126)		$5.00
1977D 31,449,106	1.00		1984P........ 26,029,000	$1.00	
1977S Proof.. (3,251,152)		$1.75	1984D 26,262,158	1.00	
1978 14,350,000	1.50		1984S Proof.. (3,065,110)		16.00
1978D 13,765,799	1.50		1985P........ 18,706,962	1.00	
1978S Proof.. (3,127,781)		2.50	1985D 19,814,034	1.00	
1979 68,312,000	1.00		1985S Proof.. (3,362,662)		15.00
1979D 15,815,422	1.00		1986P........ 13,107,633	1.00	
1979S Proof.. (3,677,175)			1986D 15,336,145	1.00	
Filled S		2.00	1986S Proof.. (3,010,497)		16.00
Clear S		15.00	1987P................	4.00	
1980P........ 44,134,000	1.00		1987D	4.00	
1980D 33,456,449	1.00		1987S Proof.. (3,792,233)		7.00
1980S Proof.. (3,554,806)		1.50	1988P........ 13,626,000	1.00	
1981P........ 29,544,000	1.00		1988D 12,000,096	1.00	
1981D 27,839,533	1.00		1988S Proof...........		10.00
1981S Proof.. (4,063,083)		1.50	1989P........ 24,542,000	1.00	
1982P........ 10,819,000	1.00		1989D 23,000,216	1.00	
1982D 13,140,102	1.00		1989S Proof...........		5.00
1982S Proof.. (3,857,479)		4.00	1990P................	1.00	
1983P........ 34,139,000	1.00		1990D	1.00	
1983D 32,472,244	1.00		1990S Proof...........		5.00

BIBLIOGRAPHY

Beistle, M. L. *Register of United States Half Dollar Die Varieties and Sub-Varieties.* Shippensburg, Pa., 1929.

Haseltine, J. W. *Type Table of United States Dollars, Half Dollars and Quarter Dollars.* Philadelphia, 1881 (reprinted 1927, 1968).

Overton, Al C. *Early Half Dollar Die Varieties 1794-1836.* Colorado Springs, 1967. Revised edition, 1970.

SILVER DOLLARS — 1794 to Date

The silver dollar was authorized by Congress April 2, 1792. Weight and fineness were specified at 416 grains and 892.4 fine. The first issues appeared in 1794 and until 1804 all silver dollars had the value stamped on the edge: HUNDRED CENTS, ONE DOLLAR OR UNIT. After a lapse in coinage of the silver dollar during the period 1804 to 1835, coins were made with either plain or reeded edges and the value was placed on the reverse side.

The weight was changed by the law of January 18, 1837 to 412½ grains, fineness .900. The coinage was discontinued by the Act of February 12, 1873 and reauthorized by the Act of February 28, 1878. The dollar was again discontinued after 1935, and since then only the copper-nickel pieces first authorized in 1971 have been coined for circulation.

ORIGIN OF THE DOLLAR

The word Dollar evolves from German Taler, the name given to the first large-sized European silver coin. Designed as a substitute for the gold Florin, the coin originated in the Tyrol in 1484. So popular did these large silver coins become during the 16th century that many other countries struck similar pieces, giving them names derived from taler. In the Netherlands the coin was called Rijksdaalder, in Denmark Rigsdaler, in Italy Tallero, in Poland Talar, in France Jocandale, in Russia Jefimok. All these names are abbreviations of "Joachimsthaler." Until the discovery of the great silver deposits in Mexican and South American mines, the mint with the greatest output of large silver coins was that of Joachimsthal in the Bohemian Erzgebirge.

The Spanish Dollar, or piece-of-eight, was widely used and familiar to everyone in the English-American colonies. It was only natural therefore that the word "dollar" was adopted officially as the standard monetary unit of the United States by Congress on July 6, 1785. The Continental Dollar of 1776 is described on page 32.

+ or − indicates change from previous year	TYPE COIN VALUES									
	G-4	F-12	EF-40	AU-50	MS-60	MS-63	MS-65	PF-60	PF-63	PF-65
Flowing Hair 1794-1795	850.00	1,400	4,250	12,000	25,000	35,000	200,000+			
Drpd Bust, SE 1795-1798	625.00	1,100	3,200+	6,500	15,000+	22,500	150,000+			
Drpd Bust, HE 1798-1804	350.00+	600.00+	1,500+	3,500+	9,500+	20,000+	150,000+	70,000		
Lib Seat-NM 1840-1866	75.00	150.00	350.00	500.00	1,200+	4,500+	30,000+	1,500+	4,000+	20,000+
Lib. Seat-WM 1866-1873	75.00	150.00	350.00	525.00	1,600+	5,200+	30,000+	1,500+	3,500+	20,000+
U.S. Trade Dol 1873-1883	47.50	75.00	175.00	285.00	650.00+	1,750	15,000+	1,100	3,200+	14,000+
Morgan Dol 1878-1921	9.00−	10.00−	11.00−	15.00−	25.00+	30.00−	350.00−	1,000+	3,000	10,000
Peace Dol 1921-1935	9.00−	10.00−	11.00−	13.00−	16.00−	35.00−	550.00			

FLOWING HAIR TYPE 1794-1795

Varieties listed are those most significant to collectors, but numerous minor variations may be found because each of the early dies was individually made. Values of variations not listed in this guide depend on collector interest and demand. Values shown here for uncirculated pieces are for well struck, attractive coins with a minimum of surface marks.

Designer Robert Scot; weight 26.96 grams; composition: .8924 silver, .1076 copper; approx. diameter 39-40 mm; edge: HUNDRED CENTS ONE DOLLAR OR UNIT with decorations between words.

AG-3 ABOUT GOOD—*Clear enough to identify.*

G-4 GOOD—*Date and letters readable. Main devices outlined, but lack details.*

VG-8 VERY GOOD—*Major details discernible. Letters well formed but worn.*

F-12 FINE—*Hair ends distinguishable. Top hairlines show, but otherwise worn smooth.*

VF-20 VERY FINE—*Hair in center shows some detail. Other details more bold.*

EF-40 EXTREMELY FINE—*Hair well defined but will show some wear.*

MS-60 UNCIRCULATED—*No trace of wear. Light blemishes.*

SILVER DOLLARS

	Quan. Minted	AG-3	G-4	VG-8	F-12	VF-20	EF-40	MS-60
1794	1,758	$4,000	$6,250	$9,500	$17,000	$25,000	$45,000	$140,000

Two Leaves Beneath
Each Wing (11 Varieties)

Three Leaves Beneath
Each Wing

		AG-3	G-4	VG-8	F-12	VF-20	EF-40	MS-60
1795 Two leaves	160,295	450.00	850.00	1,100	1,400	2,500	4,250	25,000
1795 Three leaves		450.00	850.00	1,100	1,400	2,500	4,250	25,000

DRAPED BUST TYPE, SMALL EAGLE REVERSE 1795-1798

AG-3 ABOUT GOOD—*Clear enough to identify.*
G-4 GOOD—*Bust outlined, no detail. Date readable, some leaves evident.*
VG-8 VERY GOOD—*Drapery worn except deepest folds. Hairlines smooth.*
F-12 FINE—*All drapery lines distinguishable. Hairlines near cheek and neck show some detail.*
VF-20 VERY FINE—*Left side of drapery worn smooth.*
EF-40 EXTREMELY FINE—*Drapery shows distinctly. Hair well outlined and detailed.*
MS-60 UNCIRCULATED—*No trace of wear. Light blemishes.*

		AG-3	G-4	VG-8	F-12	VF-20	EF-40	MS-60
1795 (2 varieties)	42,738	400.00	750.00	1,000	1,500	2,000	3,850	17,500

SILVER DOLLARS

Small Date

Large Date

Small Letters

Large Letters

	Quan. Minted	AG-3	G-4	VG-8	F-12	VF-20	EF-40	MS-60
1796 Sm. dt. sm. let. (3 vars.)								
All kinds	72,920	$300.00	$625.00	$825.00	$1,100	$1,850	$3,200	$15,000
1796 Sm. date, lg. let		300.00	625.00	825.00	1,100	1,850	3,200	15,000
1796 Lg. date, sm. let.		300.00	625.00	825.00	1,100	1,850	3,200	15,000
1797, 9 stars left, 7 right								
Sm. let. All kinds . .	7,776	625.00	1,200	1,700	2,200	3,300	——	——
1797, 9 stars l., 7 r., lg. let.		300.00	625.00	825.00	1,100	1,850	3,200	15,000
1797, 10 stars left, 6 right .		300.00	625.00	825.00	1,100	1,850	3,200	15,000
1798, 15 stars on obverse . .		550.00	1,100	1,500	2,200	3,000	5,500	20,000
All kinds	327,536							
1798, 13 stars on obverse . .		550.00	1,100	1,500	2,200	3,000	5,500	19,000

HERALDIC EAGLE REVERSE 1798-1804

G-4 GOOD—*Letters and date readable. E PLURIBUS UNUM obliterated.*
VG-8 VERY GOOD—*Motto partially readable. Only deepest drapery details visible. All other lines smooth.*
F-12 FINE—*All drapery lines distinguishable. Hairlines near cheek and neck show some detail.*
VF-20 VERY FINE—*Left side of drapery worn smooth.*
EF-40 EXTREMELY FINE—*Drapery is distinct. Hair well detailed.*
MS-60 UNCIRCULATED—*No trace of wear. Light blemishes.*

	Quan. Minted	G-4	VG-8	F-12	VF-20	EF-40	MS-60
1798 Large heraldic eagle, knob 9. . .		$350.00	$450.00	$600.00	$850.00	$1,600	$10,500
1798 Lg. eagle, 10 arrows		350.00	450.00	600.00	850.00	1,500	10,000
1798 Close date.		350.00	450.00	600.00	850.00	1,500	10,000
1798 Wide date, 13 arrows (11 var.) .		350.00	450.00	600.00	850.00	1,500	10,000

SILVER DOLLARS

1799 over 98, Stars 7 and 6   **Stars 8 and 5**

	Quan. Minted	G-4	VG-8	F-12	VF-20	EF-40	MS-60
1799 All kinds............	423,515						
1799 9 over 8 rev. with 15 stars		$350.00	$450.00	$600.00	$850.00	$1,500	$9,500
1799 9 over 8 rev. with 13 stars ..		350.00	500.00	650.00	900.00	1,700	10,500
1799 Irregular date, 15-star rev...		350.00	500.00	650.00	900.00	1,700	10,500
1799 Irregular date, 13-star rev...		350.00	450.00	600.00	850.00	1,500	9,500
1799 Normal date................		350.00	450.00	600.00	850.00	1,500	9,500
1799 Stars - 8 left, 5 right........		350.00	500.00	650.00	900.00	1,700	10,500
1800 All kinds............	220,920	350.00	450.00	600.00	850.00	1,500	9,500
1800 Very wide date, low 8.......		350.00	450.00	600.00	850.00	1,500	9,500
1800 "Dotted date" from die breaks		350.00	450.00	600.00	850.00	1,500	9,500
1800 Only 12 arrows.............		550.00	450.00	600.00	850.00	1,500	9,500
1800 Only 10 arrows.............		350.00	450.00	600.00	850.00	1,500	9,500
1800 AMERICAI (2 varieties).......		350.00	450.00	600.00	850.00	1,500	9,500
1801 (4 varieties)	54,454	350.00	450.00	600.00	850.00	1,500	9,500
1801 Proof restrike (rev. struck from first die of 1804 dollar).						(Proof)	70,000

1802 over 1   **Small 3**   **Large 3**

1802 All kinds............... 41,650						
1802 2 over 1, narrow date........	350.00	450.00	600.00	850.00	1,500	9,500
1802 2 over 1, wide date	350.00	450.00	600.00	850.00	1,500	9,500
1802 Narrow normal date	350.00	450.00	600.00	850.00	1,500	9,500
1802 Wide normal date.............	350.00	450.00	600.00	850.00	1,500	9,500
1802 Proof restrike					(Proof)	70,000
1803 Small 3 (5 varieties)... } 85,634	350.00	450.00	600.00	850.00	1,700	10,500
1803 Large 3 (1 variety)....	350.00	450.00	600.00	850.00	1,500	9,500
1803 Proof restrike					(Proof)	70,000

SILVER DOLLARS
THE 1804 DOLLAR

FIRST REVERSE

SECOND REVERSE

Note position of words
STATES OF
with relation to clouds.

Compare
with first
reverse.

1804 First reverse, Original (Dexter specimen sold for $990,000 in 1989.)
1804 Second reverse, Restrike (Adams specimen sold for $220,000 in 1989.)
This piece is one of the most publicized rarities in the United States series.
There are specimens known as originals (first reverse), of which eight are
known, and restrikes (second reverse), of which seven are known.

Numismatists have found that the 1804 "original" dollars were struck at the
mint in the 1834-35 period, for use in presentation proof sets. The first known
specimen, a proof, was obtained from a mint officer by Mr. Stickney on May
9, 1843, in exchange for an "Immune Columbia" piece in gold. Later, in 1859,
the pieces known as restrikes were made at the mint to supply the needs of
collectors who wanted specimens of these dollars.

Evidence that these pieces were struck during the later period is based on
the fact that the 1804 dollars differ from issues of 1803 or earlier and conform
more closely to those struck after 1836, their edges or borders having beaded
segments and raised rim, not elongated denticles such as are found on the
earlier dates.

Although the mint records state that 19,570 dollars were coined in 1804, in
no place does it mention that they were dated 1804. It was the practice in those
days to use old dies as long as they were serviceable with no regard in the
annual reports for the dating of the coins. It is probable that the 1804 total for
dollars actually covered coins that were dated 1803.

BIBLIOGRAPHY

Bolender, M. H. *The United States Early Silver Dollars from 1794 to 1803.* Freeport, Ill., 1950.
Newman, Eric P. and Bressett, Kenneth E. *The Fantastic 1804 Dollar.* Racine, Wis., 1962.
Haseltine, J. W. *Type Table of United States Dollars, Half Dollars and Quarter Dollars.* Philadelphia,
    1881 (reprinted 1927, 1968).

SILVER DOLLARS
GOBRECHT DOLLARS — 1836-1839

Suspension of silver dollar coinage was lifted in 1831; however, not until 1835 were steps taken to resume coinage. Late in that year Director R.M. Patterson ordered Engraver Christian Gobrecht to prepare a pair of dies from designs by Thomas Sully and Titian Peale. The first obverse die bore the seated figure of Liberty on the obverse with the inscription C. GOBRECHT F. (F. - FECIT - made it) below the base of Liberty. On the reverse was a large eagle flying left surrounded by twenty-six stars and the legend UNITED STATES OF AMERICA ONE DOLLAR. Public criticism forced Gobrecht's name to the base of Liberty on a new die and, with this, pieces were struck in late 1836 on the standard of 1792, 416 grains.

In early 1837 the weight was lowered to 412½ grains and pieces were struck on the new standard in March, 1837, using the dies of 1836. To distinguish the 1837 coinage from that of 1836, the reverse die was oriented in "medal" fashion.

Between 1855 and 1860 the Mint produced restrikes to satisfy collector demands. Mules (mismatched combinations of dies) were also struck in the 1850's and are rare. Restrikes and mules are seldom seen in worn condition.

Original die alignment using either "coin" ↓↑ or "medal ↑↑ turn.   **Die alignment of restrikes ↑↖ .**

Dollars issued for circulation in 1836 and 1839, and the patterns of 1836 (with name below base) and 1838 have dies oriented in normal "coin" alignment ↑↓ with the reverse inverted.

The special issue of 1837 (using dies of 1836 with name on base) have dies oriented in "medal" fashion ↑↑ with the reverse upright when turned.

All circulating issues and patterns are positioned so that the eagle will be flying upright as shown in the illustration.

Restrikes incorporate both "medal" ↑↑ and "coin" ↓↑ turns, and use the same die combinations as originals, but with the eagle flying level when rotated (see illustration). Mules with wrong edge or die combinations also exist and are all rare.

SILVER DOLLARS
CIRCULATION ISSUES AND PATTERNS

	VF-20	EF-40	Proof-60
1836 C. GOBRECHT F. below base. Rev. Eagle flying left amid stars. Plain edge ↑↓ . Pattern			$30,000
1836 C. GOBRECHT F. on base. Rev. as above. Plain edge ↑↓ . Circulation issue. 1,000 struck	$3,200	$4,200	7,000
1836 As above. Plain edge ↑↑ . Circulation issue struck in 1837 on new standard. 600 struck	3,200	4,500	7,200

	VF-20	EF-40	Proof-60
1838 Similar obv., designer's name omitted, stars added around border. Rev. Eagle flying in plain field. Reeded edge. ↑↓ . Pattern	4,000	4,750	12,000
1839 As above. Reeded edge. ↑↓. Circulation issue, regular coinage. 300 struck	3,500	4,500	10,000

RESTRIKES

Restrikes were produced between 1855 and 1860 and are not official coins. All have reverse die orientation with eagle flying level when rotated.

1836 Name below base. Eagle in plain field. Plain edge	23,000
1836 Name on base. Plain or reeded edge	—
1838 Designer's name omitted. Plain or reeded edge	25,000
1839 Same as above. Plain or reeded edge.	—

SILVER DOLLARS
LIBERTY SEATED TYPE — HERALDIC EAGLE 1840-1873

Starting in 1840 silver dollars were issued for general circulation in larger quantities than before. The seated figure of Liberty device was adopted for the obverse, but the flying eagle design was rejected in favor of the more familiar form with olive branch and arrows used for the other silver denominations.

The 1866 proof quarter, half and dollar without motto are not mentioned in the Director's Report, and were not issued for circulation.

Mint mark location is on the reverse below eagle.

Designer Christian Gobrecht; weight 26.73 grams; composition: .900 silver, .100 copper; diameter 38.1 mm; reeded edge; mints: Philadelphia, New Orleans, Carson City, San Francisco. Net weight: .77344 oz. pure silver.

VG-8 VERY GOOD—*Any 3 letters of LIBERTY at least two-thirds complete.*

F-12 FINE—*All 7 letters of LIBERTY visible though weak.*

VF-20 VERY FINE—*LIBERTY is strong but its ribbon shows slight wear.*

EF-40 EXTREMELY FINE—*Horizontal lines of shield complete. Eagle's eye plain.*

MS-60 UNCIRCULATED—*No trace of wear. Light marks or blemishes.*

	Quan. Minted	VG-8	F-12	VF-20	EF-40	MS-60	Proof-60
1840	61,005	$110.00	$170.00	$220.00	$375.00	$1,400	$3,300
1841	173,000	100.00	150.00	200.00	350.00	1,300	3,300
1842	184,618	100.00	150.00	200.00	350.00	1,300	3,300
1843	165,100	100.00	150.00	200.00	350.00	1,300	3,300
1844	20,000	150.00	185.00	235.00	400.00	2,000	3,500
1845	24,500	150.00	185.00	235.00	400.00	2,000	3,500
1846	110,600	100.00	150.00	200.00	350.00	1,300	3,300
1846O	59,000	200.00	250.00	350.00	600.00	2,500	
1847	140,750	100.00	150.00	200.00	350.00	1,300	3,300
1848	15,000	150.00	200.00	250.00	450.00	2,100	3,500
1849	62,600	100.00	150.00	200.00	350.00	1,300	3,300
1850	7,500	200.00	250.00	350.00	750.00	4,000	5,500
1850O	40,000	175.00	250.00	350.00	600.00	3,300	
1851 Original, high date	1,300	1,200	1,500	2,300	3,900	12,000	14,000
1851 Restrike, date centered							12,000
1852 Original	1,100					12,000	
1852 Restrike							10,000
1853	46,110	100.00	150.00	200.00	350.00	1,600	4,500
1854	33,140	135.00	250.00	350.00	550.00	2,400	9,000
1855	26,000	250.00	350.00	500.00	700.00	2,400	5,600
1856	63,500	150.00	210.00	275.00	400.00	2,100	5,000
1857	94,000	125.00	175.00	235.00	375.00	2,100	3,750
1858	Estimated (80)						5,000

SILVER DOLLARS

	Quan. Minted	VG-8	F-12	VF-20	EF-40	MS-60	Proof-63
1859 .... (800)	256,500	$85.00	$150.00	$200.00	$350.00	$1,800	$4,000
1859O.........	360,000	85.00	150.00	200.00	350.00	1,200	
1859S.........	20,000	200.00	275.00	400.00	700.00	3,200	
1860 .. (1,330)	218,930	100.00	150.00	200.00	350.00	1,300	4,000
1860O.........	515,000	85.00	150.00	200.00	350.00	1,200	
1861 .. (1,000)	78,500	125.00	170.00	220.00	375.00	2,000	4,000
1862 .... (550)	12,090	225.00	325.00	500.00	650.00	2,600	4,000
1863 .... (460)	27,660	150.00	200.00	250.00	450.00	2,000	4,000
1864 .... (470)	31,170	150.00	200.00	250.00	450.00	2,000	4,000
1865 .... (500)	47,000	150.00	200.00	250.00	450.00	2,000	4,000
1866 (2 known)..							——

Motto "In God We Trust" Added to Reverse

1866 .... (725)	49,625	100.00	150.00	200.00	350.00	1,600	3,500
1867 .... (625)	47,525	100.00	150.00	200.00	350.00	1,600	3,500
1868 .... (600)	162,700	100.00	150.00	200.00	350.00	1,600	3,500
1869 .... (600)	424,300	100.00	150.00	200.00	350.00	1,600	3,500
1870 .. (1,000)	416,000	100.00	150.00	200.00	350.00	1,600	3,500
1870CC	12,462	150.00	225.00	400.00	700.00	3,200	
1870S................				50,000	60,000	——	
1871 .... (960)	1,074,760	100.00	150.00	200.00	350.00	1,600	3,500
1871CC	1,376	800.00	1,000	3,500	5,000	12,000	
1872 .... (950)	1,106,450	100.00	150.00	200.00	350.00	1,600	3,500
1872CC	3,150	500.00	850.00	1,500	2,500	6,000	
1872S............	9,000	150.00	250.00	400.00	850.00	4,500	
1873 .... (600)	293,600	100.00	150.00	200.00	350.00	1,600	3,500
1873CC	2,300	1,500	2,000	3,000	5,000	18,000	
1873S.............. 700					Unknown in any collection.		

TRADE DOLLARS 1873-1885

This coin was issued for circulation in the Orient to compete with dollar-size coins of other countries. It weighed 420 grains compared to 412½ grains, the weight of the regular silver dollar.

Many of the pieces which circulated in the Orient were counterstamped with oriental characters, known as "chop marks". These are generally valued lower than normal pieces.

When first coined they were legal tender in the United States to the extent of $5.00, but with the decline in price of silver bullion Congress repealed the legal tender provision in 1876 and authorized the Treasury to limit coinage to export demand. In 1887 a law was passed authorizing the Treasury to redeem all Trade dollars which were not mutilated.

The Trade dollars of 1884 and 1885 were unknown to collectors generally

TRADE DOLLARS 1873 - 1885

until 1908. None is listed in the Director's Report and numismatists believe that they are not a part of the regular mint issue. After 1878, strikings were specimen proofs only.

The law authorizing Trade dollars was repealed in February, 1887.

Designer William Barber; weight 27.22 grams; composition: .900 silver, .100 copper; diameter 38.1 mm; reeded edge; mints: Philadelphia, Carson City, San Francisco. Net weight: .7874 oz. pure silver.

VG-8 VERY GOOD—*About half of mottoes IN GOD WE TRUST and E PLURIBUS UNUM will show. Rim on both sides well defined.*

F-12 FINE—*Mottoes and LIBERTY readable but worn.*

EF-40 EXTREMELY FINE—*Mottoes and LIBERTY are sharp. Only slight wear on rims.*

MS-60 UNCIRCULATED—*No trace of wear. Light blemishes.*

1875S
S over CC

Mint mark location on reverse above letter "D" in dollar.

	Quan. Minted	VG-8	F-12	EF-40	MS-60	Proof-63
1873 . . . . (865)	397,500	$60.00	$75.00	$185.00	$700.00	$3,300
1873CC	124,500	65.00	100.00	225.00	1,200	
1873S	703,000	60.00	75.00	175.00	700.00	
1874 . . . . (700)	987,800	60.00	75.00	175.00	650.00	3,200
1874CC	1,373,200	65.00	80.00	185.00	1,100	
1874S	2,549,000	60.00	75.00	175.00	650.00	
1875 . . . . (700)	218,900	85.00	135.00	350.00	1,300	3,200
1875CC	1,573,700	65.00	80.00	185.00	800.00	
1875S	4,487,000	60.00	75.00	175.00	650.00	
1875S, S over CC		125.00	250.00	500.00	1,500	
1876 . . . . . . (1,150)	456,150	60.00	75.00	175.00	650.00	3,200
1876CC	509,000	65.00	80.00	200.00	1,000	
1876S	5,227,000	60.00	75.00	175.00	650.00	
1877 . . . . (510)	3,039,710	60.00	75.00	175.00	650.00	3,200
1877CC	534,000	75.00	100.00	225.00	1,200	
1877S	9,519,000	60.00	75.00	175.00	650.00	
1878 . . . . (900)	900	. . . .				3,300
1878CC	*97,000	200.00	350.00	850.00	3,750	
1878S	4,162,000	60.00	75.00	175.00	725.00	
1879 . . . . (1,541)	1,541	. . . .				3,300
1880 . . . . (1,987)	1,987	. . . .				3,300
1881 . . . . (960)	960	. . . .				3,300
1882 . . . . (1,097)	1,097	. . . .				3,300
1883 . . . . (979)	979	. . . .				3,300
1884 . . . . (10)	10	. . . .				60,000
1885 . . . . (5)	5	. . . .				110,000

*44,148 Trade dollars were melted on July 19, 1878. Many of these may have been 1878CC.

BIBLIOGRAPHY

Willem, John M. *The United States Trade Dollar.* Second edition, Racine, Wis., 1965.

SILVER DOLLARS
LIBERTY HEAD OR MORGAN TYPE 1878-1921

The coinage law of 1873 made no provision for the standard silver dollar. During the lapse in coinage of this denomination the gold dollar became the unit coin and the trade dollar was used for our commercial transactions with the Orient.

The legal tender character was restored to the silver dollar by the Act of February 28, 1878, known as the Bland-Allison Act. The weight, 412½ grains and fineness .900 were to conform with the act of January 18, 1837.

George T. Morgan, formerly a pupil of Wyon in the Royal Mint in London, designed the new dollar. His initial M is found at the truncation of the neck, at the last tress. It also appears on the reverse on the left-hand loop of the ribbon.

Coinage of the silver dollar was suspended after 1904 when the bullion supply became exhausted. Under provisions of the Pittman Act of 1918, 270,232,722 silver dollars were melted and later, in 1921, coinage of the silver dollar was resumed. The Morgan design, with some slight refinements, was employed until the new Peace design was adopted later in that year.

Varieties listed are those most significant to collectors, but numerous other variations may be found. Values of variations not listed in this guide depend on collector interest and demand.

Sharply struck, "proof-like" coins have a highly reflective surface and are very scarce and usually command substantial premiums.

BIBLIOGRAPHY

Van Allen, Leroy C. and Mallis, A. George. *Comprehensive Catalogue and Encyclopedia of U.S. Morgan and Peace Silver Dollars.* New York. 1976.

Designer George T. Morgan; weight 26.73 grams; composition: .900 silver, .100 copper; diameter 38.1 mm; reeded edge; mints: Philadelphia, New Orleans, Carson City, Denver, San Francisco. Net weight: .77344 oz. pure silver.

Mint mark location is on reverse below wreath.

First Reverse

8 Tail Feathers, 1878 Philadelphia Only

Second Reverse

Parallel top arrow feather, concave breast.

Third Reverse

Slanted top arrow feather, convex breast.

SILVER DOLLARS

VF-20 VERY FINE—*Two-thirds of hairlines from top of forehead to ear must show. Ear well defined. Feathers on eagle's breast worn.*

EF-40 EXTREMELY FINE—*All hairlines strong and ear bold. Eagle's feathers all plain but slight wear on breast and wing tips.*

AU-50 ABOUT UNCIRCULATED—*Slight trace of wear. Most of mint luster is present although marred by bag marks.*

MS-60 UNCIRCULATED—*No trace of wear. Has full mint luster but may be noticeably marred by scuff marks or bag abrasions.*

MS-63 SELECT UNCIRCULATED—*No trace of wear, full mint luster, few noticeable surface marks.*

MS-65 UNCIRCULATED—*Many Morgan dollars in this grade are very rare and command much higher prices. The most common dates sell for approximately $350.00.*

See pg. 6 for information on investment grade coins.

	Quan. Minted	VF-20	EF-40	AU-50	MS-60	MS-63	Proof-63
1878, 8 tail feathers. (500)	750,000	$19.00	$24.00	$35.00	$60.00	$130.00	$3,500
1878, 7 tail feathers. (250)	9,759,550						
1878, 7 feathers, 2nd reverse		17.00	20.00	25.00	40.00	100.00	
1878, 7 feathers, 3rd reverse........		19.00	27.00	40.00	55.00	165.00	5,000
1878, 7 over 8 feathers.............		22.00	28.00	45.00	70.00	200.00	
1878CC 2,212,000		33.00	40.00	55.00	100.00	160.00	
1878S..................... 9,774,000		16.00	20.00	25.00	32.00	65.00	
1879 .... (1,100) 14,807,100		13.00	15.00	20.00	30.00	85.00	3,000
1879CC broken CC.......... 756,000		70.00	175.00	325.00	900.00	2,500	
1879CC clear CC...................		80.00	225.00	450.00	1,300	4,000	
1879O.................... 2,887,000		12.00	15.00	20.00	50.00	210.00	
1879S second reverse .... ⎱ 9,110,000		20.00	27.00	40.00	150.00	500.00	
1879S third reverse ...... ⎰		12.00	15.00	20.00	30.00	45.00	
1880, 8 over 7* .... ⎱ 12,601,355		20.00	25.00	40.00	80.00	300.00	
1880 .... (1,355) ⎰		12.00	15.00	19.00	30.00	75.00	3,000

1880CC, 80 over 79†	**1880CC, 8 over high 7***	**1880CC, 8 over low 7**

		VF-20	EF-40	AU-50	MS-60	MS-63	
1880CC all kinds............ 591,000							
1880CC, 80 over 79, 2nd rev.†.......		60.00	90.00	135.00	185.00	275.00	
1880CC, 8 over 7, 2nd rev..........		60.00	90.00	135.00	185.00	275.00	
1880CC, 8 over high 7, 3rd rev.*		55.00	80.00	125.00	175.00	250.00	
1880CC, 8 over low 7, 3rd. rev.		55.00	80.00	125.00	175.00	250.00	
1880CC third reverse		55.00	80.00	105.00	175.00	250.00	
1880O, 8 over 7* .... ⎱ 5,305,000		14.00	18.00	30.00	75.00	350.00	
1880O................... ⎰		14.00	18.00	25.00	40.00	240.00	
1880S, 8 over 7* .... ⎱		14.00	18.00	26.00	50.00	70.00	
1880S, 0 over 9 .... ⎬ 8,900,000		14.00	18.00	26.00	50.00	70.00	
1880S................. ⎰		14.00	18.00	25.00	40.00	45.00	
1881 .... (975) 9,163,975		14.00	18.00	25.00	30.00	150.00	3,000
1881CC 296,000		100.00	120.00	140.00	200.00	235.00	
1881O.................... 5,708,000		12.00	15.00	18.00	28.00	125.00	
1881S 12,760,000		12.00	15.00	20.00	30.00	45.00	
1882 .... (1,100) 11,101,100		12.00	15.00	18.00	30.00	100.00	3,000
1882CC 1,133,000		35.00	45.00	65.00	80.00	125.00	
1882O.................. ⎱ 6,090,000		12.00	15.00	18.00	28.00	100.00	
1882O, O over S* .... ⎰		12.00	15.00	20.00	40.00	110.00	

* Several die varieties. Values shown are for the most common.

† 7 and 9 show within the 80, no tip below second 8.

Proof Morgan Dollars where indicated in mintage record (quantity shown in parenthesis) are valued approximately as follows:

Proof-60 $1,000   Proof-65 $10,000

SILVER DOLLARS

	Quan. Minted	VF-20	EF-40	AU-50	MS-60	MS-63	Proof-63
1882S	9,250,000	$14.00	$18.00	$23.00	$32.00	$45.00	
1883 . . . . (1,039)	12,291,039	12.00	15.00	18.00	30.00	70.00	$3,000
1883CC	1,204,000	35.00	45.00	65.00	80.00	125.00	
1883O	8,725,000	11.00	13.00	15.00	21.00	45.00	
1883S	6,250,000	22.00	25.00	110.00	375.00	1,700	
1884 . . . . (875)	14,070,875	12.00	15.00	18.00	30.00	75.00	3,000
1884CC	1,136,000	35.00	45.00	65.00	80.00	125.00	
1884O	9,730,000	11.00	13.00	15.00	21.00	45.00	
1884S	3,200,000	20.00	32.00	200.00	4,000	15,000	
1885 . . . . (930)	17,787,767	13.00	14.00	16.00	21.00	40.00	3,000
1885CC	228,000	190.00	200.00	225.00	250.00	285.00	
1885O	9,185,000	11.00	13.00	15.00	21.00	45.00	
1885S	1,497,000	16.00	19.00	45.00	80.00	210.00	
1886 . . . . (886)	19,963,886	11.00	13.00	15.00	21.00	40.00	3,000
1886O	10,710,000	15.00	19.00	50.00	350.00	2,500	
1886S	750,000	21.00	28.00	42.00	110.00	325.00	
1887, 7 over 6 . } (710)	20,290,710	18.00	24.00	37.00	75.00	600.00	
1887		11.00	13.00	15.00	21.00	40.00	3,000
1887O, 7 over 6 . . . . . . }	11,550,000	20.00	26.00	38.00	150.00	1,500	
1887O		12.00	14.00	23.00	35.00	200.00	
1887S	1,771,000	15.00	20.00	28.00	75.00	250.00	
1888 . . . . (832)	19,183,832	12.00	14.00	16.00	30.00	75.00	3,000
1888O	12,150,000	12.00	14.00	16.00	30.00	75.00	
1888S	657,000	25.00	28.00	50.00	110.00	325.00	
1889 . . . . (811)	21,726,811	12.00	14.00	16.00	25.00	90.00	3,000
1889CC	350,000	270.00	625.00	2,300	6,000	16,000	
1889O	11,875,000	15.00	19.00	28.00	70.00	300.00	
1889S	700,000	25.00	30.00	50.00	85.00	275.00	
1890 . . . . (590)	16,802,590	12.00	14.00	16.00	35.00	70.00	3,500
1890CC	2,309,041	30.00	38.00	75.00	210.00	425.00	
1890O	10,701,000	14.00	18.00	25.00	35.00	100.00	
1890S	8,230,373	14.00	18.00	25.00	35.00	100.00	
1891 . . . . (650)	8,694,206	12.00	15.00	30.00	45.00	150.00	3,500
1891CC	1,618,000	30.00	38.00	70.00	165.00	300.00	
1891O	7,954,529	18.00	22.00	32.00	55.00	235.00	
1891S	5,296,000	14.00	18.00	25.00	45.00	125.00	
1892 . . . . (1,245)	1,037,245	17.00	24.00	45.00	100.00	225.00	3,500
1892CC	1,352,000	45.00	80.00	180.00	300.00	850.00	
1892O	2,744,000	18.00	24.00	45.00	100.00	250.00	
1892S	1,200,000	40.00	135.00	800.00	7,500	19,000	
1893 . . . . (792)	389,792	45.00	85.00	150.00	300.00	525.00	4,000
1893CC	677,000	125.00	325.00	550.00	850.00	3,500	
1893O	300,000	65.00	185.00	325.00	1,000	5,000	
1893S	100,000	1,400	3,000	8,500	20,000	50,000	
1894 . . . . (972)	110,972	215.00	350.00	525.00	850.00	1,850	5,000
1894O	1,723,000	21.00	30.00	110.00	400.00	1,500	
1894S	1,260,000	36.00	80.00	155.00	325.00	675.00	
1895† . . . . (880)	12,880			† 10,000	† 14,000		19,000
1895O	450,000	75.00	185.00	410.00	2,700	9,500	
1895S	400,000	150.00	350.00	550.00	875.00	2,500	
1896 . . . . (762)	9,976,762	12.00	14.00	16.00	21.00	45.00	3,000
1896O	4,900,000	15.00	20.00	100.00	700.00	4,500	
1896S	5,000,000	32.50	100.00	210.00	550.00	1,800	
1897 . . . . (731)	2,822,731	12.00	14.00	16.00	21.00	45.00	3,000
1897O	4,004,000	14.00	18.00	50.00	450.00	3,000	
1897S	5,825,000	14.00	18.00	25.00	45.00	110.00	

†Beware of removed mint mark. Values are for Proofs; no others are known to exist.
For Proof-60 and Proof-65 Morgan dollar prices see Pg. 177.

SILVER DOLLARS

	Quan. Minted	VF-20	EF-40	AU-50	MS-60	MS-63	Proof-63
1898 .... (735)	5,884,735	$12.00	$14.00	$16.00	$21.00	$40.00	$3,000
1898O................	4,440,000	12.00	14.00	16.00	21.00	40.00	
1898S................	4,102,000	14.00	18.00	50.00	150.00	265.00	
1899 .... (846)	330,846	30.00	42.00	60.00	70.00	135.00	3,000
1899O...............	12,290,000	12.00	14.00	16.00	23.00	45.00	
1899S................	2,562,000	14.00	21.00	60.00	90.00	225.00	
1900 .... (912)	8,830,912	12.00	14.00	16.00	21.00	40.00	3,000
1900O..............		14.00	16.00	20.00	25.00	45.00	
1900O, O over CC*... }	12,590,000	25.00	30.00	55.00	120.00	250.00	
1900S................	3,540,000	18.00	24.00	45.00	100.00	200.00	
1901 .... (813)	6,962,813	28.00	40.00	175.00	1,000	6,000	4,000
1901O................	13,320,000	13.00	16.00	22.00	30.00	50.00	
1901S................	2,284,000	23.00	32.00	80.00	235.00	450.00	
1902 .... (777)	7,994,777	12.00	16.00	26.00	37.50	85.00	3,200
1902O................	8,636,000	13.00	16.00	22.00	30.00	50.00	
1902S................	1,530,000	35.00	60.00	85.00	125.00	250.00	
1903 .... (755)	4,652,755	13.00	16.00	22.00	35.00	75.00	3,200
1903O................	4,450,000	150.00	160.00	175.00	200.00	250.00	
1903S................	1,241,000	50.00	165.00	625.00	1,800	3,500	
1904 .... (650)	2,788,650	14.00	18.00	30.00	65.00	150.00	3,500
1904O................	3,720,000	11.00	13.00	15.00	21.00	40.00	
1904S................	2,304,000	50.00	110.00	400.00	775.00	1,700	
1921	44,690,000	9.00	11.00	14.00	18.00	30.00	———
1921D................	20,345,000	9.00	11.00	15.00	25.00	55.00	
1921S................	21,695,000	9.00	11.00	15.00	25.00	55.00	

*Several die varieties.
For Proof-60 and Proof-65 Morgan dollar prices see Pg. 177.

PEACE TYPE 1921-1935

The dollar issued from 1921 to 1935 was a commemorative peace coin, which might easily have been a half dollar. The Peace Dollar, in fact, was issued without congressional sanction, under the terms of the Pittman Act, which referred to the bullion and in no way affected the design.

Anthony De Francisci, a medalist, designed this dollar. His monogram is located in the field of the coin under the neck of Liberty.

The new Peace Dollar was placed in circulation January 3, 1922. 1,006,473 pieces were struck in December, 1921.

The high relief of the 1921 design was found impractical for coinage and was slightly modified in 1922. The rare matte proof specimens of 1921 and 1922 are of the high relief style of 1921.

Mint mark location is on reverse below ONE.

SILVER DOLLARS

Legislation dated August 3, 1964 authorized the coinage of 45 million silver dollars, and 316,076 dollars of the Peace design dated 1964 were struck at the Denver mint. Plans for completing this coinage were subsequently abandoned and all of these coins were melted. None were preserved or released for circulation.

Designer Anthony De Francisci; weight 26.73 grams; composition: .900 silver, .100 copper; diameter 38.1 mm; reeded edge; mints: Philadelphia, Denver, San Francisco. Net weight: .77344 oz. pure silver.

VF-20 VERY FINE—*Hair over eye well worn. Some strands over ear well defined. Some eagle feathers on top and outside edge of right wing will show.*

EF-40 EXTREMELY FINE—*Hairlines over brow and ear are strong though slightly worn. Outside wing feathers at right and those at top are visible but faint.*

AU-50 ABOUT UNCIRCULATED—*Slight trace of wear. Most of mint luster is present although marred by contact marks.*

MS-60 UNCIRCULATED—*No trace of wear. Has full mint luster but may be noticeably marred by stains, surface marks or bag abrasions.*

MS-63 SELECT UNCIRCULATED—*No trace of wear, full mint luster, few noticeable surface marks.*

MS-65 CHOICE UNCIRCULATED—*No trace of wear, full mint luster, and only minute surface marks.*

Quan. Minted	VF-20	EF-40	AU-50	MS-60	MS-63	Matte Proof-65
1921 1,006,473	$30.00	$40.00	$60.00	$165.00	$300.00	$30,000
1922 51,737,000	9.00	11.00	13.00	16.00	35.00	30,000
1922D. . . 15,063,000	10.00	12.00	15.00	35.00	120.00	
1922S . . . 17,475,000	10.00	12.00	15.00	35.00	130.00	
1923 30,800,000	9.00	11.00	13.00	16.00	35.00	
1923D. . . . 6,811,000	10.00	12.00	15.00	35.00	120.00	
1923S . . . 19,020,000	10.00	12.00	15.00	35.00	130.00	
1924 11,811,000	10.00	13.00	18.00	25.00	45.00	
1924S 1,728,000	16.00	21.00	45.00	100.00	650.00	
1925 10,198,000	10.00	13.00	18.00	25.00	45.00	
1925S 1,610,000	13.00	19.00	30.00	85.00	315.00	
1926 1,939,000	13.00	16.00	23.00	35.00	85.00	
1926D. . . . 2,348,700	13.00	18.00	27.00	55.00	165.00	
1926S 6,980,000	13.00	16.00	20.00	45.00	135.00	
1927 848,000	18.00	24.00	32.00	75.00	200.00	
1927D. . . . 1,268,900	17.00	23.00	85.00	175.00	900.00	
1927S 866,000	16.00	21.00	50.00	110.00	450.00	
1928 360,649	115.00	140.00	160.00	225.00	500.00	
1928S* . . . 1,632,000	15.00	20.00	45.00	100.00	400.00	
1934 954,057	17.00	24.00	38.00	80.00	200.00	
1934D* . . . 1,569,500	16.00	21.00	45.00	100.00	375.00	
1934S 1,011,000	42.00	150.00	475.00	1,400	4,800	
1935 1,576,000	16.00	19.00	25.00	60.00	150.00	
1935S† . . . 1,964,000	16.00	19.00	50.00	125.00	350.00	

*Large and small mint mark varieties, see page 65.
†Varieties occur with either 3 or 4 rays below ONE.

EISENHOWER DOLLARS 1971-1978

Honoring both President Dwight D. Eisenhower and the first landing of man on the moon, this design is the work of Chief Engraver Frank Gasparro, whose initials are on the truncation and below the eagle. The reverse is an adaptation of the official Apollo 11 insignia. Collectors' coins were struck in 40% silver composition and the circulation issue is copper-nickel.

Since 1971, the dies for the Eisenhower dollar have been modified several times by changing the relief, strengthening the design and making the world above the eagle more clearly defined.

Low relief dies were used for all copper-nickel issues of 1971, all uncirculated silver of 1971, and most copper-nickel coins of 1972.

EISENHOWER DOLLARS

High relief dies were used for all proofs of 1971, all silver issues of 1972, and the reverse of some exceptional Philadelphia copper-nickel coins of 1972 (identified by round world and weakly defined continents).

Modified high relief reverse dies were used for late 1972 Philadelphia copper-nickel coins and for all subsequent issues. Modified high relief obverse dies were also used on all issues beginning in 1973.

A few 1974D and 1977D dollars in silver clad composition were made in error.

Designer Frank Gasparro. Silver issue: weight 24.59 grams; composition: outer layers of .800 silver, .200 copper bonded to inner core of .209 silver, .791 copper. Copper-nickel issue: weight 22.68 grams; composition: outer layers of .750 copper, .250 nickel bonded to inner core of pure copper. Diameter 38.1 mm; reeded edge. Net weight of silver issues: .3161 oz. pure silver.

Mint mark location is above the date.

	Quan. Minted			
	Proof	Regular	MS-63	Proof-65
1971 Copper-nickel clad		47,799,000	$2.75	
1971D Copper-nickel clad..........................		68,587,424	2.50	
1971S Silver clad	(4,265,234)	6,868,530	6.00	$8.00
1972 Copper-nickel clad		75,890,000	2.50	
1972D Copper-nickel clad..........................		92,548,511	2.50	
1972S Silver clad	(1,811,631)	2,193,056	8.00	11.00
1973 Copper-nickel clad		*2,000,056	5.50	
1973D Copper-nickel clad..........................		*2,000,000	5.50	
1973S Copper-nickel clad	(2,760,339)			7.00
1973S Silver clad	(1,013,646)	1,883,140	10.00	45.00
1974 Copper-nickel clad		27,366,000	2.50	
1974D Copper-nickel clad..........................		45,517,000	2.50	
1974S Copper-nickel clad	(2,612,568)			7.00
1974S Silver clad	(1,306,579)	1,900,156	9.00	12.00

*1,769,258 of each sold only in sets and not released for circulation. Unissued coins destroyed at mint.

BICENTENNIAL COINAGE DATED 1776-1976

The national significance of the Bicentennial of the United States was highlighted with the adoption of new reverse designs for the quarter, half dollar and dollar. Nearly a thousand entries were submitted after the Treasury announced in October of 1973 that an open contest was to be held for the selection of the new designs. After the field was narrowed down to twelve semifinalists, the judges chose the rendition of the Liberty Bell superimposed on the moon to appear on the dollar coins. This design is the work of Dennis R. Williams. The obverse remained unchanged except for the dual date 1776-1976, which appeared on all dollars made during 1975 and 1976. These dual-dated coins

BICENTENNIAL DOLLARS

were included in the various offerings of proof and uncirculated coins made by the Mint. They were also struck for general circulation.

The lettering was modified early in 1975 to produce a more attractive design.

Designers Frank Gasparro and Dennis R. Williams. Silver issue: weight 24.59 grams; composition: outer layers of .800 silver, .200 copper bonded to inner core of .209 silver, .791 copper. Copper-nickel issue: weight 22.68 grams; composition: outer layers of .750 copper, .250 nickel bonded to inner core of pure copper. Diameter 38.1 mm; reeded edge. Net weight of silver issues: .3161 oz. pure silver.

Obverse and Reverse Variety II   **Reverse Var. I**

Variety I: Design in low relief, bold lettering on reverse. Variety II: Sharp design, delicate lettering on reverse.

	Quan. Minted	MS-63	Proof-65
1776-1976 Copper-nickel clad, variety I	4,019,000	$2.50	
1776-1976 Copper-nickel clad, variety II	113,318,000	2.50	
1776-1976D Copper-nickel clad, variety I	21,048,710	2.50	
1776-1976D Copper-nickel clad, variety II	82,179,564	2.50	
1776-1976S Copper-nickel clad, variety I	(2,845,450)		$8.00
1776-1976S Copper-nickel clad, variety II	(4,149,730)		5.50
1776-1976S Silver clad, variety I	* 11,000,000	8.00	
1776-1976S Silver clad, variety I	*(4,000,000)		13.00

*Approximate mintage.

EAGLE REVERSE RESUMED

1977 Copper-nickel clad	12,596,000	2.50	
1977D Copper-nickel clad	32,983,006	2.50	
1977S Copper-nickel clad	(3,251,152)		5.00
1978 Copper-nickel clad	25,702,000	2.50	
1978D Copper-nickel clad	33,012,890	2.50	
1978S Copper-nickel clad	(3,127,781)		5.50

SUSAN B. ANTHONY DOLLARS 1979 To 1981

Intended to honor this pioneer in women's rights, legislation dated October 10, 1978, provided for the issuance of the Susan B. Anthony dollar coin. Both obverse and reverse designs were the work of Chief Engraver of the U.S. Mint, Frank Gasparro. His initials FG are located below the portrait and the eagle.

Placement of Susan B. Anthony's likeness on the new dollar represented the first time that a woman, other than a mythical figure, has appeared on a circulating U.S. coin. The reverse design is the same as that used on the Eisenhower dollar. Mint marks P, D or S appear on the obverse, slightly above Anthony's right shoulder.

Because its small size often caused confusion with the quarter and half dollar coins in circulation, the Anthony dollar failed to gain widespread public acceptance and was discontinued in 1981.

Designer Frank Gasparro; weight 8.1 grams; composition: outer layers of copper-nickel (.750 copper, .250 nickel) bonded to inner core of pure copper; diameter 26.5 mm; reeded edge.

ANTHONY DOLLARS

 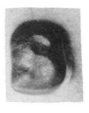

Clear S   **Filled S**

	Quan. Minted	MS-63	Proof-65		Quan. Minted	MS-63	Proof-65
1979P*	360,222,000	$1.75		1980D	41,628,708	$1.75	
1979D	288,015,744	1.75		1980S	20,422,000	2.25	
1979S	109,576,000	2.00		1980S Proof	(3,554,806)		$7.00
1979S Proof	(3,677,175)			1981P	3,000,000	4.75	
Filled S			$8.00	1981D	3,250,000	4.75	
Clear S			85.00	1981S	3,492,000	4.75	
1980P	27,610,000	1.75		1981S Proof	(4,063,083)		7.00

* The obverse design was modified in 1979 to widen the border rim. Late issues of 1979P and all subsequent issues have the wide rim. The 1979P with wide rim is very scarce.

GOLD

Gold has served as money or established the monetary value of currencies longer than any other material. The use of gold coins was widespread in Europe by the fourth century B.C.

The earliest coins circulated in the United States were foreign coins, mostly gold, brought from Europe. The Coinage Act in 1792 established an independent monetary system with the dollar as the basic United States monetary unit containing 24¾ grains of fine gold, based on the world price of $19.39 a troy ounce (480 grains). Congress changed the gold specification in 1834 and again in 1837, when it set the dollar price of gold at $20.67 an ounce.

In 1934, United States citizens were prohibited from holding monetary gold in this country; this was extended in 1961 to gold held abroad as well. The dollar price was then set at $35 per ounce. Use of gold in international trade was further restricted as the price rose. The government revalued it at $38 per ounce in 1972, then $42.22 in 1973. It has fluctuated boldly over the past few years. All restrictions on holding gold were removed in 1975.

GOLD DOLLARS 1849-1889

Coinage of the gold dollar was authorized by the Act of March 3, 1849. The weight was 25.8 grains, fineness .900. The first type, struck until 1854, is known as the Liberty Head or small-sized type.

In 1854 the piece was made larger in diameter and thinner. The design was changed to a feather headdress on a female, generally referred to as the Indian Head or large-sized type. In 1856 the type was changed slightly by enlarging the size of the head.

+ or − indicates change from previous year	**TYPE COIN VALUES**									
	F-12	VF-20	EF-40	AU-50	MS-60	MS-63	MS-65	PF-60	PF-63	PF-65
Liberty Hd 1849-1854	110.00 –	160.00 –	200.00 –	250.00 –	600.00 –	3,000 +	16,000 +			
Indian Hd Type II 1854-1856	175.00	300.00 –	550.00 –	1,350 –	4,500 –	15,000 +	45,000 +			
Indian Hd Type III 1856-1889	110.00 –	160.00 –	200.00 –	235.00 –	550.00 –	2,300 +	6,500 +	2,000	5,000 +	20,000 +

Values of common gold coins have been based on the current bullion price of gold, and may vary with the prevailing spot price.
The weight and content of these coins is stated in the introduction to each series, and may be used to recalculate bullion value.

LIBERTY HEAD TYPE 1849-1854

Designer James B. Longacre; weight 1.672 grams; composition: .900 gold, .100 copper; diameter 13 mm; reeded edge. Net weight: .04837 oz. pure gold.

VF-20 VERY FINE—*LIBERTY on headband complete and readable. Knobs on coronet are defined.*

EF-40 EXTREMELY FINE—*Slight wear on Liberty's hair. Knobs on coronet sharp.*

AU-50 ABOUT UNCIRCULATED—*Trace of wear on headband. Nearly full luster.*

MS-60 UNCIRCULATED—*No trace of wear. Light marks and blemishes.*

Type 1
With open or closed wreath.

Mint mark is below wreath.

	Quan. Minted	VF-20	EF-40	AU-50	MS-60
1849 Open wreath—All kinds*	688,567	$160.00	$200.00	$250.00	$600.00
1849 Closed wreath (ends closer to numeral)		160.00	200.00	250.00	600.00
1849C Closed wreath	} 11,634	325.00	650.00	1,100	3,250
1849C Open wreath (Ex. rare)		——	——	——	——
1849D Open wreath	21,588	325.00	650.00	1,100	3,250
1849O Open wreath	215,000	200.00	250.00	350.00	1,400
1850	481,953	160.00	200.00	250.00	600.00
1850C	6,966	400.00	600.00	1,000	3,250
1850D	8,382	400.00	600.00	1,000	3,250
1850O	14,000	275.00	450.00	575.00	1,800

*The variety with smaller head and no L on truncation is valued higher.

GOLD DOLLARS

	Quan. Minted	VF-20	EF-40	AU-50	MS-60	Proof-63
1851	3,317,671	$160.00	$200.00	$250.00	$600.00	
1851C	41,267	325.00	550.00	850.00	2,200	
1851D	9,882	350.00	600.00	1,000	2,750	
1851O	290,000	200.00	250.00	300.00	1,000	
1852	2,045,351	160.00	200.00	250.00	600.00	
1852C	9,434	300.00	550.00	900.00	2,400	
1852D	6,360	350.00	600.00	1,100	2,900	
1852O	140,000	200.00	250.00	300.00	1,000	
1853	4,076,051	160.00	225.00	250.00	600.00	
1853C	11,515	350.00	600.00	950.00	3,250	
1853D	6,583	350.00	650.00	1,100	3,250	
1853O	290,000	200.00	250.00	350.00	950.00	
1854	855,502	160.00	225.00	250.00	600.00	——
1854D	2,935	600.00	1,100	1,900	5,000	
1854S	14,632	300.00	500.00	800.00	2,500	

INDIAN HEAD TYPE, Small Head 1854-1856

Standards same as previous issue. Diameter changed to 15 mm.

Type 2

VF-20 VERY FINE—Feather curl tips outlined but details worn.

EF-40 EXTREMELY FINE—Slight wear on tips of feather curls on headdress.

AU-50 ABOUT UNCIRCULATED—Trace of wear on feathers, nearly full luster.

MS-60 UNCIRCULATED—No trace of wear. Light marks and blemishes.

	Quan. Minted	VF-20	EF-40	AU-50	MS-60	Proof-63
1854	783,943	300.00	550.00	1,350	4,500	——
1855	758,269	300.00	550.00	1,350	4,500	——
1855C	9,803	750.00	1,200	2,600	11,000	
1855D	1,811	3,000	5,500	8,500	20,000	
1855O	55,000	500.00	1,000	2,000	7,500	
1856S	24,600	500.00	950.00	1,900	7,500	

INDIAN HEAD TYPE, Large Head 1856-1889

Type 3

VF-20 VERY FINE—Curled feathers have slight detail. Details worn smooth at eyebrow, hair below headdress and behind ear and bottom curl.

EF-40 EXTREMELY FINE—Slight wear above and to right of eye and on top of curled feathers.

AU-50 ABOUT UNCIRCULATED—Trace of wear on feathers, nearly full luster.

MS-60 UNCIRCULATED—No trace of wear. Light marks and blemishes.

	Quan. Minted	VF-20	EF-40	AU-50	MS-60	Proof-63
1856 Upright 5	} 1,762,936	200.00	275.00	550.00	1,000	
1856 Slant 5		160.00	200.00	235.00	550.00	$7,500
1856D	1,460	3,000	4,750	7,000	19,000	
1857	774,789	160.00	200.00	235.00	550.00	7,500
1857C	13,280	450.00	600.00	950.00	3,000	
1857D	3,533	550.00	900.00	1,750	4,750	
1857S	10,000	300.00	400.00	700.00	2,500	
1858	117,995	160.00	200.00	235.00	550.00	7,500
1858D	3,477	850.00	1,200	2,200	6,000	
1858S	10,000	300.00	400.00	800.00	2,300	
1859	(80) 168,244	160.00	200.00	235.00	550.00	6,750
1859C	5,235	550.00	850.00	1,400	4,000	
1859D	4,952	550.00	900.00	1,600	4,600	
1859S	15,000	300.00	400.00	725.00	2,300	
1860	(154) 36,668	160.00	200.00	235.00	550.00	6,000
1860D	1,566	2,700	5,000	7,500	16,500	
1860S	13,000	300.00	425.00	750.00	2,300	
1861	(349) 527,499	160.00	200.00	235.00	550.00	6,000

GOLD DOLLARS

	Quan. Minted	VF-20	EF-40	AU-50	MS-60	Proof-63
1861D		$5,250	$8,500	$15,000	$28,000	
1862 .... (35)	1,361,390	160.00	200.00	235.00	550.00	$8,500
1863 .... (50)	6,250	450.00	650.00	1,000	3,000	8,500
1864 .... (50)	5,950	400.00	600.00	950.00	2,500	8,500
1865 .... (25)	3,725	400.00	600.00	950.00	3,000	8,500
1866 .... (30)	7,130	325.00	500.00	800.00	1,500	8,000
1867 .... (50)	5,250	350.00	600.00	900.00	2,000	8,000
1868 .... (25)	10,525	300.00	525.00	725.00	1,500	8,000
1869 .... (25)	5,925	325.00	550.00	800.00	1,600	8,000
1870 .... (35)	6,335	300.00	525.00	725.00	1,700	8,000
1870S		3,000	625.00	1,000	1,900	3,000	
1871 .... (30)	3,930	300.00	525.00	725.00	1,350	7,500
1872 .... (30)	3,530	300.00	525.00	725.00	1,500	7,500
1873 Closed 3 .... (25)	1,825	300.00	550.00	825.00	2,200	9,000
1873 Open 3	123,300	160.00	200.00	235.00	550.00	
1874 .... (20)	198,820	160.00	200.00	235.00	550.00	7,500
1875 .... (20)	420	2,200	3,200	4,500	8,000	25,000
1876 .... (45)	3,245	225.00	325.00	500.00	1,500	6,750
1877 .... (20)	3,920	250.00	350.00	450.00	1,600	6,750
1878 .... (20)	3,020	250.00	350.00	450.00	1,200	6,750
1879 .... (30)	3,030	250.00	350.00	450.00	1,200	6,750
1880 .... (36)	1,636	225.00	300.00	450.00	1,500	6,750
1881 .... (87)	7,707	200.00	250.00	325.00	900.00	6,000
1882 .... (125)	5,125	200.00	250.00	325.00	900.00	6,000
1883 .... (207)	11,007	200.00	250.00	325.00	900.00	6,000
1884 .... (1,006)	6,236	200.00	250.00	325.00	900.00	5,000
1885 .... (1,105)	12,261	200.00	250.00	325.00	900.00	5,000
1886 .... (1,016)	6,016	200.00	250.00	325.00	900.00	5,000
1887 .... (1,043)	8,543	200.00	250.00	325.00	900.00	5,000
1888 .... (1,079)	16,580	200.00	250.00	325.00	900.00	5,000
1889 .... (1,779)	30,729	200.00	250.00	325.00	900.00	5,000

BIBLIOGRAPHY

Akers, David W., *Gold Dollars*. Englewood, Ohio, 1975. (and other gold denominations)
Breen, Walter, *Major Varieties of U.S. Gold Dollars*. Chicago. 1964. (and other gold denominations)
Bowers, Q. David, *United States Gold Coins. An Illustrated History*. Wolfeboro, NH, 1982.

QUARTER EAGLES ($2.50 GOLD PIECES)—1796-1929

Authorized by the Act of April 2, 1792, they weighed 67.5 grains, 916 2/3 fine until the weight was changed to 64.5 grains, fineness 899.225, by the Act of June 28, 1834. The Act of January 18, 1837 established fineness at .900. Most dates before 1834 are rare. The first issue was struck in 1796, most of which had no stars on the obverse.

Proofs of some dates prior to 1855 are known to exist, and all are rare.

+ or – indicates change from previous year		TYPE COIN VALUES								
	F-12	VF-20	EF-40	AU-50	MS-60	MS-63	MS-65	PF-60	PF-63	PF-65
Cap Bust Right-NS 1796	9,000–	17,000+	25,000+	32,000	45,000	65,000				
Cap Bust Right 1796-1807	2,750–	4,000–	5,200–	8,000–	17,500+	45,000+	50,000+			
Cap Bust Left-Lg. 1808	9,000+	13,000	20,000+	27,000	47,500	75,000+				
Cap Bust Left-Sm. 1821-1827	3,400	5,000	7,000	10,000	17,000	20,000	40,000			
Cap. Bust Left-Sm. 1829-1834	3,000	4,000	5,750	8,500	13,500	17,000	30,000			
Classic Head 1834-1839	200.00–	300.00	475.00+	850.00	2,400+	11,000+	30,000+			
Lib Coronet 1840-1907	125.00	175.00–	200.00–	250.00–	500.00–	1,600–	6,000+	2,000–	7,000+	22,000+
Indian Head 1908-1929	115.00–	150.00–	175.00–	200.00–	375.00–	1,400–	9,000+	3,250–	9,000+	25,000+

CAPPED BUST TO RIGHT 1796-1807

Designer Robert Scot; weight 4.37 grams; composition: .9167 gold, .0833 copper; approx. diameter 20 mm; reeded edge.

F-12 FINE—*Hair worn smooth on high spots. E PLURIBUS UNUM weak but readable.*

VF-20 VERY FINE—*Some wear on high spots.*

EF-40 EXTREMELY FINE—*Only slight wear on hair and cheek.*

MS-60 UNCIRCULATED—*No trace of wear. Light blemishes.*

QUARTER EAGLES

No Stars on Obverse 1796 Only **Stars on Obverse 1796-1807**

	Quan. Minted	F-12	VF-20	EF-40	MS-60
1796 No stars on obverse	963	$9,000	$17,000	$25,000	$45,000
1796 Stars on obverse	432	7,500	12,000	17,000	38,000
1797	427	5,500	8,000	12,000	22,000
1798	1,094	4,000	5,000	7,000	18,000
1802, 2 over 1	3,035	2,750	4,000	5,200	17,500
1804, 13-Star reverse	} 3,327	5,000	10,000	17,000	35,000
1804, 14-Star reverse		2,750	4,000	5,250	17,500
1805	1,781	2,750	4,000	5,250	17,500
1806, 6 over 4, stars 8 left, 5 right	1,136	2,750	4,000	5,250	17,500
1806, 6 over 5, stars 7 left, 6 right	480	3,500	5,500	8,000	22,000
1807	6,812	2,750	4,000	6,000	17,500

CAPPED BUST TO LEFT, Large Size 1808

Designer John Reich. Standards same as previous issue.

F-12 FINE—*E PLURIBUS UNUM and LIBERTY on headband readable but weak.*
VF-20 VERY FINE—*Motto and LIBERTY clear.*
EF-40 EXTREMELY FINE—*All details of hair are plain.*
MS-60 UNCIRCULATED—*No trace of wear. Light blemishes.*

1808	2,710	9,000	13,000	20,000	47,500

CAPPED HEAD TO LEFT 1821-1834

Those dated 1829 through 1834 are smaller in diameter than the 1821-1827 pieces. They also have smaller letters, dates and stars.

Standards same as previous issue. Diameter changed to approximately 18.5 mm.

1821	6,448	3,400	5,000	7,000	17,000
1824, 4 over 1	2,600	3,400	5,000	7,000	17,000
1825	4,434	3,400	5,000	7,000	17,000
1826	760	4,500	6,000	9,000	30,000
1827	2,800	3,400	5,000	7,000	17,000

Reduced Size 1829-1834

1829	3,403	3,200	4,250	6,200	13,500
1830	4,540	3,000	4,000	5,750	13,500
1831	4,520	3,000	4,000	5,750	13,500
1832	4,400	3,000	4,000	5,750	13,500
1833	4,160	3,000	4,000	5,750	13,500
1834 (Motto)	4,000	6,000	9,000	14,000	28,000

QUARTER EAGLES
CLASSIC HEAD TYPE, No Motto on Reverse 1834-1839

In 1834 the quarter eagle was redesigned. A ribbon binding the hair, bearing the word LIBERTY, replaces the Liberty cap. The motto was omitted from the reverse. In 1840 a coronet and smaller head were designed to conform in appearance with that of the larger gold coins.

Designer William Kneass; weight 4.18 grams; composition: .8992 gold, .1008 copper; diameter 18.2 mm; reeded edge.

F-12 FINE—*LIBERTY readable and complete. Curl under ear outlined but no detail.*

VF-20 VERY FINE—*LIBERTY plain. Hair curl has detail.*

EF-40 EXTREMELY FINE—*Small amount of wear on top of hair and below L in LIBERTY. Wear evident on wing.*

AU-50 ABOUT UNCIRCULATED—*Trace of wear on coronet and hair above ear.*

MS-60 UNCIRCULATED—*No trace of wear. Light blemishes.*

Mint mark location.

	Quan. Minted	F-12	VF-20	EF-40	AU-50	MS-60
1834 No motto	112,234	$200.00	$300.00	$475.00	$850.00	$2,400
1835	131,402	200.00	300.00	475.00	850.00	2,400
1836	547,986	200.00	300.00	475.00	850.00	2,400
1837	45,080	200.00	325.00	500.00	950.00	2,700
1838	47,030	200.00	325.00	500.00	950.00	2,700
1838C	7,880	400.00	550.00	1,200	1,500	6,200
1839	27,021	200.00	325.00	500.00	950.00	2,700
1839C	18,140	375.00	525.00	1,000	1,400	6,000
1839D	13,674	400.00	550.00	1,200	1,500	5,500
1839O	17,781	300.00	400.00	750.00	1,100	4,500

1839, 9 over 8 varieties exist for P, C and D mints.

CORONET TYPE 1840-1907

Mint mark location.

Designer Christian Gobrecht; weight 4.18 grams; composition: .900 gold, .100 copper; diameter 18 mm; reeded edge. Net weight: .12094 oz. pure gold.

	Quan. Minted	VF-20	EF-40	AU-50	MS-60
1840	18,859	$275.00	$325.00	$450.00	$1,300
1840C	12,822	450.00	750.00	1,100	3,200
1840D	3,532	1,200	2,250	4,000	6,200
1840O	33,580	250.00	300.00	450.00	1,400
1841 Proofs only	15,000	30,000	40,000	60,000
1841C	10,281	425.00	750.00	1,200	2,500
1841D	4,164	800.00	1,400	2,500	4,750
1842	2,823	500.00	800.00	1,300	3,250
1842C	6,729	500.00	800.00	1,200	2,600
1842D	4,643	700.00	1,300	2,400	4,500
1842O	19,800	275.00	500.00	1,000	2,000
1843	100,546	250.00	275.00	400.00	1,000
1843C Small date, crosslet 4	2,988	1,400	2,750	4,000	6,000
1843C Large date, plain 4	23,076	500.00	900.00	1,300	2,300
1843D Small date, crosslet 4	36,209	450.00	850.00	1,200	2,750
1843O Small date, crosslet 4	288,002	250.00	275.00	400.00	1,100
1843O Large date, plain 4	76,000	250.00	275.00	400.00	1,100

[188]

QUARTER EAGLES

	Quan. Minted	VF-20	EF-40	AU-50	MS-60
1844	6,784	$300.00	$500.00	$1,000	$2,000
1844C	11,622	400.00	650.00	1,200	3,000
1844D	17,332	500.00	800.00	1,300	3,000
1845	91,051	225.00	250.00	375.00	1,000
1845D	19,460	500.00	800.00	1,300	3,500
1845O	4,000	950.00	1,500	2,500	9,000
1846	21,598	250.00	400.00	600.00	1,200
1846C	4,808	600.00	1,000	1,600	3,750
1846D	19,303	550.00	850.00	1,500	3,500
1846O	62,000	225.00	250.00	450.00	1,200
1847	29,814	225.00	250.00	400.00	1,000
1847C	23,226	400.00	500.00	1,000	2,750
1847D	15,784	500.00	800.00	1,100	3,000
1847O	124,000	225.00	300.00	500.00	1,100
1848	7,497	425.00	650.00	1,000	2,500

CAL. Above Eagle on Reverse

California Gold Quarter Eagle

In 1848 about two hundred and thirty ounces of gold were sent to Secretary of War Marcy by Col. R. B. Mason, Military Governor of California. The gold was turned over to the mint and made into quarter eagles. The distinguishing mark "CAL." was punched above the eagle on the reverse side, while the coins were in the die. Two specimens with proof surface are known.

	Quan. Minted	VF-20	EF-40	AU-50	MS-60
1848 CAL. above eagle	1,389	4,500	7,500	12,500	30,000
1848C	16,788	425.00	700.00	1,200	2,500
1848D	13,771	550.00	750.00	1,300	3,000
1849	23,294	250.00	300.00	500.00	1,000
1849C	10,220	450.00	750.00	1,200	2,500
1849D	10,945	500.00	950.00	1,400	2,800
1850	252,923	200.00	240.00	375.00	1,000
1850C	9,148	450.00	700.00	1,000	2,200
1850D	12,148	450.00	850.00	1,350	2,500
1850O	84,000	225.00	250.00	600.00	1,000
1851	1,372,748	200.00	240.00	300.00	700.00
1851C	14,923	450.00	700.00	1,000	2,200
1851D	11,264	450.00	800.00	1,350	2,500
1851O	148,000	225.00	240.00	400.00	900.00
1852	1,159,681	200.00	240.00	300.00	650.00
1852C	9,772	400.00	750.00	1,200	2,500
1852D	4,078	550.00	1,000	2,000	3,750
1852O	140,000	225.00	240.00	400.00	1,100
1853	1,404,668	200.00	240.00	300.00	650.00
1853D	3,178	600.00	1,200	2,000	3,750
1854	596,258	200.00	240.00	300.00	750.00
1854C	7,295	450.00	700.00	1,100	2,400
1854D	1,760	2,400	4,000	6,000	12,000
1854O	153,000	200.00	240.00	350.00	1,000
1854S	246		20,000	40,000	——
1855	235,480	200.00	240.00	300.00	750.00
1855C	3,677	750.00	1,400	2,500	4,500
1855D	1,123	2,600	4,250	7,000	18,000
1856	384,240	200.00	240.00	300.00	700.00
1856C	7,913	500.00	800.00	1,500	2,750

QUARTER EAGLES

	Quan. Minted	VF-20	EF-40	AU-50	MS-60	Proof-63
1856D	874	$3,200	$8,000	$13,000	$25,000	
1856O	21,100	250.00	300.00	500.00	1,100	
1856S	72,120	235.00	275.00	475.00	1,000	
1857	214,130	200.00	240.00	300.00	700.00	$17,000
1857D	2,364	650.00	1,200	2,000	4,250	
1857O	34,000	235.00	275.00	450.00	1,000	
1857S	69,200	235.00	300.00	500.00	1,200	
1858	47,377	225.00	250.00	400.00	900.00	15,000
1858C	9,056	400.00	650.00	1,100	2,750	

A modified reverse design (smaller letters and arrowheads) was used on all Philadelphia issues from 1859 through 1907, and on San Francisco issues of 1877 through 1879.

		Quan. Minted	VF-20	EF-40	AU-50	MS-60	Proof-63
1859	(80)	39,444	225.00	240.00	300.00	900.00	12,000
1859D		2,244	600.00	900.00	2,200	4,250	
1859S		15,200	225.00	325.00	450.00	1,000	
1860	(112)	22,675	225.00	240.00	350.00	900.00	8,000
1860C		7,469	400.00	700.00	1,100	2,750	
1860S		35,600	235.00	300.00	450.00	1,000	

1862, 2 0ver 1

		Quan. Minted	VF-20	EF-40	AU-50	MS-60	Proof-63
1861	(90)	1,283,878	200.00	240.00	300.00	700.00	8,000
1861S		24,000	250.00	300.00	600.00	1,100	
1862, 2 over 1			900.00	1,500	3,000	——	
1862	(35)	98,543	225.00	250.00	350.00	700.00	9,000
1862S		8,000	450.00	800.00	1,000	2,200	
1863 Proofs only	(30)	30					45,000
1863S		10,800	300.00	500.00	800.00	1,800	
1864	(50)	2,874	1,000	1,750	3,000	5,500	13,000
1865	(25)	1,545	1,000	1,750	3,000	5,500	14,000
1865S		23,376	250.00	350.00	550.00	1,100	
1866	(30)	3,110	350.00	500.00	900.00	1,800	10,000
1866S		38,960	250.00	350.00	550.00	1,200	
1867	(50)	3,250	300.00	500.00	800.00	1,600	9,000
1867S		28,000	250.00	300.00	550.00	1,100	
1868	(25)	3,625	275.00	375.00	650.00	1,400	9,000
1868S		34,000	225.00	300.00	500.00	1,100	
1869	(25)	4,345	275.00	325.00	600.00	1,100	9,000
1869S		29,500	225.00	300.00	500.00	1,100	
1870	(35)	4,555	275.00	350.00	600.00	1,200	9,000
1870S		16,000	250.00	325.00	425.00	1,200	
1871	(30)	5,350	275.00	350.00	500.00	1,200	9,000
1871S		22,000	200.00	240.00	350.00	1,000	
1872	(30)	3,030	300.00	400.00	600.00	1,200	9,000
1872S		18,000	200.00	240.00	300.00	800.00	
1873 Closed 3	(25)	55,225	200.00	240.00	300.00	700.00	9,000
1873 Open 3		122,800	200.00	240.00	300.00	700.00	
1873S		27,000	250.00	300.00	600.00	1,000	
1874	(20)	3,940	275.00	350.00	600.00	1,000	10,000
1875	(20)	420	2,000	4,000	6,500	9,500	25,000
1875S		11,600	250.00	300.00	425.00	1,000	
1876	(45)	4,221	250.00	350.00	600.00	1,200	9,000
1876S		5,000	250.00	325.00	450.00	1,500	
1877	(20)	1,652	450.00	650.00	850.00	1,800	10,000

QUARTER EAGLES

	Quan. Minted	VF-20	EF-40	AU-50	MS-60	Proof-63
1877S	35,400	$200.00	$240.00	$300.00	$700.00	
1878 .... (20)	286,260	200.00	240.00	300.00	700.00	$10,000
1878S	178,000	200.00	240.00	300.00	700.00	
1879 .... (30)	88,990	200.00	240.00	300.00	700.00	9,000
1879S	43,500	200.00	240.00	300.00	700.00	
1880 .... (36)	2,996	250.00	325.00	400.00	1,100	9,000
1881 .... (51)	691	900.00	1,500	2,750	4,000	10,000
1882 .... (67)	4,067	250.00	300.00	400.00	1,100	8,500
1883 .... (82)	2,002	275.00	350.00	425.00	1,200	8,500
1884 .... (73)	2,023	275.00	350.00	425.00	1,200	8,500
1885 .... (87)	887	750.00	1,100	2,000	3,000	9,750
1886 .... (88)	4,088	250.00	300.00	400.00	1,000	8,500
1887 .... (122)	6,282	235.00	250.00	350.00	1,000	8,000
1888 .... (97)	16,098	200.00	240.00	300.00	700.00	8,000
1889 .... (48)	17,648	200.00	240.00	300.00	700.00	8,000
1890 .... (93)	8,813	250.00	275.00	325.00	1,000	8,000
1891 .... (80)	11,040	250.00	275.00	325.00	1,000	8,000
1892 .... (105)	2,545	275.00	375.00	500.00	1,000	7,750
1893 .... (106)	30,106	175.00	200.00	275.00	600.00	7,750
1894 .... (122)	4,122	225.00	275.00	350.00	700.00	7,500
1895 .... (119)	6,119	200.00	240.00	300.00	700.00	7,500
1896 .... (132)	19,202	175.00	200.00	250.00	550.00	7,500
1897 .... (136)	29,904	175.00	200.00	250.00	550.00	7,500
1898 .... (165)	24,165	175.00	200.00	250.00	550.00	7,500
1899 .... (150)	27,350	175.00	200.00	250.00	550.00	7,000
1900 .... (205)	67,205	175.00	200.00	250.00	500.00	7,000
1901 .... (223)	91,323	175.00	200.00	250.00	500.00	7,000
1902 .... (193)	133,733	175.00	200.00	250.00	500.00	7,000
1903 .... (197)	201,257	175.00	200.00	250.00	500.00	7,000
1904 .... (170)	160,960	175.00	200.00	250.00	500.00	7,000
1905* .... (144)	217,944	175.00	200.00	250.00	500.00	7,000
1906 .... (160)	176,490	175.00	200.00	250.00	500.00	7,000
1907 .... (154)	336,448	175.00	200.00	250.00	500.00	7,000

*Pieces dated 1905S are counterfeit.

> Values of common gold coins have been based on the current bullion price of gold, and may vary with the prevailing spot price.

INDIAN HEAD TYPE 1908-1929

The new type represents a departure from all preceding coin types in the United States series. Bela Lyon Pratt was the designer of this and the half eagle piece. The coin has no raised milling and the main devices and legends are incuse.

Designer Bela Lyon Pratt; weight 4.18 grams; composition: .900 gold, .100 copper; diameter 18 mm; reeded edge. Net weight: .12094 oz. pure gold.

VF-20 VERY FINE—*Hair cord knot distinct. Feathers at top of head clear. Cheekbone worn.*

EF-40 EXTREMELY FINE—*Cheekbone, war bonnet and headband feathers slightly worn.*

AU-50 ABOUT UNCIRCULATED—*Trace of wear on cheekbone and headdress.*

MS-60 UNCIRCULATED—*No trace of wear. Light blemishes.*

Mint mark location is on reverse left of arrows.

	Quan. Minted	VF-20	EF-40	AU-50	MS-60	Matte Proof-63
1908 .... (236)	565,057	$115.00	$175.00	$200.00	$375.00	$9,000
1909 .... (139)	441,899	115.00	175.00	200.00	450.00	9,000

QUARTER EAGLES

	Quan. Minted	VF-20	EF-40	AU-50	MS-60	Matte Proof-63
1910 .... (682)	492,682	$115.00	$175.00	$200.00	$375.00	$9,000
1911 .... (191)	704,191	115.00	175.00	200.00	375.00	9,000
1911D........................	55,680	700.00	850.00	1,500	4,000	
1912 .... (197)	616,197	115.00	175.00	200.00	450.00	9,000
1913 .... (165)	722,165	115.00	175.00	200.00	375.00	9,000
1914 .... (117)	240,117	125.00	225.00	250.00	500.00	9,000
1914D........................	448,000	115.00	175.00	200.00	425.00	
1915 .... (100)	606,100	115.00	175.00	200.00	375.00	9,000
1925D........................	578,000	115.00	175.00	200.00	375.00	
1926	446,000	115.00	175.00	200.00	375.00	
1927	388,000	115.00	175.00	200.00	375.00	
1928	416,000	115.00	175.00	200.00	375.00	
1929	532,000	115.00	175.00	200.00	375.00	

THREE DOLLAR GOLD PIECES — 1854-1889

The three dollar gold piece was authorized by the Act of February 21, 1853. The coin was first struck in 1854. It was never popular and saw very little circulation.

The coin weighs 77.4 grains, .900 fine. The head on the obverse represents an Indian princess with hair tightly curling over the neck, head crowned with a circle of feathers, the band of which is inscribed LIBERTY. A wreath of tobacco, wheat, corn and cotton occupies the field of the reverse, with the denomination and date within it.

Restrikes of some years were made at the Mint; particularly 1873 and 1876.

In the year 1854 only, the word DOLLARS is in much smaller letters than in years 1855 through 1889. The 1856 proof has DOLLARS in large letters cut over the same word in small letters.

+ or – indicates change from previous year	**TYPE COIN VALUES**									
	F-12	VF-20	EF-40	AU-50	MS-60	MS-63	MS-65	PF-60	PF-63	PF-65
Indian Head 1854-1889	375.00	550.00–	750.00–	1,100–	3,200–	8,000+	24,000+	4,000–	12,500+	45,000+

Designer James B. Longacre, weight 5.015 grams; composition: .900 gold, .100 copper; diameter 20.5 mm; reeded edge. Net weight: .14512 oz. pure gold.

VF-20 VERY FINE—*Eyebrow, hair about forehead and ear and bottom curl are worn smooth. Curled feather-ends have faint details showing.*

EF-40 EXTREMELY FINE—*Light wear above and to right of eye. and on top of curled feathers.*

AU-50 ABOUT UNCIRCULATED—*Trace of wear on top of curled feathers and in hair above and to right of eye.*

MS-60 UNCIRCULATED—*No trace of wear. Light blemishes.*

Mint mark location is on reverse below wreath.

	Quan. Minted	VF-20	EF-40	AU-50	MS-60	Proof-63
1854	138,618	$550.00	$750.00	$1,100	$3,200	$25,000
1854D........................	1,120	6,500	11,000	20,000	——	
1854O........................	24,000	600.00	800.00	1,400	4,000	
1855	50,555	600.00	800.00	1,300	3,500	30,000
1855S........................	6,600	825.00	1,300	2,000	8,500	
1856	26,010	600.00	800.00	1,300	3,500	22,000
1856S*........................	34,500	700.00	1,200	1,600	5,000	
1857	20,891	600.00	800.00	1,300	4,000	20,000
1857S........................	14,250	725.00	1,200	1,600	5,000	
1858	2,133	775.00	1,300	1,700	5,500	18,000
1859 .... (80)	15,638	600.00	800.00	1,300	4,000	16,000

*Small and medium S varieties exist.

THREE DOLLAR GOLD PIECES

	Quan. Minted	VF-20	EF-40	AU-50	MS-60	Proof-63
1860 .... (119)	7,155	$700.00	$1,200	$1,400	$4,000	$13,000
1860S. (2,592 melted at Mint)	7,000	800.00	1,400	1,700	———	
1861 .... (113)	6,072	700.00	1,200	1,400	4,000	13,000
1862 .... (35)	5,785	700.00	1,200	1,400	4,000	13,000
1863 .... (39)	5,039	750.00	1,300	1,500	4,000	13,000
1864 .... (50)	2,680	750.00	1,300	1,500	4,000	13,000
1865 .... (25)	1,165	950.00	1,500	2,000	6,000	18,000
1866 .... (30)	4,030	750.00	1,300	1,500	4,000	13,000
1867 .... (50)	2,650	750.00	1,300	1,500	4,000	13,000
1868 .... (25)	4,875	750.00	1,300	1,500	4,000	13,000
1869 .... (25)	2,525	750.00	1,300	1,500	4,000	13,000
1870 .... (35)	3,535	750.00	1,300	1,500	4,000	13,000
1870S (Unique)	1	687,500	U.S. Gold Sale, 1982			
1871 .... (30)	1,330	850.00	1,350	1,600	5,000	13,000
1872 .... (30)	2,030	750.00	1,300	1,500	4,000	13,000
1873 Closed 3................		2,500	4,000	5,000	9,000	20,000
1873 Open 3 (Original) ... (25)	25					30,000
1874 .... (20)	41,820	550.00	750.00	1,100	3,200	17,500
1875 Proofs only........ (20)	20		Carter Sale, 1984			121,000
1876 Proofs only........ (45)	45		Carter Sale, 1984			35,200
1877 .... (20)	1,488	950.00	1,750	2,100	6,000	18,000
1878 .... (20)	82,324	550.00	750.00	1,100	3,200	17,500
1879 .... (30)	3,030	750.00	1,300	1,500	4,000	13,000
1880 .... (36)	1,036	850.00	1,300	1,600	4,000	13,000
1881 .... (54)	554	1,000	1,700	2,100	6,000	14,000
1882 .... (76)	1,576	750.00	1,300	1,500	4,000	11,000
1883 .... (89)	989	850.00	1,300	1,600	4,500	11,000
1884 .... (106)	1,106	850.00	1,300	1,600	4,000	10,000
1885 .... (109)	910	900.00	1,400	1,700	4,000	10,000
1886 .... (142)	1,142	750.00	1,300	1,600	4,500	10,000
1887 .... (160)	6,160	675.00	900.00	1,300	3,500	10,000
1888 .... (291)	5,291	675.00	900.00	1,300	3,500	10,000
1889 .... (129)	2,429	675.00	900.00	1,300	3,500	10,000

FOUR DOLLAR GOLD OR "STELLA"

These pattern coins were first suggested by the Hon. John A. Kasson, then U.S. Minister to Austria; and it was through the efforts of Dr. W. W. Hubbell, who patented the goloid metal used in making the goloid metric dollars, that we have these beautiful and interesting pieces.

There are two distinct types in both years of issue. Charles E. Barber designed the flowing hair type, and George T. Morgan the coiled hair. They were struck in gold, aluminum, copper and white metal. Only those struck in gold are listed.

	Quan. Minted	EF-40	Proof-60	Proof-63	Proof-65
1879 Flowing hair	(425)	$20,000	$35,000	$45,000	$100,000
1879 Coiled hair...............	(10)		75,000	100,000	165,000
1880 Flowing hair	(15)		45,000	75,000	125,000
1880 Coiled Hair...............	(10)		100,000	135,000	200,000

HALF EAGLES — 1795-1929

($5.00 GOLD PIECES)

The half eagle was the first gold coin actually struck for the United States. The $5.00 piece was authorized to be coined by the Act of April 2, 1792, and the first type weighed 135 grains, 916 2/3 fine. The Act of June 28, 1834 changed the weight to 129 grains, 899.225 fine. Fineness became .900 by the Act of January 18, 1837.

There are many varieties among the early dates caused by changes in the number of stars, style of eagle, overdates, and differences in the size of figures in the dates. Those dated prior to 1807 do not bear any mark of value. The 1822 half eagle is considered the most valuable regular issue coin of the entire United States series. Proofs of some dates prior to 1855 are known to exist, and all are rare. The half eagle was the only U.S. denomination struck in each of the eight mints.

+ or − indicates change from previous year	TYPE COIN VALUES									
	F-12	VF-20	EF-40	AU-50	MS-60	MS-63	MS-65	PF-60	PF-63	PF-65
Cap Bust-Sm. Eag. 1795-1798	5,500	8,000	11,000	14,000	27,500+	60,000+	125,000+			
Cap Bust-Lg. Eag. 1795-1807	1,200	1,750	2,750	4,250	9,500	20,000+	60,000+			
Cap Draped Bust 1807-1812	1,100	1,600	2,400	4,000	8,000−	18,000+	70,000+			
Cap Head 1813-1834	1,500	2,000	3,000	5,500	11,000	20,000	75,000+			
Classic Head 1834-1838	250.00	300.00	500.00+	1,200+	2,500+	15,000+	50,000+			
Lib Coronet-NM 1839-1866	135.00−	175.00−	225.00−	350.00	1,800+	13,000+	60,000+	6,000+	20,000+	55,000+
Lib. Coronet 1866-1908	125.00−	150.00−	175.00−	200.00−	250.00−	2,000+	11,000+	2,800+	11,000+	40,000+
Indian Head 1908-1929	175.00−	225.00−	250.00−	300.00−	650.00−	4,200+	30,000+	6,000+	13,000+	35,500+

CAPPED BUST TO RIGHT, SMALL EAGLE 1795-1798

This type was struck from mid-1795 to early 1798, when the small eagle reverse was changed to the large or "heraldic" eagle. Note that the 1795 and 1797 dates exist for both types, but the heraldic reverses of these dates were probably struck under emergency conditions in late 1798.

Designer Robert Scot; weight 8.75 grams; composition: .9167 gold, .0833 copper; approx. diameter 25 mm; reeded edge.

F-12 FINE—*Hair worn smooth but with distinct outline. For heraldic type, E PLURIBUS UNUM is faint but readable.*

VF-20 VERY FINE—*Slight to noticeable wear on high spots such as hair, turban, eagle's head and wings.*

EF-40 EXTREMELY FINE—*Slight wear on hair and highest part of cheek.*

MS-60 UNCIRCULATED—*No trace of wear. Light blemishes.*

	Quan. Minted	F-12	VF-20	EF-40	MS-60
1795 Small eagle*.........................	8,707	$5,500	$8,000	$11,000	$27,500

*One variety has final S in STATES over D.

1796, 6 over 5	**1797, 15 Stars**	**1797, 16 Stars**

1796, 6 over 5	6,196	5,500	8,000	11,000	30,000

HALF EAGLES

	Quan. Minted	F-12	VF-20	EF-40	MS-60
1797, 15 stars..........................	} 3,609	$7,000	$10,000	$15,000	$30,000
1797, 16 stars..........................		7,500	11,000	16,000	32,000
1798 Small eagle *(7 known)*............		——	75,000	100,000	——

CAPPED BUST TO RIGHT, HERALDIC EAGLE 1795-1807

		F-12	VF-20	EF-40	MS-60
1795 Heraldic eagle*..........................		6,000	9,000	14,500	32,000
1797, 7 over 5*..............................		5,250	8,000	12,000	23,000
1797, 16 star obverse* *(Unique)*...............			——		
1798 Small 8 .... }	24,867	1,200	1,750	2,750	9,500
1798 Large 8, 13 star reverse..........		1,200	1,750	2,750	11,000
1798 Large 8, 14 star reverse.......... }		1,600	2,600	4,000	17,000
1799..................................	7,451	1,200	1,750	2,750	9,500

*These three pieces are thought to have been struck in 1798 and included in the mintage figure for that year.

1802 over 1	**1803 over 2**		**Small 8 over Large 8**		
1800.................................		37,628	1,200	1,750	2,750	9,500
1802, 2 over 1.......................		53,176	1,200	1,750	2,750	9,500
1803, 3 over 2.......................		33,506	1,200	1,750	2,750	9,500
1804 Small 8 .... }		30,475	1,200	1,750	2,750	9,500
1804 Small 8 over large 8			1,200	1,750	2,750	9,500
1805.................................		33,183	1,200	1,750	2,750	9,500

Pointed 6, 8 and 5 Stars		**Round Top 6, 7 and 6 Stars**			
1806 Pointed top 6....................	9,676	1,200	1,750	3,000	11,000
1806 Round top 6.....................	54,417	1,200	1,750	2,750	9,500
1807.................................	32,488	1,200	1,750	2,750	9,500

HALF EAGLES
CAPPED DRAPED BUST TO LEFT 1807-1812

Designer John Reich. Standards same as previous issue.

F-12 FINE—*LIBERTY readable but partly weak.*

VF-20 VERY FINE—*Headband edges slightly worn. LIBERTY is bold.*

EF-40 EXTREMELY FINE—*Slight wear on highest portions of hair. 80% of major curls are plain.*

MS-60 UNCIRCULATED—*No trace of wear. Light blemishes.*

	Quan. Minted	F-12	VF-20	EF-40	MS-60
1807	51,605	$1,100	$1,600	$2,500	$9,750

1808, 8 over 7	**Normal Date**		**1809, 9 over 8**

	Quan. Minted	F-12	VF-20	EF-40	MS-60
1808, 8 over 7	} 55,578	1,100	1,600	2,400	8,000
1808		1,100	1,600	2,400	8,000
1809, 9 over 8	33,875	1,100	1,600	2,400	8,000

Small Date	**Large Date**	**Large 5**	**Tall 5**

	Quan. Minted	F-12	VF-20	EF-40	MS-60
1810 Small date, small 5		3,000	4,500	9,000	
1810 Small date, tall 5	100,287	1,100	1,600	2,400	8,000
1810 Large date, small 5		1,250	2,500	4,000	11,000
1810 Large date, large 5		1,100	1,600	2,400	8,000
1811 Small 5	99,581	1,100	1,600	2,400	8,000
1811 Tall 5		1,100	1,600	2,400	8,000
1812	58,087	1,100	1,600	2,400	8,000

CAPPED HEAD TO LEFT (large diameter) 1813-1829

	Quan. Minted	F-12	VF-20	EF-40	MS-60
1813	95,428	1,500	2,000	3,000	11,000
1814, 4 over 3	15,454	1,750	2,800	4,000	15,000
1815	635			70,000	150,000
1818 Normal dies		1,500	2,000	3,000	11,000
1818 STATESOF one word	48,588	1,500	2,000	3,000	11,000
1818, 5D over 50		1,500	2,000	3,000	13,000
1819	51,723		——	30,000	50,000
1819, 5D over 50				30,000	50,000

[196]

HALF EAGLES

Curved Base 2	Square Base 2	Small Letters	Large Letters

	Quan. Minted	F-12	VF-20	EF-40	MS-60
1820 Curved-base 2, small letters.....	⎫	$1,500	$2,000	$3,200	$13,000
1820 Curved-base 2, large letters.....	⎬ 263,806	1,500	2,000	3,200	13,000
1820 Square-base 2..................	⎭	1,500	2,000	3,200	13,000
1821..................................	34,641	3,000	6,500	9,000	25,000

1825, 5 over 1	1825, 5 over 4

	Quan. Minted	F-12	VF-20	EF-40	MS-60
1822 (3 known)	17,796	—	687,500	—	
1823.................................	14,485	2,300	3,300	4,300	18,000
1824.................................	17,340	5,500	9,000	18,000	33,000
1825, 5 over 1	⎫	3,000	4,500	7,500	22,500
1825, 5 over 4 (2 known)	⎬ 29,060			140,000	220,000
1826.................................	18,069	6,500	9,500	27,500	
1827.................................	24,913	9,000	19,000	35,000	

Large Date	Small Date

	Quan. Minted	F-12	VF-20	EF-40	MS-60
1828, 8 over 7	⎫ 28,029	5,000	7,000	16,500	35,000
1828...............................	⎭	6,500	9,500	21,000	35,000
1829 Large date	57,442	——	——	——	100,000

The half eagles dated 1829 (small date) through 1834 are smaller in diameter than the earlier pieces. They also have smaller letters, dates and stars.

HALF EAGLES
CAPPED HEAD TO LEFT (reduced diameter) 1829-1834

Standards as before. Modified design by William Kneass. Diameter 23.8 mm.

	Large 5D	Small 5D	13 Stars Square Base 2

	Quan. Minted	F-12	VF-20	EF-40	MS-60
1829 Small date .... inc. above			$18,500	$27,500	$75,000
1830 Small or large 5 D 126,351		$2,200	3,750	5,250	16,000
1831 Small or large 5 D 140,594		2,200	3,750	5,250	16,000
1832 Curved-base 2, 12 stars *(6 known)* } 157,487		—	—	45,000	——
1832 Square-base 2, 13 stars		4,750	6,750	10,000	21,000
1833 Large date .... } 193,630		2,200	3,750	5,250	16,000
1833 Small date		2,200	3,750	6,750	17,000

 Plain 4   Crosslet 4

	Quan. Minted	F-12	VF-20	EF-40	MS-60
1834 Plain 4........................ } 50,141		2,200	3,750	5,250	15,000
1834 Crosslet 4		2,200	3,750	5,250	15,000

CLASSIC HEAD TYPE 1834-1838

As on the quarter eagle of 1834, the motto E PLURIBUS UNUM was omitted from the new, reduced size half eagle in 1834, to distinguish the old coins which had become worth more than face value.

Designer William Kneass; weight 8.36 grams; composition: .8992 gold, .1008 copper; diameter 22.5 mm; reeded edge.

	Quan. Minted	F-12	VF-20	EF-40	MS-60
1834 Plain 4........................ } 657,460		250.00	300.00	500.00	2,500
1834 Crosslet 4		275.00	425.00	800.00	4,750
1835............................... 371,534		250.00	300.00	500.00	2,500
1836............................... 553,147		250.00	300.00	500.00	2,500
1837............................... 207,121		250.00	300.00	550.00	3,000
1838............................... 286,588		250.00	300.00	500.00	2,750
1838C.............................. 17,179		825.00	1,200	2,500	7,750
1838D.............................. 20,583		825.00	1,200	2,500	7,750

[198]

HALF EAGLES
CORONET TYPE, No Motto Above Eagle 1839-1866

Designer Christian Gobrecht; weight 8.359 grams; composition: .900 gold, .100 copper; diameter (1839-40) 22.5 mm. (1840-1929) 21.6 mm; reeded edge. Net weight: .24187 oz. pure gold.

VF-20 VERY FINE—*LIBERTY bold. Major lines show in neck hair.*

EF-40 EXTREMELY FINE—*Neck hair details clear. Slight wear on top and lower part of coronet, and hair.*

AU-50 ABOUT UNCIRCULATED—*Trace of wear on coronet and hair above eye.*

MS-60 UNCIRCULATED—*No trace of wear. Light blemishes.*

Mint mark above date 1839 only, below eagle 1840-1908.

	Quan. Minted	VF-20	EF-40	AU-50	MS-60
1839	118,143	$250.00	$375.00	$700.00	$3,000
1839C	17,205	550.00	1,000	1,500	3,500
1839D	18,939	550.00	1,000	1,500	3,500
1840*	137,382	225.00	275.00	800.00	3,000
1840C*	18,992	550.00	1,000	1,500	3,500
1840D*	22,896	550.00	1,000	2,000	4,000
1840O*	40,120	400.00	650.00	1,100	2,500
1841	15,833	325.00	450.00	850.00	2,250
1841C	21,467	450.00	850.00	1,500	3,500
1841D	29,392	475.00	950.00	1,750	3,500
1841O (Unconfirmed in any collection)	50				

*Scarce varieties of the 1840 coins have the large diameter and wide rims of the 1839 issues.

1842 Large Date   **Large Letters**   **Small Letters**   **Extra 7 at border**

	Quan. Minted	VF-20	EF-40	AU-50	MS-60
1842 Small letters	27,578	250.00	450.00	675.00	2,000
1842 Large letters		250.00	450.00	675.00	2,000
1842C Small date	27,432	1,000	1,600	3,000	5,000
1842C Large date		425.00	700.00	1,200	3,200
1842D Small date	59,608	500.00	800.00	1,300	3,300
1842D Large date		550.00	1,000	1,800	3,700
1842O	16,400	350.00	700.00	1,000	2,300
1843	611,205	175.00	225.00	350.00	1,800
1843C	44,277	425.00	700.00	1,400	2,500
1843D	98,452	425.00	800.00	1,500	3,500
1843O Small letters	19,075	300.00	500.00	800.00	2,500
1843O Large letters	82,000	300.00	500.00	700.00	2,200
1844	340,330	175.00	225.00	350.00	1,800
1844C	23,631	500.00	900.00	1,500	3,500
1844D	88,982	425.00	700.00	1,500	3,400
1844O	364,600	275.00	400.00	725.00	2,100
1845	417,099	175.00	225.00	350.00	1,800
1845D	90,629	425.00	700.00	1,300	3,000
1845O	41,000	350.00	500.00	900.00	2,300

HALF EAGLES

	Quan. Minted	VF-20	EF-40	AU-50	MS-60	Proof-63
1846	395,942	$175.00	$225.00	$350.00	$1,900	
1846C	12,995	600.00	1,000	1,450	3,500	
1846D	} 80,294	475.00	725.00	1,200	3,000	
1846D high second D over D		500.00	800.00	1,500	3,200	
1846O	58,000	350.00	500.00	1,000	2,300	
1847	915,981	175.00	225.00	350.00	1,800	
1847, top of extra very low 7 at border	——	——				
1847C	84,151	425.00	800.00	1,300	3,000	
1847D	64,405	425.00	800.00	1,300	3,000	
1847O	12,000	475.00	1,000	1,300	3,000	
1848	260,775	175.00	225.00	350.00	1,800	
1848C	64,472	500.00	800.00	1,200	2,750	
1848D	47,465	500.00	800.00	1,200	3,000	
1849	133,070	200.00	250.00	375.00	1,900	
1849C	64,823	500.00	800.00	1,200	3,000	
1849D	39,036	500.00	800.00	1,400	3,400	
1850	64,491	175.00	225.00	350.00	1,800	
1850C	63,591	500.00	800.00	1,200	3,500	
1850D	43,984	500.00	800.00	1,300	3,500	
1851	377,505	175.00	225.00	350.00	1,800	
1851C	49,176	500.00	800.00	1,200	3,000	
1851D	62,710	500.00	800.00	1,200	3,000	
1851O	41,000	350.00	500.00	800.00	2,100	
1852	573,901	175.00	225.00	350.00	1,800	
1852C	72,574	500.00	800.00	1,200	3,000	
1852D	91,584	500.00	800.00	1,200	3,000	
1853	305,770	175.00	225.00	350.00	1,800	
1853C	65,571	500.00	800.00	1,200	3,000	
1853D	89,678	500.00	800.00	1,200	3,000	
1854	160,675	175.00	225.00	350.00	1,800	
1854C	39,283	500.00	800.00	1,200	3,000	
1854D	56,413	500.00	800.00	1,200	3,000	
1854O	46,000	300.00	500.00	855.00	2,750	
1854S	268	——	——	187,000	——	
1855	117,098	175.00	225.00	350.00	1,800	——
1855C	39,788	500.00	800.00	1,200	3,000	
1855D	22,432	500.00	800.00	1,200	3,000	
1855O	11,100	500.00	800.00	1,200	3,250	
1855S	61,000	300.00	450.00	500.00	2,000	
1856	197,990	175.00	225.00	350.00	1,800	——
1856C	28,457	500.00	800.00	1,200	3,000	
1856D	19,786	500.00	800.00	1,200	3,000	
1856O	10,000	550.00	950.00	1,400	3,500	
1856S	105,100	175.00	225.00	350.00	1,800	
1857	98,188	175.00	225.00	350.00	2,000	——
1857C	31,360	500.00	800.00	1,200	3,000	
1857D	17,046	500.00	800.00	1,200	3,000	
1857O	13,000	500.00	800.00	1,200	3,000	
1857S	87,000	175.00	225.00	350.00	1,800	
1858	15,136	250.00	375.00	550.00	2,000	——
1858C	38,856	500.00	800.00	1,200	3,000	
1858D	15,362	500.00	800.00	1,200	3,000	
1858S	18,600	400.00	750.00	900.00	2,200	
1859	(80) 16,814	300.00	500.00	900.00	2,500	$18,000
1859C	31,847	500.00	800.00	1,200	3,000	
1859D	10,366	500.00	900.00	1,500	3,500	
1859S	13,220	300.00	500.00	900.00	2,200	

HALF EAGLES

	Quan. Minted	VF-20	EF-40	AU-50	MS-60	Proof-63
1860 . . . . (62)	19,825	$300.00	$500.00	$900.00	$2,500	$22,000
1860C	14,813	500.00	800.00	1,200	3,000	
1860D	14,635	500.00	1,000	1,700	4,000	
1860S	21,200	400.00	900.00	2,000		
1861 . . . . (66)	688,150	175.00	225.00	350.00	1,800	20,000
1861C	6,879	1,200	2,100	3,750	8,000	
1861D	1,597	4,000	7,000	10,000	22,000	
1861S	18,000	350.00	800.00	1,500	——	
1862 . . . . (35)	4,465	350.00	800.00	1,500	——	20,000
1862S	9,500	500.00	1,000	2,000	——	
1863 . . . . (30)	2,472	600.00	900.00	1,500	3,300	20,000
1863S	17,000	400.00	750.00	1,000	3,000	
1864 . . . . (50)	4,220	425.00	650.00	1,300	4,000	20,000
1864S	3,888	1,000	2,200	3,000	——	
1865 . . . . (25)	1,295	850.00	1,200	2,000	——	20,000
1865S	27,612	500.00	1,000	2,000	——	
1866S	9,000	500.00	1,100	2,100	——	

Variety 2 — Motto Above Eagle 1866-1908

Designer Christian Gobrecht; weight 8.359 grams; composition: .900 gold, .100 copper; diameter 21.6 mm; reeded edge. Net weight: .24187 oz. pure gold.

VF-20 VERY FINE—*Half of hairlines above coronet missing. Hair curls under ear evident, but worn. Motto and its ribbon sharp.*

EF-40 EXTREMELY FINE—*Small amount of wear on top of hair and below L in LIBERTY. Wear evident on wing tips and neck of eagle.*

AU-50 ABOUT UNCIRCULATED—*Trace of wear on tip of coronet and hair above eye.*

MS-60 UNCIRCULATED—*No trace of wear. Light blemishes.*

	Quan. Minted	VF-20	EF-40	AU-50	MS-60	Proof-63
1866 . . . . (30)	6,730	350.00	550.00	850.00	2,000	15,000
1866S	34,920	325.00	550.00	850.00	1,600	
1867 . . . . (50)	6,920	350.00	600.00	900.00	2,000	15,000
1867S	29,000	300.00	550.00	900.00	——	
1868 . . . . (25)	5,725	350.00	550.00	900.00	2,000	15,000
1868S	52,000	275.00	500.00	900.00	——	
1869 . . . . (25)	1,785	650.00	800.00	1,300	2,750	15,000
1869S	31,000	250.00	400.00	600.00	1,400	
1870 . . . . (35)	4,035	350.00	650.00	900.00	1,700	15,000
1870CC	7,675	2,400	4,000	6,000		
1870S	17,000	300.00	550.00	1,000	——	
1871 . . . . (30)	3,230	400.00	650.00	1,100	——	15,000
1871CC	20,770	700.00	1,200	1,800	3,350	
1871S	25,000	250.00	450.00	800.00	1,600	
1872 . . . . (30)	1,690	600.00	900.00	1,300	2,500	15,000
1872CC	16,980	650.00	1,000	1,500	3,350	
1872S	36,400	250.00	400.00	650.00	1,200	
1873 Closed 3 . . . . (25) ⎫	112,505	175.00	200.00	300.00	750.00	15,000
1873 Open 3 . . . . ⎭		175.00	200.00	275.00	600.00	
1873CC	7,416	700.00	1,200	2,000	3,700	
1873S	31,000	400.00	800.00	1,200	2,000	
1874 . . . . (20)	3,508	450.00	850.00	1,300	2,100	15,000
1874CC	21,198	425.00	800.00	1,000	2,500	
1874S	16,000	250.00	500.00	800.00	——	
1875 . . . . (20)	220	——	——	——	——	——
1875CC	11,828	550.00	1,200	1,800	2,800	
1875S	9,000	375.00	900.00	1,300	2,500	

HALF EAGLES

	Quan. Minted	VF-20	EF-40	AU-50	MS-60	Proof-63
1876 .... (45)	1,477	$600.00	$950.00	$1,500	$2,600	$10,000
1876CC	6,887	600.00	1,200	1,800	3,100	
1876S............................	4,000	800.00	1,500	2,000	3,000	
1877 .... (20)	1,152	600.00	1,000	1,700	3,500	12,000
1877CC	8,680	600.00	1,200	1,800	3,100	
1877S........................	26,700	175.00	275.00	350.00	800.00	
1878 .... (20)	131,740	175.00	200.00	250.00	425.00	12,000
1878CC	9,054	1,500	2,700	3,700		
1878S........................	144,700	175.00	200.00	250.00	425.00	
1879 .... (30)	301,950	175.00	200.00	250.00	375.00	10,000
1879CC	17,281	375.00	550.00	1,000	2,000	
1879S........................	426,200	175.00	200.00	250.00	375.00	
1880 .... (36)	3,166,436	175.00	200.00	250.00	375.00	10,000
1880CC	51,017	350.00	650.00	750.00	1,500	
1880S........................	1,348,900	175.00	200.00	250.00	375.00	
1881, 1 over 0		300.00	500.00	850.00	——	
1881 .... (42)	5,708,802	150.00	175.00	200.00	300.00	8,500
1881CC	13,886	400.00	600.00	1,200	1,900	
1881S........................	969,000	150.00	175.00	200.00	300.00	
1882 .... (48)	2,514,568	150.00	175.00	200.00	300.00	8,500
1882CC	82,817	275.00	325.00	500.00	1,200	
1882S........................	969,000	150.00	175.00	200.00	300.00	
1883 .... (61)	233,461	150.00	175.00	200.00	300.00	8,500
1883CC	12,958	375.00	650.00	1,000	1,400	
1883S........................	83,200	150.00	175.00	200.00	350.00	
1884 .... (48)	191,078	150.00	175.00	200.00	350.00	8,500
1884CC	16,402	375.00	650.00	1,000	1,400	
1884S........................	177,000	150.00	175.00	200.00	350.00	
1885 .... (66)	601,506	150.00	175.00	200.00	300.00	8,500
1885S........................	1,211,500	150.00	175.00	200.00	300.00	
1886 .... (72)	388,432	150.00	175.00	200.00	300.00	8,500
1886S........................	3,268,000	150.00	175.00	200.00	300.00	
1887 Proofs only....... (87)	87					20,000
1887S........................	1,912,000	150.00	175.00	200.00	300.00	
1888 .... (95)	18,296	175.00	250.00	300.00	500.00	8,000
1888S........................	293,900	175.00	200.00	250.00	375.00	
1889 .... (45)	7,565	275.00	450.00	575.00	1,300	8,000
1890 .... (88)	4,328	325.00	650.00	900.00	1,800	8,000
1890CC	53,800	225.00	300.00	500.00	900.00	
1891 .... (53)	61,413	175.00	200.00	250.00	425.00	8,000
1891CC	208,000	225.00	250.00	400.00	850.00	
1892 .... (92)	753,572	150.00	175.00	200.00	300.00	8,000
1892CC	82,968	225.00	275.00	400.00	850.00	
1892O........................	10,000	650.00	850.00	1,350	3,000	
1892S........................	298,400	175.00	200.00	250.00	425.00	
1893 .... (77)	1,528,197	150.00	175.00	200.00	300.00	8,000
1893CC	60,000	225.00	275.00	450.00	1,200	
1893O........................	110,000	225.00	275.00	475.00	1,200	
1893S........................	224,000	175.00	200.00	250.00	400.00	
1894 .... (75)	957,955	150.00	175.00	200.00	300.00	8,000
1894O........................	16,600	250.00	350.00	450.00	950.00	
1894S........................	55,900	175.00	200.00	250.00	450.00	
1895 .... (81)	1,345,936	150.00	175.00	200.00	300.00	8,000
1895S........................	112,000	175.00	200.00	250.00	425.00	
1896 .... (103)	59,063	175.00	200.00	250.00	425.00	8,000
1896S........................	155,400	175.00	200.00	250.00	425.00	
1897 .... (83)	867,883	150.00	175.00	200.00	250.00	8,000
1897S........................	354,000	150.00	175.00	200.00	300.00	

HALF EAGLES

	Quan. Minted	VF-20	EF-40	AU-50	MS-60	Proof-63
1898 . . . . (75)	633,495	$150.00	$175.00	$210.00	$300.00	$11,000
1898S	1,397,400	150.00	175.00	210.00	300.00	
1899 . . . . (99)	1,710,729	150.00	175.00	200.00	250.00	11,000
1899S	1,545,000	150.00	175.00	210.00	300.00	
1900 . . . . (230)	1,405,730	150.00	175.00	200.00	250.00	11,000
1900S	329,000	150.00	175.00	210.00	300.00	
1901 . . . . (140)	616,040	150.00	175.00	200.00	250.00	11,000
1901S, 1 over 0 . . . . ⎱		150.00	225.00	300.00	400.00	
1901S . . . . ⎰	3,648,000	150.00	175.00	200.00	250.00	
1902 . . . . (162)	172,562	150.00	175.00	200.00	275.00	11,000
1902S	939,000	150.00	175.00	200.00	250.00	
1903 . . . . (154)	227,024	150.00	175.00	200.00	250.00	11,000
1903S	1,855,000	150.00	175.00	200.00	250.00	
1904 . . . . (136)	392,136	150.00	175.00	200.00	275.00	11,000
1904S	97,000	150.00	175.00	200.00	300.00	
1905 . . . . (108)	302,308	150.00	175.00	200.00	250.00	11,000
1905S	880,700	150.00	175.00	200.00	300.00	
1906 . . . . (85)	348,820	150.00	175.00	200.00	275.00	11,000
1906D	320,000	150.00	175.00	200.00	275.00	
1906S	598,000	150.00	175.00	200.00	300.00	
1907 . . . . (92)	626,192	150.00	175.00	200.00	250.00	11,000
1907D	888,000	150.00	175.00	200.00	275.00	
1908	421,874	150.00	175.00	200.00	250.00	

Values of common gold coins have been based on the current bullion price of gold, and may vary with the prevailing spot price.

INDIAN HEAD TYPE 1908-1929

This type conforms to the quarter eagle of the same date. The incuse designs and lettering make this a unique series, along with the quarter eagle, in our United States coinage.

Designer Bela Lyon Pratt; weight 8.359 grams; composition: .900 gold, .100 copper; diameter 21.6 mm; reeded edge. Net weight: .24187 oz. pure gold.

Mint mark location.

VF-20 VERY FINE—*Noticeable wear on large middle feathers and tip of eagle's wing.*
EF-40 EXTREMELY FINE—*Cheekbone, war bonnet and headband feathers slightly worn. Feathers on eagle's upper wing show considerable wear.*
AU-50 ABOUT UNCIRCULATED—*Trace of wear on cheekbone and headdress.*
MS-60 UNCIRCULATED—*No trace of wear. Light blemishes.*

Scarcer coins with well struck mint marks command higher prices.

						Matte Proof-63
1908 . . . . (167)	578,012	225.00	250.00	300.00	650.00	$13,000
1908D	148,000	225.00	250.00	300.00	650.00	
1908S	82,000	300.00	450.00	750.00	2,500	
1909 . . . . (78)	627,138	225.00	250.00	325.00	750.00	13,000
1909D	3,423,560	225.00	250.00	300.00	650.00	
1909O*	34,200	600.00	1,000	1,750	7,000	
1909S	297,200	225.00	300.00	500.00	1,300	
1910 . . . . (250)	604,250	225.00	250.00	300.00	650.00	13,000

*Beware spurious "O" mint mark.

HALF EAGLES

	Quan. Minted	VF-20	EF-40	AU-50	MS-60	Matte Proof-63
1910D	193,600	$225.00	$250.00	$325.00	$1,000	
1910S	770,200	250.00	285.00	350.00	2,000	
1911 (139)	915,139	225.00	250.00	300.00	650.00	$13,000
1911D	72,500	350.00	400.00	800.00	4,750	
1911S	1,416,000	250.00	300.00	350.00	1,250	
1912 (144)	790,144	225.00	250.00	300.00	650.00	13,000
1912S	392,000	250.00	300.00	500.00	1,650	
1913 (99)	916,000	225.00	250.00	300.00	650.00	13,000
1913S	408,000	260.00	325.00	550.00	3,000	
1914 (125)	247,125	250.00	285.00	350.00	800.00	13,000
1914D	247,000	225.00	250.00	300.00	750.00	
1914S	263,000	250.00	285.00	350.00	1,200	
1915* (75)	588,075	225.00	250.00	300.00	650.00	14,000
1915S	164,000	260.00	300.00	425.00	2,600	
1916S	240,000	250.00	285.00	400.00	1,100	
1929	662,000	3,000	4,000	5,000	7,500	

*Pieces dated 1915D are counterfeit.

EAGLES ($10.00 Gold Pieces) — 1795-1933

Coinage authority including specified weights and fineness of the eagle conforms to that of the half eagle. The small eagle reverse was used until 1797 when the large, heraldic eagle replaced it. The early dates have variations in the number of stars, the rarest date being 1798. Many of these early pieces show file scratches from the mint's practice of adjusting weight. No eagles were struck dated 1805 to 1837. Proofs of some dates prior to 1855 are known to exist, and all are rare.

+ or – indicates change from previous year	TYPE COIN VALUES									
	F-12	VF-20	EF-40	AU-50	MS-60	MS-63	MS-65	PF-60	PF-63	PF-65
Cap Bust-Sm. Eag. 1795-1797	6,000	8,500	12,000	19,000	32,000+	45,000	75,000+			
Cap Bust-Lg. Eag. 1797-1804	2,250	3,200	4,750	7,500	15,000	20,000	50,000+			
Lib Coronet-NM 1838-1866	230.00–	250.00–	275.00–	500.00	3,000+	25,000+	85,000+	8,000–	27,500+	150,000+
Lib. Coronet 1866-1907	230.00–	240.00–	250.00–	265.00–	325.00–	2,200–	11,000+	4,500	13,500+	55,000+
Indian Head-NM 1907-1908	325.00	450.00–	500.00–	600.00–	750.00–	2,250–	13,000+	7,000–	15,000–	40,000+
Indian Head 1908-1933	325.00+	425.00–	450.00–	485.00–	550.00–	2,000–	11,000+	5,500–	15,000	40,000+

CAPPED BUST TO RIGHT, SMALL EAGLE 1795-1797

Designer Robert Scot; weight 17.50 grams; composition: .9167 gold, .0833 copper; approx. diameter 33 mm; reeded edge.

F-12 FINE—*Details on turban and head obliterated.*

VF-20 VERY FINE—*Neck hairlines and details under turban and over forehead are worn but distinguishable.*

EF-40 EXTREMELY FINE—*Definite wear on hair to left of eye and strand of hair across and around turban, also on eagle's wing tips.*

MS-60 UNCIRCULATED—*No trace of wear. Light blemishes.*

	Quan. Minted	F-12	VF-20	EF-40	MS-60
1795 9 leaves below eagle	} 5,583	$7,500	$9,500	$15,000	$40,000
1795 13 leaves below eagle		6,000	8,500	12,000	32,000
1796	4,146	6,000	8,500	12,000	32,000
1797 Small eagle	3,615	6,000	8,500	12,000	32,000

EAGLES
CAPPED BUST TO RIGHT, HERALDIC EAGLE 1797-1804

	Quan. Minted	F-12	VF-20	EF-40	MS-60
1797 Large eagle	10,940	$2,250	$3,500	$5,500	$18,000
1798, 8 over 7, 9 stars left, 4 right	900	4,500	7,500	12,000	25,000
1798, 8 over 7, 7 stars left, 6 right	842	10,000	22,000	——	——
1799	37,449	2,250	3,200	4,750	15,000
1800	5,999	2,250	3,200	4,750	17,000

1801	44,344	2,250	3,200	4,750	15,000
1803	15,017	2,250	3,200	4,750	17,000
1804	3,757	3,000	4,500	7,500	23,000
1804 Plain 4. Proof. (4 known)					40,000

CORONET TYPE, No Motto Above Eagle 1838-1866

In 1838 the weight and diameter of the eagle were reduced and the obverse and reverse were redesigned. Liberty now faces left and the word LIBERTY is placed on the coronet. A more natural appearing eagle is used on the reverse. The value, TEN D., is shown for the first time on this denomination.

Designer Christian Gobrecht; weight 16.718 grams; composition: .900 gold, .100 copper, diameter 27 mm; reeded edge. Net weight: .48375 oz. pure gold.

Mint mark location on reverse below eagle.

VF-20 VERY FINE—*Hairlines above coronet partly worn. Curls under ear worn but defined.*

EF-40 EXTREMELY FINE—*Small amount of wear on top of hair and below L in LIBERTY. Wear evident on wing tips and neck of eagle.*

AU-50 ABOUT UNCIRCULATED—*Trace of wear on tip of coronet and hair above eye.*

MS-60 UNCIRCULATED—*No trace of wear. Light blemishes.*

EAGLES

	Quan. Minted	VF-20	EF-40	AU-50	MS-60	Proof-63
1838	7,200	$850.00	$ 1,750	$3,000	$9,000	
1839 Large letters	25,801	550.00	1,200	2,800	8,000	

The Liberty head style of 1838 and 1839 (large letters) differs from that used for subsequent issues.

**1853,
3 over 2**

	Quan. Minted	VF-20	EF-40	AU-50	MS-60	Proof-63
1839 Small letters	12,447	800.00	1,450	2,500	7,000	
1840	47,338	375.00	450.00	650.00	3,750	
1841	63,131	375.00	450.00	650.00	3,750	
1841O	2,500	600.00	1,250	1,900	6,500	
1842 Small date	18,623	375.00	450.00	650.00	3,500	
1842 Large date	62,884	375.00	450.00	650.00	3,500	
1842O	27,400	375.00	450.00	750.00	4,500	
1843	75,462	375.00	450.00	650.00	3,250	
1843O	175,162	350.00	425.00	650.00	3,250	
1844	6,361	500.00	900.00	1,250	4,000	
1844O	118,700	350.00	425.00	700.00	3,250	
1845	26,153	350.00	450.00	750.00	3,500	
1845O	47,500	350.00	500.00	700.00	3,250	
1846	20,095	350.00	450.00	650.00	3,250	
1846O	81,780	350.00	500.00	750.00	3,250	
1847	862,258	250.00	275.00	500.00	3,000	
1847O	571,500	350.00	400.00	650.00	3,000	
1848	145,484	250.00	275.00	500.00	3,000	
1848O	35,850	375.00	500.00	750.00	3,500	
1849	653,618	250.00	275.00	500.00	3,000	
1849O	23,900	375.00	500.00	750.00	3,500	
1850 Large date	} 291,451	250.00	275.00	500.00	3,000	
1850 Small date		375.00	600.00	——		
1850O	57,500	375.00	500.00	750.00	3,500	
1851	176,328	350.00	400.00	650.00	3,000	
1851O	263,000	350.00	400.00	650.00	3,000	
1852	263,106	250.00	275.00	500.00	3,000	
1852O	18,000	425.00	575.00	800.00	3,500	
1853, 3 over 2	} 201,253	425.00	800.00			
1853		250.00	275.00	500.00	3,000	
1853O	51,000	375.00	500.00	750.00	3,500	
1854	54,250	350.00	450.00	750.00	3,000	
1854O Large or small date	52,500	350.00	425.00	750.00	3,750	
1854S	123,826	350.00	425.00	725.00	3,100	
1855	121,701	250.00	275.00	500.00	3,000	——
1855O	18,000	425.00	550.00	800.00	3,100	
1855S	9,000	700.00	1,300	1,600	4,500	——
1856	60,490	250.00	275.00	600.00	3,000	
1856O	14,500	400.00	550.00	800.00	3,250	
1856S	68,000	350.00	450.00	650.00	3,000	

EAGLES

	Quan. Minted	VF-20	EF-40	AU-50	MS-60	Proof-63
1857	16,606	$375.00	$450.00	$700.00	$3,000	——
1857O	5,500	900.00	1,400	2,000	5,500	
1857S	26,000	350.00	450.00	650.00	3,000	
1858*	2,521	3,500	6,000	8,000	22,000	——
1858O	20,000	375.00	450.00	675.00	3,900	
1858S	11,800	400.00	550.00	700.00	3,900	
1859 (80)	16,093	375.00	450.00	650.00	3,750	$30,000
1859O	2,300	1,250	2,500	3,600	6,000	
1859S	7,000	800.00	1,500	2,000	4,000	
1860 (50)	15,105	350.00	425.00	600.00	3,500	27,500
1860O	11,100	400.00	600.00	750.00	4,250	
1860S	5,000	750.00	1,250	1,900	5,000	
1861 (69)	113,233	250.00	275.00	500.00	3,000	27,500
1861S	15,500	350.00	425.00	750.00	3,400	
1862 (35)	10,995	350.00	425.00	750.00	3,400	27,500
1862S	12,500	350.00	425.00	750.00	3,400	
1863 (30)	1,248	2,500	4,500	6,000	8,000	34,000
1863S	10,000	425.00	850.00	1,150	3,750	
1864 (50)	3,580	850.00	1,350	1,850	4,250	30,000
1864S	2,500	2,000	3,500			
1865 (25)	4,005	775.00	1,150	1,550	4,500	29,500
1865S	} 16,700	775.00	1,150	1,550	4,500	
1865S, 865 over inverted 186		950.00	1,500			
1866S	8,500	1,200	2,000	3,000	5,000	

*Beware removed mint mark.

Variety 2 — Motto Above Eagle 1866-1907

Mint mark location is on the reverse below the eagle.

VF-20 VERY FINE—*Half of hairlines over coronet visible. Curls under ear worn but defined. IN GOD WE TRUST and its ribbon are sharp.*

EF-40 EXTREMELY FINE—*Small amount of wear on top of hair and below IN GOD WE TRUST. Plain tips and neck of eagle.*

AU-50 ABOUT UNCIRCULATED—*Trace of wear on hair above eye and on coronet.*

MS-60 UNCIRCULATED—*No trace of wear. Light blemishes.*

		VF-20	EF-40	AU-50	MS-60	Proof-63
1866 (30)	3,780	475.00	650.00	900.00	2,100	21,000
1866S	11,500	425.00	600.00	750.00	2,000	
1867 (50)	3,140	475.00	650.00	900.00	2,100	18,000
1867S	9,000	450.00	650.00	850.00	1,700	
1868 (25)	10,655	425.00	600.00	750.00	1,400	18,000
1868S	13,500	425.00	600.00	750.00	1,400	
1869 (25)	1,855	750.00	1,500	2,000	2,500	18,000
1869S	6,430	450.00	900.00	1,200	1,700	
1870 (35)	4,025	450.00	700.00	900.00	2,100	18,000
1870CC	5,908	1,300	4,000	6,000		
1870S	8,000	450.00	700.00	900.00	1,800	
1871 (30)	1,820	700.00	1,200	1,900	4,500	18,000
1871CC	8,085	800.00	1,600	2,500		
1871S	16,500	375.00	550.00	700.00	1,400	

EAGLES

	Quan. Minted	VF-20	EF-40	AU-50	MS-60	Proof-63
1872 . . . . (30)	1,650	$900.00	$1,600	$2,250	$3,700	$17,000
1872CC	4,600	700.00	1,200	1,500	3,800	
1872S	17,300	375.00	550.00	700.00	1,400	
1873 . . . . (25)	825	1,250	2,800	4,000	8,000	26,000
1873CC	4,543	1,050	1,750	3,000	6,000	
1873S	12,000	375.00	550.00	700.00	1,400	
1874 . . . . (20)	53,160	300.00	350.00	500.00	700.00	21,000
1874CC	16,767	425.00	600.00	750.00	2,000	
1874S	10,000	400.00	525.00	675.00	1,300	
1875 . . . . (20)	120		40,000	——		——
1875CC	7,715	650.00	1,000	1,500	3,000	
1876 . . . . (45)	732	1,250	3,000	4,500	7,800	21,000
1876CC	4,696	900.00	1,500	2,000	3,600	
1876S	5,000	500.00	750.00	1,100	2,200	
1877 . . . . (20)	817	1,600	3,000	4,200	9,000	26,000
1877CC	3,332	1,000	1,600	2,200	3,900	
1877S	17,000	325.00	450.00	650.00	900.00	
1878 . . . . (20)	73,800	300.00	325.00	400.00	700.00	19,000
1878CC	3,244	1,100	1,700	2,750	4,200	
1878S	26,100	300.00	400.00	500.00	700.00	
1879 . . . . (30)	384,770	240.00	275.00	300.00	425.00	18,000
1879CC	1,762	2,500	4,500	7,500	12,000	
1879O	1,500	1,200	2,500	3,500	7,500	
1879S	224,000	240.00	275.00	300.00	425.00	
1880 . . . . (36)	1,644,876	240.00	275.00	300.00	425.00	17,000
1880CC	11,190	350.00	500.00	700.00	1,200	
1880O	9,200	350.00	500.00	800.00	1,200	
1880S	506,250	240.00	250.00	265.00	350.00	
1881 . . . . (40)	3,877,260	240.00	250.00	265.00	350.00	17,000
1881CC	24,015	325.00	450.00	650.00	1,100	
1881O	8,350	350.00	475.00	700.00	1,350	
1881S	970,000	240.00	250.00	265.00	325.00	
1882 . . . . (40)	2,324,480	240.00	250.00	265.00	325.00	17,000
1882CC	6,764	350.00	500.00	750.00	1,750	
1882O	10,820	325.00	475.00	675.00	900.00	
1882S	132,000	240.00	250.00	265.00	325.00	
1883 . . . . (40)	208,740	240.00	250.00	265.00	325.00	17,000
1883CC	12,000	350.00	500.00	800.00	1,400	
1883O	800	2,100	3,400	5,750	12,000	
1883S	38,000	250.00	275.00	300.00	425.00	
1884 . . . . (45)	76,905	250.00	275.00	300.00	425.00	25,000
1884CC	9,925	400.00	600.00	900.00	1,400	
1884S	124,250	240.00	250.00	275.00	375.00	
1885 . . . . (65)	253,527	240.00	250.00	275.00	375.00	16,000
1885S	228,000	240.00	250.00	275.00	375.00	
1886 . . . . (60)	236,160	240.00	250.00	275.00	375.00	16,000
1886S	826,000	240.00	250.00	275.00	375.00	
1887 . . . . (80)	53,680	240.00	250.00	275.00	375.00	16,000
1887S	817,000	240.00	250.00	275.00	375.00	
1888 . . . . (75)	132,996	240.00	250.00	275.00	375.00	16,000
1888O	21,335	250.00	350.00	425.00	775.00	
1888S	648,700	250.00	275.00	300.00	425.00	
1889 . . . . (45)	4,485	425.00	600.00	950.00	1,500	17,000
1889S	425,400	240.00	250.00	275.00	375.00	
1890 . . . . (63)	58,043	250.00	300.00	425.00	800.00	14,500
1890CC	17,500	350.00	375.00	500.00	900.00	
1891 . . . . (48)	91,868	250.00	275.00	300.00	425.00	14,500
1891CC	103,732	250.00	275.00	300.00	700.00	

EAGLES

	Quan. Minted	VF-20	EF-40	AU-50	MS-60	Proof-63
1892 .... (72)	797,552	$240.00	$250.00	$300.00	$375.00	$14,500
1892CC	40,000	325.00	450.00	650.00	1,200	
1892O........................	28,688	250.00	275.00	400.00	600.00	
1892S........................	115,500	240.00	275.00	300.00	425.00	
1893 .... (55)	1,840,895	240.00	250.00	265.00	325.00	14,500
1893CC	14,000	400.00	550.00	750.00	1,300	
1893O........................	17,000	325.00	425.00	550.00	850.00	
1893S........................	141,350	240.00	250.00	275.00	375.00	
1894 .... (43)	2,470,778	240.00	250.00	265.00	325.00	14,500
1894O........................	107,500	250.00	275.00	300.00	475.00	
1894S........................	25,000	250.00	275.00	300.00	600.00	
1895 .... (56)	567,826	240.00	250.00	265.00	325.00	14,500
1895O........................	98,000	250.00	275.00	300.00	425.00	
1895S........................	49,000	250.00	275.00	400.00	1,200	
1896 .... (78)	76,348	240.00	250.00	275.00	375.00	14,500
1896S........................	123,750	250.00	275.00	300.00	425.00	
1897 .... (69)	1,000,159	240.00	250.00	265.00	325.00	14,500
1897O........................	42,500	250.00	275.00	300.00	425.00	
1897S........................	234,750	250.00	275.00	300.00	475.00	
1898 .... (67)	812,197	240.00	250.00	265.00	325.00	14,500
1898S........................	473,600	250.00	275.00	300.00	425.00	
1899 .... (86)	1,262,305	240.00	250.00	265.00	325.00	13,500
1899O........................	37,047	250.00	275.00	300.00	475.00	
1899S........................	841,000	240.00	250.00	275.00	375.00	
1900 .... (120)	293,960	240.00	250.00	265.00	325.00	13,500
1900S........................	81,000	240.00	250.00	275.00	375.00	
1901 .... (85)	1,718,825	240.00	250.00	265.00	325.00	13,500
1901O........................	72,041	250.00	275.00	300.00	400.00	
1901S........................	2,812,750	240.00	250.00	265.00	325.00	
1902 .... (113)	82,513	250.00	275.00	300.00	375.00	13,500
1902S........................	469,500	240.00	250.00	265.00	325.00	
1903 .... (96)	125,926	240.00	250.00	275.00	375.00	13,500
1903O........................	112,771	250.00	275.00	300.00	400.00	
1903S........................	538,000	240.00	250.00	265.00	325.00	
1904 .... (108)	162,038	240.00	250.00	275.00	375.00	13,500
1904O........................	108,950	250.00	275.00	300.00	425.00	
1905 .... (86)	201,078	240.00	250.00	275.00	375.00	13,500
1905S....	369,250	250.00	275.00	300.00	475.00	
1906 .... (77)	165,497	240.00	250.00	275.00	375.00	13,500
1906D........................	981,000	240.00	250.00	265.00	325.00	
1906O........................	86,895	250.00	275.00	300.00	475.00	
1906S........................	457,000	250.00	275.00	300.00	475.00	
1907 .... (74)	1,203,973	240.00	250.00	265.00	325.00	13,500
1907D........................	1,030,000	240.00	250.00	265.00	325.00	
1907S........................	210,500	250.00	275.00	300.00	475.00	

> Values of common gold coins have been based on the current bullion price of gold, and may vary with the prevailing spot price.

INDIAN HEAD TYPE 1907-1933

Augustus Saint-Gaudens, considered by many the greatest of modern sculptors introduced a new high standard of art in United States coins evidenced by his eagle and double eagle types of 1907. The obverse of the eagle shows the head of Liberty crowned with an Indian war bonnet while an impressively majestic eagle dominates the reverse side. A departure from older standards is found on the edge of the piece, where 46 raised stars are arranged signifying the

EAGLES

states of the Union, instead of a lettered or reeded edge. (48 stars 1912 and later.)

The first eagles struck had no motto IN GOD WE TRUST as did the later issues starting in 1908. President Theodore Roosevelt personally objected to the use of the Deity's name on coins. The motto was restored to the coins by an Act of Congress in 1908.

Designer Augustus Saint-Gaudens. Standards same as previous issue. Edge 1907-1911: 46 raised stars; 1912-1933: 48 raised stars. Net weight: .48375 oz. pure gold.

VF-20 VERY FINE—*Bonnet feathers worn near band. Hair high points show wear.*

EF-40 EXTREMELY FINE—*Slight wear on cheekbone and headdress feathers. Eagle's eye and left wing will show slight wear.*

AU-50 ABOUT UNCIRCULATED—*Trace of wear on hair above eye and on forehead.*

MS-60 UNCIRCULATED—*No trace of wear. Light blemishes.*

Variety 1 — No Motto on Reverse 1907-1908

No Motto

Mint mark location is above left tip of branch on 1908-D no motto, and at left of arrow points thereafter.

Choice uncirculated (MS-65) coins are rare and worth substantial premiums.

	Quan. Minted	VF-20	EF-40	AU-50	MS-60	Proof-63
1907 Wire rim, periods	500			$6,500	$12,000	$20,000
1907 Rounded rim, periods before and after •E•PLURIBUS•UNUM•	*42				30,000	——
1907 No periods	239,406	$450.00	$500.00	600.00	750.00	
1908 No motto	33,500	550.00	650.00	800.00	1,200	
1908D No motto	210,000	450.00	500.00	600.00	750.00	

*19,958 melted at Mint.

Variety 2 — Motto on Reverse 1908-1933

With Motto
IN GOD WE TRUST

						Matte Proof-63
1908 .... (116)	341,486	425.00	450.00	485.00	550.00	$15,000
1908D	836,500	425.00	450.00	550.00	1,000	
1908S	59,850	425.00	450.00	800.00	3,000	
1909 .... (74)	184,863	425.00	450.00	485.00	600.00	15,000
1909D	121,540	425.00	450.00	550.00	1,000	
1909S	292,350	425.00	450.00	550.00	1,200	
1910 .... (204)	318,704	425.00	450.00	485.00	550.00	15,000

EAGLES

	Quan. Minted	VF-20	EF-40	AU-50	MS-60	Matte Proof-63
1910D	2,356,640	$425.00	$450.00	$485.00	$550.00	
1910S	811,000	425.00	450.00	485.00	1,400	
1911 (95)	505,595	425.00	450.00	485.00	550.00	$15,000
1911D	30,100	550.00	750.00	1,150	5,500	
1911S	51,000	425.00	450.00	600.00	2,000	
1912 (83)	405,083	425.00	450.00	485.00	550.00	15,000
1912S	300,000	425.00	450.00	485.00	2,000	
1913 (71)	442,071	425.00	450.00	485.00	550.00	15,000
1913S	66,000	575.00	750.00	1,250	7,500	
1914 (50)	151,050	425.00	450.00	485.00	650.00	17,500
1914D	343,500	425.00	450.00	485.00	650.00	
1914S	208,000	425.00	450.00	550.00	1,400	
1915 (75)	351,075	425.00	450.00	485.00	600.00	17,500
1915S	59,000	425.00	450.00	650.00	3,000	
1916S	138,500	425.00	450.00	600.00	1,200	
1920S	126,500	4,500	7,500	12,000	17,500	
1926	1,014,000	425.00	450.00	485.00	550.00	
1930S	96,000	3,000	4,500	7,500	1,400	
1932	4,463,000	425.00	450.00	485.00	550.00	
1933	312,500				70,000	

DOUBLE EAGLES ($20.00 Gold Pieces) — 1849-1933

This largest denomination of all regular United States issues was authorized to be coined by the Act of March 3, 1849. Its weight was 516 grains, .900 fine. The 1849 double eagle is a unique pattern and reposes in the Smithsonian. The rarest date obtainable is 1883. The 1861 reverse design by Anthony C. Paquet was withdrawn soon after striking. Very few specimens are known.

+ or − indicates change from previous year	TYPE COIN VALUES									
	F-12	VF-20	EF-40	AU-50	MS-60	MS-63	MS-65	PF-60	PF-63	PF-65
Lib Coronet-NM 1849-1866	450.00−	500.00−	525.00−	700.00−	2,800+	12,500+	65,000+	11,000−	35,000+	150,000+
Lib (Twenty D.) 1866-1876	450.00−	475.00−	500.00−	525.00−	800.00	10,000+	60,000+	8,000−	25,000+	150,000+
Lib 1877-1907	450.00−	460.00−	475.00−	500.00−	550.00−	1,400−	10,000+	6,000−	20,000+	85,000+
Saint-Gaudens-RN, HR 1907	2,750	3,500	4,500−	6,000−	8,500−	16,000	45,000+			
Saint-Gaudens 1907-1932	450.00−	460.00−	475.00−	500.00−	575.00−	850−	3,200−	9,000−	25,000+	60,000+

Designer James B. Longacre; weight 33.436 grams; composition: .900 gold, .100 copper; diameter 34 mm; reeded edge. Net weight: .96750 oz. pure gold.

VF-20 VERY FINE—*LIBERTY is bold. Jewels on crown defined. Lower half worn flat. Hair worn about ear.*

EF-40 EXTREMELY FINE—*Trace of wear on rounded prongs of crown and down hair curls. Minor bag marks.*

AU-50 ABOUT UNCIRCULATED—*Trace of wear on hair over eye and on coronet.*

MS-60 UNCIRCULATED—*No trace of wear. Light blemishes.*

Mint mark location is below the eagle.   1861S Paquet Reverse

[211]

DOUBLE EAGLES
Without Motto on Reverse 1849-1866
See pg. 6 for information on investment grade coins.

	Quan. Minted	VF-20	EF-40	AU-50	MS-60	Proof-63
1849	1				Smithsonian collection	
1850	1,170,261	$550.00	$600.00	$850.00	$3,500	
1850O	141,000	700.00	900.00	1,200	4,750	
1851	2,087,155	500.00	525.00	700.00	2,800	
1851O	315,000	700.00	850.00	1,000	4,500	
1852	2,053,026	500.00	525.00	700.00	2,800	
1852O	190,000	700.00	850.00	1,000	4,500	

1853, 3 over 2

	Quan. Minted	VF-20	EF-40	AU-50	MS-60	Proof-63
1853, 3 over 2	} 1,261,326	—	—		—	
1853		500.00	525.00	700.00	2,800	
1853O		675.00	800.00	1,200	5,000	
1854	757,899	500.00	525.00	700.00	2,800	
1854O	3,250	20,000	33,000	50,000		
1854S	141,468	550.00	600.00	775.00	3,750	
1855	364,666	500.00	525.00	700.00	2,800	
1855O	8,000	2,000	3,500	5,500	——	
1855S	879,675	500.00	525.00	700.00	3,200	
1856	329,878	500.00	525.00	700.00	2,800	
1856O	2,250	25,000	35,000	57,000		
1856S	1,189,750	500.00	525.00	700.00	2,800	
1857	439,375	500.00	525.00	700.00	3,000	
1857O	30,000	700.00	850.00	1,300	6,000	
1857S	970,500	500.00	525.00	700.00	2,800	
1858	211,714	500.00	525.00	700.00	3,000	
1858O	35,250	700.00	850.00	1,800	6,500	
1858S	846,710	500.00	525.00	700.00	3,000	
1859 (80)	43,597	550.00	600.00	775.00	3,800	——
1859O	9,100	1,650	2,750	4,750	9,500	
1859S	636,445	500.00	525.00	700.00	2,800	
1860 (59)	577,670	500.00	525.00	700.00	3,000	——
1860O	6,600	2,200	3,500	5,000	12,000	
1860S	544,950	500.00	525.00	700.00	2,800	
1861 (66)	2,976,453	500.00	525.00	700.00	2,800	$43,000
1861O	17,741	1,200	2,300	3,400	9,000	
1861S	768,000	500.00	525.00	700.00	3,000	
1861 — A.C. Paquet rev. (Tall letters)		(Norweb Auction 1988)			660,000	
1861S—A.C. Paquet rev. (Tall letters)		5,000	6,750	9,000	——	
1862 (35)	92,133	550.00	600.00	775.00	5,000	37,500
1862S	854,173	500.00	525.00	700.00	3,200	
1863 (30)	142,790	550.00	600.00	775.00	5,000	35,000
1863S	966,570	500.00	525.00	700.00	3,000	
1864 (50)	204,285	550.00	600.00	775.00	3,500	35,000
1864S	793,660	500.00	525.00	700.00	3,000	
1865 (25)	351,200	550.00	600.00	775.00	3,400	37,500
1865S	1,042,500	500.00	525.00	700.00	3,000	
1866S	incl. below	675.00	800.00	1,350	5,500	

DOUBLE EAGLES
Motto Above Eagle, Value TWENTY D. 1866-1876

	Quan. Minted	VF-20	EF-40	AU-50	MS-60	Proof-63
1866 . . . . (30)	698,775	$525.00	$600.00	$650.00	$2,000	$25,000
1866S	842,250	525.00	600.00	650.00	1,750	
1867 . . . . (50)	251,065	525.00	600.00	650.00	1,900	25,000
1867S	920,750	525.00	600.00	650.00	1,750	
1868 . . . . (25)	98,600	525.00	600.00	650.00	2,100	25,000
1868S	837,500	525.00	600.00	650.00	1,750	
1869 . . . . (25)	175,155	525.00	600.00	650.00	1,750	25,000
1869S	686,750	525.00	600.00	650.00	1,750	
1870 . . . . (35)	155,185	525.00	600.00	650.00	1,750	25,000
1870CC 3,789		15,000	27,500	——	——	
1870S	982,000	525.00	600.00	650.00	2,000	
1871 . . . . (30)	80,150	525.00	600.00	650.00	1,800	25,000
1871CC 17,387		1,400	2,750	3,800		
1871S	928,000	525.00	600.00	650.00	1,500	
1872 . . . . (30)	251,880	525.00	600.00	650.00	1,300	25,000
1872CC 26,900		775.00	1,000	1,500	3,500	
1872S	780,000	475.00	500.00	525.00	800.00	
1873 Closed 3 . . . . (25) ⎱ 1,709,825		650.00	750.00	950.00	1,800	25,000
1873 Open 3 . . . . ⎰		475.00	500.00	525.00	800.00	
1873CC Closed 3 22,410		750.00	850.00	1,300	2,750	
1873S	1,040,600	475.00	500.00	525.00	800.00	
1874 . . . . (20)	366,800	475.00	500.00	525.00	800.00	27,500
1874CC 115,085		675.00	800.00	1,100	2,000	
1874S	1,214,000	475.00	500.00	525.00	800.00	
1875 . . . . (20)	295,740	475.00	500.00	525.00	800.00	——
1875CC 111,151		675.00	800.00	1,100	2,000	
1875S	1,230,000	475.00	500.00	525.00	800.00	
1876 . . . . (45)	583,905	475.00	500.00	525.00	800.00	25,000
1876CC 138,441		675.00	750.00	900.00	1,800	
1876S	1,597,000	475.00	500.00	525.00	800.00	

TWENTY DOLLARS 1877-1907

[213]

DOUBLE EAGLES

	Quan. Minted	VF-20	EF-40	AU-50	MS-60	Proof-63
1877 .... (20)	397,670	$475.00	$500.00	$550.00	$650.00	$21,000
1877CC	42,565	750.00	800.00	1,000	1,800	
1877S	1,735,000	475.00	500.00	550.00	650.00	
1878 .... (20)	543,645	475.00	500.00	550.00	650.00	21,000
1878CC	13,180	750.00	900.00	1,350	3,000	
1878S	1,739,000	475.00	500.00	550.00	650.00	
1879 .... (30)	207,630	475.00	500.00	550.00	650.00	20,000
1879CC	10,708	850.00	1,500	2,100	4,250	
1879O	2,325	2,500	3,750	5,500	12,000	
1879S	1,223,800	475.00	500.00	550.00	650.00	
1880 .... (36)	51,456	475.00	550.00	600.00	1,000	20,000
1880S	836,000	475.00	500.00	550.00	650.00	
1881 .... (61)	2,260	2,250	4,500	7,250	10,500	30,000
1881S	727,000	475.00	500.00	550.00	600.00	
1882 .... (59)	630	3,500	9,000	15,000	30,000	45,000
1882CC	39,140	700.00	800.00	950.00	1,750	
1882S	1,125,000	475.00	500.00	550.00	600.00	
1883 Proofs only .... (92)	92					——
1883CC	59,962	700.00	800.00	950.00	1,750	
1883S	1,189,000	475.00	500.00	550.00	600.00	
1884 Proofs only .... (71)	71					——
1884CC	81,139	700.00	800.00	950.00	1,750	
1884S	916,000	460.00	475.00	500.00	550.00	
1885 .... (77)	828	3,500	8,000	12,500	21,000	35,000
1885CC	9,450	900.00	1,300	2,000	3,800	
1885S	683,500	460.00	475.00	500.00	550.00	
1886 .... (106)	1,106	4,000	9,000	13,500	22,500	42,500
1887 Proofs only ...... (121)	121					45,000
1887S	283,000	475.00	500.00	550.00	650.00	
1888 .... (105)	226,266	475.00	500.00	550.00	650.00	20,000
1888S	859,600	475.00	500.00	550.00	650.00	
1889 .... (41)	44,111	475.00	500.00	575.00	750.00	20,000
1889CC	30,945	650.00	750.00	900.00	2,200	
1889S	774,700	460.00	475.00	500.00	600.00	
1890 .... (55)	75,995	460.00	500.00	550.00	650.00	20,000
1890CC	91,209	650.00	750.00	800.00	1,750	
1890S	802,750	460.00	500.00	550.00	600.00	
1891 .... (52)	1,442	1,250	2,750	4,250	8,500	21,000
1891CC	5,000	1,200	2,200	3,000	5,500	
1891S	1,288,125	460.00	475.00	500.00	550.00	
1892 .... (93)	4,523	1,000	1,850	2,350	5,000	21,000
1892CC	27,265	650.00	800.00	1,200	2,200	
1892S	930,150	460.00	475.00	500.00	550.00	
1893 .... (59)	344,339	460.00	475.00	500.00	550.00	20,000
1893CC	18,402	675.00	825.00	1,300	2,600	
1893S	996,175	460.00	475.00	500.00	550.00	
1894 .... (50)	1,368,990	460.00	475.00	500.00	550.00	20,000
1894S	1,048,550	460.00	475.00	500.00	550.00	
1895 .... (51)	1,114,656	460.00	475.00	500.00	550.00	20,000
1895S	1,143,500	460.00	475.00	500.00	550.00	
1896 .... (128)	792,663	460.00	475.00	500.00	600.00	20,000
1896S	1,403,925	460.00	475.00	500.00	550.00	
1897 .... (86)	1,383,261	460.00	475.00	500.00	550.00	20,000
1897S	1,470,250	460.00	475.00	500.00	550.00	
1898 .... (75)	170,470	460.00	475.00	500.00	700.00	20,000
1898S	2,575,175	460.00	475.00	500.00	550.00	
1899 .... (84)	1,669,384	460.00	475.00	500.00	550.00	20,000

DOUBLE EAGLES

	Quan. Minted	VF-20	EF-40	AU-50	MS-60	Proof-63
1899S	2,010,300	$460.00	$475.00	$500.00	$650.00	
1900 (124)	1,874,584	460.00	475.00	500.00	550.00	$20,000
1900S	2,459,500	460.00	475.00	500.00	550.00	
1901 (96)	111,526	460.00	475.00	500.00	650.00	20,000
1901S	1,596,000	460.00	475.00	500.00	600.00	
1902 (114)	31,254	460.00	475.00	500.00	750.00	20,000
1902S	1,753,625	460.00	475.00	500.00	550.00	
1903 (158)	287,428	460.00	475.00	500.00	550.00	20,000
1903S	954,000	460.00	475.00	500.00	600.00	
1904 (98)	6,256,797	460.00	475.00	500.00	550.00	20,000
1904S	5,134,175	460.00	475.00	500.00	550.00	
1905 (92)	59,011	460.00	475.00	500.00	750.00	20,000
1905S	1,813,000	460.00	475.00	500.00	650.00	
1906 (94)	69,690	460.00	475.00	500.00	750.00	20,000
1906D	620,250	460.00	475.00	500.00	650.00	
1906S	2,065,750	460.00	475.00	500.00	550.00	
1907 (78)	1,451,864	460.00	475.00	500.00	550.00	20,000
1907D	842,250	460.00	475.00	500.00	650.00	
1907S	2,165,800	460.00	475.00	500.00	600.00	

Values of common gold coins are based on the current bullion price of gold, and may vary with the prevailing spot price.

SAINT-GAUDENS TYPE 1907-1933

The $20 gold piece designed by Augustus Saint-Gaudens is considered to be the most beautiful United States coin. The first coins issued were 11,250 high relief pieces struck for general circulation. The relief is much higher than later issues and the date 1907 is in Roman numerals. A few of the proof coins were made using the lettered edge collar from the extremely high relief version. These can be distinguished by a pronounced bottom left serif on the N in UNUM, and other minor differences. Flat-relief double eagles were issued later in 1907 with Arabic numerals, and continued through 1933.

The field of the rare extremely high relief experimental pieces is excessively concave and connects directly with the edge without any border, giving it a sharp knifelike appearance; Liberty's skirt shows two folds on the side of her right leg; the Capitol building in the background at left is very small; the sun, on the reverse side, has 14 rays, as opposed to the regular high relief coins that have only 13 rays extending from the sun. High relief proofs are trial or experimental pieces.

Designer Augustus Saint-Gaudens. Standards same as previous issue. Edge: E. PLURIBUS UNUM with words divided by stars. One specimen of the high relief variety with plain edge is known.

VF-20 VERY FINE—*Minor wear on legs and toes. Eagle's left wing and breast feathers worn.*

EF-40 EXTREMELY FINE—*Drapery lines on chest visible. Wear on left breast, knee and below. Eagle's feathers on breast and right wing are bold.*

AU-50 ABOUT UNCIRCULATED—*Trace of wear on nose, breast and knee. Wear visible on eagle's wings.*

MS-60 UNCIRCULATED—*No trace of wear. Light marks or blemishes.*

See pg. 6 for information on investment grade coins.

Extremely High Relief Patterns of 1907

	Proof
1907 Ex. high relief, plain edge (*Unique*)	——
1907 Ex. high relief, lettered edge	$225,000

DOUBLE EAGLES

	Quan. Minted	VF-20	EF-40	AU-50	MS-60	Proof
1907 High relief, Roman numerals (MCMVII), wire rim	} 11,250	$3,500	$4,500	$6,000	$8,500	——
1907 Same, flat rim		3,500	4,500	6,000	8,500	——

Arabic Numerals

No Motto

	Quan. Minted	VF-20	EF-40	AU-50	MS-60
1907 Arabic numerals........	361,667	600.00	750.00	850.00	1,000
1908	4,271,551	500.00	550.00	600.00	700.00
1908D.....................	663,750	500.00	550.00	600.00	800.00

With Motto IN GOD WE TRUST, 1908-1933

Mint mark location is on obverse above date.

						Matte Proof-63
1908 .... (101)	156,359	460.00	500.00	575.00	700.00	$29,000
1908D........................	349,500	460.00	500.00	575.00	800.00	
1908S........................	22,000	750.00	1,000	1,400	4,000	

DOUBLE EAGLES

Double eagles from 1907 to 1911 have 46 stars on the obverse and 48 stars from 1912 to 1933.

1909, 9 over 8

	Quan. Minted	VF-20	EF-40	AU-50	MS-60	Matte Proof-63
1909, 9 over 8	⎱	$500.00	$600.00	$700.00	$900.00	
1909 .... (67)	161,282	500.00	600.00	700.00	1,000	$29,000
1909D........................	52,500	600.00	750.00	1,000	2,500	
1909S......................	2,774,925	460.00	475.00	500.00	700.00	
1910 .... (167)	482,167	460.00	475.00	500.00	575.00	27,500
1910D........................	429,000	500.00	525.00	550.00	700.00	
1910S........................	2,128,250	460.00	475.00	500.00	600.00	
1911 .... (100)	197,350	460.00	475.00	500.00	600.00	25,000
1911D........................	846,500	475.00	500.00	550.00	700.00	
1911S........................	775,750	475.00	500.00	550.00	700.00	
1912 .... (74)	149,824	500.00	600.00	700.00	900.00	25,000
1913 .... (58)	168,838	500.00	525.00	550.00	600.00	25,000
1913D........................	393,500	460.00	475.00	500.00	575.00	
1913S........................	34,000	550.00	650.00	800.00	1,200	
1914 .... (70)	95,320	460.00	475.00	500.00	575.00	25,000
1914D........................	453,000	460.00	475.00	500.00	575.00	
1914S........................	1,498,000	460.00	475.00	500.00	575.00	
1915 .... (50)	152,050	460.00	475.00	500.00	575.00	27,500
1915S........................	567,500	460.00	475.00	500.00	575.00	
1916S........................	796,000	460.00	475.00	500.00	700.00	
1920	228,250	460.00	475.00	500.00	575.00	
1920S........................	558,000	6,500	9,000	10,000	16,000	
1921	528,500	7,500	12,000	14,000	20,000	
1922	1,375,500	460.00	475.00	500.00	575.00	
1922S........................	2,658,000	500.00	650.00	800.00	1,200	
1923	566,000	460.00	475.00	500.00	575.00	
1923D........................	1,702,250	460.00	475.00	500.00	575.00	
1924	4,323,500	460.00	475.00	500.00	575.00	
1924D........................	3,049,500	800.00	1,200	1,500	2,250	
1924S........................	2,927,500	800.00	1,200	1,500	2,100	
1925	2,831,750	460.00	475.00	500.00	575.00	
1925D........................	2,938,500	800.00	1,200	1,500	2,400	
1925S........................	3,776,500	800.00	1,200	1,500	2,500	
1926	816,750	460.00	475.00	500.00	575.00	
1926D........................	481,000	900.00	1,200	1,600	2,800	
1926S........................	2,041,500	650.00	900.00	1,100	1,800	
1927	2,946,750	460.00	475.00	500.00	575.00	
1927D........................	180,000				200,000	
1927S........................	3,107,000		4,200	6,000	10,000	
1928	8,816,000	460.00	475.00	500.00	575.00	
1929	1,779,750		4,500	6,000	10,000	
1930S........................	74,000		10,000	13,000	20,000	
1931	2,938,250		8,000	10,000	15,000	
1931D........................	106,500		9,000	12,000	17,500	
1932	1,101,750		10,000	13,000	18,500	
1933	445,500		None placed in circulation			

COMMEMORATIVE COINS

Commemorative coins have been popular since the days of the Greeks and Romans. In the beginning they served to record and honor important events and in the absence of newspapers they proved highly useful in passing along news of the day.

Many modern nations have issued commemorative coins and such pieces are highly esteemed by collectors. Yet no nation has surpassed our own country when it comes to commemorative coins and in this we have reason to be proud.

The unique position occupied by commemoratives in United States coinage is largely due to the fact that with few exceptions all commemorative coins have a real historical significance. The progress and advance of people in the New World are presented in an interesting and instructive manner on the commemorative issues. Such a record of facts artistically presented on our gold and silver memorial issues appeals strongly to the collector who favors the historical side of numismatics. It is the historical features of the commemoratives, in fact, which create interest among many people who would otherwise have little interest in coins.

Commemorative issues are considered for coinage by two committees of Congress — The Committee on Banking, Housing and Urban Affairs, and the Committee on Banking and Currency of the House. Congress is guided to a great extent by the reports of these committees when passing upon bills authorizing commemorative coins.

These special coins are usually issued either to commemorate events or to help pay for monuments or celebrations that commemorate historical persons, places or things. The commemorative coins are offered in most instances by a commission in charge of the event to be commemorated, and sold at a price in advance of the face value of the piece. All are of the standard weight and fineness of traditional gold and silver coins, and all are legal tender.

Commemorative coins are popularly collected either by major types or in sets with mint mark varieties. In many years no special commemorative coins were issued. Some regular coins such as the Lincoln cent of 1909, Washington quarter of 1932, and Bicentennial issues of 1976 are also considered to be commemoratives.

Unless otherwise stated, the coinage figures given represent the total outstanding coinage. In many cases, larger quantities were minted but were not all sold. The unsold coins were usually returned to the mint and melted, although some were placed in circulation at face value.

Note: The commemorative coins listed on pages 217-237 are arranged alphabetically. The modern commemorative coin section on pages 241-248 is arranged chronologically.

High quality brilliant uncirculated commemoratives (MS-65) are worth far more than the uncirculated (MS-60) pieces which are often dull, cleaned, or blemished by contact marks.

A limited number of proof strikings or presentation pieces were made for some of these issues. All are very rare and valuable.

COMMEMORATIVE SILVER — Isabella Quarter, Alabama, Albany
ISABELLA QUARTER DOLLAR

In 1893 the Board of Lady Managers of the Columbian Exposition petitioned for a souvenir quarter dollar. Authority was granted March 3, 1893. The coin known as the Isabella quarter was designed by C. E. Barber. These souvenir quarters were sold for $1.00. The obverse has the crowned bust of Queen Isabella of Spain. The kneeling female on the reverse with distaff and spindle is emblematic of women's industry.

	Quan. Issued	AU-50	MS-60	MS-63	MS-65
1893 Columbian Exposition, Chicago.....	24,214	$210.00	$425.00	$875.00	$5,500

ALABAMA CENTENNIAL

The Alabama half dollars were authorized in 1920 for the centennial which was celebrated in 1919, but they were not struck until 1921. The coins, designed by Laura Gardin Fraser, were offered first during President Harding's visit to Birmingham, October 26, 1921. The St. Andrews cross, an emblem on the state flag, appears on a part of the issue between the figures 22 indicating the twenty-second state of the Union. The obverse has busts of W. W. Bibb, first governor of Alabama, and T. E. Kilby, governor at the time of the centennial. This is the first instance of the use of a living person's portrait on a United States coin.

2x2 in Field

1921 Alabama Centennial, with 2 x 2 in field of obverse	6,006	150.00	275.00	650.00	7,750
1921 Alabama Centennial, no 2 x 2	59,038	85.00	250.00	550.00	7,750

ALBANY, NEW YORK CHARTER

The 250th anniversary of the granting of a charter to the city of Albany was the occasion for a commemorative half dollar. The reverse design shows Governor Dongan, Peter Schuyler and Robert Livingston. The obverse has a beaver gnawing on a maple branch. Gertrude K. Lathrop of Albany was the designer.

1936 Albany, New York	17,671	275.00	325.00	400.00	1,300

COMMEMORATIVE SILVER — Antietam, Arkansas

BATTLE OF ANTIETAM

A souvenir half dollar was designed by William Marks Simpson and struck in 1937 to commemorate the seventy-fifth anniversary of the famous Civil War battle to thwart Lee's invasion of Maryland. The opposing generals McClellan and Lee are featured on the obverse while the Burnside Bridge, an important tactical objective, is shown on the reverse. The Battle of Antietam, on September 17, 1862, was one of the bloodiest single-day battles of the war with total losses of about 25,000 men.

	Quan. Minted	AU-50	MS-60	MS-63	MS-65
1937 Battle of Antietam 1862-1937	18,028	$350.00	$425.00	$500.00	$1,100

ARKANSAS CENTENNIAL

This souvenir issue marked the one hundredth anniversary of the admission of Arkansas into the Union. Edward Everett Burr designed the piece and models were prepared by Emily Bates of Arkansas. Although 1936 was the centennial year the first of several issues was brought out in 1935 from all three mints. During 1936 a new design was authorized by Congress. The late Senator Joseph T. Robinson consented to have his portrait placed on the reverse side of the coins which were struck in January 1937 at the Philadelphia Mint. The 1937 and 1938 issues were the same as those of 1935 except for the dates. They were sold by the distributors at $8.75 per set of three coins. The reverse shows accolated heads of an Indian chief of 1836 and an American girl of 1936.

	Quan. Issued		MS-60	MS-63	MS-65
1935 Arkansas Centennial	13,012				
1935D Same type D mint	5,505	Set $300.00		$400.00	$3,500
1935S Same type S mint	5,506				
1936 Arkansas Centennial, same as 1935— date 1936 on rev	9,660				
1936D Same type D mint	9,660	Set 300.00		400.00	3,500
1936S Same type S mint	9,662				
1937 Arkansas Centennial (same as 1935)	5,505				
1937D Same type D mint	5,505	Set 300.00		400.00	3,500
1937S Same type S mint	5,506				
1938 Arkansas Centennial (same as 1935)	3,156				
1938D Same type D mint	3,155	Set 450.00		550.00	4,500
1938S Same type S mint	3,156				
1939 Arkansas Centennial (same as 1935)	2,104				
1939D Same type D mint	2,104	Set 875.00		1,200	5,500
1939S Same type S mint	2,105				
Single, type coin	Abt. Unc.	$85.00	100.00	135.00	1,250

COMMEMORATIVE SILVER — Bay Bridge, Boone

BAY BRIDGE SAN FRANCISCO- OAKLAND

The opening of the San Francisco Bay Bridge was the occasion for a special souvenir fifty-cent piece. The designs were the work of Jacques Schnier, a San Francisco artist. A California grizzly bear dominates the obverse. The famous bridge is shown on the reverse. The coins were struck at the San Francisco Mint in November 1936. The bear depicted was Monarch II.

	Quan. Issued	AU-50	MS-60	MS-63	MS-65
1936S San Francisco-Oakland Bay Bridge	71,424	$125.00	$200.00	$250.00	$1,000

DANIEL BOONE BICENTENNIAL

Date added in field.

This coin, issues for which covered several dates, was struck to commemorate the two hundredth anniversary of the famous frontiersman's birth. The commemorative date, 1934, was removed after the first issue. The change of date to 1935 for the next year's coinage brought about the addition of 1934 above the words PIONEER YEAR. Coinage covered several years similar to the schedule for the Texas issues. The models for this coin were prepared by Augustus Lukeman. The obverse bears a portrait of Daniel Boone. The reverse shows Boone with Chief Black Fish.

	Quan. Issued		MS-60	MS-63	MS-65
1934 Daniel Boone Bicentennial	10,007		$100.00	$150.00	$525.00
1935 Same type	10,010				
1935D Same type D mint	5,005	Set 375.00		450.00	1,500
1935S Same type S mint	5,005				
1935 Daniel Boone same as 1934					
sm. 1934 on rev	10,008				
1935D Same type D mint	2,003	Set 900.00		1,200	3,250
1935S Same type S mint	2,004				
1936 Daniel Boone (same as 1934)	12,012				
1936D Same type D mint	5,005	Set 375.00		450.00	1,600
1936S Same type S mint	5,006				
1937 Daniel Boone (same as 1934)	9,810				
1937D Same type D mint	2,506	Set 650.00		750.00	1,900
1937S Same type S mint	2,506				
1938 Daniel Boone (same as 1934)	2,100				
1938D Same type D mint	2,100	Set 850.00		1,100	2,600
1938S Same type S mint	2,100				
Single, type coin .... Abt. Unc.	$85.00		100.00	150.00	525.00

COMMEMORATIVE SILVER — Bridgeport, California, Cincinnati

BRIDGEPORT, CONNECTICUT CENTENNIAL

In commemoration of the one hundredth anniversary of the incorporation of the city of Bridgeport a special fifty-cent piece was authorized May 15, 1936. Henry Kreiss designed this coin which somewhat resembles the Connecticut Tercentenary issue. The head of P. T. Barnum, who was Bridgeport's best known citizen, occupies the obverse. An ultra-modernistic eagle dominates the reverse.

	Quan. Issued	AU-50	MS-60	MS-63	MS-65
1936 Bridgeport, Conn., Centennial	25,015	$130.00	$170.00	$210.00	$1,500

CALIFORNIA DIAMOND JUBILEE

The California half dollar was designed by Jo Mora, a noted California sculptor. The obverse bears a kneeling figure of a forty-niner. The reverse shows a walking grizzly bear, the state emblem. The celebration for which these coins were struck marked the seventy-fifth anniversary of the admission of California into the Union. The jubilee was held in 1925.

1925S California Diamond Jubilee	86,394	120.00	150.00	350.00	2,300

CINCINNATI MUSIC CENTER

Although the head of Stephen Foster, "America's Troubadour," dominates the obverse of this special issue the anniversary celebrated bears no relation to him. The coins, designed by Constance Ortmayer of Washington, D. C., were struck to commemorate the fiftieth anniversary in 1936 of Cincinnati as a center of music. The coins were struck at the three mints and were sold only in sets at $7.75, the highest initial cost of a new type.

1936 Cincinnati Music Center	5,005 ⎫				
1936D Same type D	5,005 ⎬ Set		950.00	1,200	6,000
1936S Same type S	5,006 ⎭				
Single, type coin		280.00	335.00	385.00	2,200

CLEVELAND GREAT LAKES EXPOSITION

A special coinage of fifty-cent pieces was authorized in commemoration of the centennial celebration of Cleveland, Ohio on the occasion of the Great Lakes Exposition held there in 1936. The designs were prepared by Brenda Putnam. Although half the coinage was struck in 1937 all were dated 1936. The obverse has a bust of Moses Cleaveland and the reverse displays a map of the Great Lakes region with a compass pointed at Cleveland. Nine Great Lakes cities are marked by stars.

	Quan. Issued	AU-50	MS-60	MS-63	MS-65
1936 Cleveland, Great Lakes Exposition	50,030	$85.00	$110.00	$135.00	$1,400

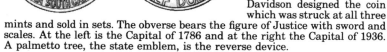

COLUMBIA, SOUTH CAROLINA SESQUICENTENNIAL

Souvenir half dollars were authorized to help finance the extensive celebrations marking the sesquicentennial of the founding of Columbia in 1786. A. Wolfe Davidson designed the coin which was struck at all three mints and sold in sets. The obverse bears the figure of Justice with sword and scales. At the left is the Capital of 1786 and at the right the Capital of 1936. A palmetto tree, the state emblem, is the reverse device.

1936 Columbia, S.C., Sesquicentennial	9,007 ⎫				
1936D Same type D mint	8,009 ⎬ Set	700.00	800.00	1,800
1936S Same type S mint	8,007 ⎭				
Single, type coin		250.00	275.00	325.00	650.00

COLUMBIAN EXPOSITION HALF DOLLAR

The first United States commemorative coin was the Columbian half dollar. C. E. Barber designed the obverse showing the bust of Columbus; and G. T. Morgan designed the reverse having a representation of Columbus' flagship the Santa Maria above two hemispheres. The coins were sold for $1.00 each at the World's Columbian Exposition in Chicago during 1893. A great many remained unsold and a substantial quantity was later released for circulation at face value. Approximately 100 brilliant proofs were struck for each date.

1892 Columbian Exp. Chicago	950,000	25.00	85.00	550.00	4,500
1893 Same type	1,550,405	20.00	85.00	550.00	5,000

COMMEMORATIVE SILVER — Connecticut, Delaware, Elgin

CONNECTICUT TERCENTENARY

In commemoration of the three hundredth anniversary of the founding of the Colony of Connecticut a souvenir half dollar was struck. Henry Kreiss designed the coin. The famous "Charter Oak" is the main device on the reverse. According to tradition the Royal Charter was secreted in the tree during the reign of James II who wished to revoke it. The Charter was produced after the king's overthrow in 1688 and the Colony continued under its protection.

	Quan. Issued	AU-50	MS-60	MS-63	MS-65
1935 Connecticut Tercentenary	25,018	$210.00	$250.00	$335.00	$2,400

DELAWARE TERCENTENARY

The three hundredth anniversary of the landing of the Swedes in Delaware was the occasion for a souvenir issue of half dollars. The colonists landed on a spot which is now Wilmington and established a church which is the oldest Protestant church still used for worship. Their ship "Kalmar Nyckel" is shown on the reverse of the coin and the Old Swedes Church is on the obverse. Designs were chosen from a competition which was won by Carl L. Schmitz. This coin was authorized in 1936, struck in 1937 and dated 1938 on the reverse and 1936 on the obverse. The anniversary was celebrated in 1938 both in Sweden and America. A two kronor coin was issued in Sweden to commemorate the same event.

1936 Delaware Tercentenary	20,993	200.00	250.00	325.00	1,500

ELGIN, ILLINOIS CENTENNIAL

The one hundredth anniversary of the founding of Elgin was marked by a special issue of half dollars in 1936. The proceeds were devoted to financing a Pioneer Memorial statue, which is depicted on the reverse of the coin. The year 1673 bears no relation to the event but refers to the year in which Joliet and Marquette entered Illinois Territory. The designs were prepared by Trygve Rovelstad who also designed the Memorial.

1936 Elgin, Illinois, Centennial	20,015	250.00	275.00	320.00	1,500

COMMEMORATIVE SILVER — Gettysburg, Grant, Hawaiian

BATTLE OF GETTYSBURG

On June 16, 1936 Congress authorized a coinage of fifty-cent pieces in commemoration of the Battle of Gettysburg. The models were prepared by Frank Vittor, a Pittsburgh sculptor. Portraits of a Union and a Confederate veteran are shown on the obverse. Two shields representing the Union and Confederate armies separated by a double-bladed fasces are on the reverse.

	Quan. Issued	AU-50	MS-60	MS-63	MS-65
1936 Battle of Gettysburg 1863-1938.....	26,928	$210.00	$250.00	$300.00	$1,800

GRANT MEMORIAL

This coin was struck during 1922 as a centenary souvenir of Ulysses S. Grant's birth. A star which appeared on the first issues was later removed, creating a second variety. The star has no particular significance. Laura Gardin Fraser designed both the Grant half dollar and gold dollar. The reverse shows a log cabin in Point Pleasant, Ohio, where Grant was born April 27, 1822.

Star in obverse field

(Fake stars have flattened spot on reverse.)

1922 Grant Memorial. Star in obv. field...	4,256	350.00	700.00	2,500	20,000
1922 Same, no star	67,405	85.00	125.00	350.00	3,000

HAWAIIAN SESQUICENTENNIAL

This small issue was struck to commemorate the 150th anniversary of the rediscovery of the Hawaiian Islands by Captain James Cook in 1778. The design was sketched by Juliette May Fraser of Honolulu and executed by Chester Beach. Captain Cook is shown on the obverse and a native chief on the reverse. The coins were distributed in 1928 and sold for $2.00 each, the highest initial sale price up to that time.

1928 Hawaiian Sesquicentennial..........	9,958	725.00	850.00	1,800	12,000
1928 Hawaiian Sesquicentennial —					
sandblast proof presentation piece......	50				

HUDSON, NEW YORK SESQUICENTENNIAL

This souvenir half dollar marked the one hundred and fiftieth anniversary of the founding of Hudson, New York, which was named after the explorer Hendrik Hudson. The designs by Chester Beach show Hudson's flagship the "Half Moon" on the obverse and the seal of the City of Hudson on the reverse. Details of the seal include representations of Neptune with trident on a spouting whale and a mermaid blowing a conch shell.

	Quan. Issued	AU-50	MS-60	MS-63	MS-65
1935 Hudson, N.Y. Sesquicentennial	10,008	$400.00	$500.00	$750.00	$4,000

HUGUENOT-WALLOON TERCENTENARY

Settling of the Huguenots and Walloons in the New World was the occasion commemorated by this issue. New Netherlands, now New York, was founded in 1624 by a group of Dutch colonists. The persons represented on the obverse were not directly concerned with the occasion, however. They are Admiral Coligny and William the Silent. The reverse shows the vessel "Nieu Nederland." G. T. Morgan prepared the models for this coin.

1924 Huguenot-Walloon Tercentenary	142,080	70.00	110.00	235.00	2,100

ILLINOIS CENTENNIAL

The obverse was designed by G. T. Morgan and the reverse by J. R. Sinnock. The obverse shows the head of Lincoln taken from the statue by Andrew O'Connor in Springfield, Illinois. The reverse is based on the Illinois State Seal. This coin was authorized to commemorate the one hundredth anniversary of the admission of Illinois into the Union, the first souvenir piece for such an event.

1918 Illinois Centennial	100,058	75.00	125.00	200.00	1,750

COMMEMORATIVE SILVER — Iowa, Lexington, Long Island

IOWA CENTENNIAL

This half dollar, commemorating the one hundredth anniversary of Iowa's statehood, was designed by Adam Pietz of Philadelphia. The reverse shows the Iowa state seal and the obverse has the first stone capitol building at Iowa City. This issue was sold first to the residents of Iowa and only a small remainder to others. The entire issue was disposed of in a few weeks.

	Quan. Issued	AU-50	MS-60	MS-63	MS-65
1946 Iowa Centennial	100,057	$75.00	$100.00	$125.00	$475.00

LEXINGTON-CONCORD SESQUICENTENNIAL

The two famous battles fought in 1775 are commemorated on this coin. A statue of the familiar Minute Man is depicted on the obverse, and the old Belfry at Lexington is the reverse device. Chester Beach designed the coin. The famous statue by Daniel Chester French located in Concord was used for the design.

1925 Lexington-Concord Sesquicentennial	162,013	50.00	65.00	185.00	2,400

LONG ISLAND TERCENTENARY

This souvenir issue was authorized to commemorate the three hundredth anniversary of the first white settlement on Long Island which was at Jamaica Bay by Dutch colonists. The design was prepared by Howard Kenneth Weinman, son of the sculptor A. A. Weinman who designed the regular Liberty walking type half dollar. Accolated heads depicting a Dutch settler and an Indian are shown on the obverse, while a Dutch sailing vessel is the reverse device. This was the first issue for which a date was specified (1936) irrespective of the year minted or issued.

1936 Long Island Tercentenary	81,826	85.00	100.00	135.00	2,000

COMMEMORATIVE SILVER — Lynchburg, Maine, Maryland

LYNCHBURG, VIRGINIA SESQUICENTENNIAL

The issuance of a charter to the city of Lynchburg in 1786 was commemorated in 1936 by a special coinage of half dollars. The models for the coin were prepared by Charles Keck. The obverse bears a portrait of Senator Carter Glass, a native of Lynchburg and former Secretary of the Treasury, who objected to the idea of using portraits of living men on coins. Despite his protests his likeness was incorporated on the coin. The reverse shows Liberty standing, with the old Lynchburg courthouse in the background.

	Quan. Issued	AU-50	MS-60	MS-63	MS-65
1936 Lynchburg, Va., Sesquicentennial...	20,013	$200.00	$225.00	$300.00	$1,500

MAINE CENTENNIAL

Congress authorized the Maine Centennial half dollar May 10, 1920, to be sold at the Centennial celebration at Portland. They were received too late for this event and were sold by the state Treasurer until all

were sold. Anthony de Francisci modeled this coin according to specifications furnished him. The latin word DIRIGO means: I direct. The obverse device is the arms of the state of Maine.

1920 Maine Centennial	50,028	90.00	115.00	325.00	2,200

MARYLAND TERCENTENARY

The three hundredth anniversary of the founding of the Maryland Colony by Cecil Calvert (known as Lord Baltimore) was the occasion for this special coin. The profits from the sale of this issue were used to finance the celebration in Baltimore during 1934. Hans Schuler designed the coin which shows the facing head of Lord Baltimore on the obverse and the arms of Maryland on the reverse, reminiscent of the Maryland colonial pieces.

1934 Maryland Tercentenary............	25,015	125.00	150.00	225.00	1,600

COMMEMORATIVE SILVER — Missouri, Monroe, New Rochelle

MISSOURI CENTENNIAL

The one hundredth anniversary of the admission of Missouri to the Union was celebrated at Sedalia during August, 1921. To mark the occasion Congress authorized the coinage of a fifty-cent piece. Robert Aitken designed the piece which shows the bust of a frontiersman on the obverse, and another frontiersman and Indian on the reverse. The first coins struck show 2★4 incused, indicating that Missouri was the twenty-fourth star in the flag. The type without the star was struck later, but was the first to be sold.

2★4 in field

	Quan. Issued	AU-50	MS-60	MS-63	MS-65
1921 Missouri Centennial 2★4 in field	5,000	$210.00	$425.00	$1,300	$15,000
1921 Missouri Centennial, no 2★4	15,428	200.00	400.00	1,000	15,000

MONROE DOCTRINE CENTENNIAL

The motion picture industry promoted this issue in conjunction with a motion picture exposition in June 1923. The obverse shows the heads of James Monroe and John Quincy Adams who were identified with the Monroe Doctrine. The Western Hemisphere is portrayed on the reverse by two female figures. Chester Beach prepared the models for this coin.

1923S Monroe Doctrine Centennial..... 274,077	25.00	65.00	275.00	7,500

NEW ROCHELLE, NEW YORK

To observe the founding of New Rochelle in 1688 by French Huguenots, a special half dollar was issued in 1938. The title to the land which the Huguenots purchased from John Pell provided that a fattened calf be given away every year on June 20th. This will explain the appearance of the calf and figure representing John Pell on the obverse of the coin. The fleur-de-lis which is shown on the reverse is adopted from the Seal of the city. Both sides of the coin were designed by Gertrude K. Lathrop.

1938 New Rochelle, N.Y. 1688-1938 15,266	375.00	400.00	450.00	1,000

COMMEMORATIVE SILVER — Norfolk, Oregon
NORFOLK, VIRGINIA BICENTENNIAL

To provide funds for the celebration of Norfolk's anniversary of its growth from a township in 1682 to a royal borough in 1736, Congress first passed a law for the striking of medals. The proponents, however, being dissatisfied finally succeeded in winning authority for half dollars commemorating the 300th anniversary of the original Norfolk land grant and the 200th anniversary of the establishment of the borough. William Marks Simpson and his wife Marjorie Emory Simpson designed the piece. The obverse shows the Seal of the City of Norfolk with a three-masted ship as the central device. The reverse features the Royal Mace of Norfolk presented by Lieutenant Governor Dinwiddie in 1753.

	Quan. Issued	AU-50	MS-60	MS-63	MS-65
1936 Norfolk, Va. Bicentennial..........	16,936	$525.00	$600.00	$650.00	$800.00

OREGON TRAIL MEMORIAL

This memorial coin was struck in commemoration of the Oregon trail and in memory of the pioneers, many of whom lie buried along the famous 2,000 mile highway of history. James Earle Fraser and his wife, Laura Gardin Fraser, prepared the designs. The original issue was struck at Philadelphia and San Francisco in 1926. The coin was reissued in 1928 (released in 1933), 1933, 1934, 1936, and 1938. The 1933 half dollar was the first commemorative coin struck at the Denver Mint.

1926	Oregon Trail Memorial..........	47,955	90.00	120.00	195.00	750.00
1926S	Same type S mint...............	83,055	90.00	120.00	195.00	625.00
1928	Oregon Trail Mem. (same as 1926)	6,028	140.00	225.00	300.00	1,000
1933D	Oregon Trail Memorial, same D mint....................	5,008	225.00	275.00	375.00	1,600
1934D	Oregon Trail Memorial, same D mint....................	7,006	125.00	200.00	300.00	1,600
1936	Oregon Trail Mem. (same as 1926)	10,006	120.00	165.00	200.00	900.00
1936S	Same type S mint................	5,006	135.00	235.00	300.00	950.00
1937D	Oregon Trail Memorial D mint...	12,008	100.00	125.00	225.00	625.00
1938	Oregon Trail Memorial (same as 1926)....................	6,006				
1938D	Same type D mint	6,005	Set	550.00	725.00	1,700
1938S	Same type S mint...............	6,006				
1939	Oregon Trail (same as 1926)	3,004				
1939D	Same type D mint	3,004	Set	1,300	1,650	3,600
1939S	Same type S mint...............	3,005				
	Single, type coin		90.00	120.00	195.00	625.00

COMMEMORATIVE SILVER — Panama-Pacific, Pilgrim

PANAMA-PACIFIC EXPOSITION

This half dollar was designed by C. E. Barber. The exposition held in San Francisco in 1915 celebrated the opening of the Panama Canal. The coins were struck at the San Francisco Mint and were sold at $1.00 each during the exposition. The Panama-Pacific coins have the distinction of being the first commemorative coins to carry the motto. IN GOD WE TRUST appears above the eagle. A representation of Columbia with the golden gate in the background is the principal feature of the obverse.

	Quan. Issued	AU-50	MS-60	MS-63	MS-65
1915S Panama-Pacific Exposition........	27,134	$210.00	$400.00	$950.00	$4,600

PILGRIM TERCENTENARY

To commemorate the landing of the Pilgrims at Plymouth, Massachusetts in 1620, Congress authorized a special half dollar May 12, 1920. Cyrus E. Dallin, a Boston sculptor, executed the designs furnished him by the Commission. The obverse has a portrait of Governor Bradford. The reverse shows the "Mayflower." The first issue had no date on the obverse. The coins struck in 1921 show that date in addition to 1620-1920. There was a large coinage of both issues and not all were sold. A total of 128,000 were returned to the mint and melted.

1920 Pilgrim Tercentenary.............	152,112	50.00	65.00	150.00	1,800

With 1921 date Added in Field on Obverse

1921 Same type	20,053	90.00	125.00	200.00	2,200

COMMEMORATIVE SILVER — Rhode Island, Roanoke, Robinson

RHODE ISLAND TERCENTENARY PROVIDENCE

The three hundredth anniversary of Roger Williams' founding of Providence was the occasion for this special half dollar in 1935. The designs were the work of Arthur Graham Carey and John Howard Benson. The obverse shows Roger Williams in a canoe being welcomed by an Indian. The reverse has the anchor of Hope with a shield and mantling in the background. Although the founding of Providence was being celebrated, no mention of the city is to be found on the coin.

	Quan. Issued		AU-50	MS-60	MS-63	MS-65
1936 Rhode Island Tercentenary	20,013					
1936D Same type D mint..............	15,010	} Set		$350.00	$450.00	$3,500
1936S Same type S mint	15,011					
Single, type coin			$95.00	110.00	145.00	1,300

ROANOKE ISLAND, NORTH CAROLINA

A celebration was held in Old Fort Raleigh in 1937 to commemorate the 350th anniversary of Sir Walter Raleigh's "Lost Colony" and the birth of Virginia Dare, the first white child born on the American continent. A special half dollar for the occasion was designed by William Marks Simpson of Baltimore. The obverse bears a portrait of Sir Walter Raleigh and the reverse has a figure representing Eleanor Dare holding the child Virginia Dare.

1937 Roanoke Island, N.C., 1587-1937 ... 29,030   185.00   225.00   300.00   850.00

ROBINSON-ARKANSAS CENTENNIAL

A new reverse design for the Arkansas Centennial coin was authorized by the Act of June 26, 1936. Senator Joseph T. Robinson is the subject for the new issue designed by Henry Kreiss. The obverse, designed by Everett Burr, was unchanged. The law specified a change in the reverse, because of the fact that the obverse side is that which bears the date. From a numismatic viewpoint, however, the side which has the portrait is usually considered the obverse. Thus in this instance, the side with the eagle device is often considered the reverse.

1936 Arkansas Centennial (Robinson) ... 25,265   100.00   115.00   160.00   1,500

COMMEMORATIVE SILVER — San Diego, Sesquicentennial

SAN DIEGO-CALIFORNIA-PACIFIC EXPOSITION

Congress approved the coinage of souvenir half dollars for the exposition on May 3, 1935. Robert Aitken designed the coin which was struck at the San Francisco Mint. The same type with date 1936 was struck at the Denver Mint, under authority of the special Recoinage Act of May 6, 1936, which specified that 180,000 pieces could be recoined with the date 1936 irrespective of the year of issue. The obverse displays a seated female with spear and a bear in the left background. The reverse shows the observation tower and the State of California building at the Exposition.

	Quan. Issued	AU-50	MS-60	MS-63	MS-65
1935S San Diego, California-Pacific Exp. S mint	70,132	$85.00	$110.00	$150.00	$375.00
1936D San Diego, California-Pacific Exposition D mint (same as 1935)	30,092	100.00	125.00	160.00	475.00

SESQUICENTENNIAL OF AMERICAN INDEPENDENCE

The one hundred and fiftieth anniversary of the signing of the Declaration of Independence was the occasion for an International Fair held in Philadelphia in 1926. To help raise funds for financing the fair special issues of half dollars and quarter-eagles were authorized by Congress. For the first time a portrait of a president appeared on a coin struck during his lifetime. President Coolidge and Washington are depicted on the obverse of the half dollar. The reverse bears an accurate model of the Liberty Bell. John R. Sinnock, Chief Engraver of the United States mint, designed the sesquicentennial coins. The dies were in very low relief causing much loss of detail in the coin.

1926 Sesquicentennial of American Independence	141,120	50.00	65.00	275.00	15,000

COMMEMORATIVE SILVER — Old Spanish Trail, Stone Mountain, Texas

OLD SPANISH TRAIL

This coin commemorated the four hundredth anniversary of the overland trek of the Cabeza de Vaca Expedition through the gulf states in 1535. L. W. Hoffecker designed the coin models which were prepared by Edmund J. Senn. The explorer's name literally translated means "head of a cow;" therefore this device was chosen for the obverse. The reverse bears a yucca tree and a map showing the Old Spanish Trail.

	Quan. Issued	AU-50	MS-60	MS-63	MS-65
1935 Old Spanish Trail 1535-1935	10,008	$600.00	$725.00	$875.00	$2,200

STONE MOUNTAIN MEMORIAL

The models for this coin were prepared by Gutzon Borglum. The first coins were struck at Philadelphia January 21, 1925, General Thomas "Stonewall" Jackson's birthday. General Robert E. Lee and Jackson, mounted, are shown on the obverse. The reverse has an eagle and the words MEMORIAL TO THE VALOR OF THE SOLDIER OF THE SOUTH. The funds received from the sale of this large issue of half dollars were devoted to the expense of carving figures of Confederate leaders and soldiers on Stone Mountain in Georgia. The carving was completed and dedicated in 1970.

1925 Stone Mountain Memorial	1,314,709	30.00	50.00	100.00	700.00

TEXAS CENTENNIAL

This issue commemorated the independence of Texas. The first of several dates was offered in 1934. The later dates were struck at all three mints. The models were prepared by Pompeo Coppini. The reverse shows

the kneeling figure of winged Victory, and on each side, medallions with portraits of General Sam Houston and Stephen Austin, founders of the Republic and State of Texas. The large five-pointed star behind the eagle on the obverse carries out the "Lone star" tradition.

1934 Texas Centennial	61,463		145.00	200.00	550.00

COMMEMORATIVE SILVER — Texas,
Vancouver, Vermont

	Quan. Issued	AU-50	MS-60	MS-63	MS-65
1935 Texas Centennial (same as 1934) ...	9,996				
1935D Same type D mint..............	10,007	Set	$425.00	$600.00	$1,650
1935S Same type S mint	10,008				
1936 Texas Centennial (same as 1934) ...	8,911				
1936D Same type D mint..............	9,039	Set	425.00	600.00	1,650
1936S Same type S mint	9,055				
1937 Texas Centennial (same as 1934) ...	6,571				
1937D Same type D mint..............	6,605	Set	425.00	600.00	1,650
1937S Same type S mint	6,637				
1938 Texas Centennial (same as 1934) ...	3,780				
1938D Same type D mint..............	3,775	Set	675.00	900.00	2,400
1938S Same type S mint	3,814				
Single, type coin		$120.00	145.00	200.00	550.00

FORT VANCOUVER CENTENNIAL

Dr. John McLaughlin, shown on the obverse of this coin, built Fort Vancouver on the Columbia River in 1825. The sale of the coins at $1.00 each helped to finance the pageant staged for the celebration. Laura Gardin Fraser prepared the models for this coin which was minted in San Francisco. The S Mint mark was omitted. The reverse has a pioneer settler in buckskin suit with a musket in his hands. Fort Vancouver is in the background.

1925 Fort Vancouver Centennial	14.994	250.00	375.00	550.00	3.500

VERMONT SESQUICENTENNIAL

This souvenir issue commemorates the 150th Anniversary of the Battle of Bennington and the Independence of Vermont. Authorized in 1925, it was not coined until 1927. The models were prepared by Charles Keck. The obverse shows the head of Ira Allen, founder of Vermont. The reverse bears a catamount on a pedestal.

1927 Vermont Sesquicentennial (Bennington).................	28,142	155.00	225.00	325.00	3,000

COMMEMORATIVE SILVER — B. T. Washington, Washington-Carver

BOOKER T. WASHINGTON MEMORIAL

This commemorative coin was issued to perpetuate the ideals and teachings of Booker T. Washington and to construct memorials to his memory. Issued from all mints, it received wide distribution from the start. The reverse has the legend FROM SLAVE CABIN TO HALL OF FAME. His log cabin birthplace is shown beneath. Designed by Isaac Scott Hathaway, as was the Washington-Carver half dollar issued under the same authority.

		Quan. Minted		MS-60	MS-63	MS-65
1946	Booker T. Washington	*1,000,546				
1946D	Same type D mint	200,113	Set	$40.00	$65.00	$375.00
1946S	Same type S mint	500,279				
1947	Same type as 1946	100,017				
1947D	Same type D mint	100,017	Set	55.00	75.00	450.00
1947S	Same type S mint	100,017				
1948	Same type as 1946	8,005				
1948D	Same type D mint	8,005	Set	100.00	145.00	450.00
1948S	Same type S mint	8,005				
1949	Same type as 1946	6,004				
1949D	Same type D mint	6,004	Set	110.00	160.00	475.00
1949S	Same type S mint	6,004				
1950	Same type as 1946	6,004				
1950D	Same type D mint	6,004	Set	100.00	150.00	450.00
1950S	Same type S mint	512,091				
1951	Same type as 1946	510,082				
1951D	Same type D mint	7,004	Set	85.00	125.00	475.00
1951S	Same type S mint	7,004				
	Single, type coin			15.00	22.00	125.00

*Minted; quantity melted unknown.

WASHINGTON-CARVER

Designed by Isaac Scott Hathaway, this coin shows the conjoined busts of two prominent black Americans. Booker T. Washington was a lecturer, educator,

and principal of Tuskegee Institute. He urged training to advance independence and efficiency for his race. George Washington Carver was an agricultural chemist who worked to improve the economy of the south. He spent his life teaching crop improvement and new uses for soybeans, peanuts, sweet potatoes and cotton waste.

COMMEMORATIVE SILVER — Washington-Carver, Wisconsin, York County

Money obtained from the sale of these commemoratives was to be used "to oppose the spread of communism among Negroes in the interest of national defense."

		Quan. Minted		MS-60	MS-63	MS-65
1951	Washington-Carver	110,018				
1951D	Same type D mint	10,004	Set	$65.00	$90.00	$900.00
1951S	Same type S mint	10,004				
1952	Same type as 1951	2,006,292				
1952D	Same type D mint	8,006	Set	70.00	100.00	1,000
1952S	Same type S mint	8,006				
1953	Same type as 1951	8,003				
1953D	Same type D mint	8,003	Set	80.00	120.00	1,400
1953S	Same type S mint	108,020				
1954	Same type as 1951	12,006				
1954D	Same type D mint	12,006	Set	65.00	90.00	1,250
1954S	Same type S mint	122,024				
	Single, type coin			16.00	24.00	275.00

WISCONSIN TERRITORIAL CENTENNIAL

The one hundredth anniversary of the Wisconsin Territorial government was the occasion for a special half dollar issue. The original design was made by David Parsons, a University of Wisconsin student. Benjamin Hawkins, a New York artist, made changes to conform with technical requirements. The reverse has the Territorial Seal, which includes a forearm holding a pickaxe over a mound of lead ore, and the inscription 4th DAY OF JULY ANNO DOMINI 1836. The obverse shows a badger on a log, the state emblem, and arrows representing the Black Hawk War of the 1830's.

	Quan. Issued	AU-50	MS-60	MS-63	MS-65
1936 Wisconsin Centennial	25,015	$210.00	$250.00	$300.00	$700.00

YORK COUNTY, MAINE TERCENTENARY

A souvenir half dollar was authorized by Congress upon the three hundredth anniversary of the founding of York County, Maine. Brown's Garrison on the Saco River was the site of a town which was settled in 1636. The designs were made by Walter H. Rich of Portland. The obverse design shows a stockade and the reverse has an adaptation of the York County seal.

1936 York County, Maine Tercentenary	25,015	200.00	225.00	285.00	700.00

LAFAYETTE DOLLAR

The heads of Washington and Lafayette appear on this commemorative issue, which was the first commemorative coin of one dollar denomination, and the first authorized United States coin to bear a portrait of one of our presidents. The dies were prepared by C. E. Barber. The statue on the reverse is similar to the monument of General Lafayette which was erected in Paris as a gift of the American people. The coins were sold by the Lafayette Memorial Commission for $2.00 each.

	Quan. Issued	AU-50	MS-60	MS-63	MS-65
1900 Lafayette Dollar	36,026	$300.00	$800.00	$2,600	$18,500

COMMEMORATIVE GOLD — Grant, Lewis & Clark, Louisiana Purchase

GRANT MEMORIAL GOLD DOLLARS

Like the half-dollar commemorative coins, the gold dollars were issued first with a star which was removed for the later issues. The designs by Laura Gardin Fraser are the same as for the half-dollar coinage.

		Quan. Issued	AU-50	MS-60	MS-63	MS-65
1922	Grant Memorial Dollar with star..	5,016	$1,500	$1,900	$3,500	$6,000
1922	Grand Memorial Dollar no star ...	5,000	1,500	1,900	3,400	6,200

LEWIS AND CLARK EXPOSITION

The Lewis and Clark Centennial Exposition was held in Portland, Oregon in 1905. A souvenir issue of gold dollars was struck to mark the event with the dates 1904 and 1905. The two famous explorers are represented on each side of the coin which was designed by C. E. Barber. A bronze memorial of the Indian guide, Sacagawea, who assisted in the famous expedition, was erected in Portland, Oregon and financed by the sale of these coins.

		Quan. Issued	AU-50	MS-60	MS-63	MS-65
1904	Lewis and Clark Dollar.........	10,025	$575.00	$1,300	$4,000	$18,500
1905	Lewis and Clark Dollar.........	10.041	575.00	1,450	4,750	35,000

LOUISIANA PURCHASE EXPOSITION

The first souvenir gold coins were authorized for the Louisiana Purchase Exposition held in St. Louis in 1904. There are two varieties of gold dollars — one with the head of Jefferson who was president when the Louisiana Territory was purchased from France; and the other President William McKinley who sanctioned the Exposition. The reverse is the same for each variety. The designs were by C. E. Barber.

		Quan Issued	AU-50	MS-60	MS-63	MS-65
*1903	Louisiana Pur. Jefferson Dol......	17,500	$400.00	$700.00	$1,850	$6,500
*1903	Louisiana Pur. McKinley Dol	17,500	400.00	700.00	1,850	6,500

*Proofs exist of each type

COMMEMORATIVE GOLD — McKinley, Panama-Pacific

McKINLEY MEMORIAL GOLD DOLLARS

The sale of the McKinley dollars aided in paying for a memorial building at Niles, Ohio, the martyred president's birthplace. The obverse showing a profile of McKinley was designed by C. E. Barber; the reverse with the memorial building was designed by G. T. Morgan.

		Quan. Issued	AU-50	MS-60	MS-63	MS-65
1916	McKinley Memorial Dollar	9,977	$350.00	$800.00	$1,700	$6,000
1917	McKinley Memorial Dollar	10,000	375.00	850.00	1,800	9,000

PANAMA-PACIFIC EXPOSITION

Charles Keck designed the gold dollar, the obverse of which has the head of a man representing a Panama Canal laborer. Two dolphins encircle ONE DOLLAR on the reverse.

The quarter-eagle was the work of Charles E. Barber and George T. Morgan. It was the first commemorative coin of this denomination. The obverse shows Columbia with a caduceus in her left hand seated on a hippocampus typifying the use of the Panama Canal. An American eagle with raised wings is shown on the reverse.

The fifty-dollar gold piece was designed by Robert Aitken and was issued in round and octagonal form. The obverse bears the helmeted head of Minerva; the owl, symbol of wisdom, is on the reverse. The octagonal issue has eight dolphins in the angles on both sides. The devices are smaller on the octagonal variety.

	Quan. Issued	AU-50	MS-60	MS-63	MS-65
1915S Panama-Pacific Exposition Dollar. .	15,000	$375.00	$750.00	$1,700	$6,000

1915S Panama-Pacific Exposition $2.50. . .	6,749	900.00	1,900	3,800	8,500

COMMEMORATIVE GOLD — Panama-Pacific, U.S. Sesquicentennial

	Quan. Issued	AU-50	MS-60	MS-63	MS-65
1915S Panama-Pacific $50 Round 483		$22,000	$32,000	$46,000	$115,000

	Quan. Issued	AU-50	MS-60	MS-63	MS-65
1915S Panama-Pacific $50 Octagonal 645		17,000	25,000	38,000	110,000

UNITED STATES SESQUICENTENNIAL—QUARTER EAGLES

The obverse of this special gold issue has a standing female figure symbolic of Liberty, holding in one hand a scroll representing the Declaration of Independence and in the other the Torch of Freedom. The reverse bears a representation of Independence Hall in Philadelphia. The coin was designed by J. R. Sinnock.

	Quan. Issued	AU-50	MS-60	MS-63	MS-65
1926 United States Sesquicent. $2.50..... 46,019		$325.00	$625.00	$1,300	$18,000

MODERN COMMEMORATIVES — Washington, Los Angeles

GEORGE WASHINGTON

This coin, the first commemorative half dollar issued since 1954, commemorates the 250th anniversary of the birth of George Washington. It is also the first 90% silver coin produced by the U.S. Mint since 1964. Designed by Elizabeth Jones, Chief Sculptor and Engraver of the United States, the obverse features George Washington astride a horse. The reverse depicts the eastern facade of Mount Vernon. The uncirculated version was struck at Denver and the proof at San Francisco.

		Quan. Issued	MS-65	Proof-65
1982D	Geo. Washington-250th Anniversary	2,210,458	$10.00	
1982S	Same, Proof	4,894,044		$9.00

LOS ANGELES XXIII OLYMPIAD

Three distinctive coins were issued to commemorate the 1984 Los Angeles Summer Olympic Games. The silver dollar dated 1983 was designed by Elizabeth Jones, Chief Engraver of the Mint. On the obverse is a representation of the traditional Greek discus thrower inspired by the ancient work of the sculptor Myron. The reverse depicts the head and upper body of an American eagle.

	Quan. Issued	MS-65	Proof-65
1983P Discus Thrower Silver Dollar	294,543	$20.00	
1983D Same type D mint	174,014	30.00	
1983S Same type S mint (1,577,025)	174,014	22.00	$22.00

The 1984 Olympic silver dollar was designed by Robert Graham, an American sculptor who created the sculpture placed at the entrance to the Los Angeles Memorial Coliseum. The obverse depicts Graham's sculpture with the Coliseum in the background. The reverse features an American eagle.

MODERN COMMEMORATIVES — Los Angeles, Statue of Liberty

	Quan. Issued	MS-65	Proof-65
1984P Olympic Coliseum Silver Dollar	217,954	$20.00	
1984D Same type D mint	116,675	60.00	
1984S Same type S mint	(1,801,210) 116,675	50.00	$22.00

Mintage of a commemorative gold coin for the 1984 Olympics was the first U.S. gold piece issued in over 50 years. The weight, size and fineness are the same as the last ten dollar coin issued in 1933. It is the first coin ever to bear the W mint mark for West Point.

The obverse depicts two runners bearing the Olympic torch aloft, and was designed by John Mercanti from a concept by James Peed, an artist at the Mint. The eagle on the reverse is modeled after the Great Seal.

		MS-65	Proof-65
1984P Olympic Gold Eagle	(33,309)		425.00
1984D Olympic Gold Eagle	(34,533)		300.00
1984S Olympic Gold Eagle	(48,551)		275.00
1984W Olympic Gold Eagle	(381,085)	75,886 205.00	205.00

STATUE OF LIBERTY

[243]

MODERN COMMEMORATIVES — Statue of Liberty

The first clad half dollar commemorative depicts this country's heritage as a nation of immigrants. The obverse, designed by Edgar Steever, pictures a ship of immigrants steaming into New York harbor, with the Statue of Liberty greeting them in the foreground and the New York skyline in the distance. The reverse, designed by Sherl Joseph Winter, has a scene of an immigrant family with their belongings on the threshold of America.

	Quan. Issued	MS-65	Proof-65
1986D Statue of Liberty	928,008	$7.00	
1986S Same type S mint	(6,925,627)		$8.50

Designed by Mint artist John Mercanti, this .900 fine silver dollar commemorates Ellis Island as the "Gateway to America." The obverse features a classic pose of Liberty in the foreground, with the Ellis Island Immigration Center standing behind her. On the reverse is a silhouette of Liberty's torch, along with the words "Give me your tired, your poor, your huddled masses yearning to breathe free." Matthew Peloso assisted in the model work on the reverse.

1986P Statue of Liberty Silver Dollar	723,635	19.00	
1986S Same type S mint	(6,414,638)		18.00

The commemorative half eagle is also the first of this denomination to be minted in over fifty years. Standards for weight and size are the same as previous gold coins. The design is the creation of the Mint's chief engraver, Elizabeth Jones. The obverse features an unusual close-up view of Liberty's face in sharp relief with the inscription 1986 LIBERTY. An eagle in flight adorns the reverse. All were minted at West Point and bear the W mint mark.

1986W Statue of Liberty $5	(404,013)	95,248	175.00	175.00

MODERN COMMEMORATIVES — Constitution, Olympiad 1988

CONSTITUTION BICENTENNIAL

The silver dollar commemorating the 200th anniversary of the United States Constitution was designed by Patricia Lewis Verani using standard weight, size and fineness. A quill pen, a sheaf of parchment and the words WE THE PEOPLE are depicted on the obverse. The reverse portrays a cross section of Americans from various periods representing contrasting lifestyles.

	Quan. Issued	MS-65	Proof-65
1987P U.S. Constitution Silver Dollar	451,629	$15.00	
1987S Same type S mint	(2,747,116)		$15.00

A modernistic design by Marcel Jovine was selected for the $5 gold coin of standard weight, size and purity commemorating the bicentennial of the United States Consitution. The obverse portrays a stylized eagle holding a massive quill pen. Another large quill pen is featured on the reverse. To the left are nine stars signifying the first colonies that ratified the Constitution. Four stars to the right represent the remaining original states. Both uncirculated and proof versions were minted at West Point.

1987W U.S. Constitution $5.........	(651,659)......... 214,225	130.00	140.00

OLYMPIAD 1988

The 1988 Olympic silver dollar commemorates the U.S. participation in the Seoul Olympiad. Its size and weight are identical to other silver dollars. Design of the obverse is by Patricia Lewis Varani. The reverse is by Mint Sculptor Engraver Sherl J. Winter.

	Quan. Issued	MS-65	Proof-65
1988D Olympic Silver Dollar	191,368	$27.50	
1988S Olympic Silver Dollar	1,354,366		$30.00

The 1988 $5 gold Olympic coin was designed by Elizabeth Jones, Chief Sculptor and Engraver of the U.S. Mint. The obverse features Nike, goddess of Victory, in a crown of olive leaves. The reverse features Marcel Jovine's stylized Olympic flame, evoking the spectacle of the Games and the renewal of the Olympic spirit every four years.

		MS-65	Proof-65
1988W Olympic $5	(281,465) 62,913	225.00	235.00

CONGRESS BICENTENNIAL

The obverse is designed by sculptor Patricia I. Verani and features a detailed bust of the Statue of Freedom. The reverse, designed by William Woodward offers a full view of the Capitol Building accented by a wreath of stars. The composition is 92% copper, 8% nickel.

	MS-65	Proof-65
1989D Congress Bicentennial Half Dollar	$7.00	
1989S Congress Bicentennial Half Dollar		$9.00

MODERN COMMEMORATIVES — Congress, Eisenhower

Designed by muralist William Woodward, the obverse features the Statue of Freedom which towers atop the Capitol dome. The reverse shows the Mace of the House of Representatives which resides in the House Chamber whenever the House is in session. The Mace's staff is topped by an eagle astride a world globe.

	MS-65	Proof-65
1989D Congress Silver Dollar	$30.00	
1989S Congress Silver Dollar		$35.00

The Capitol Dome is depicted on the obverse of this coin and is the work of Mint Engraver John Mercanti. The reverse features a majestic eagle atop the canopy overlooking the Old Senate Chamber.

	MS-65	Proof-65
1989W Congress Bicentennial Gold $5.00	$215.00	$225.00

EISENHOWER CENTENNIAL

The unusual design on this coin features the profile of President Eisenhower facing right, which is superimposed over his own left-facing profile as a five-star general. It is the creation of Mint Engraver John Mercanti. The reverse shows the Eisenhower home at Gettysburg, a National Historic Site, and was designed by Marcel Jovine. The coins was issued to celebrate the 100th anniversary of the birth of the 34th president.

	MS-65	Proof-65
1990W Eisenhower Silver Dollar	$26.00	
1990P Eisenhower Silver Dollar		$30.00

BIBLIOGRAPHY

Bullowa, David M. *The Commemorative Coinage of the United States 1892-1938.* New York, 1938.
Mosher, Stuart. *The Commemorative Coinage of the United States 1892-1938.* New York, 1940.
Slabaugh, Arlie. *United States Commemorative Coinage.* Racine, 1975.
Swiatek, Anthony and Breen, Walter. *The Encyclopedia of United States Silver and Gold Commemorative Coins 1892-1954.* New York, 1981.
Taxay, Don. *An Illustrated History of U.S. Commemorative Coinage.* New York, 1967.

PRIVATE OR TERRITORIAL GOLD COINS

The words "Private Gold," used with reference to coins struck outside of the United States Mint, are a general term. In the sense that no state or territory had authority to coin money, private gold simply refers to those interesting necessity pieces of various shapes, denominations and degrees of intrinsic worth which were circulated in isolated areas of our country by individuals, assayers, bankers, etc. Some will use the words "Territorial" and "State" to cover certain issues because they were coined and circulated in a territory or state. While the state of California properly sanctioned the ingots stamped by F. D. Kohler as state assayer, in no instance were any of the gold pieces struck by authority of any of the territorial governments.

The stamped ingots put out by Augustus Humbert, the United States assayer of gold, were not recognized at the United States Mint as an official issue of coins, but simply as ingots, though Humbert placed the value and fineness on the pieces as an official agent of the federal government.

Private coins were circulated in most instances because of a shortage of regular coinage. In the western states particularly, money became so scarce that the very commodity which the pioneers had come so far to acquire was converted into a local medium of exchange.

Ephraim Brasher's New York doubloon of 1787 described on page 40 also falls into this class.

BIBLIOGRAPHY

Adams, Edgar H. *Private Gold Coinage of California 1849-1855.* Brooklyn, N.Y., 1913.
Adams, Edgar H. *Official Premium Lists of Private and Territorial Gold Coins.* Brooklyn, N.Y., 1909.
Bowers, Q. David. *The History of United States Coinage as Illustrated by the Garrett Collection.* Los Angeles, Cal., 1979.
Breen, Walter. *California Pioneer Fractional Gold.* Santa Barbara, Cal., 1983.
Clifford, Henry H. *Pioneer Gold Coinage in the West- 1848-1861.* Reprint from "The Westerners Brand Book- Book Nine." Los Angeles Corral, 1961.
Doering, David. *California Fractional Gold.* Seal Beach, Cal., 1982.
Griffin, Clarence. *The Bechtlers and Bechtler Coinage and Gold Mining in North Carolina 1814-1830.* Spindale, N.C., 1929.
Kagin Donald H. *Private Gold Coins and Patterns of the United States,* New York, 1981.
Lee, Kenneth W. *California Gold — Dollars, Half Dollars, Quarter Dollars.* Santa Ana, Cal., 1979.
Seymour, Dexter C. *The 1830 Coinage of Templeton Reid.* American Numismatic Society Museum Notes No. 22. New York, 1977.

TEMPLETON REID
Georgia 1830

The first private gold coinage under the Constitution was struck by Templeton Reid, a jeweler and gunsmith, in Milledgeville, Georgia in July, 1830. To be closer to the mines, he moved to Gainesville where most of his coins were made. Although weights were accurate, Reid's assays were not and his coins were slightly short of claimed value. Accordingly, he was severely attacked in the newspapers and soon lost the public's confidence. He closed his mint before the end of October, 1830 and his output amounted only to about 1,600 coins. Denominations struck were $2.50, $5.00 and $10.00.

1830 $2.50	V.F.	$20,000
1830 $5.00	V.F.	75,000

TEMPLETON REID — GEORGIA

1830 TEN DOLLARS	V.G.	$60,000
(No date) TEN DOLLARS	V.G.	40,000

TEMPLETON REID
"California Gold 1849"

The enigmatic later issues of Templeton Reid were probably made from California gold. Reid, who never went to California, was then a cotton gin maker in Columbus, Georgia, where he died in 1851. The coins were in denominations of ten and twenty-five dollars. Struck copies of both exist in various metals.

The only specimen known of the $25 piece was stolen from the Cabinet of the U.S. Mint on August 16, 1858. It was never recovered.

1849 TEN DOLLAR CALIFORNIA GOLD (Smithsonian Collection)	*Unique*
1849 TWENTY-FIVE DOLLARS CALIFORNIA GOLD	*Unknown*

THE BECHTLERS
Rutherford County, N. C. 1830-1852

Two skilled German metallurgists, Christopher Bechtler and his son August, and later Christopher Bechtler, Junior, a nephew of Christopher the elder, operated a "private" mint at Rutherfordton, North Carolina. Rutherford county in which Rutherfordton is located was the principal source of the nation's gold supply from 1790 to 1840.

The coins minted by the Bechtlers were of only three denominations, but they cover a wide variety of weights and sizes.

THE BECHTLERS

The Bechtlers have the distinction of producing the first gold dollar in the United States. The government mint did not release the first regular series until 1849.

The inscription "Aug. 1, 1834" on one variety of the five-dollar piece has a special significance. The Secretary of the Treasury recommended to the Director of the Mint that the gold coins of the reduced weight bear the date "Aug. 1, 1834." Instead of this, however, a new U.S. gold design was used (the motto was omitted). Christopher Bechtler evidently acted on the official recommendation to avoid any difficulty with Treasury authorities.

CHRISTOPHER BECHTLER

	V. Fine	E. Fine	Unc.
ONE DOLLAR CAROLINA, 28 gr. N reversed	$800.00	$1,250	$3,500
ONE DOLLAR N. CAROLINA, 28 gr. centered, no star ...	1,600	2,750	7,000
ONE DOLLAR N. CAROLINA, 28 gr. high, no star.......	4,500	6,000	9,500

| ONE DOLLAR N. CAROLINA, 30 gr..................... | 1,000 | 2,000 | 4,500 |
| $2.50 CAROLINA, 67 gr. 21 carats .... | 1,600 | 3,200 | 6,200 |

$2.50 CAROLINA, 70 gr. 20 carats	2,000	3,200	6,500
$2.50 GEORGIA, 64 gr. 22 carats	2,200	3,750	7,000
$2.50 GEORGIA, 64 gr. 22 carats — even 22..........	2,500	4,000	8,000

$2.50 NORTH CAROLINA, 75 gr. 20 carats.			
RUTHERFORD in a circle. Border of lg. beads	4,500	6,500	10,000
$2.50 NORTH CAROLINA, without 75 G..............	4,500	6,250	9,500

THE BECHTLERS

	V. Fine	E. Fine	Unc.
$2.50 NORTH CAROLINA, without 75 G, CAROLINA above 250 instead of GOLD			(Unique)
$2.50 NORTH CAROLINA, 20 carats on obv. 75 gr. on rev. Border finely serrated	$5,000	$8,000	——

5 DOLLARS CAROLINA, RUTHERFORD, 140 gr. 20 carats. Date August 1, 1834.			
Plain edge	3,000	4,500	$8,500
Reeded edge	3,500	5,500	9,000
BECHTLER without star and C.	——		
5 DOLLARS CAROLINA, 134 gr. 21 carats, with star	3,000	4,500	8,500
5 DOLLARS CAROLINA, 134 gr. 21 carats, no star,......	——	——	
(Reverse of A. Bechtler shown on page 253)			

5 DOLLARS GEORGIA, RUTHERFORD, 128 gr. 22 carats	3,700	5,500	8,500
Similar. Colon before 22 and after 128 G...........	——	——	
5 DOLLARS GEORGIA, RUTHERF. 128 gr. 22 carats......	3,200	4,500	8,500
5 DOLLARS CAROLINA, RUTHERF. 140 gr. 20 carats. Date August 1, 1834	3,000	4,000	7,500
Similar. 20 distant from carats...................	5,500	9,500	——

Without 150 G

5 DOLLARS NORTH CAROLINA, 150 gr. 20 carats	3,250	6,000	15,000
5 DOLLARS. Same as last variety without 150 G	4,000	7,000	15,500

THE BECHTLERS
AUGUST BECHTLER
1842-1852

	V. Fine	E. Fine	Unc.
1 DOLLAR CAROLINA, 27 gr. 21 carats...............	$700.00	$1,000	$2,800
5 DOLLARS CAROLINA, 134 gr. 21 carats..............	2,400	3,500	7,500

| 5 DOLLARS CAROLINA, 128 gr. 22 carats.............. | 4,000 | 5,500 | 11,000 |
| 5 DOLLARS CAROLINA, 141 gr. 20 carats.............. | 4,000 | 5,500 | 11,000 |

(Restrikes in "proof" exist from original dies.)

NORRIS, GREGG & NORRIS
San Francisco 1849

Edgar H. Adams considered this piece the first of the California private gold coins. A newspaper account dated May 31, 1849, described a five-dollar gold coin, struck at Benicia City, though with the imprint San Francisco. It mentioned the private stamp of Norris, Gregg and Norris. The initials N. G. and N. were not identified until 1902 when the coins of Augustus Humbert were sold.

	Fine	V. Fine	E. Fine	Unc.
1849 HALF EAGLE — Plain edge	$2,500	$3,250	$6,000	$16,000
1849 HALF EAGLE — Reeded edge	2,500	3,400	6,500	17,000
1850 HALF EAGLE with STOCKTON beneath date				(Unique)

MOFFAT & CO.
San Francisco 1849-1853

The firm of Moffat and Company was perhaps the most important of the California private coiners. The assay office they conducted was semi-official in character. The successors to this firm, Curtis, Perry and Ward, later established the United States Branch mint of San Francisco.

In June or July, 1849, Moffat & Co. began to issue small rectangular pieces of gold owing to lack of coin in the locality, in values from $9.43 to $264. The $9.43, $14.25 and $16.00 varieties are the only types known today.

The unique specimens of the $9.43 and $14.25 ingots are in the National Coin Collection in the Smithsonian.

$9.43 Ingot (*Unique*)	—
$14.25 Ingot (*Unique*)	—
$16.00 Ingot	$21,000

The dies for the $10 piece were cut by a Bavarian, Albert Kuner. The words MOFFAT & CO. appear on the coronet of Liberty instead of the word LIBERTY as in regular United States issues.

	Fine	V. Fine	E. Fine	Unc.
1849 FIVE DOL. (All varieties)	$700.00	$1,000	$2,750	$9,000
1850 FIVE DOL. (All varieties)	700.00	1,000	2,750	9,000
1849 TEN DOL.	1,500	2,200	5,000	13,000
1849 TEN D.	1,500	2,200	5,000	13,000

United States Assay Office
AUGUSTUS HUMBERT
U. S. Assayer 1851

Augustus Humbert, a New York watchcase maker, was appointed United States Assayer, and he placed his name and the government stamp on the ingots of gold issued by Moffat & Co. The assay office, a Provisional Government Mint, was a temporary expedient to accommodate the Californians until the establishment of a permanent branch mint.

The fifty-dollar gold piece was accepted as legal tender on a par with standard U.S. gold coins and was known variously as a slug, quintuple eagle or five-eagle piece. It was officially termed an ingot.

LETTERED EDGE VARIETIES

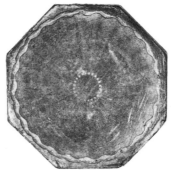

	Fine	V. Fine	E. Fine	A. Unc.
1851 50 D C 880 THOUS., no 50 on Reverse. Sunk in edge: AUGUSTUS HUMBERT UNITED STATES ASSAYER OF GOLD CALIFORNIA 1851..................	$7,000	$10,000	$15,000	$24,000

Reverse, Rays from Central Star

	Fine	V. Fine	E. Fine	A. Unc.
1851 50 D C Similar to last variety, but 50 on Reverse	8,000	12,000	——	——
1851 Similar to last variety, but 887 THOUS......................	8,000	11,000	——	——
1851 50 D C 887 THOUS., no 50 on Reverse.........................	——	——	——	
1851 50 D C 880 THOUS. Rev. Rays from central star (Unique)				——

REEDED EDGE VARIETIES

 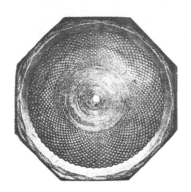

	Fine	V. Fine	E. Fine	A. Unc	Unc.
1851 FIFTY DOLLS 880 THOUS. "Target" Reverse	$5,250	$7,000	$12,000	$18,000	$30,000
1851 FIFTY DOLLS 887 THOUS. "Target" Reverse	5,500	7,500	13,000	18,000	30,000
1852 FIFTY DOLLS. 887 THOUS.	5,500	7,500	13,000	18,000	30,000

A unique proof specimen of the 1851 with 887 THOUS. was sold at the Garrett II auction in 1980 for $500,000.

The withdrawal of the discredited private coins of $5, $10 and $20 denominations as a result of the new U.S. Assay operations caused a new turn of affairs for Californians.

The fractional currency coins of almost every nation were pressed into service by the Californians, but the supply was too small to help to any extent. Moffat & Co. proceeded in January, 1852 to issue a new ten-dollar piece bearing the stamp MOFFAT & CO.

1852 TEN D. MOFFAT & CO. (Close date)	2,000	3,000	5,000	9,000	——
1852 TEN D. MOFFAT & CO. (Wide date)	2,000	3,000	5,000	9,000	——

MOFFAT — HUMBERT

	Fine	V. Fine	E. Fine	A. Unc	Unc.
1852 TWENTY DOLS. 1852, 2 over 1.	$2,750	$4,000	$6,500	$9,000	——

1852 TEN DOLS. 1852, 2 over 1.....	1,200	2,000	3,250	6,500	——
1852 TEN DOLS.	900.00	1,700	2,500	5,000	$9,000

UNITED STATES ASSAY OFFICE OF GOLD

1852

The firm of Moffat & Co. dissolved and a new reorganized company known as the United States Assay Office of Gold, composed of Curtis, Perry and Ward took over the contract.

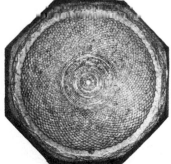

1852 FIFTY DOLLS. 887 THOUS.	5,000	7,000	11,000	18,000	28,000
1852 FIFTY DOLLS. 900 THOUS.	5,000	8,000	12,500	20,000	30,000

UNITED STATES ASSAY OFFICE

	Fine	V. Fine	E. Fine	A. Unc	Unc.
1852 TEN DOLS 884 THOUS.	$750.00	$1,300	$2,250	$4,000	$8,500

	Fine	V. Fine	E. Fine	A. Unc	Unc.
1853 TEN D. 884 THOUS.	3,000	6,000	10,000	13,000	——
1853 TEN D. 900 THOUS.	1,800	3,000	5,000	7,000	——

	Fine	V. Fine	E. Fine	A. Unc	Unc.
1853 TWENTY D. 884 THOUS.	5,000	8,000	11,000	17,000	22,000

	Fine	V. Fine	E. Fine	A. Unc	Unc.
1853 TWENTY D. 900 THOUS.	1,200	2,000	3,500	6,000	10,000

U. S. ASSAY — MOFFAT

The last Moffat issue was the 1853 twenty dollar piece which is very similar to the U.S. double eagle of that period. It was struck after the retirement of Mr. Moffat from the Assay Office.

	Fine	V. Fine	E. Fine	Unc.
1853 TWENTY D.	$1,750	$3,250	$4,500	$9,000

J. H. BOWIE

Joseph H. Bowie joined his cousins in San Francisco in 1849 and produced a limited coinage of $5.00 gold pieces. A trial piece of the dollar denomination is known in copper, but may never have reached the coinage stage. Little is known about the company or reason for issuing these coins which were all valued above face and quickly melted for their gold content.

1849 5 DOLLARS. (2 known) ....

CINCINNATI MINING & TRADING CO.

The origin and location of this company are unknown.

	E. Fine	Unc.
1849 FIVE DOLLARS	Unique	
1849 TEN DOLLARS — Garrett Sale, 1980	$270,000	——

(Beware of spurious specimens cast in base metal with word TRACING in place of TRADING.)

MASSACHUSETTS AND CALIFORNIA COMPANY
San Francisco 1849

This company was believed to have been organized in Northampton, Mass. in May 1849.

	Fine	Unc.
1849 FIVE D.	$35,000	$100,000

MINERS' BANK
San Francisco 1849

The institution of Wright & Co., exchange brokers located in Portsmouth Square, San Francisco, was known as the Miners' Bank.

A ten dollar piece was issued in the autumn of 1849, but the coins were not readily accepted because they were worth less than face value. The firm dissolved January 14, 1850. Unlike most issues, the gold in these coins was alloyed with copper.

	V. Fine	E. Fine	Unc.
(1849) TEN. D.	$7,500	$12,000	$35,000

(Specimen sold in Garrett sale, 1980 — MS-65, $135,000)

J. S. ORMSBY
Sacramento 1849

The initials J. S. O. which appear on certain issues of California privately coined gold pieces represent the firm of J. S. Ormsby & Co. They struck both five and ten dollar denominations, all undated.

	V. Fine
(1849) 5 DOLLS. Plain edge (Unique)	$150,000
(1849) 5 DOLLS. Reeded edge (Unique)	150,000
(1849) 10 DOLLS. — Garrett Sale, 1980	100,000

PACIFIC COMPANY
San Francisco 1849

The origin of the Pacific Co. is very uncertain. All data regarding the firm is based on conjecture.

Edgar H. Adams wrote that he believed that the coins bearing the stamp of the Pacific Company were produced by the coining firm of Broderick and Kohler. The coins were probably handstruck, with the aid of a sledgehammer.

1849 5 DOLLARS
   Coles Sale, 1983
   Ex. Fine................ $57,500

1849 10 DOLLARS
   A. Unc.......... $132,000

F. D. KOHLER
California State Assayer 1850

The State Assay Office was authorized April 12, 1850. Governor Burnett appointed F. D. Kohler that year who thereupon sold his assaying business to Baldwin & Co. He served at both San Francisco and Sacramento Offices. The State Assay Offices were discontinued at the time the U. S. Assay Office was established Feb. 1, 1851.

Ingots issued ranged from $36.55 to $150. An Ex. F. specimen sold in the Garrett Sale, 1980 for $200,000.

$36.55 Sacramento ....　——
$47.71 Sacramento ....　——
$37.31 San Francisco ....　——
$40.07 San Francisco ....　——
Note: $40.07 stolen from the Mint Cabinet in 1858 and was never recovered.
$41.68 San Francisco ....　——
$45.34 San Francisco ....　——
$50.00 San Francisco Ex.F $200,000
$54.09 San Francisco ....　——

DUBOSQ & COMPANY
San Francisco 1850

Theodore Dubosq, a Philadelphia jeweler, took melting and coining machinery to San Francisco in 1849.

	V. Fine
1850 FIVE D.	$30,000
1850 TEN D.	35,000

BALDWIN & COMPANY
San Francisco 1850

George C. Baldwin and Thomas S. Holman were in the jewelry business in San Francisco and were known as Baldwin & Co. They were the successors to F. D. Kohler & Co., taking over their machinery and other equipment in May, 1850.

	Fine	V. Fine	E. Fine	Unc.
1850 FIVE DOL.	$3,000	$5,000	$8,000	$17,000
1850 TEN DOLLARS — Horseman type.	12,000	24,000	40,000	——

1851 TEN D.	5,000	8,000	16,000	——

The Baldwin & Co. $20 piece was the first of that denomination issued in California.

BALDWIN & COMPANY

Baldwin coins were believed to have contained about twenty-thousandths copper alloy.

	E. Fine	Unc.
1851 TWENTY D...	$65,000	——

Beware of spurious specimens cast in base metal.

SHULTZ & COMPANY
San Francisco 1851

The firm located in back of Baldwin's establishment operated a brass foundry beginning in 1851. Judge G. W. Shultz and William T. Garratt were partners in the enterprise.

	Fine	V. Fine	A. Unc
1851 FIVE D	$12,000	$25,000	$40,000

DUNBAR & COMPANY
San Francisco 1851

Edward E. Dunbar operated the California Bank in San Francisco. Mr. Dunbar later returned to New York and organized the famous Continental Bank Note Co.

	E. Fine
1851 FIVE D..	$55,000

WASS, MOLITOR & COMPANY
San Francisco 1852-1855

The gold smelting and assaying plant of Wass, Molitor & Co. was operated by two Hungarian patriots, Count S. C. Wass and A. P. Molitor. They maintained an excellent laboratory and complete apparatus for analysis and coinage of gold.

The company struck five, ten, twenty and fifty dollar coins. In 1852 they produced a ten dollar piece similar in design to the five dollar denomination. The difference is in the reverse legend which reads: s.m.v. (Standard Mint Value) CALIFORNIA GOLD TEN D.

No pieces were coined in 1853 or 1854, but they brought out the twenty dollar and fifty dollar pieces in 1855. A considerable number of the fifty dollar coins were made. There was a ten dollar piece issued in 1855 also, with the Liberty head and small close date.

Large Head, Pointed Bust

	Fine	V. Fine	E. Fine	Unc.
1852 FIVE DOLLARS. Small head with rounded bust	$2,000	$3,500	$6,500	$16,000
1852 FIVE DOLLARS. Large head with pointed bust	2,200	3,750	6,500	16,000

Large Head　　　　　　　　　　　　**Small Head**

Small Date

1852 TEN D. Large head	1,500	3,000	4,500	——
1852 TEN D. Small head	3,000	4,500	8,000	——
1852 TEN D. Small close date.............		(Ex. Rare)		
1855 TEN D..............................	6,500	12,000	16,500	——

WASS, MOLITOR & COMPANY

Large Head   **Small Head**

	Fine	V.Fine	E. Fine	Unc.
1855 TWENTY DOL. Large head		——	$40,000	——
1855 TWENTY DOL. Small head	$6,000	$11,000	15,000	——

1855 50 DOLLARS	11,000	15,000	24,000	120,000

KELLOGG & COMPANY
San Francisco 1854-1855

John G. Kellogg came to San Francisco October 12, 1849, from Auburn, New York. At first he was employed by Moffat and Company, and remained with that organization when control passed to Curtis, Perry and Ward. When the United States Assay Office was discontinued December 14, 1853, Mr. Kellogg became associated with G. F. Richter, who had been an assayer in the government assay office. These two set up business as Kellogg & Richter December 19, 1853.

When the U. S. Assay Office ceased operations a period ensued during which no private firm was striking gold. The new San Francisco branch mint did not produce coins for some months after Curtis & Perry took the contract for the government. The lack of coin was again keenly felt by businessmen who petitioned Kellogg & Richter to "supply the vacuum" by issuing private coin.

Their plea was soon answered, for on February 9, 1854, Kellogg & Co. placed their first twenty-dollar piece in circulation.

	Fine	*V. Fine*	*E. Fine*	*Unc.*
1854 TWENTY D.	$1,500	$2,000	$3,500	$8,000

The 1855 twenty-dollar piece is similar to that dated 1854. The letters on the reverse side are larger and the arrows longer on one 1854 variety. There are several die varieties of both issues.

1855 TWENTY D.	1,400	2,000	3,500	11,000

The firm dissolved late in 1854 and reorganized as Kellogg & Humbert. The latter partner was Augustus Humbert, for some time identified as U.S. Assayer.

Regardless of the fact that the branch mint was then producing coins, Kellogg & Humbert issued coins in 1855 in a quantity greater than before.

	Proof
1855 FIFTY DOLLS. — Carter Sale 1984	$154,000

OREGON EXCHANGE COMPANY
Oregon City, 1849
THE BEAVER COINS OF OREGON

Upon the discovery of gold in California there was a great exodus of settlers who joined in the hunt for the precious metal. Soon returning gold seekers offered their gold dust, which became the accepted medium of exchange. As in other western areas of that time the uncertain qualities of the gold and weighing devices tended to irk the tradespeople and petitions were made to the legislature for a standard gold coin issue.

On February 16, 1849, the legislature passed an act providing for a mint and specified five- and ten-dollar gold coins without alloy. Oregon City, the largest city in the territory with a population of about 1000, was designated as the location for the mint. At the time this act was passed Oregon had been brought into the United States as a territory by act of Congress. When the new governor arrived March second, he declared the coinage act unconstitutional.

The public-spirited people, however, continued to work for a convenient medium of exchange and soon took matters into their own hands by starting a private mint. Eight men of affairs whose names were Kilborne, Magruder, Taylor, Abernethy, Willson, Rector, Campbell and Smith set up the Oregon Exchange Company.

The coins struck were of virgin gold as specified in the original act. Ten-dollar dies were made later, and were of finer design and workmanship.

	Fine	V. Fine	E. Fine	Unc.
1849 5 d .... (6,000 minted)	$6,000	$12,000	$16,000	——

1849 TEN d .... (2,850 minted)	17,500	25,000	40,000	——

MORMON GOLD PIECES
Salt Lake City, Utah 1849-1860

The first name given to the organized Mormon Territory was the "State of Deseret," the last word meaning "honey bee." The beehive, which is shown on the reverse of the five-dollar 1860 piece, was a favorite device of the followers of Joseph Smith and Brigham Young. The clasped hands appear on most Mormon coins and exemplify strength in unity. "Holiness to the Lord" was an inscription frequently used.

MORMON GOLD PIECES

Brigham Young was the instigator of the coinage system and personally supervised the mint which was housed in a little adobe building in Salt Lake City.

The mint was inaugurated late in 1849 as a public convenience.

	Fine	V. Fine	E. Fine	Unc.
1849 TWO AND HALF DO.................	$2,750	$5,000	$7,000	$20,000
1849 FIVE DOLLARS	2,500	3,750	5,000	12,000

	Fine
1849 TEN DOLLARS..	$80,000

	Fine	V. Fine
1849 TWENTY DOLLARS..	$22,000	$50,000

The Mormon twenty-dollar piece was the first of that denomination to be coined in this country.

1850 FIVE DOLLARS	
Fine	$2,500
V. Fine...................	4,250
Ex. Fine.................	6,000
Unc.	—

MORMON GOLD PIECES

1860 5D
Fine	$4,500
V. Fine	7,200
Ex. Fine	14,000
Unc.	25,000

COLORADO GOLD PIECES
Clark, Gruber & Co. — Denver 1860-1861

Clark, Gruber and Co. was a well-known private minting firm in Denver, Colo. in the early sixties.

	Fine	V. Fine	E. Fine	Unc.
1860 2½ D	$750.00	$1,250	$1,800	$8,000
1860 5D	1,000	1,600	3,000	10,000

1860 TEN D	3,000	4,500	7,500	16,000
1860 TWENTY D	18,000	30,000	50,000	——

The $2.50 and five-dollar pieces of 1861 follow closely the designs of the 1860 issues. The main difference is found in the legends. The reverse side now has CLARK GRUBER & CO. DENVER. PIKES PEAK is on the coronet of Liberty.

1861 2½ D	750.00	1,250	2,400	8,000
1861 FIVE D	1,000	1,750	3,000	10,000
1861 TEN D	1,500	2,000	3,500	10,000

COLORADO GOLD PIECES

	Fine	V. Fine	E. Fine	Unc.
1861 TWENTY D	$4,500	$8,000	$16,000	——

JOHN PARSONS & COMPANY
Tarryall Mines — Colorado 1861

Very little is known regarding the mint of John Parsons and Co., although it is reasonably certain that it operated in the South Park of Colorado, near the original town of Tarryall, in the summer of 1861.

PIKES PEAK GOLD

		V. Fine
(1861)	Undated 2½ D...	$37,500
(1861)	Undated FIVE D...	50,000

J. J. CONWAY & COMPANY
Georgia Gulch, Colorado, 1861

Records show that the Conway Mint operated for a short while in 1861. As in all gold mining areas the value of gold dust caused disagreement among the merchants and the miners. The firm of J. J. Conway & Co. solved this difficulty by bringing out its gold pieces in August, 1861.

(1861)	Undated 2½ DOLL'S.......................................	40,000
(1861)	Undated FIVE DOLLARS	60,000
(1861)	Undated FIVE DOLLARS, Similar.	
	Variety without numeral 5 on reverse	40,000

J.J. CONWAY & COMPANY

(1861) Undated
    TEN DOLLARS....   ——

CALIFORNIA SMALL DENOMINATION GOLD

There was a scarcity of small coins during the California gold rush and starting in 1852, quarter, half and dollar pieces were privately minted from native gold to alleviate the shortage. The need and acceptability of these pieces declined after 1856 and they then became popular as souvenirs. Private coinage became illegal with passage of the Act of 1864, but production continued until 1882 before the law was enforced.

The designs of the early issues were similar to those of the larger territorials. Later issues showed greater variety, had lower intrinsic value, and were often struck from highly polished dies giving prooflike surfaces. In contrast to the tokens which lack the denomination and were often back dated, California small denomination gold was mostly made in the year indicated. Authentic pieces all have CENTS, DOLLAR, or an abbreviation thereof on the reverse.

A total of about 10,000 pieces still exist; of these nearly 500 different varieties have been identified, many of them very rare. Although some of the early pieces are machine made with reeded edges, most are hand struck and have crude designs and incomplete features. Many bear the maker's initials: D, DN, N, NR, L, H, G, GG, FD, or DERI. Major types are listed below; values are for the commonest varieties of each type. The tokens are much less valuable. Modern restrikes and replicas have no numismatic value.

Values are only for genuine coins with the denomination on the reverse expressed as: CENTS, DOL., DOLL., *or* DOLLAR.

	EF-40	AU-50	MS-60
25c Octagonal: Large Liberty head/Wreath..........	$70.00	$110.00	$200.00
Small Liberty head/Wreath..........	70.00	110.00	200.00
Liberty head/Beaded circle	100.00	175.00	250.00
Small Liberty head/Shield and wreath	110.00	185.00	275.00
Large Indian head/Wreath	100.00	175.00	250.00
Small Indian head/Wreath..........	150.00	225.00	325.00
Washington head/Wreath............	300.00	500.00	800.00
25c Round: Large Liberty head/Wreath..............	80.00	125.00	225.00
Small Liberty head/Wreath	80.00	125.00	225.00
Small Liberty head/Shield and wreath...	150.00	250.00	350.00
Large Indian head/Wreath..............	110.00	185.00	275.00
Small Indian head/Wreath..............	125.00	200.00	325.00
Washington head/Wreath...............	400.00	700.00	900.00

CALIFORNIA SMALL DENOMINATION GOLD

	EF-40	AU-50	MS-60
50c Octagonal: Liberty head/Wreath	$100.00	$150.00	$250.00
Liberty head/Legend and wreath	125.00	200.00	325.00
Liberty head/Beaded circle	110.00	175.00	250.00
Liberty head/Eagle	750.00	950.00	1,800
Large Indian head/Wreath	225.00	325.00	500.00
Small Indian head/Wreath	250.00	350.00	500.00
50c Round: Liberty head/Wreath	115.00	150.00	250.00
Liberty head/Legend and wreath	125.00	175.00	275.00
Large Indian head/Wreath	150.00	200.00	375.00
Small Indian head/Wreath	175.00	250.00	450.00
$1.00 Octagonal: Liberty head/Legend and wreath	225.00	350.00	550.00
Liberty head/Eagle	1,250	2,000	3,000
Liberty head/Beaded circle	225.00	350.00	550.00
Indian head/Legend and wreath	400.00	500.00	800.00
Small Indian head/Wreath	450.00	550.00	900.00
$1.00 Round: Liberty head/Legend and wreath	1,000	1,500	2,200
Indian head/Legend and wreath	1,200	1,700	2,500

See bibliography on page 249.

CIVIL WAR TOKENS — 1861-1864

Civil War Tokens are generally divided into two groups: tradesmen's tokens, and anonymously issued pieces with political or patriotic themes. They came into existence only because of the scarcity of government coins and disappeared as soon as the bronze coins of 1864 met the public demand for small copper change.

From the outset of the Civil War, government cents were insufficient in number, widely hoarded and worth a premium over all other currencies. As a result of this scarcity of cent pieces, private copper coins were issued by many individuals. Their wide circulation was made possible by the scarcity of copper-nickel cents and the public dislike of fractional paper money.

The tradesmen's tokens were issued by various firms to provide change and advertise the dealers' wares. They usually bore an implied or an explicit promise of redemption in goods or money. The second type was simply unauthorized substitutes for government coins, produced at a profit by private manufacturers and put into general circulation through various agencies.

These tokens are of great variety in composition and design. A number were more or less faithful imitations of the copper-nickel cent. A few of this type have the word "NOT" in very small letters above the words "ONE CENT."

Many pieces, especially of the tradesmen token type, were individual in device and size, representing any caprice of design or slogan that appealed to the maker. Some were political or patriotic in character, carrying the likeness of some military leader such as McClellan or bearing such inscriptions as "Millions for contractors, not one cent for the widows." An estimated 50,000,000 or more of these pieces were issued. Approximately 10,000 different varieties have been recorded.

The legal status of the Civil War Tokens was uncertain. Mint Director Pollock thought they were illegal; however, there was no law prohibiting the issue of tradesmen's tokens or of private coins not in imitation of United States coins. A law was passed April 22, 1864 prohibiting the issue of any one or two-cent coins, tokens, or devices for use as money, and on June 8 another law was passed which abolished private coinage of every kind.

	Fine	V. Fine	E.F.	Unc.
Copper or Brass Tokens	$3.00	$5.00	$8.00	$30.00
Nickel or German Silver Tokens	27.50	45.00	55.00	75.00
White Metal Tokens	27.50	45.00	55.00	75.00
Copper-Nickel Tokens	40.00	70.00	90.00	125.00
Silver Tokens	85.00	140.00	175.00	250.00

CONFEDERATE STATES OF AMERICA
CONFEDERATE 1861 HALF DOLLAR

The half dollar struck by the Confederacy was unknown to collectors until 1879. A specimen of the coin and both dies were found in the possession of Dr. B. F. Taylor of New Orleans. Mr. E. Mason, Jr. of Philadelphia purchased Dr. Taylor's specimen and the reverse die and later sold them to J. W. Scott and Company of New York.

CONFEDERATE STATES OF AMERICA — 1861

Five hundred genuine 1861 half dollars from the New Orleans mint were acquired by J. W. Scott and Company. The reverses were planed off and then restamped with the Confederate die. These are known as restrikes. The restrikes have flattened obverses.

According to records only four originals were struck. These were made on a hand press. Original silver half dollar planchets were used, as well as the original obverse die. One of the coins was given to the Secretary of the Confederacy Memminger who passed it on to President Jefferson Davis for his approval. Another was given to Prof. J. L. Riddell of the University of Louisiana. Dr. E. Ames of New Orleans received a third specimen, the last being kept by Chief Coiner B. F. Taylor, who sold it later as mentioned above.

Lack of bullion prevented the Confederate government from proceeding with any coinage plans that might have been made.

J. W. Scott struck some tokens in white metal using the Confederate reverse die and a special die bearing the inscription:

4 ORIGINALS STRUCK BY ORDER OF C. S. A. IN NEW ORLEANS 1861 ******* REV. SAME AS U.S. (FROM ORIGINAL DIE SCOTT)

Confederate Reverse　　**Scott Obverse**

	Quan. Minted	V. Fine	Unc.
1861 HALF DOL. (Ex. Rare)	4	—	—
1861 HALF DOL. Restrike	500	$950.00	$2,750
1861 Scott Token obverse. Confederate reverse	500	200.00	600.00

THE CONFEDERATE CENT

An order to make cents for the Confederacy was placed with Mr. Robert Lovett Jr., an engraver and die-sinker of Philadelphia, through a jewelry firm of that city. Fearing arrest by the United States government for giving assistance to the enemy, Mr. Lovett decided against delivering the coins to the Confederate government and hid the coins and dies in his cellar.

The original dies were later purchased by Capt. John W. Haseltine who made restrikes from the dies.

1861 Cent Original (copper-nickel)	Unc.	12	$20,000
1861 Cent Restrike (copper)	Proof	55	4,000
1861 Cent Restrike (gold)	Proof	7	18,000
1861 Cent Restrike (silver)	Proof	12	6,000

LESHER REFERENDUM DOLLARS

Coined by Joseph Lesher in 1900 and 1901 at Victor, Colorado. Used in trade to some extent, and stocked by various merchants who redeemed them in goods. Coins were numbered and a blank space left at bottom of 1901 issues, in which were stamped names of businessmen who bought them. All are quite rare, many varieties extremely rare. Composition is .950 fine silver alloyed with copper.

	V.Fine	Unc.
1900 First Type, no business name.....................	$650.00	$1,600
1900 A.B. Bumstead, with or without scrolls............	600.00	1,500
1900 Bank Type (9 known)	—	—
1901 Imprint Type, no name..........................	600.00	1,500
1901 Imprint Type, various names	$600-$3,500	$1,500-$6,000

FEUCHTWANGER CENT 1837

Dr. Lewis Feuchtwanger produced a metal which was really a variety of German silver consisting of nickel, copper and some zinc. He suggested as early as 1837 to Congress that his metal be substituted for copper, and made one-cent and three-cent trial pieces.

One Cent... Fine $40.00 Ex. Fine $175.00
Three-Cent piece.. V. Scarce

**HARD TIMES
TOKENS
1834-1844**

In addition to the coins issued by the United States government, numismatists include in their collections the Hard Times and Civil War tokens which circulated as money during two periods in this country's history when nearly all the minor coin was hoarded.

The Hard Times tokens were issued in the period 1834-1844 and are the size of the large U. S. cent. They were generally struck in copper and are of two general groups: political tokens whose theme centered around President Jackson's fight against the United States Bank, and those issued by merchants (tradesmen's cards). Many different varieties exist. The most common pieces are generally valued $4.00 Good to $50.00 Ex. Fine.

COINS AND TOKENS OF HAWAII

The first official coins of Hawaii were the copper cents of 1847 issued by King Kamehameha III. The five cent piece of 1881 and the eighth dollar piece of 1883 are patterns. In 1883 Kalakaua I issued silver dimes, quarters, halves and dollars bearing his bust and showing the Hawaiian coat of arms on the reverse. By 1937 most of these silver coins had been withdrawn and melted. The plantation tokens listed here were all used as small change on the Islands.

One Cent 1847   Ten Cents 1883

	Quan. Minted	Fine	V. Fine	E. Fine	MS-60	MS-65	Proof
1847 Cent	100,000	$150.00	$225.00	$325.00	$650.00	$2,000	
1881 Five Cents		2,250	3,000	4,000	5,000	7,000	$8,000
1883 Ten Cents	250,000	30.00	45.00	200.00	900.00	3,000	11,000
1883 Eighth Dollar (12½ c)							35,000
1883 Quarter Dollar	500,000	25.00	40.00	85.00	275.00	450.00	11,000
1883 Half Dollar	700,000	60.00	90.00	200.00	1,000	3,000	11,500
1883 Dollar	500,000	185.00	210.00	650.00	4,000	13,000	16,000

HAWAIIAN TOKENS

Thomas Hobron Token 1879   Haiku Plantation 1882

Wailuku Plantation 1880

Wailuku Plantation 1871

	Fine	V. Fine	E. Fine
Waterhouse Token 1862. Bust of Kamehameha IV ..	$350.00	$550.00	$800.00
Wailuku Plantation Token 1871	125.00	200.00	300.00
Wailuku Plantation Token 1880	150.00	225.00	400.00
Wailuku Plantation Token, Half Real 1880	250.00	350.00	450.00
Thomas Hobron Token 1879	75.00	100.00	200.00
Haiku Plantation Token	100.00	150.00	225.00
Grove Ranch Plantation Token 1886	125.00	175.00	250.00
Grove Ranch Plantation Token 1887	150.00	200.00	300.00

ALASKA RURAL REHABILITATION CORPORATION
TOKENS OF 1935

These tokens were issued by the U. S. Government for the use of the colonists of the Matanuska Valley Colnization Project to supply them with much needed Federal aid. They were redeemable only at the ARRC stores. The "Bingles," as they were called, were in use only about six months during 1935-1936 after which they were redeemed for regular U. S. money and destroyed. They were issued on a basis of family dependents. Each token is the size of the corresponding U. S. coin with the exception of the one cent piece which is octagonal. The design is the same on both sides of each denomination.

Aluminum				Quan. Mtd.	V. Fine	Unc.
	Quan. Minted	V. Fine	Unc.	50c 2,500	$30.00	$50.00
1c 5,000		$12.50	$25.00	$1.00 2,500	40.00	75.00
5c 5,000		12.50	25.00	**Brass**		
10c 5,000		12.50	25.00	$5.00 1,000	65.00	100.00
25c 3,000		17.50	35.00	$10.00 1,000	75.00	125.00

PHILIPPINES UNDER SOVEREIGNTY OF THE U.S.

The 1903-19 issues were struck at Philadelphia and San Francisco. 1920 and after were struck at Manila. Because of World War II the 1944-45 coins were minted at Philadelphia, Denver and San Francisco.

Bronze

	E.Fine	Unc.
½ Centavo 1903-08........	$2.00	$11.00
1 Centavo 1903-36........	2.00	13.00

PHILIPPINES UNDER SOVEREIGNTY OF THE U.S.

Copper Nickel

Copper-Nickel

	E. Fine	Unc.
5 Centavos 1937-41...	$2.00	$10.00

	E. Fine	Unc.
5 Centavos 1903-28...	$2.50	$13.00
5 Centavos 1918 Rev. of 20 Centavos (Mule) Fine $125.00	500.00	1,600

Copper-Nickel-Zinc
Same Type as Cop.-Nic.

5 Centavos 1944-45...	.20	1.00

Reduced Size

5 Centavos 1930-35...	3.00	40.00

Silver

10 Centavos 1937-45...	.75	1.50
20 Centavos 1937-45...	1.00	2.00
50 Centavos 1944-45...	2.50	5.00

Silver

10 Centavos 1903-06...	3.00	25.00
20 Centavos 1903-06...	4.50	32.00
50 Centavos 1903-06...	13.00	85.00
1 Peso 1903-06.......	20.00	125.00

COMMEMORATIVE ISSUES

Establishment of the
Commonwealth
Quezon and Murphy

Size Reduced

10 Centavos 1907-35...	2.50	22.00
20 Centavos 1907-29...	3.50	25.00
20 Centavos 1928 Rev. of 5 Centavos (Mule).............	75.00	400.00
50 Centavos 1907-21	6.00	27.50
1 Peso 1907-12.......	11.00	80.00

50 Centavos 1936	40.00	65.00
1 Peso 1936..........	70.00	125.00

Roosevelt and Quezon

COMMONWEALTH ISSUES

Bronze

1 Centavo 1937-44....	.20	1.00

1 Peso 1936..........	70.00	125.00

MISSTRUCK COINS

With the production of millions of coins each year, it is natural that a few abnormal pieces escape inspection and are inadvertently released for circulation, usually in original bags or rolls of new coins. Once generally unappreciated, today these pieces are eagerly sought for the information they shed on minting techniques, and as a variation from normal date and mint series collecting.

Nearly every misstruck coin is unique in some way, and prices may vary from coin to coin. They may all be classified in general groups related to the kind of manufacturing malfunction involved. Collectors value these pieces according to the scarcity of each kind of error for each type of coin.

The following listings show current average values for the most frequently encountered kinds of errors, in uncirculated condition for modern issues and extremely fine for obsolete types, when unmarred by serious marks or scratches. Exceptions are valued higher or lower. Rare date errors generally do not command a premium beyond their normal values.

1. CLIPPED PLANCHET: An incomplete coin, missing 10-25% of the metal.
2. LAMINATION: A flaw of approximately 25% peeled off the coin's surface.
3. WRONG PLANCHET: A coin struck on a blank intended for another denomination.
4. DEFECTIVE DIE: Coin shows raised metal from a large die crack or small rim break.
5. BLANK PLANCHET: A blank of metal intended for coinage but not struck.
6. OFF CENTER: Approximately 10-20% of design missing from obsolete type coins; 20-60% missing from modern coins.
7. BROCKAGE: Mirror image of one coin impressed on another.
8. MULTIPLE STRIKE: Coin has additional image from being struck again approximately 80% off center. Value increases with number of strikes.

	1	2	3	4	5	6	7	8
Large Cent	$50.	$15.		$15.	$25.	$100.	$175.	$400.
Indian 1c	20.	2.	$600.-$975.	10.	5.	50.	100.	150.
Lincoln 1c	2.	1.	80.-150.	10.	1.	2.	20.	15.
Steel 1c	12.	15.	150.-400.	15.	10.	45.	80.	150.
Liberty 5c	25.	10.	500.-600.	30.	30.	70.	100.	300.
Buffalo 5c	20.	5.	300.-600.	15.	3.	50.	75.	300.
Jefferson 5c	3.	4.	20.-100.	10.	3.	5.	40.	25.
Wartime 5c	10.	3.	200.-300.	15.	150.	50.	100.	150.
Barber 10c	20.	10.		10.	65.	100.	200.	
Mercury 10c	15.	5.		20.	10.	20.	50.	175.
Roosevelt 10c (S)	4.	5.		20.	10.	15.	30.	50.
Roosevelt 10c (C)	2.	6.		15.	2.	6.	25.	30.
Washington 25c (S)	9.	15.	50.- 125.	20.	32.	40.	75.	150.
Washington 25c (C)	3.	10.	30.- 100.	10.	5.	15.	50.	50.
Bicentennial 25c	15.	25.	250.-350.	50.		50.	200.	200.
Franklin 50c	50.	18.	150.-500.	100.	25.	300.	500.	400.
Kennedy 50c (S)	18.	18.	150.-300.	50.	25.	200.	400.	400.
Kennedy 50c (C)	10.	15.	125.-500.	20.	12.	70.	300.	125.
Bicentennial 50c	25.	20.	300.-750.	75.		150.	——	400.
Silver $1	125.	40.			225.	1000.		2000.
Eisenhower $1	30.	30.			20.	450.	500.	800.
Bicentennial $1	50.	40.	1500.-2500.	——		600.	——	1000.
Anthony $1	40.	30.	300.- 1500.	350.	100.	500.	500.	1000.

UNITED STATES BULLION COINS
Gold

The gold American Eagle bullion coins are made in four denominations that contain 1 oz., ½ oz., ¼ oz. and 1/10 oz. of gold. The obverse features a modified rendition of the Augustus Saint-Gaudens design used on U.S. twenty dollar gold pieces from 1907 until 1933. The reverse displays a "family of eagles" motif designed by Mrs. Miley Busiek and engraved by Sherl J. Winter.

Designers: Augustus Saint-Gaudens (obverse), Miley Busiek (reverse); composition, 91.67% gold, 3% silver, 5.33% copper; reeded edge; mints: Philadelphia, West Point.
$50 diameter 32.7mm; weight 33.931 grams; net weight one oz. fine gold.
$25 diameter 27mm; weight 16.966 grams; net weight ½ oz. fine gold.
$10 diameter 22mm; weight 8.483 grams; net weight ¼ oz. fine gold.
$ 5 diameter 16.5mm; weight 3.393 grams; net weight 1/10 oz. fine gold.

		Quan. Issued	Unc.	Proof
$ 5	MCMLXXXVI (1986)	912,609	$55.00	
$ 5	MCMLXXXVII (1987)	580,266	55.00	
$ 5	MCMLXXXVIII (1988)	159,500	55.00	
$ 5	MCMLXXXVIII (1988)P	143,881		$75.00
$ 5	MCMLXXXIX (1989)	264,790	35.00	
$ 5	MCMLXXXIX (1989)P			75.00
$ 5	MCMXC (1990)		55.00	
$ 5	MCMXC (1990)P			75.00
$10	MCMLXXXVI (1986)	726,031	120.00	
$10	MCMLXXXVII (1987)	269,255	120.00	
$10	MCMLXXXVIII (1988)	49,000	140.00	
$10	MCMLXXXVIII (1988)P	98,028		150.00
$10	MCMLXXXIX (1989)	81,789	55.00	
$10	MCMLXXXIX (1989)P			75.00
$10	MCMXC (1990)		55.00	
$10	MCMXC (1990)P			75.00
$25	MCMLXXXVI (1986)	599,566	235.00	
$25	MCMLXXXVII (1987)	131,255	235.00	
$25	MCMLXXXVII (1987)P	(143,398)		260.00
$25	MCMLXXXVIII (1988)	45,000	245.00	
$25	MCMLXXXVIII (1988)P	76,528		325.00
$25	MCMLXXXIX (1989)	44,829	235.00	
$25	MCMLXXXIX (1989)P			325.00
$25	MCMXC (1990)		235.00	
$25	MCMXC (1990)P			325.00
$50	MCMLXXXVI (1986)	1,362,650	450.00	
$50	MCMLXXXVI (1986)W	(446,290)		480.00
$50	MCMLXXXVII (1987)	1,045,500	450.00	
$50	MCMLXXXVII (1987)W	(147,498)		480.00
$50	MCMLXXXVIII (1988)	465,000	485.00	
$50	MCMLXXXVIII (1988)W	87,133		600.00
$50	MCMLXXXIX (1989)	415,790	450.00	
$50	MCMLXXXIX (1989)W			625.00
$50	MCMXC (1990)		450.00	
$50	MCMXC (1990)W			650.00

UNITED STATES BULLION COINS

Silver

The silver eagle is a one ounce bullion coin with a face value of one dollar. The obverse has Adolph A. Weinman's Walking Liberty design used on the half dollar coins from 1916 through 1947. His initials are on the hem of the gown. The reverse design is a rendition of a heraldic eagle by John Mercanti.

Designers: Adolph A. Weinman (obverse), John Mercanti (reverse); composition 99.93% silver, .07% copper; weight 31.101 grams; diameter 40.6mm; net weight one oz. fine silver; reeded edge; mints: Philadelphia, San Francisco.

		Quan. Issued	Unc.	Proof			Quan. Issued	Unc.	Proof
$1	1986	5,393,005	$15.00		$1	1988S	(557,370)		$85.00
$1	1986S	(1,446,778)		$35.00	$1	1989	5,203,327	$9.50	
$1	1987	11,442,335	9.00		$1	1989S			40.00
$1	1987S	(904,732)		23.00	$1	1990		9.00	
$1	1988	5,004,500	11.00		$1	1990S			30.00

INDEX

INDEX — *Continued*

INDEX — *Continued*

INDEX — *Continued*

The following numismatic magazines are obtainable by subscription. They are published monthly or as indicated below. Information or sample copies may be obtained by writing to the individual publisher.

The Numismatist
Published by the American
Numismatic Association
818 North Cascade Ave.
Colorado Springs, Colo.   80903

Numismatic News (Weekly)
700 E. State Street
Iola, Wisconsin   54990

Coins Magazine
700 E. State Street
Iola, Wisconsin   54990

Coin World (Weekly)
P.O. Box 150
Sidney, Ohio   45367

The Canadian Numismatic Journal
Published by the Canadian
Numismatic Association
P.O. Box 226
Barrie, Ontario, Canada

COINage Magazine
2660 E. Main St.
Ventura, California   93003

BULLION VALUE OF SILVER COINS

Silver Bullion	Wartime Nickel .05626 oz.	Dime .07234 oz.	Quarter .18084 oz.	Half Dollar .36169 oz.	Silver Clad Half Dollar .14792 oz.	Silver Dollar .77344 oz.
$ 4.00	$ .23	$ .29	$ .72	$ 1.45	$ .59	$ 3.10
4.50	.25	.32	.81	1.63	.66	3.48
5.00	.28	.36	.90	1.81	.74	3.87
5.50	.31	.40	1.00	1.99	.81	4.26
6.00	.34	.44	1.09	2.17	.89	4.64
6.50	.36	.47	1.18	2.35	.96	5.03
7.00	.40	.51	1.27	2.53	1.04	5.42
7.50	.42	.55	1.36	2.72	1.11	5.80
8.00	.45	.58	1.45	2.90	1.19	6.19
8.50	.48	.62	1.54	3.08	1.26	6.58
9.00	.50	.65	1.63	3.26	1.33	6.96
9.50	.53	.69	1.72	3.44	1.42	7.35
10.00	.56	.72	1.81	3.62	1.48	7.73
11.00	.62	.80	1.99	3.98	1.63	8.51
12.00	.68	.87	2.17	4.34	1.78	9.28
13.00	.73	.94	2.35	4.70	1.92	10.05
14.00	.79	1.01	2.53	5.06	2.07	10.83
15.00	.84	1.09	2.71	5.43	2.22	11.60

BULLION VALUE OF GOLD COINS

Price Per Ounce	$5.00 Liberty Head 1839-1908 Indian Head 1908-1929	$10.00 Liberty Head 1838-1907 Indian Head 1907-1933	$20.00 1849-1933
$ 200.00	$ 48.37	$ 96.75	$ 193.50
225.00	54.42	108.85	217.69
250.00	60.47	120.94	241.88
275.00	66.52	133.03	266.07
300.00	72.50	145.13	290.25
325.00	78.60	157.22	314.44
350.00	84.65	169.31	338.63
375.00	90.70	181.40	362.81
400.00	96.75	193.50	387.00
425.00	102.80	205.60	411.19
450.00	108.84	217.69	435.38
475.00	114.89	229.78	459.56
500.00	120.94	241.87	483.75
525.00	126.98	253.97	507.94
550.00	133.03	266.06	532.13
575.00	139.08	278.16	556.31
600.00	145.12	290.25	580.50

The U.S. bullion coins first issued in 1986 are unlike the older regular issues. They contain the following amounts of pure metal: Gold $50, 1 oz.; $25, ½ oz.; $10, ¼ oz.; $5, 1/10 oz. Silver $1, 1 oz.

Providing Coin Collectors with Quality Hobby Supplies for over 40 years.

For more information on available
WHITMAN Coin Products write:

WHITMAN Coin Products M.S. 438R
Western Publishing Company, Inc.
1220 Mound Avenue
Racine, WI 53404

LIMITED EDITION, COMMEMORATIVE MEDAL

To celebrate Whitman's *A Guide Book of United States Coins* ("Red Book") 44th edition, Whitman Coin Products is issuing a limited edition, proof-like, one ounce silver medal to honor the occasion. This collector's medal was exclusively designed and struck for Whitman. It is comprised of one ounce of .999 pure silver in an attractive collector's case.

Your Whitman "Red Book" medal will be complemented later this year by the issuance of Whitman's *Handbook of United States Coins* ("Blue Book") medal. The two medals will complete your limited edition set, so watch for further details in the 1991 edition Blue Book available in August, 1990.

To receive your limited edition Red Book medal, and free display holder, order now while supplies last.

To order, fill in and mail the order blank below (or a copy of it) with check or money order for $10.95 U.S. (plus sales tax where applicable) plus the proof of purchase label from the front cover of this book for a Red Book medal with case. (Only one medal may be ordered per proof of purchase.)

I understand I may return the medal within 14 days and receive a full refund if not completely satisfied.

Mail To:
Whitman Coin Department
Western Publishing Company, Inc.
P.O. Box 700, M.S. #438RB
Racine, WI 53401

```
┌─────────────────────────┐
│                         │
│    Place Proof of       │
│  Purchase Label Here    │
│                         │
└─────────────────────────┘
```

NAME _____
                          Please Print

ADDRESS _____

CITY _____ STATE _____ ZIP _____

PLACE OF PURCHASE _____

Offer expires January 31, 1991. This is a limited offer which may be cancelled at any time without notice subject to availability and dependent on bullion price of silver. Good only in Continental U.S.A., Alaska, Hawaii, and Canada. **Allow 6-8 weeks for delivery.** Copyright ©1990. Western Publishing Company, Inc. All rights reserved. Printed in U.S.A. Whitman, Whitman & Design, Official Blue Book of United States Coins, and Official Red Book of United States Coins are registered trademarks of Western Publishing Company, Inc.

cut along line